THE VIRGIN TRAVEL HEALTH HANDBOOK

MICHAEL WRIGHT

CHECKED FOR MEDICAL ACCURACY
BY THE TRAVEL CLINIC, HOSPITAL
FOR TROPICAL DISEASES, LONDON

Other titles in the same series published by Virgin Books:

The Virgin Travellers' Handbook
The Virgin Guide to Working Abroad
The Virgin 2003 Alternative Guide to British Universities

First published in Great Britain in 2003 by
Virgin Books Ltd
Thames Wharf Studios
Rainville Road
London W6 9HA

Series style by Smith & Gilmour
This book designed by Judith Robertson
Printed and bound in Great Britain by CPD, Wales

IMPORTANT NOTES

The author, checkers and publisher of this book have taken great care to ensure that it is accurate and up-to-date in the light of present medical knowledge. However, no book can be a substitute for personal consultation with a qualified doctor, and mention of any treatment or remedy should not be taken as a recommendation or endorsement. The author, checkers and publisher accept no responsibility for any loss, injury or inconvenience, whether direct or indirect, sustained as a result of using any information or advice included in the book. It is always important to consult your doctor.

Great care has also been taken to ensure that addresses, telephone numbers, website addresses and other similar information are as accurate and up-to-date as possible at the date of writing. However, such details are liable to change, and we cannot accept any responsibility arising from the use of such information. The mention of any clinic, hospital or other institution is not to be taken as a recommendation or endorsement.

We would be pleased to receive any updates, corrections and suggestions for inclusion in the next edition. Please e-mail *travelhealth@virgin-books.co.uk*.

CONTENTS

INTRODUCTION

Long-distance travel is exciting, adventurous, sometimes daunting – and enormous fun. It should stay that way. You certainly don't want your trip of a lifetime to be ruined by illness or a disabling accident. There are definitely hazards out there in the wide world, but with this book you can judge the risks, know how to avoid them, or – if the worst really comes to the worst – find out how to get help and deal with them.

Low-cost air travel has put within the reach of almost all of us areas of the planet that were considered inaccessible except to well-equipped expeditions only a few decades ago. Even if you're thinking only of a package holiday, you can choose Bangkok or Brazil rather than Benidorm; Gambia or Goa instead of the Greek islands. But if you do so, you could come up against unexpected – sometimes life-threatening – health hazards.

Many people visit such once-outlandish places quite unprepared, expecting perhaps that the spread of the Western urban lifestyle, combined with the constantly-trumpeted advances of modern medicine, have made the health threat of travel a thing of the past. Unfortunately, some less than scrupulous people in the travel industry perpetuate the idea, not wanting to put off potential customers. (A frightening proportion of travellers venture without protection into areas where malaria is a real risk, for example, and tourists are still assured that some African lakes – popular for water sports – are free of bilharzia when this is simply not true.)

Package tourists and backpackers alike may, in many parts of the world, come into contact with potentially fatal diseases ranging from malaria and rabies to HIV and hepatitis. And many of these – far from being eliminated – are on the increase. Did you know, for example, that more than 2000 people are treated for malaria each year in Britain alone? Or that 30 000 people die of rabies every year in India? Or that dengue (or 'breakbone') fever – usually mild, but fatal in a small number of cases – has reached epidemic proportions, with 50 to 100 million cases a year worldwide? Even the journey itself can present hazards – although only rarely life-threatening ones.

The last thing I want to do is scare you off travelling, so remember that the great majority of travellers get nothing worse than a nasty attack of Dehli belly or Montezuma's revenge. This book is designed to give you guidance and advice before, during and after your trip. Browse in it before you go, paying particular attention to the risks that I've highlighted for the places you're planning to visit. Take the proper precautions and record them, with your other medical details, on the form on page 276 so you can refer to them if needed. Find a corner in your backpack or luggage for the book, and it will be there to refer to if you fall ill or need to contact consular authorities for help in locating a doctor or other medical assistance (see pp. 182–273).

The book is organised pretty simply. The first part deals systematically with preparations for your trip, and the second all the major hazards you're likely to encounter virtually anywhere in the world – ranging from insect bites to dangerous snakes and mammals, from altitude sickness to things you can catch from contaminated food. (The only things I've ignored are extreme rarities and commonplace diseases that you're as likely to encounter at home as anywhere else in the world.) In each case, I explain what it is, what it does, how you can avoid it, when you need help and how it's treated.

The third part contains a region-by-region rundown of the health risks and precautions you need to take in more than 100 popular travellers' destinations worldwide – and how to get help, including contact details for consulates and medical facilities. And when communication gets difficult, the brief multilingual dictionary of key words (*see p.280*) is there to help you to summon assistance and explain basic symptoms.

I hope you never have to use the book 'in anger', that your travels are as uneventful, healthwise, as you yourself would wish. But I hope you find it helpful if and when you do need it.

If you have any suggestions, comments or criticisms, don't hesitate to get in touch; email me at *travelhealth@virgin-books.co.uk*.

GETTING THERE

Sensible preparations help you to make sure you stay healthy during your travels

Any trip – whether you're setting off on a round-the-world adventure, a pack on your back, or a shorter visit to an exotic destination – can be spoiled by ill-health. This part of the book helps you to plan and prepare in a way that minimises that risk and makes you as ready as you can be to face any health problems that do confront you.

It's a process that needs to start several weeks – preferably two months or more – before departure, so you have plenty of time to consult experts on what vaccinations and other protective measures you should take, and to get the necessary jabs in good time. There are more mundane practicalities to consider too, including what first-aid and other medical supplies it's sensible to take with you. I've covered separately the special considerations women travellers need to think about.

If you have a particular medical problem already, then of course you have to take this into account and consult your doctor and possibly other specialists. But I've included general guidance for many more or less common conditions that might make it more troublesome to travel – or, in some cases, mean that you should delay your flight or consult the airline about special equipment or facilities you may need. Finally there's the very small but universal problem of in-flight health – particularly the risk of deep-vein thrombosis and how to avoid it ruining your trip before it's even begun.

ARE YOU TRAVEL-FIT?

Fit as a fiddle or a built-in medical problem? Plan your trip accordingly.

You'd be forgiven for thinking, after browsing through the later pages of this book, that the major problem you face on a long trip, healthwise, is the myriad exotic diseases that lurk in foreign parts, waiting to pounce on you. Sorry to disappoint the ghouls, but it's simply not true, statistically speaking.

Of course there are strange bugs and nasty diseases in many parts of the world that you need to be aware of – otherwise there'd be no point in me writing and you reading this book! – but the truth is that you're far more likely to have an accident or fall prey to what insurance companies call a pre-existing condition. That's why travel insurance forms always ask if you have any existing illness or condition (and why you'd be foolish not to declare anything relevant on the form, or you may find yourself without cover).

I'll come on to the special problems of people with pre-existing conditions in a moment, but first there are issues that affect all long-distance travellers. It's a bit OTT to suggest having a pre-trip medical exam – unless you're worried about your health, or the insurance company demands it, or you're going somewhere really outlandish. But do take into account any plans for new or unusual activities during your trip. Hiking; surfing; sailboarding? Not too demanding, but you'll enjoy them all the more if you're fit. Scuba diving? You'll need a medical at some point, and you'll probably find it cheaper and more convenient to have it before you leave home rather than on the trip. Trekking at high altitude? That's getting more serious; it'd be as well to start fitness training, although it won't affect the risk of getting altitude sickness.

Even if you don't plan such activities, and even if you have nothing basically wrong with you, I wouldn't advise trying to turn yourself from a couch-potato into an around-the-world backpacker overnight. It pays to get fit and lose unnecessary flab before you start travelling, but don't go at it too quickly. As I explain in the next section (*p.12*), you need to plan the vaccinations and other medical precautions for your trip, and preferably spread them over a period of several weeks. You'll need even longer to get properly fit, so make up your mind to start as early as possible to tone up those trekking muscles!

Walk (with a weighted backpack if you're really keen) or bike rather than taking the bus, train or car; use the stairs rather than the lift; go to the gym or pool if that's your style; and get into the habit of eating a healthy, balanced, low-fat diet with plenty of fruit, vegetables and other complex carbohydrates.

Pay a visit to the dentist. Emergency dentistry in an outlandish spot can be awkward and expensive – if you can find a competent dentist. You'd be far better off getting any problems fixed by your regular dentist before you leave home. The same applies to an eye test; take a copy of your prescription.

It's worth knowing your blood group before you set off, too, so why not donate blood? You'll need to do it *before* you start a course of vaccinations.

Pre-existing conditions

It's emphaticatically not true that having an existing medical condition makes long-distance travel impossible or dangerous. You do have to take your condition into account, perhaps make special plans or take special precautions, maybe search around for suitable insurance. But it needn't stop you having an amazing trip. Good luck, and go for it!

If common sense tells you that something might affect your ability to travel safely, it's important to distinguish things that aren't going to 'get better' if you decide to delay your trip a few weeks or months, rather than travel right now, from those that affect your immediate fitness to get on an aircraft for a long flight. (For example, asthma and diabetes come into the first category, but major surgery or a heart attack usually into the second.) I've covered immediate fitness to fly separately, on page 17; here I'll concentrate on travelling with common chronic medical conditions (in the broadest sense), outlining your best approach and points to consider before you go.

If you do have a long- or short-term medical condition the first stop for more specific advice is your regular doctor or medical specialist. Secondly, contact the patient-support organisation for your condition if there is one; many such bodies publish travellers' guides with valuable advice (and can often point you to firms who'll provide travel health insurance). A third approach – although it's liable to be more patchy and may be less reliable – is to browse the Web for discussion groups covering your situation.

First, a few points that apply whatever your existing medical condition:–

→ Get a full doctor's note detailing your condition and regular medication, plus copy prescriptions listing both generic (chemical) and proprietary (trade) names. Keep all these with your passport, and copy the details in outline on the medical record form on page 276 of this book, together with contact details for your next-of-kin and doctor(s), and other medical data.

→ If you need regular medication while you travel, take ample supplies, to last until you reach a country where you can be sure of getting more. (If possible, check availability at your destination before departure.) Except in the case of insulin for diabetes (*see below*), divide the medication between your hand and hold luggage in case anything goes astray.

→ If you have a condition such as diabetes or epilepsy, where there's a risk of unconsciousness or other crisis, wear a medical alert bracelet or tag.

→ Before you set off, find out contact details for local support organisations at your main destination(s).

Diabetes Here the problems range from keeping track of your medication as you change time zones (it's advisable to stay on 'home time' until a suitable pause in your travels) to coping with unusual foods, and possibly diarrhoea, vomiting or unaccustomed exercise upsetting your sugar balance. There's also an increased risk of the foot problems that tend to bedevil diabetics.

If you're an insulin-dependent ('Type 1') diabetic, particularly, you may be more likely to have a 'hypo' – hypoglycaemic shock attack (*see p. 176*) – partly because you may be more active, and thus have a lower blood-sugar level. If you don't already do so, perhaps now's the time to start doing your own blood-glucose tests to monitor your control. In remote areas especially, it's advisable to travel with a companion who knows how to help in an crisis. Non-insulin-dependent ('Type 2') diabetics usually have fewer problems, although vomiting or diarrhoea again may upset your intake of medication.

Discuss all these and other questions – including how best to reschedule your medication as you cross time zones – with your doctor. Make sure you have adequate supplies of medication and (if necessary) glucose, and know exactly when and how to use each type (including short- and longer-acting insulin if you're on a combination regime). An insulin 'pen' is easier to use and less likely to arouse security queries than a syringe, but carry a doctor's letter in case you encounter over-zealous security officials. This is particularly necessary because you should carry all insulin supplies in hand luggage rather than in the hold, where they might be damaged by freezing. (If in doubt, let the airline know beforehand that you'll be carrying a diabetic kit.)

Epilepsy If your epilepsy is well controlled, there's no reason why you shouldn't travel unless you've had a recent 'grand mal' seizure (*see p. 18*), but it always makes sense to take medical advice on your precise condition. Certain antimalarial drugs – notably chloroquine and mefloquine ('Lariam'; *see p. 115*) can make you prone to seizures, and some others may react with your epilepsy-control medication. So make sure that you mention your condition when consulting a travel clinic about malaria prophylaxis.

Heart and circulatory problems Again, unless you've had a recent heart attack (*see p. 18*) or have some other poorly-controlled heart condition, there may or may not be a reason not to travel – you should always take your doctor's specific advice. If you have a pacemaker fitted, see the notes on page 18 about interference from airport security scanners.

If you take pills to control your blood pressure, be sure to carry adequate supplies (and a copy prescription) with you, as it can be dangerous to suddenly stop taking them if you run out. If the pills include diuretics – or if you take diuretics ('water pills') for any other reason – don't be tempted to stop for the sake of convenience while you're flying. As with medication for diabetes, keep to 'home time' while you're travelling, then gradually shift to a more convenient time (by an hour or two a day) once you arrive.

Taking anticoagulants (such as warfarin) can cause bleeding problems if you have a vaccine injection into a muscle, so again tell the travel clinic doctor or nurse. These drugs also increase your risk of serious bleeding if you have an accident, making it more likely that you'll need a blood transfusion – particularly risky in some parts of the world – so make arrangements for emergency blood supplies if needed (*see p. 172*). Also make arrangements to continue your regular blood tests at your destination on a lengthy trip.

Immunodeficiency You'll probably think of HIV/AIDS (*see p.146*), but a lot of other things can also suppress your immune system, including certain other diseases, long-term steroid treatment, treatment for cancer, and the use of immunosuppressive drugs after transplant surgery. Apart from the effects of the immunodeficiency itself, the main problem for such travellers involves vaccinations. In some cases (and depending on your CD4 count in the case of HIV infection), it may be advisable to avoid vaccines containing live viruses and possibly live bacteria too; some vaccines are known to be safe, including inactivated vacines, but the latter may give only limited immunity. It's essential to discuss your travel plans with your specialist doctor and also tell the staff of your travel clinic about your condition. This is one case in which it can seriously influence where in the world you can safely go.

HIV-positive travellers of course have their own special problems, including restrictions on entry to some countries (nowadays generally applying only to people wanting work permits or long-term residence). There may also be an interaction between the medications you take against HIV and certain other drugs, including antimalarials. Ask your HIV clinic or an HIV charity for more information on travelling with the virus.

Splenectomy – removal of the spleen, usually after an accident – causes a particular type of immunodeficiency that makes the victim prone to both pneumoccocal (lung) disease and meningitis (*see p.163*). If you're in this category you need regular booster vaccinations, and it makes sense to carry an emergency course of antibiotics in case you get a chest infection. You may also be prone to other infections, and malaria is a serious danger. It's probably worth avoiding altogether going to parts of the world where the malaria risk is very high (*see p.107 & pp.182–273*).

Kidney disease Long-distance travel may be a daunting prospect if you need regular kidney dialysis, but it is possible if you plan carefully – although wilderness areas may be beyond your reach. As an example and encouragement, the reciprocal health agreement between the UK and Australia reportedly covers dialysis in public hospitals; you have to make prior arrangements, but it's possible! The same applies (although the treatment won't necessarily be free) in most other developed parts of the world. As ever, discuss your plans – or dreams – with your doctors and get information from support organisations. At a more mundane level, if you're prone to kidney stones, take particular care to keep up your fluid intake in hot climates, where stones are more likely to develop.

Pregnancy Yes, I know that pregnancy isn't an illness, but the truth remains that medical complications can arise during pregnancy and no one can foresee whether any will arise and, if so, what. Some obstetricians are highly conservative and advise against any inessential travel – particularly long-distance, or to a remote area. Others say that if you feel fit and well, and your tests are OK, then go for it! Only you can decide, after discussing your plans with your doctors, but here are a few points to bear in mind:–

→ If at all possible, get all your vaccinations *before* you become pregnant, as vaccination can be risky during pregnancy. If you're not already vaccinated, discuss it very carefully with your doctor and travel clinic, as a balance has to be struck between the risk of infection and the risk of damaging your baby. If necessary, change your planned route.

→ Don't skip any of your routine antenatal checks, but if necessary arrange for some to be carried out overseas in a reliable hospital.

→ Travel health insurance may be a problem, and almost impossible for a baby born overseas. Double-check your airline's dates policy (see p.18).

→ The best time to travel is the second three months (when you'll probably feel most like it anyway) – ie, from about the 12th to the 24th–26th weeks. (Some obstetricians advise waiting until the 18th week.) This avoids the periods of highest risk of nausea, miscarriage and premature birth.

→ Certain diseases are particularly dangerous during pregnancy, including chickenpox, hepatitis E (see p.51) and malaria (see p.107). *Warning*: Some suggest it's safer for mother or baby to avoid taking antimalarial pills in pregnancy; *not true* – but certain pills aren't suitable for pregnant women.

→ Continue to follow dietary advice and keep taking your folic acid; take particularly care with food and drink safety (see p.28).

Physical disabilities A lot depends on the nature and severity of your disability and whether you have a supportive companion to travel with, but even complete immobility need be no bar to travel. The worst practical problem if you're wheelchair-bound may be using a plane's toilet. Advice and assistance is available from many support organisations for disabled people.

Respiratory problems If you're prone to asthmatic attacks, travelling may mean you encounter more asthma triggers, ranging from cold, damp, high altitude, air pollution and dust to aggressive air conditioning and simple anxiety. (Such conditions may even be enough to reawaken a 'dormant' childhood tendency to asthma.) Plan your trip accordingly – for example, avoiding high-altitude cities with heavy pollution, such as Mexico City. On the other hand, some destinations may actually be better for your asthma.

Make sure you have adequate inhaler(s), and know how and when to use it/them – including the warning signs of trouble. As mentioned on page 18, your doctor may advise taking preventive steroids before you fly. Also discuss having a flu jab and a pneumococcal vaccination before setting off. If you can, check on inhaler availablity at your destination; some types may not be available in certain countries, or may go under different names.

If you need oxygen or a nebuliser during a flight, the airline will usually supply them if you make arrangements in advance (see p.19). If you need a respirator, it's usually possible to take a battery-powered one on an aircraft with you; also check in advance with the airline.

PRE-TRIP PRACTICALITIES

Organise your vaccinations, travel health insurance and medical kit.

Amid all the excitement of planning, searching for bargain flights, working out your budget and a million other things, it's easy to forget or delay essentials for ensuring that your trip – particularly if it's long-distance – isn't spoiled unnecessarily by medical trouble. Being prepared for the worst isn't just a boring extra, it's the key to taking many of the worries out of your adventure and leaving you free to have the greatest fun. There are three main areas: making sure that you're protected against dangerous diseases, arranging insurance so that you have the resources and protection to get cured if you are ill, and packing the essentials to deal with problems en route.

Vaccinations and prophylaxis

It's important to realise that vaccinations – and prophylactic (preventive) drugs against such diseases as malaria – aren't the ultimate answer to keeping healthy. Many diseases aren't (yet) vaccine-preventable, and few vaccines are 100 per cent effective, so you'll often need to protect yourself physically as well – eg, by taking care of what you eat and drink (*see p.28*) and preventing mosquito bites (*see p.75*). But vaccination against many diseases is vital. You may be able to get certain vaccines from your usual doctor at low cost in the UK and some other countries with national health-insurance schemes, but for others you'll have to go to a specialist travel clinic (found in any major city) and usually pay a fee. (Vaccines are often pricey enough to figure in your travel budget once you've added them all up.) In any case, travel clinics are a better source of advice than GPs or pharmacists.

If possible, you should contact the clinic at least two months before you set off, to discuss which vaccinations and drugs you need, and when. The long lead time is needed because some vaccines can't be given at the same time as (or just after) others, and many need two or more doses at intervals of days or weeks. They all need some time to become effective. The checklist (*opposite*) lists the main vaccines available and the page reference for further details. For more information on recommended vaccines for various parts of the world, see the regional articles on pages 182–273, but always take a travel clinic's expert advice. The medical record chart on pages 276–279 is a convenient place to record your vaccinations and when you'll need boosters.

Travel health insurance

About one in five travellers who contact British consulates abroad for help don't have any form of travel health insurance. In some countries, reciprocal agreements provide emergency treatment at no or low cost – see the details in the regional articles on pages 182–273. But these arrangements don't usually cover routine or long-term treatments, or evacuation/repatriation back home if you're seriously ill. So you need travel insurance as well – and certainly in other parts of the world. If you have a pre-existing condition (*see p.9*), it may be best to contact a patient-support organisation, but others

VACCINATION/PROPHYLAXIS CHECKLIST

The vaccinations (or boosters) you need depend on where in the world you're planning to go, and sometimes the season when you plan to travel. These are the main vaccines currently available (not necessarily in all countries); for more information refer to the pages indicated:–

→ **Cholera** (*see p.44*) – modern types include ones (in some countries) combined with typhoid (*see below*) or ETEC diarrhoea (*see p.34*).

→ **Diphtheria** (*see p.166*) – usually combined with tetanus (*see below*).

→ **Flu** and **pneumoccocal disease** – the former a regular for elderly and many other people; the latter often a worthwhile extra for many.

→ **Hepatitis A** (*see p.51*) – also available combined with hepatitis B or with typhoid (*see below*).

→ **Hepatitis B** (*see p.148*) – also available combined with hepatitis A.

→ **Japanese encephalitis** (*see p.128*).

→ **Meningitis** (*see p.163*).

→ **Polio** (*see p.165*).

→ **Rabies** (*see p.139*) – pre-exposure; further vaccinations if bitten.

→ **Tetanus** (*see p.166*) – usually combined with diphtheria (*see above*).

→ **Tick-borne encephalitis** (*see p.133*).

→ **Tuberculosis** (*see p.160*) – but not generally used in USA (*see p.161*).

→ **Typhoid** (*see p.46*) – also available combined with hepatitis A or, in some countries, cholera (*see above*).

→ **Yellow fever** (*see p.123*).

In addition, you may need prophylactic (preventive) drugs for:–

→ **Loiasis** (*see p.132*) – for west and central Africa only.

→ **Malaria** (*see p.107*) – get advice on which drugs to take (*see p.115*).

can get insurance from tour operators and travel agents (including long-haul flight specialists), banks, or direct from insurance companies and brokers.

Terms, conditions and prices vary, so make some comparisons before you buy, and don't agree to any policy without reading it in full. Does it exclude long-term trips to remote areas, if that's your intention, or any activities you may want to do, such as winter sports, scuba diving, climbing, motor-biking or manual work? Does it cover emergency helicopter evacuation, and repatriation if you need it? Emergency blood supplies? Is the cover adequate for the worst-case scenario? (It may seem high, but cover for *at the very least* £2 million –$US3 million or $A5 million – is advisable for a long trip.)

How easy will it be to get payment if you need treatment? Hospitals and doctors in many places demand immediate cash payment – not even a credit card will do – and you may have trouble persuading them to deal directly with your insurer, especially if it doesn't have a local agent. This is linked to what emergency assistance the company gives; ideally, if you're going somewhere

IF YOU'RE A WOMAN...

Quite apart from sexual prejudice you may face in some parts of the world, travelling as a woman of course presents its own personal hurdles. Two primarily female ailments – cystitis and thrush (see pp.157 & 158) – can be particularly troublesome when you travel, but the main problems are to do with personal safety, contraception and menstruation.

Safety is largely outside the scope of this book, but if you're going on a long trip it pays to plan well ahead of departure what you intend to do about the others, since they may be linked and any change in your regime may take time to settle down. If, like many women travellers, you opt for some form of hormonal contraception, consult your doctor, gynaecologist or family-planning clinic several months before you set off. If a new method turns out to have side-effects you don't like, then you'll still have time to change your mind. If (as often happens) it causes erratic periods at first, there's a good chance your cycle will have settled down before departure day.

Contraceptive options

The first thing to be said is that, whatever main method of contraception you adopt, make sure you take a supply of condoms (male and/or female) for the sake of safer sex (see p.145) and as a back-up. Pills, coils or diaphragms won't protect you from HIV. Even if you're travelling with your regular partner, and both of you are faithful to each other, remember that a dose of the trots, a course of antibiotics (or certain other medicines), or simple forgetfulness can make the Pill ineffective (see box, p.39). I would also suggest taking one or two packs of emergency 'morning-after' contraception in case of accidents or other need. (For more information on this and other sexual emergencies, including abortion, see page 179.)

The Pill doesn't, of course, suit all women, but in most of its forms it does have some advantages when you travel – particularly in regulating and in some cases eliminating your periods, which tend to become irregular on a long trip. If you're taking the normal combined (oestrogen–progestogen) Pill, with seven Pill-free days between packs, you can do away with your periods altogether – certainly for three or four months – by going straight on to a new pack (ie, with no Pill-free days). If your brand involves taking Pills in a continuous 28-day cycle, ask your doctor for advice.

out of the way or where there's likely to be a language barrier, you need on-the-spot help. Various firms claim to provide this over greater or lesser parts of the world, but many travel insurance policies offer only a telephone 'hot line' – very much second-best if a decision has to be agreed on what's best for you, medically. You may have to pay more for a policy that includes local assistance, if you can get it at all, but I think it's worthwhile for long-distance trips. Be sure to declare any medical problem – or if you're pregnant.

The conventional Pill also has disadvantages. In particular, it may worsen the swollen ankles that some people get in hot climates (see p.58) and it raises (slightly) the risk of blood clots when you fly (see p.21) or climb high. There are claims that 'second-generation' Pills are better in this respect than 'third-generation' ones (ask your doctor). Progestogen-only 'mini-Pills' also don't have these side-effects, but they're more prone to result in accidental pregnancy if you're forgetful or have a stomach upset.

Whatever type of Pill you use, take a copy prescription; you should be able to get your usual brand or a close equivalent in Australia, Canada, New Zealand or the USA, but this may not be true elsewhere. The mini-Pill is reportedly difficult to get in much of Asia, and all hormonal contraception may be expensive in Japan. So carry adequate supplies with you (but take into account Japan's strict import controls on pharmaceuticals; see p.245).

You can avoid many of these problems by using an implanted or injected contraceptive. Best known is the IUD or 'coil', which can be effective for five years but doesn't regulate your periods. (It may in fact cause irregular bleeding, especially at first.) A progestogen-releasing IUD (eg, 'Mirena') is equally effective but also partially or completely eliminates your periods. You get much the same effect from an injected ('depo') contraceptive such as 'Depo-Provera' or 'Noristerat', which is effective for two or three months, or from a progestogen implant (eg, 'Implanton'), which lasts up to three years. Before you get too excited, however, remember that all these methods, like Pills, have side-effects that may make them unsuitable. That's why you need to discuss your needs with an expert well in advance.

Menstrual problems

Even if you don't use any hormonal form of contraception, you may want to delay a period by taking norethisterone, a progestogen that can be used for up to 14 days; you'll need a prescription. You should have no problem getting your favourite type of tampon or towel in big cities and advanced countries around the world, but it may be a different matter in less developed areas. So pack ample supplies – in double plastic bags to prevent damp seeping in – unless you're prepared to use local products that may, in some places, seem primitive in the extreme. If you're prone to PMT or period pains, take plenty of your normal remedy for those, too.

First-aid and medical kits

First rule: Make sure you know how and when to use any medicines or other medical supplies you take with you, including the correct dose and duration of treatment for all drugs. Carry a legible copy prescription for all prescribed drugs. Secondly, don't overload yourself, but do take sensible supplies in relation to the chance of being able to restock. If in doubt, discuss your needs with your doctor, the staff of a travel clinic or a reputable travel store.

Basics Apart from medications you need to deal with a pre-existing medical condition, items you should consider taking on any trip – if it's more than a couple of weeks' holiday to a developed area, hotel or resort – include:–

→ Sticky plasters; non-adherent dressings (eg, 'Melolin'); microporous sticky tape; blister dressings; possibly 'butterfly' closures (eg, 'Steri-Strips'); 8cm (3in) crepe bandage and safety pins; scissors; tweezers.

→ Clinical thermometer – the disposable liquid-crystal type is best for long-distance travel; in any case, keep it cool and protected from damage.

→ Cotton balls and/or buds; antiseptic surgical wipes (baby wipes are a good substitute); antiseptic cream containing cetrimide or chlorhexidine; povidone-iodine paint and/or dry spray (eg, 'Betadine' or 'Videne'), or tincture of iodine and/or potassium permanganate crystals (*see p.178*).

→ Mild painkiller – paracetamol (acetaminophen; eg, 'Tylenol') or soluble aspirin (*note*: aspirin and remedies containing it are *not suitable for children under 12*); possibly ibuprofen. Stronger painkiller – eg, codeine with aspirin or paracetamol (but codeine may be regarded as a 'controlled substance' in some places). Sore-throat and cough remedies.

→ Antihistamine tablets (consult your doctor or pharmacist). If you're prone to serious allergic reactions if bitten or stung, take a preloaded adrenaline (epinephrine) syringe and wear a medical alert bracelet or tag.

→ Sunscreen lotion and sunblock (*see p.56*); calamine or similar lotion, or crotamiton cream or lotion (eg, 'Eurax'); possibly ibuprofen skin gel; 1 per cent hydrocortosone cream (eg, 'HC45'; 'Lanacort'); insect-repellent containing DEET (*see p.77*); anti-fungal ('athlete's foot') cream or powder.

STERILE SURGICAL/TRANSFUSION KITS

Some doctors feel it's worth taking a kit of sterile syringes, injection needles and sutures for use in an emergency, especially to areas where HIV/AIDS and hepatitis B are common and hygiene standards poor. The idea is to ask medical staff to use the sterile instruments instead of their own, possibly contaminated equipment. (Some such 'AIDS' kits also include intravenous transfusion fluid for use before safe blood supplies can be obtained, but this adds greatly to the bulk and in any case is likely to be inadequate after a serious accident.)

It's a controversial subject. Unless you carry the kit in your day-pack, it won't be much use if you're knocked down in the street; and there have been cases of sterile kits being produced but not used. Only you (in consulation with your travel doctor) can decide; but if you do take such a kit, make sure it's properly packaged and labeled, so you're not mistaken for a junkie.

→ For women, thrush remedy (*see p. 158*) and possibly course of antibiotics against cystitis (discuss with your doctor). Also condoms (both sexes) and emergency contraception (*see p. 180*).

→ Eye and/or ear drops if you're prone to problems (consult your doctor).

Hot-climate travel In addition to the above you may need:–

→ Antimalarial pills (*see above*); permethrin-impregnated mosquito net (*see p. 76*); possibly insecticide spray (but don't take an aerosol container on an aircraft; best bought locally).

→ Water-purification chemicals and/or filter (*see p.32*). Oral rehydration salts (or take measuring spoon and get sugar and salt at your destination; *see p.41*); anti-diarrhoeal drugs such as loperamide (eg, 'Arret'; 'Imodium'; *but see pp.41–42*); perhaps bismuth subsalicylate (*see p.38*).

→ Aciclovir (acyclovir; 'Zovirax') cream if you're prone to cold sores.

Other long-distance travel If you're heading for an outlandish place, or going on any very long-term/distance trip, consult your doctor (or a specialist travel doctor) about prescription drugs (eg, antibiotics for severe diarrhoea, chest infections or persistent tropical ulcers; emergency malaria treatment; stronger painkillers; sleeping tablets; drugs against altitude sickness) it may be wise to take – and precisely when and how they should be used. Temporary dental fillings are useful if you have tooth problems in the wild.

ON YOUR WAY!

Make sure your flight itself is comfortable, safe and trouble-free.

The waiting and planning are over, you're on the plane and about to leave behind all the worries, nagging relatives and general pre-trip hassles. Are you ready? I hope, in fact, that you're reading this *before* you board (or even set off for the airport), as there are some things you should have done or thought about already to make sure the flight itself goes without a hitch, medically speaking. They range from matters of comfort and convenience to a few quite serious (though rare) medical risks associated with flying.

Fit to fly?

First, do you have any medical condition that stops you flying? (This is slightly different from asking whether you're fit to go on a round-the-world backpacking trip, or whatever you're planning; *see p.7*.) I mean '*stops* you flying'; you must report certain conditions to the airline – often on a special form – as well as your travel insurer. The reason may be the risk of reduced cabin air-pressure or immobility making your condition worse, or simply the risk of an attack that the aircrew can't cope with. If in any doubt, discuss it with your doctor and if appropriate tell the airline's medical department. If you don't, you might get away with it; but if you get into medical trouble the consequences – medical and financial – could be severe. Not worth it.

In general you shouldn't fly without medical clearance if you...

→ Have any kind of respiratory problem (eg, emphysema or chronic bronchitis) that makes you breathless when sitting down; you're probably OK if you can walk at least 50m (165ft) or climb 12 stairs without getting breathless. Don't fly with a collapsed lung (pneumothorax) or pulmonary embolism. If you have asthma, discuss your plans with your doctor; you may need extra medication (eg, steroids) before flying.

→ Have had a heart attack, or suffered serious heart failure or angina, within the past two (possibly more) weeks – take a specialist's advice. Also take advice if you're being treated for any other kind of heart problem or have a pacemaker (which may be affected by some airport security systems – so carry a doctor's letter and ask to be hand-searched).

→ Have any kind of severe anaemia. Also take the advice of your specialist if you have full-blown sickle-cell disease or have had a sickle-cell 'crisis' within the last 10–14 days.

→ Have had a stroke (whether a cerebral haemorrhage, thrombosis or embolism), especially within three weeks – take a specialist's advice.

→ Have had recent deep-vein thrombosis (DVT; see also p.21) – depends on how well your treatment is going, so discuss it with your doctor.

→ Have epilepsy – depends on how well controlled your attacks are, so take a specialist doctor's advice; you may need extra medication.

→ Have a brain tumour; consult a specialist about any other form of cancer.

→ Have a mental illness; consult a psychiatrist and the airline if necessary.

→ Have broken a bone within the last two days (or had a skull fracture within seven to ten days). Your plaster-cast may need to be split to allow for expansion at high altitude; if you have a large leg cast you may have to pay for two seats or get upgraded to make sure you have enough room.

→ Have ear problems or have had ear surgery – take expert advice, but generally delay your flight until the surgery has healed or infection cured.

→ Have had any other type of recent major surgery – take the surgeon's advice, but as a rough guide the limits are four weeks for chest surgery; three weeks for eye surgery; two weeks for abdominal or skull surgery.

→ Have had gastrointestinal bleeding – other than from haemorrhoids (piles) – within three weeks.

→ Have been scuba diving within 48 hours – longer for deep dives. Avoid flying for at least ten days after any attack of the 'bends' or 'staggers'.

→ Are more than 34–35 weeks (most international routes) or 36 weeks (many internal flights) pregnant (or as little as 24 weeks if you're expecting twins, or have had bleeding, early contractions or a previous miscarriage or premature birth) – ask the airline its rules, and discuss with your doctor.

→ Are travelling with a new-born baby (less than a week old in many cases, but sometimes OK after two days, with clearance; longer for premature babies) – take a paediatrician's advice.

→ Have a serious infectious disease, or one that causes vomiting or diarrhoea – take a doctor's advice and get the airline's clearance.

It's a long list, but it doesn't affect very many people who are flying for pleasure. (There are special considerations and rules for people flying to get treatment, who are usually accompanied by a nurse.) In any case there's no absolute bar in many cases, but you and/or the airline may need to take special precautions. For example, certain heart, blood or lung conditions may mean you need oxygen or a nebuliser; the airline will usually provide but often make a charge. And even this list isn't exhaustive: In general, if you have *any* chronic medical condition, discuss your plans with your doctor.

General comfort

To some extent this overlaps into preventing DVT (*see p.21*), but whereas DVT affects only a small number of travellers, everyone can make their journey more comfortable and pleasant by taking a few simple precautions. Most ill-effects come from four things:–

→ Low cabin humidity;
→ Low cabin air pressure (and particularly sometimes low oxygen pressure);
→ Staying immobile in one position for a long time; and/or
→ Infection from fellow passengers.

There's not much you can do about the last of these, short of wearing a surgical mask for the whole trip (and risk odd looks from fellow passengers convinced you're either paranoid or seriously infectious). As for the others…

Cabin pressure Lowered oxygen pressure doesn't affect most healthy people; when it does have an effect, it comes into the 'Fit to fly?' category (*see above*). For most people, the worst that low overall cabin pressure – at cruising height, it's usually equivalent to the air on top of a 2000m (6500ft) mountain – does is to cause some discomfort. Any air pockets trapped in your body may expand dangerously (which is why you shouldn't fly too soon after an operation) but much more common is simply a bloated stomach. You can minimise it by drinking still, not fizzy, drinks and avoiding 'windy' foods such as beans, cabbage and curries before you fly. Most important of all, wear loosely fitting, comfortable clothes. (Shell suits come back; all is forgiven!)

The best-known pressure effect is to the ears; usually, they simply pop or click as air pressure inside the middle ear equalises with cabin pressure (via the narrow eustachian tube, which connects the middle ear with your throat). But if the eustachian tube is blocked you may feel some discomfort or even pain – mainly when you're coming in to land (when cabin pressure is increasing). The standard 'cures' are chewing gum (try the menthol type), sucking sweets, yawning or massaging just behind the ears to get the tube to open. There's also the grandly-named Valsalva manoeuvre: Simply close your mouth, pinch your nose and gently try to breathe out to increase the air pressure in your throat. But if you have a cold, nothing may help except perhaps a nasal decongestant such as pseudoephedrine (eg, 'Sudafed').

Humidity The air in an aircraft cabin is very dry; it leads to dry skin (easily corrected with moisturiser) and, more important, dehydration. This has all sorts of side-effects, from thirst, headaches, drowsiness and a congested nose (adding to the problem of popping ears; *see above*) to the much more serious effect of increasing the risk of DVT. It can also worsen jet lag (*see p.23*) and make contact lenses uncomfortable. (If you wear lenses, you'd be better off taking them out and wearing glasses for the duration of the flight.)

The real trouble is that drinking alcohol – which, to many people, goes hand-in-hand with flying – only adds to your dehydration, since alcohol is a diuretic. Caffeine is too, so (if you can resist) *don't* drink alcoholic drinks (even weak ones like beer), tea or coffee, but *do* drink plenty of water or soft (preferably non-fizzy) drinks. I'm not talking about those dinky 'airline-size' cans, either; you should try to drink at least 0.6 litre (1 pint) – that's two full standard-size soft-drink cans – every three hours. You may be hard-put to squeeze that much drink out of the cabin crew, so take a big bottle or two with you, collect the freebies whenever the cabin attendants come round, and stock up during stopovers. (Incidentally, airline food tends to be a bit on the dry side, too, so eat only what you really need, and take some fruit.)

Immobility The obvious result of this is discomfort, but far more important is that it encourages dehydration and DVT, as it has been found to encourage fluid to move into the body's tissues from the bloodstream, causing the blood to thicken. As a side-effect, this fluid flow can cause swelling of the ankles, as fluid 'pools' at the bottom of your legs – not to be confused with the painful swelling caused directly by DVT. The effect is usually short-lived and should clear up within, at most, a day or two of reaching your destination.

You probably won't be able to do much about the space you have in the plane, but airlines' seat spacing does vary and you can find out how much legroom they each allow; if you can, choose to fly with one that gives you more room. It may also be possible, if you check in early, to get extra space by choosing a seat next to an emergency exit (in which case, the airline may want to be sure that you can respond rapidly and sensibly in an emergency) or behind a bulkhead (although some airlines reserve those for familiies with young children). Otherwise, I prefer an aisle seat and forego the view. As suggested in the article on DVT, it's important to get up from your seat and move around the aircraft cabin at intervals, and also do leg exercises when sitting.

Travel sickness

This is usually far more of a problem when travelling on land or sea than in a jet airliner, although some people feel queasy at the slightest provocation, and severe turbulence may make others feel sick. Short hops on lower-flying propeller aircraft are much more likely to be bumpy than cruising at 11 000m (36 000ft). The central part of the cabin, near the wings, is the most stable. If you're prone to travel sickness, you probably know what – if anything – is best for you, but these measures help at least some people:–

→ Lie as flat and still as possible, your head firmly against the head-rest.
→ Keep your eyes closed.
→ If you must look, keep your eyes fixed on the outside horizon.
→ Don't read or watch the movie, but do keep your mind occupied by listening to an in-flight entertainment channel.
→ Wrist bands (claimed to act on acupressure points) may help – although there's little or no scientific proof of whether and how they do so.
→ Avoid drinking alcohol.

Various drugs undoubedly can help. For short journeys, many doctors recommend hyoscine (scopolamine) tablets (eg, 'Joy-Rides'; 'Kwells'), which act quickly (in about 30 minutes) but last only about four to six hours. For longer trips you could try a skin-patch version (eg, 'Scopoderm'). The snag is hyoscine's side-effects: often drowsiness, a dry mouth and sometimes blurred vision. If you've tried it without success, or you don't like the side-effects, ask your doctor or a pharmacist about alternatives, such certain antihistamines (although most of these also have side-effects).

DEEP-VEIN THROMBISIS (DVT)

'Economy-class syndrome' can affect any long-distance traveller.

DVT is nothing new; it has been recognised for over 50 years. It also seems to be quite common – I say *seems* because information is still unclear – but, if so, it goes completely unnoticed in the vast majority of cases. There are differing estimates of the number of people who actually have symptoms during or after a flight – complicated by the fact that DVT affects something like 1 in 2000 people each year among the general population. It's generally agreed that a long-haul flight – and long-distance road or rail travel – does increase the risk, but mostly among certain groups of people who are most prone to DVT. Of those who do have symptoms, 'only' about 1 in 100 die of it – but those, of course, are the ones who make the headlines.

What it is Sitting still a long time without taking exercise makes the blood circulation in the legs rather sluggish, and immobility and dehydration together tend to make the blood stickier. As a result, small blood clots tend to form in the deep veins, particularly in the calves. (Clotting in a varicose vein just under the skin is quite different and much less serious.) These small clots may occur in as many as one in ten long-haul passengers, according to a recent study, but in the vast majority of cases the clots dissolve again as soon as the person gets moving, and s/he never realises they had formed. In a few cases, a clot gets big enough to obstruct blood-flow, causing symptoms (*see below*). In an even smaller number, the clot breaks loose and reaches the lungs, causing a life-threatening pulmonary embolism.

Who is most at risk Some people are inherently more prone to DVT, while the risk for everyone may be increased if they don't take simple precautions (*see below*). The greatest risk is in people who...

→ Have or have previously had DVT or a pulmonary embolism.
→ Have (or have a family history of) a tendency to form blood clots.
→ Have recently had a stroke or heart disease.
→ Have had recent major surgery (especially involving the hips or knees).
→ Currently have cancer or are undergoing chemotherapy.
→ Are unable to move their legs.

Such people should take expert medical advice on whether to fly at all; if they do, they should wear compression stockings (*see below*) and in some cases may need an injection of an anticoagulant drug such as heparin before flying.

There's a less serious but slightly increased risk in people who...

→ Are aged over 40.
→ Are very overweight and/or smoke.
→ Are women who are pregnant, have recently given birth, or are taking the combined contraceptive Pill or HRT (especially, according to some doctors, 'third-generation' types; ask your doctor about this).

Again, compression stockings are a worthwhile precaution, and (subject to medical advice) taking a low-dose (or half a standard-dose) aspirin before take-off *may* reduce the tendency of blood to clot (although it's not proven).

How to reduce the risk Elastic graduated compression (support) stockings – or shorter 'flight socks', although these may dig into your upper calves,

---

EXERCISING YOUR CIRCULATION

You can reduce the risk of DVT by following this routine:–

→ Get up and walk around the cabin at least every two to three hours (if allowed); get as much exercise as possible during refuelling stops.

→ Make sure the edge of the seat doesn't dig into your thighs as you sit; don't cross your legs. Keep your foot space clear of hand luggage.

→ While sitting, bend and stretch your legs at least every half-hour: Hold each leg in turn with your hands around the knee, and raise, lower and tense it; hold for 10–15 seconds and repeat several times.

→ Also at least every half-hour, press down hard with the balls of your feet on the floor or foot-rest, then raise your toes as hard as possible while pressing down with your heels; again hold and repeat several times. Then rotate your ankles several times in each direction.

→ Do shoulder-rotating and upper-body stretching exercises at least every hour. Take some deep breaths (but try not to hyperventilate).

causing discomfort – force your circulation to work harder and reduce the risk of clots. I'd advise anyone – and particularly people at increased risk (*above*) – to wear them on a long-haul (five-hours-plus) flight. If you have the time, break your journey so you don't fly longer than 10–12 hours without a day or two's stopover. Apart from this, drink lots of fluids (but not alcoholic drinks, tea or coffee; *see p.20*) and avoid sleeping pills, which encourage immobility, in flight. Also follow the in-flight exercise suggestions in the box.

What it does to you The symptoms of a DVT clot serious enough to need treatment usually arise some time after you've landed – typically days later; rarely on the flight itself, or weeks later – and include...

→ Pain in a calf, accompanied by swelling that's harder and quite distinct from the simple ankle swelling caused by immobility (*see p.20*).
→ Often reddening or darkening of the skin in the area, which feels hot.

If the blood clot breaks off and lodges in the lung, it causes sudden pain and breathlessness. The bigger the breakaway clot the greater the risk of death.

How it's treated DVT always needs urgent treatment, but a clot in the lung is a real emergency. Both leg and lung types need hospital diagnosis and treatment with blood-thinning drugs to dissolve the clot.

JET LAG

As well as travel-induced fatigue, your body (and especially sleep) can be seriously disturbed by crossing time zones. Travelling north–south causes few problems because your body clock stays synchonised with real time. But travelling long-haul east to west or – worse – west to east means you have to adjust your body clock to a later or earlier day. (It's usually easier to stay awake late than to go to sleep early; that's why west–east travel is worse.) Many people need up to a day to adjust for each time-zone crossed – ie, for each hour from 'home' time – and until they do they're liable to feel dreadful. Sleeping pills can help, but are best left until after you reach your destination.

Various methods are said to speed up the process, but nothing's *proven* to work for everyone. Many people swear by melatonin – a natural hormone whose concentration in the body rises at night. This isn't sold in Britain, but is available in US 'health' stores. Timing is critical. The most convincing reports – and a number of doctors agree – advocate a small dose of melatonin (3mg) in the late afternoon (about 5pm) to help bring your body-day forward after eastbound travel, or in the very early morning (about 6am) to move your day later. A more complicated scheme suggests calculating the equivalent 'home' time, and starting to take the pills at that time a day before take-off.

You could combine this with regulating your exposure to bright light, which also works for many people. Get out in the sun early in the day (and keep in the dark in the afternoon) if you've travelled eastwards, and vice-versa if you've travelled west. However, if you've crossed more than six time zones in whatever direction, it's best simply to get plenty of light around midday.

TRAVEL HEALTH HAZARDS

Things that can go wrong when you travel – what they are and how to deal with them

There are hundreds of diseases that could in theory afflict you, wherever you may go. Some are localised, some widespread. Many have become rarities – even eliminated altogether – in the parts of the world that most readers of this book call home. Other places, and their inhabitants, aren't so fortunate; through chance, lack of public health resources or intrinsic local factors, diseases occur that we in developed countries no longer fear. If you travel widely, you have to face the fact that you may encounter them.

Remember, too, that you're no less (and sometimes more) likely to catch 'conventional' illnesses, such as chickenpox, flu, measles and so on, on your travels than you are at home. In this book for travellers, I've concentrated mainly on the diseases and other conditions that are less familiar and more likely to be encountered away from your cosy home environment. The most common and important of them are grouped here in seven categories:–

Hazards from food and drink 27
Heat, cold and other environmental hazards 53
Things that bite, sting and burrow 72
Diseases from insects and other biters 106
Sexually-transmitted infections 144
Skin and other infections 152
Accidents, injuries and emergencies 169

If it seems that you're surrounded on all sides by such hazards on your travels, you do need to get the risks into perspective. As pointed out in connection with travel fitness (*see p. 7*), if you go away with an inbuilt medical problem, that's far more of a threat than all the exotic infections you might encounter. Death is, admittedly, rather a drastic measure of how widespread a problem is, but surveys have shown that fewer that one in twenty of all those who die during their travels do so because of an infectious disease.

Way ahead in the list of causes of death, at almost 70 per cent, are heart attacks and related diseases – the great majority in people aged over 50. (Perhaps not surprisingly, the over-50s have overall the highest death rate abroad.) But the second most common cause – and by far the leading cause among people in their 20s – is an accident or injury. Overall, these account for more than one in five travellers' deaths, and about one in three among those aged under 30. Road accidents are the biggest single cause, followed by swimming accidents; alcohol is often involved in both.

Having said that, how do other risks compare? It's difficult to get accurate estimates, since many illnesses go unreported, but sources include the number of calls or claims made to insurance companies and what travellers say they've had wrong with them on their travels. (Only about 1 in 500 travellers actually call their insurer's helpline while overseas.)

By far the most common is travellers' diarrhoea, which can range from a brief bout of 'tummy trouble' to persistent giardiasis or amoebic dysentery; overall, diarrhoea is reckoned to hit around 40 to 50 per cent of travellers spending a month in a developing country. (The figure is much lower, but still 20 to 30 per cent, if you include those taking much shorter trips.) Chest and related problems come second, affecting around 3 per cent of travellers.

What about the more notorious travel afflictions, such as malaria and typhoid? Among people visiting west Africa for a month without taking suitable malaria pills, about 2.4 per cent will get the disease; the figures are lower for east Africa, at 0.5 per cent, and Latin America, at about 0.05 per cent. About 0.4 per cent will get a sexual-transmitted infection or typhoid (in Africa or India; fewer elsewhere). Pretty low figures, you might think. (Maths fiends will calculate that 2.4 per cent equates to odds of 42 to 1 against; 0.4 per cent to 250 to 1.) But why accept even such long odds – particularly since many of these diseases can threaten your life – when sensible precautions can reduce the risk...well, not quite to zero, but certainly to far lower levels?

That's the purpose of this part of the book: To set out the facts about the most important travellers' hazards, show you how best to avoid them, and give guidance on the kind of help you'll need if you draw the short straw and turn out to be that one in 42 – or 250, or 10 000, or whatever – who succumbs.

Making sense of symptoms

If you get ill, you may have some idea of what's wrong (particularly if it's happened before), but unless you're medically trained it's very unlikely you'll know for sure. What you will have are symptoms (things that you can sense, such as pain, or that can be detected – eg, with a thermometer) and signs (which can be seen – eg, jaundice or a rash). These, together with the history or development of your condition, are the main clues a doctor uses to make an initial diagnosis, but s/he may need lab or other tests for confirmation. Self-diagnosis can be dangerous, but if you're far from medical help, it's useful to have some idea of what common symptoms may mean and when they indicate that you should get help. These are some important ones:–

Fever Normal body temperature is about 37°C (98.6°F). The most common cause of fever – a rise in temperature – is a cold or flu. But all sorts of other infections can cause it, from malaria and dengue (transmitted by insects) to hepatitis A, typhoid and some types of diarrhoea (from contaminated food or drink). For a clearer diagnosis, other symptoms have to be taken into account – eg, a headache, rash, swelling, pain, diarrhoea, etc. A high temperature – particularly 40°C (104°F) or more – always needs to be investigated.

Jaundice Yellowing of the skin and the 'whites' of the eyes – more obvious of course in black-skinned people – indicates liver trouble. Hepatitis of one type or another is the most common cause, but others can include malaria, glandular fever (mononucleosis), drug or alcohol abuse, or yellow fever.

Pain An important diagnosic aid, whose position, nature and severity are all significant. Chest pain can indicate simple 'heartburn' or indigestion, or at the other extreme a heart attack – in which case, it's usually dull, crushing and in the middle of the chest (but often spreading to the neck, shoulder or arm). Abdominal pain often accompanies diarrhoea, but if sharper might indicate appendicitis or a stomach ulcer. Any severe pain needs investigation.

Rash This is common, but the distinctive features may be easier to see than to describe. The most significant type is a rash of dark red or purplish spots that form blotches and don't pale if you press a glass on them. This indicates bleeding under the skin, and can be a sign of meningococcal disease or a haemorrhagic fever, such as dengue haemorrhagic fever; both of these are life-threatening, so the rash needs very urgent investigation.

Stools Diarrhoea and constipation are both common; the former is usually due to an intestinal infection, but can also result from malaria and other diseases. Black, tarry stools are a sign of intestinal bleeding.

Urination Pain, or a frequent need to urinate, may indicate a urinary or sexually-transmitted infection; the urine may be cloudy or smelly. Other signs (such as blood in the urine) often need laboratory tests to detect.

Vomiting This may be caused by travel sickness, but most often by eating contaminated food; it's also a symptom of many other diseases. Vomit like 'coffee grounds' indicates stomach bleeding, and may be serious.

When to get help

It's even more dangerous to set arbitrary time limits for seeking a doctor's help than it is to try to diagnose what is wrong with yourself. However, you should certainly seek immediate medical attention if...

→ You (or the patient) are/is elderly or a child;
→ You're obviously ill or have serious symptoms noted above;
→ You are or have recently been in a malarial area and develop symptoms of the disease, especially the *falciparum* form (see p. 107) – whether or not you've been taking your malaria pills regularly;
→ There's any reason to think you may have meningitis (see p. 163); or
→ You have any other set of symptoms that seem to be getting worse.

Otherwise, it's usually reasonable to wait 48 hours to see if the condition improves; if it doesn't or if it gets worse, then get medical help straight away. But after 48 hours many illnesses are on the way to clearing themselves up spontaneously – or, if not, the pattern of symptoms will often be clearer.

But let me repeat: **If in any doubt, get (or get to) a doctor.**

HAZARDS FROM FOOD AND DRINK

'Maybe it was something I ate.' Very likely indeed, in fact! An 'upset stomach' – diarrhoea and/or vomiting – is far and away the most common complaint to afflict travellers, especially in the developing world or anywhere else where food hygiene standards aren't up to scratch. So much so that it's commonly known as travellers' diarrhoea. However, in strict medical terms, that name covers a number of distinct infections, caused by various species of bacteria, protozoans and viruses that can get into you via contaminated food or drink – stomach bugs to you and me.

But those aren't the only afflications that may be served up on a plate or in a glass. Among the most serious are typhoid fever – caused by a bug closely related to some responsible for diarrhoea, and yet that symptom is quite rare in typhoid – and hepatitis A. And, although diarrhoea is often misnamed 'food poisoning' (it's caused by a bug, not a poison), true poisoning by toxins in food is possible (though rare) in some parts of the world. So are worms, although they're more likely to revolt you than do any real long-term damage.

All in all, however, while you're very likely to get travellers' diarrhoea if you travel long and far, your risk of catching anything worse is small so long as you take sensible precautions about what you eat and the establishments you choose to eat it in. New eating and drinking experiences are part of the excitement and adventure of travel, so enjoy them, but know what to do if and when those bugs catch up with you!

SAFE FOOD AND DRINK

'Waiter, what's in this salad apart from salmonella?'

– an anonymous American tourist in India

You can regard eating on your travels as a challenge and an adventure, an opportunity for mind- (and possibly stomach-) blowing experiences and for 'going native' in a big way. Or you can take the paranoid viewpoint, and see it as a necessary but unwelcome obstacle course – essential for survival, but to be negotiated as rapidly and safely as possible.

Like many keen and seasoned travellers, I guess I fall somewhere between these extremes, but definitely nearer the first than the second category – a cautious adventurer, if you like. I'm not mad keen to sample strange bits of animals' anatomy, or for that matter creepy-crawlies that I'm assured are the greatest delicacy on Earth but to my mind belong where they came from – under a rock or log. But I certainly don't want to survive on fish-'n'-chips, pizza, fried chicken, and tea like mother makes.

The global spread of regional cuisines – even if they are somewhat diluted versions of the real thing – has made most of us incomparably more adventurous in our eating than our parents' or grandparents' generations. But the scientist in me sounds a note of caution: I know I'm fortunate enough to live most of the time where I can pick up produce at the supermarket, confident that (give or take an additive or two) it's almost certainly clean, fresh and wholesome. If I turn the tap, I can expect – *almost* 100 per cent – that the water that emerges isn't a thriving culture of micro-organisms. I can even use the local swimming pool without too much risk to my guts.

Not so, of course, in many of the parts of the world that are the most attractive to travellers. As explained in the article on travellers' diarrhoea *(p.34)*, the very fact of leaving your home turf can bring you into contact with micro-organisms your stomach can't cope with – and the more outlandish the places you travel to, the more outlandish the bugs are liable to be. It's not just those that send you trotting to the loo that you need to be aware of. Brucellosis, typhoid, hepatitis, liver flukes, a whole variety of worms...*stop!* I'm falling into that paranoid trap again.

My own attitude, when I'm out there exploring the world, is to eat and enjoy what I fancy, avoid what I don't, but always be aware of the risks and choose sensibly to minimise them. So what I'll try to do here is give you some general guidelines and pointers on safe and unsafe things and ways to eat – inevitably going OTT a bit, and concentrating on the precautions you need to take in the least developed regions (you can usually take things more easily elsewhere) – and wish you luck and enjoyment. By all means ignore my advice; you may very well come to no harm at all. On the other hand, I can't guarantee you won't pick up something nasty even if you follow my advice to the letter; there's always an element of luck involved. All I can do is show you how to stack the odds a bit more in your own favour.

Basic precautions Food is by and large a much greater source of risk than drink in countries with lower hygiene standards than you're used to. However, water is far from risk-free, and I've covered it later in this article. In both cases, increased risk comes down mainly to economics. Sure, you can (and somebody reading this undoubtedly will) catch a nasty dose of travellers' diarrhoea anywhere in the 'advanced' Western world, but it's far more likely in a country where many of the people (including a lot of those engaged in producing, cooking and serving the food you eat) live below or little above subsistence level. So it's common sense, not prejudice, to tailor your level of caution to your location.

Any food can get contaminated where it lives and grows, while it's being collected and processed, while it's being transported, prepared and cooked, from the plate or eating utensils used for serving or eating it – or from your own fingers if you pick it up. So, first of all, it's back to basic hygiene: When in a higher-risk environment, be much more fastidious than at home. Particularly after going to the loo and before eating, wash your hands thoroughly with soap (including under your fingernails), and dry them properly on a clean towel. (If there aren't proper facilities, use a disinfectant baby wipe.) If you're in a group and have had a stomach upset, don't handle or prepare anyone else's food.

Make sure that plates, glasses, knives, forks, chopsticks and so on are all clean – and if necessary, give them the baby-wipe treatment, too (or use neat gin, vodka or other spirits on a tissue). In Asia, and in Asian restaurants and cafes elsewhere, disposable chopsticks are widely used, and are safer (if paper-wrapped) than reusable ones. You can buy them very cheaply from supermarkets, and it's worth getting a pack and using them whenever you're in doubt about what's provided. Personally, in some places I go so far as to take a plastic plate and mug (or disposable paper ones) in my day pack – not to use in proper restaurants (if they looked that bad, I'd avoid them) but for street food and drink. Food served on a bed of rice is out of direct contact with the dish, so it *may* be a bit safer so long as you leave the bottom layer.

What and what not to eat Food-preparation standards come down in part to the place where it's prepared and sold, and I'll come on to that in a moment. But think for a moment about the fate of any bugs that do get (or remain) in food: Cooking is the most efficient way of killing them, while keeping food nice and warm is the surest way for those bugs to thrive and breed. (Cooking food, allowing it to slowly cool, then rewarming it again and again is worst of all – so avoid a 'chef's special' that's likely to be warmed-up leftovers.)

Always go for freshly cooked, piping-hot (steaming or sizzling) cooked food. Then it doesn't matter so much whether the cook's toilet habits are as hygienic as you'd like them to be. Avoid buffets like the plague in developing regions, especially in the tropics. It's not just the food-poisoning bacteria brewing up heartily in the warm buffet you need to worry about, but also how easy it is for sneezes, fingers or flies to infect the food in the first place. Go for

SOME THINGS TO AVOID IN RISKY AREAS

→ Salads.

→ Fresh fruit juices and other home-made cold drinks.

→ Ice cream and other frozen desserts; sorbets made from acidic fruit (eg, citrus) are safer, but not 100 per cent.

→ Anything cooked well in advance – eg, quiche, pies, samosas, pizza, rotas, spring rolls, etc, that aren't freshly cooked.

→ Rare or undercooked meat or fish.

→ All shellfish, unless you're *sure* it's very well cooked.

→ Fruit salads; ready-peeled fruit; unpeelable fruit (eg, strawberries).

→ Mayonnaise, relishes and salsa left in the open.

→ Unpasteurised/unsterilised milk and dairy products. (Even pasteurised milk is best boiled in the Indian subcontinent and some other areas.)

→ Any finger-food that's not freshly cooked and sizzling-hot.

→ Ice and anything mixed with ice – eg, lassi (made from yoghurt, water and ice); drinks, butter or fruit chilled by directly adding ice.

→ Fried rice – it's usually made with yesterday's leftovers, and often contains food-poisoning bacteria (*see p.35*).

SOME THINGS TO GO FOR

→ Dry foods such as biscuits, cakes and bread (freshly baked or packaged), but *not* cream cakes.

→ Tinned food (so long as it's not past its 'sell by' date); clean the top of the can before opening.

→ Other non-perishable prepacked food (keep an emergency supply).

→ Major-brand canned drinks (safer than bottled, which can sometimes be faked refills; see text about cleaning and opening).

→ Major-brand *sealed* bottled water, from a reliable source.

→ Hot drinks such as tea or coffee without milk, unless pasteurised or preferably boiled.

à la carte, prepared-to-order dishes instead. If in doubt, choose something that has to be freshly prepared, such as an omelet or a freshly fried dish. As a very general rule, cooked vegetable dishes are safer than meat or shellfish (particularly if either isn't cooked thoroughly).

The flip-side is, of course that cold food is potentially much riskier. I've eaten salads in south-east Asia and lived to tell the tale, but I wouldn't recommend you to follow suit. Remember that in many parts of the tropics and beyond, 'night soil' is often the only fertiliser there is, so something like lettuce, which is difficult if not impossible to clean thoroughly, should be off your menu. Rinsing in chlorine, iodine or potassium permanganate ('inky-pinky') water will get rid of *some* of the bugs. But, unless it gets a long soak, then a soak in vinegar and a thorough rinsing in boiled or reliable bottled water, you can't be sure it's safe to eat (and maybe not even then). As one long-term resident of Nepal put it, the only safe lettuce in Kathmandu is a boiled one!

Use common sense: Undamaged tomatoes or peppers, whose skin is much easier to clean properly (using the above method) are much safer. The same rules apply to fruit: Avoid anything you have to eat whole but can't wash properly, such as berries. Bananas are great, because you can peel them without contaminating what's inside. Fruit that needs a knife to peel, such as pineapples and mangoes, should be washed thoroughly first in clean water, then peeled with your own clean knife (another must in my day pack).

There are several variations on the slogan, but it bears repeating: *Boil it, cook it, peel it, or forget it!*

Where and where not to eat Apparent luxury is no guarantee of kitchen standards, so if you're unsure go for a busy place (where there's a rapid turnover of food, meaning it's more likely to be fresh) over a quiet, 'romantic' one (where low lighting makes it difficult to see how clean things are). A place with the kitchen in full view is a good choice – so long as it looks OK.

What about street food? It's a way of life and a part of the overall experience in many parts of the world, but it's not difficult to see the hygiene problems if there are feral dogs and flies around, and uncooked food stacked on the ground. On the other hand, you can actually see the cook at work.

Judge food stalls and their wares in the same way as any other food source: Does the vendor handle the food only with clean utensils, or take the hands-on approach? Does the food look clean and fresh? Or is it made in the morning and left out in the open all day to collect fly droppings and other unmentionables? Personally, I'd choose a freshly prepared stir-fry or a well-cooked char-grilled satay from a stall in south-east Asia anytime – so long as they were made in clean surroundings and preferably served on my own plate – over a slice of pizza kept warm in a glass case on a London street.

Water and other drinks Travellers generally worry much more about what they drink than what they eat, and while clean food is more important, you do need clean water too. You can't always rely on local people's – even expats' – advice on whether tap water is safe, since long exposure gives a measure of immunity to local bugs. I'd advise you to treat with suspicion any tap water outside the developed world, and certainly outside major cities. (There's general guidance for popular destinations in the section on health risks around the world, starting on page 182.) If in doubt, don't let tap water in your mouth, even for cleaning your teeth, and use sterilised (*see box, p.32*) or reliable bottled water instead.

Many hotels in the tropics supply boiled water in rooms – but do use your common sense and make inquiries about it before you drink it. Is it the kind of establishment you'd basically trust? Do they properly boil the water? Is it in a stoppered container, or is it open to contamination after boiling? Is unused water thrown out and fresh supplied each day? (If not, you'd best empty the container yourself each morning.) If it's cooled, how? Ice is only as clean as the water it's made from, so be suspicious of ice *in* the water.

In the past 25 years, bottled water has appeared all over the world, and there's no doubt it's a great boon to travellers, particularly in developing regions. But it's not infallible – local brands in some countries have been found to contain bacteria (10 out of 13 brands tested by a consumer organisation in India, for example), and bottles can be refilled with local tap water and resold. So look for well-known brands if possible, and certainly make sure that any bottle you buy is properly sealed. (Glass bottles are slightly easier to refill and seal than plastic, but fizzy water is usually not worth anyone faking.) And without wanting to deprive street vendors of a living, I'd personally prefer to buy from a well-established supermarket.

The same applies, only perhaps more so, to branded fizzy drinks – colas, fruit drinks and beer. Bottles aren't difficult to fake-refill and seal, even with a proper-looking metal cap, but again you're more at risk from street vendors than from supermarkets or hotels. Make sure the bottle is opened in front of you. Cans are far safer, but to be sure you'd best wipe the top clean with an antiseptic wipe before opening and drinking it.

As mentioned above, ice is always a risk – even if it was made in a modern

MAKING WATER SAFE TO DRINK

Outside the developed world, drinking water needs treating to kill the micro-organisms in it, and if you can't get water that you're sure someone else has reliably treated, you'll have to do it yourself. There are three basic methods (some of which you need to use in combination): boiling, filtering and chemical treatment. But first, if there's any option, choose water from the cleanest source in the first place: Tap, spring or well water, or rainwater collected in a clean container, are likely to be purer than water from a river, stream or pool. (Seawater is a special case, needing a solar still to completely evaporate and then condense salt-free water.)

Boiling This is the most effective method, if you have a suitable container and source of heat. (A small electric heater element is an option if you anticipate having to boil water regularly and will have access to electricity.) As a minimum, keep the water boiling for a minute, or longer if you're at high altitude. A full five minutes is best above 3000m (10 000ft). It'll taste better if you allow it to cool, covered, for a few hours, then part-fill a clean bottle with the water and shake to re-aerate it.

Filtering If you intend to take a water filter on your travels, consult a specialist supplier. Some filters are designed to remove only relatively large particles, simply to clarify water before it's boiled or chemically hygienic factory, there's no telling how it might have got contaminated on its way to your glass. Use it *around* your drink, never *in* it. 'Fresh' fruit drinks should be given a miss in developing countries, but coconut water (direct, preferably through a clean straw, from a fresh green coconut) is usually safe – and delicious – so long as the tool used to open the coconut was clean. And don't forget that boiling-hot drinks – coffee, teas of all kinds, hot lemon – are intrinisically safer than cold ones so long as the cup is clean.

Never drink water from a natural spring or stream in the developing world, however clean it looks. You can't see disease organisms, and a friend caught giardiasis (a very unpleasant type of diarrhoea; *see p.43*) by drinking water from a seemingly pure Himalayan stream; he's still living with the aftermath, several years later. Always boil or otherwise sterilise it first (*see box below*).

Swimming pools and the sea can't be sterilised (even a big dose of chlorine won't kill all possible bugs), so try very hard not to swallow the water of even the cleanest pool. Perhaps it's that paranoia again, but I'd avoid any swimming pool that doesn't smell of chlorine and I wouldn't swim in the sea anywhere near human habitation in areas that lack proper sewage disposal.

A final word With all the emphasis in this article on caution – 'defensive' eating and drinking – you might be tempted to find one kind of safe food and then stick to it, like a student living on nothing but baked beans or pot

---

treated. Others remove micro-organisms more or less completely – some still need chemical treatment for complete safety – but must be used and cleaned carefully to remain effective. Most experts don't recommend activated-charcoal filters, because they only trap disease organisms on the charcoal surface and may let them back into the water if overloaded.

Chemical treatment The two main options are iodine (eg, 'Potable Aqua') or chlorine (eg, 'Puritabs'). Iodine is generally more effective but shouldn't be used too long or it may cause thyroid problems. (Some of the most effective water filtering devices use an iodine-resin filter, so you shouldn't treat such water again with more iodine.)

A simple method for occasional use is to add six drops of 2 per cent tincture of iodine (double if you suspect *Giardia* in the water) to a litre (1¾ pints) of water. Even cheaper is to keep a teaspoonful of iodine crystals in a small, stoppered glass bottle of water (the iodine will attack plastics) and shake it occasionally; simply add 10ml (2 teaspoons) of this iodine solution (but none of the crystals) to a litre of water for drinking, then top up the small bottle for next time. Iodine-treated water should be left to stand for 20–30 minutes before drinking; you can improve the taste by adding vitamin C (ascorbic acid) – try half an effervescent tablet for starters, but not until just before you want to drink the water as it stops the iodine working.

noodles. Please don't. Have fun eating the exotic foods you find, and try to get a balanced diet that includes...

→ Proteins: Properly cooked meat, fish, eggs, beans, lentils, other pulses.
→ Carbohydrates: Rice, potatoes, pasta, noodles, bread, tortillas, chapattis – wholemeal when you can get it, to help keep your bowels regular.
→ Properly cooked or cleaned fresh vegetables and fruit.

Enjoy them all – they're much better than a handful of vitamin pills!

TRAVELLERS' DIARRHOEA

From Dehli belly to Montezuma's revenge, it's almost universal.

Diarrhoea – call it gastroenteristis, a stomach upset, the trots, the squits or what you will – is the number one ailment affecting travellers, hitting an estimated half to two-thirds of all those who travel abroad. And ways of avoiding it and treating it are a pretty popular topic of conversation wherever backpackers and other long-distance travellers get together, too! So, before going any farther, let's clear up a few basics and dispell a few myths:–

→ Diarrhoea isn't a disease or disorder in itself; it's a symptom that can be caused by lots of different things, some serious and some relatively trivial.

→ The term 'diarrhoea' refers simply to loose stools or bowel movements, ranging from soft or semi-liquid, runny faeces to watery movements with bits floating in them.

→ 'Dysentery' implies that there's blood and mucus (slime) in the stools.

→ Diarrhoea may or may not be accompanied by vomiting – and this can be a clue as to the precise cause. (Sometimes there's vomiting alone.)

→ There may or may not be other symptoms such as stomach cramps and/or a fever – but with dysentery you usually get both.

→ Travellers' diarrhoea is mainly a problem of food and (less often) drink hygiene – ie, you 'catch' it from contaminated food. (Not to put too fine a point on it, bacteria or other germs from an infected person's faeces or vomit get into the food you eat, whether from hands, flies, the ground, blown dust or whatever.) To this extent the term 'food poisoning' is OK. But true poisoning by toxins (poisons) in food – as in ciguatera poisoning (*see p.48*) – is a quite separate issue.

This doesn't mean that you can ignore the problem of contaminated water – that's also an important cause of travellers' diarroea and other problems. It's just that diarrhoea bugs are liable to multiply alarmingly in contaminated food that isn't kept properly – the bugs themselves feeding on the food – so that far more of them may build up to infect you than in contaminated water. So, statistically, bad food causes more diarrhoea than bad water.

This article deals mostly with the relatively simple, uncomplicated kinds of diarrhoea and dysentery, with or without vomiting. In separate short articles afterwards (see p.43), some specific varieties are covered in a bit more detail. It also points you to separate coverage of more serious conditions that can cause similar symptoms, such as cholera and (sometimes) typhoid fever.

What it is Travellers' diarrhoea germs act in either (or both) of two ways: They produce toxins that attack the body cells forming the inner lining of your gut (intestines), and/or they directly invade and infect those cells (and sometimes travel farther into your body). Either way, one of the main results is that much more water (and salt) than normal flows out from your tissues and into your intestines – far more than your large intestine (lower down the 'pipeline') can re-absorb. Or, in some cases, the re-absorption mechanism in the large intestine itself fails.

The result: watery or fluid stools – ie, diarrhoea itself – causing fluid loss that can be enough to dehydrate you. And dehydration is the big (occasionally fatal) danger of travellers' diarrhoea, made worse if you're in a hot climate where you're probably losing a lot of fluid anyway, through sweating. Blood and/or mucus come from the damaged cells lining the intestines, and the infection can cause a fever. And, of course, in your stools are a fine crop of diarrhoea germs just waiting for the chance to infect someone else.

All the main types of micro-organisms crop up among the parade of causes of travellers' diarrhoea. The exact pattern of the symptoms they cause varies, along with how fast and how badly they affect you, so these patterns can help a doctor to make a precise diagnosis. (However, in quite a large proportion of cases the exact cause of diarrhoea is unknown.)

Bacteria probably account for well over half of all cases of travellers' diarrhoea. There are getting on for a dozen individual species (kinds) of bacteria that can hit you in the gut, ranging from those that normally act within a few hours to much more slow-acting types that take many hours or even several days to cause symptoms. The most common single cause of travellers' diarrhoea is a toxic form of a bacterium that everyone has in their intestines, called *Escherichia coli* (or simply *E. coli*). The toxic form that mostly affects travellers is known in full as *enterotoxigenic E. coli*, or ETEC; fortunately the diarrhoea it causes doesn't usually last long, and most people eventually build up some immunity to it. (It's different from *E. coli* 0157, the form causing recent serious outbreaks in Britain and the USA sometimes resulting in kidney failure in children; this form rarely affects travellers.)

Fast workers include *Staphylococcus aureus*, the bug responsible for boils, styes and other skin infections (and so all too easily transferred to food from a careless cook's hands); and *Bacillus cereus*, which grows on cooked rice and is a particular risk if you eat reheated rice dishes (eg, fried rice). Both often cause vomiting, diarrhoea or both, usually within a few hours.

Among the slowcoaches are bacteria called *Campylobacter* and *Shigella* (which is so powerful that as few as ten individual bacteria may be enough to make you ill); after a delay of a few days they can can go off like a time-bomb, causing nasty 'explosive' dysentery with blood in your stools. In between are bacteria that usually take about 12 to 36 hours to strike, such as certain types of *Salmonella*. (However, *Salmonella* sometimes causes a fever, with or without rigors [shivering], but no diarrhoea at all.)

One other important type of diarrhoea bacterium, *Vibrio cholerae*, causes cholera, a disease that's often almost indistinguishable from severe watery diarrhoea from other bugs; it's covered separately (see p.44).

Protozoans are tiny single-celled animal parasites. Those that can give you travellers' diarrhoea include an amoeba called *Entamoeba histolytica*. This is the cause of amoebic dysentery (see p.43), which is often very similar to the type of dysentery caused by bacteria ('bacilliary dysentery'). Another is called *Giardia*, and results in a very unpleasant and often long-lasting bout of diarrhoea called giardiasis (see p.43). Neither of these is particularly common in travellers, although giardiasis is much more so among people whose diarrhoea lingers on after they return home.

Two other protozoans have only quite recently been nailed as causes of diarrhoea: *Cryptosporidium* (see p.43), which is quite common worldwide and is a difficult bug to both prevent and treat; and *Cyclospora* (see p.43), a particular risk in Nepal and parts of South America, which is treatable.

Viruses can spread in coughs and sneezes as well as directly in food, and several types cause diarrhoea and vomiting. (The name 'gastric flu' – often used loosely, like 'food poisoning', for any diarrhoeal illness – is justifiable here.) They aren't a very common cause of diarrhoea in travellers, but are particularly important in 'closed' environments such as cruise ships (where they can be passed around like wildfire and are difficult to eliminate) and young children (who can become seriously ill and dehydrated).

Non-infective causes It isn't only micro-organisms that can cause diarrhoea and/or vomiting. Apart from the fish toxins mentioned above and covered on page 48, poisonous mushrooms and other plants, pesticides, certain drugs and other chemical toxins can all do so; if you suspect you might have consumed any of these, you need to get medical attention ASAP. Long-term causes (whose sufferers probably already know the score) include irritable bowel syndrome and inflammatory bowel disease (Crohn's disease and ulcerative colitis); they can all strike travellers and non-travellers alike.

Specifically travel-related factors include stress, jet lag, excess alcohol consumption, and heavy doses of spices and other substances in new, unusual foods that your stomach simply isn't used to. However, the diarrhoea and/or vomiting these cause is generally pretty short-lived, and the rest of this article concentrates on the infective variety.

Where you can get it Simple answer: Anywhere. More complicated answer: The less developed the area (and thus the more primitive the sanitation) and the hotter the climate (and thus the more difficult it is to keep food fresh), the more likely you are to get travellers' diarrhoea – *particularly if you travel from somewhere with an equal or lower risk*.

You can divide the world roughly into three zones. The risk is lowest in Australia and New Zealand, north-western Europe, Japan, and the USA and Canada. There's an in-between level of risk in southern Europe (bordering the Mediterranean), in the Caribbean, and in eastern Europe and the former Soviet Union. Most of the rest of the world – specifically Africa, Latin America and the rest of Asia – forms a high-risk zone.

The safest thing to do (although of course it won't guarantee that you'll avoid diarrhoea) is to stay at home. This is because everybody has some built-in immunity to the bugs they're liable to come across on their own home patch. Even going to a low-risk country from another one increases the likelihood of getting hit – partly because you'll be eating out more, and relying on other people's hygiene practices. But the greatest risk comes from travelling from a low-risk area to one of high risk. Then you probably have at least a 40 to 50 per cent chance of catching travellers' diarrhoea.

It's worth remembering, however, that after some time in even a high-risk zone you should build up a degree of resistance, certainly to ETEC bacteria and probably to some other causes of diarrhoea too. And even within high-risk zones, some places and situations are riskier than others; which comes into the realm of...

How you can avoid it Since most diarrhoea-causing bugs get a free ride in the food you eat, food hygiene and taking care about where and what you eat are the number one precaution. It's so important, to avoid both diarrhoea and a number of other diseases, that I've covered it in a separate article (*see p.28*). Remember, too, that your own hands can easily get contaminated – both in the loo and when handling everyday objects – and carry infection not only to food you handle but also directly to your mouth. So wash them regularly and thoroughly with soap, and dry them properly on a clean towel.

It's somewhat less important (as already indicated), but still vital, to ensure also that you drink clean water and other drinks, including ice (*see p.32*). This applies equally to anything that accidentally passes your lips – eg, from a swimming pool or the sea. Even a chlorinated swimming pool can contain a flourishing colony of *Cryptosporidium, Cyclospora* and maybe other diarrhoea organisms. And in many regions – including a surprising proportion of the so-called developed world – raw sewage is pumped straight into the sea or inland waterways. A UN report in 2002 said that the most sewage-polluted coasts were in southern Asia; only slightly better were coasts in eastern Asia and the north-west Pacific, and in west and central Africa. You may spot 'floaters', but in most cases the pollution is invisible. (In Europe, the Blue Flag scheme is a valuable but not infallible sign of clean seawater.)

Vaccination against travellers' diarrhoea isn't an option for most people – yet. Several vaccines against the most common cause, ETEC bacteria (*see above*), are in the advanced stages of testing, and other vaccines are being developed. At the time of writing, the only such vaccine on the market – a drinkable vaccine against ETEC and cholera called 'Dukoral' – is only licensed in New Zealand, Norway, Sweden and a dozen or so less-developed countries. But if the trials go well, you may soon be able to get vaccinated against not only ETEC but also *Campylobacter, Shigella* and possibly other diarrhoea bugs. Ask a travel doctor before you set off.

Meanwhile, what about taking protective drugs? Taking antibiotics as a routine is controversial to say the least, but you might like to note that the antibiotic doxycycline, recommended in many regions as a good option for preventing malaria (*see p.107*), has the side-effect of giving some protection against diarrhoea organisms. (But it mustn't be taken by pregnant or breast-feeding women or children, and itself occasionally causes mild diarrhoea.) Mainstream medical opinion suggests that you should discuss with your doctor (or a travel specialist) the option of taking preventive antibiotics...

→ If you have strong personal reasons for avoiding a bout of diarrhoea, such as an important meeting, a sports event or other vital need to keep to your pre-arranged plans.
→ If you are weakened by a long-standing condition such as diabetes, HIV infection, or heart or liver disease.
→ Or if you have a stomach or duodenal ulcer and may be at higher than normal risk of getting travellers' diarrhoea.

One preventive option taken by many Americans is a four-times-daily dose of bismuth subsalicylate ('Pepto-Bismol'), which is also sometimes used as an antacid to treat indigestion. It should only be taken for short trips of up to three weeks, and shouldn't be used by children, but in adults it significantly reduces the risk of getting travellers' diarrhoea. The snags are that it turns your stools and tongue black (without causing any permanent harm) and leaves an unpleasant taste in the mouth; more important, it shouldn't be taken at the same time as aspirin (which also contains salicylate). It's available over the counter in the USA in tablet form, but in Britain only comes as a liquid suspension – a bit bulky for your backpack.

Many people swear by eating live yoghurt or special preparations containing 'friendly' bacteria such as *Lactobacillus acidophilus* as a way of both preventing and treating travellers' diarrhoea. The theory is that these bacteria displace or suppress harmful ones – or, if you are hit, restore the natural bacterial balance of your intestines. As far as I know there haven't been any rigorous field trials of their effectiveness, but they're pretty safe and, so long as you don't ignore other precautions, could well help. They're available in capsule and powder form, a much safer proposition for travellers than locally produced live yoghurt (which by definition isn't pasteurised).

What it does to you The differing effects of the various diarrhoea micro-organisms have a bearing on diagnosis and the best treatment. The pattern of symptoms is usually one of the following:–

MEDICATIONS, THE PILL, AND STOMACH UPSETS

It's pretty obvious that if you throw up soon after you've swallowed a tablet or other medication, your body won't have had much time to absorb it; this applies as much to malaria pills and the contraceptive Pill as to other drugs. *Subject to what your doctor may advise*, if you vomit within about one hour of taking any medication, repeat the dose. In the case of oral contraceptives – particularly the mini-Pill – take other contraceptive precautions for the remainder of that menstrual cycle.

→ *Vomiting only*, or vomiting combined with diarrhoea (which is properly called gastroenteritis), starting very soon after the suspect meal. This is usually caused by the bacterial toxins produced by *Bacillus cereus* (the rice bug) or *Staphylococcus aureus* (from skin infections), or by a virus; in the latter case there will usually be both vomiting and diarrhoea, and also a flu-like fever.

→ *Watery diarrhoea* lasting three to five days – during which time, you may have to 'go' anything up to 40 times – but without significant vomiting or blood in the stools. There are various possible causes, including ETEC bacteria, *Salmonella*, *Clostridium*, *Vibrio*, a delayed action by *Bacillus cereus*, or others. Cholera (*see p.44*) is an extreme version of this pattern.

→ *Dysentery* – diarrhoea plus fever plus blood and/or mucus (slime) in the stools. There are two types: bacilliary dysentery, usually caused by *Shigella* or *Campylobacter* bacteria but sometimes by others, which usually starts abruptly, with a fever; and amoebic dysentery (*see p.43*), caused by the protozoan *Entamoeba histolytica*, which usually builds up more gradually, with no fever at first.

→ *Diarrhoea lasting more than about two weeks* – often due to giardiasis (*see p.43*) caused by another protozoan, *Giardia*, or some other prolonged bacterial infection of the intestines. Sometimes it's an aftereffect of the initial ('primary') infection, which may have damaged your intestines. You definitely need a medical investigation to sort out which you have.

→ *A prolonged high fever* combined with a headache and stomach pains, plus diarrhoea (or alternatively just the opposite – constipation). **These could be symptoms of typhoid fever (*see p.46*), which is dangerous and needs urgent medical attention.**

How it's treated In most cases, travellers' diarrhoea clears up within two to three days without any specific medical treatment. However, a great deal of body fluid can be lost in this time, so fluid replacement is the main priority (*see box, p.40*). **This is particularly important with children, who can become dangerously dehydrated in a matter of hours, and with elderly people.** Get professional medical help if you feel very ill or in any of the following cases:–

→ If, because of persistent vomiting, fluids won't stay down.

→ If the diarrhoea lasts more than 36–48 hours.

→ If, at any time, there's blood in the stools.

→ If there's a fever of more than about 38°C (100.4°F).

→ If there's any other underlying illness or chronic condition.

Even though the pattern of symptoms and onset of the problem can be a good clue as to what's causing your diarrhoea, and thus the best treatment, no doctor can be sure without carrying out tests, normally on a stool sample. (This should be no problem so long as you are reasonably near decent medical facilities, as medical labs in most 'high-risk' parts of the world are well used to testing for causes of diarrhoea.)

If the cause is a bacterial infection – and in some cases even if there's no positive confirmation – you're likely to be given a course of antibiotics such as ciprofloxacin (not for children, and not effective against some resistant

REPLACING BODY FLUIDS

If you eat and drink normally, in a normal climate, your food and drink supply about 2–3 litres (3½–5 pints) of fluid each day, and you lose a similar amount in your breath, sweat, urine and faeces. In hot conditions or if you sweat a lot for any other reason – or particularly if you have watery diarrhoea and/or vomiting – you can easily lose as much again. If you don't replace what you've lost, you'll become dehydrated (see p.58).

With children the normal consumption and fluid-loss figures are lower, *but they have a far lower tolerance of fluid loss and can easily become seriously dehydrated in a matter of hours.* Kids usually can't tell you when they're dehydrated – and neither can adults in many cases; they just feel generally awful. So watch out for the danger signs:–

→ Drowsiness; listlessness; dizziness on standing up; even fainting.

→ Dry mouth and tongue; flabby, flaccid skin (try pinching it); sunken eyes.

→ Small quantities of concentrated (dark and smelly) urine – or even no urine passed at all.

→ A weak, rapid pulse.

Any child showing such signs, and particularly a baby, needs to be taken to a doctor urgently. Meanwhile, try to make sure that as much fluid is taken by mouth as possible – and this applies to adults too. If everything that goes down comes straight up again, try small sips. Tepid drinks are better than either hot or ice-cold ones.

What to drink? In an emergency, it doesn't much matter, so long as it's clean and safe. But far better is a rehydration solution containing both glucose (sugar) and a little salt (which together help the body to absorb strains) or azithromycin ('Zithromax'). Rifaximin may soon be available as an alternative; at the time of writing it's only licensed in a few countries. At one time, a common remedy for travellers' diarrhoea was a combination treatment called co-trimoxazole ('Bactrim' or 'Septrin'); this may still be prescribed by doctors in some countries, but many diarrhoea bacteria are resistant to it and it can (rarely) have serious side-effects, so it's usually best avoided. (An exception is in treating *Cyclospora*, when it still works.)

If you're confirmed as having ameobic dysentery or giardiasis – or if the cause isn't clear but antibiotics don't work – you may be given metronidazole ('Flagyl') or tinidazole ('Fasigyn'). But beware: you'll have the mother of all hangovers if you're tempted to take alcohol (not that you're likely to feel much like it!), and even without you may get a nasty taste in your mouth.

There's always a temptation to treat yourself with antidiarrhoeal drugs that simply 'block' you up without actually tackling the cause, but these can make

both water and nourishment). You can buy ready-made rehydration salts in sachets or as fizzy tablets, at home or in most countries around the world, under such names as 'Dioralyte', 'Electrolade', 'Oralit' and 'Rehidrat'. Just dissolve them in the recommended quantity of clean – boiled and cooled, or reliable bottled – water. (Some mixtures contain powdered starch, which is just as good.)

Or it's very easy and much cheaper to make your own: For 1 litre (1¾ pints) of clean water use 8 level teaspoons of sugar – it doesn't matter what type so long as it's clean: white, brown, palm-sugar or honey – plus ½ teaspoon of salt; for a better flavour, add squeezed lemon, orange or lime juice. If you've got nothing else, add a small pinch of salt to a can of soft drink. Ideally, a caffeine-free fruit drink is better than a cola, flat is better than fizzy, and regular is better than a 'diet' variety – for once you really want that sugar. But use whatever you can get.

How much to drink? Simple answer: Enough to make you feel better, and ensure that you pass normal quantities of normal-looking urine again. You may need several litres at first, **but this isn't a one-off 'cure'; keep taking the rehydration mixture until your bout of diarrhoea is cured.** As a rule of thumb, adults and older children should drink at *least* one large glass – 300ml, or ½ pint – for every visit to the loo, *plus* another glass every hour (a bit less for children under ten – say 100–250ml for each stool, depending on their age). Children who are being bottle-fed should have their normal feed *plus* at least 1½ times this quantity of rehydration solution – but, as I've already said, **they should be under a doctor's care**. Breast-feeding may supply enough fluid, but the mother will need to drink more – and, again, **medical guidance is vital**.

the condition worse in the long term, and it's usually best to let the offending micro-organisms escape rather than trapping them in your gut. However, there are some circumstances when blockers are justified – for instance, if you're taking part in an event that can't be postponed, of if you're going on a long journey (which again can't be put off) in a bus or train with poor or non-existent loos. In that case, you could take loperamide ('Immodium' or 'Arret'), or (with a prescription) diphenoxylate ('Lomotil') or codeine phosphate; but these are morphine-related, and you need to keep strictly to recommended doses and not give them to children.

Other alternatives include bismuth subsalicylate ('Pepto-Bismol'; *see above*), which can be effective in slowing down your diarrhoea but again isn't for children; and kaolin mixtures (eg, 'KLN' and 'Kaopectate'), which contain powdered clay that 'mops up' the diarrhoea but may have a short-lived effect.

You'll probably come across numerous other diarrhoea 'remedies' in pharmacies, general shops and markets on your travels. I'd advise you to treat them all – apart from rehydration mixtures and the drugs I've specifically mentioned, sourced from a qualified pharmacy – with extreme scepticism. One in particular you might recognise by name: clioquinol ('Entero-Vioform'). This used to be popular in the UK and is still sold in many countries, but the consensus is that it does little or nothing for diarrhoea and is in fact toxic. Avoid it. For *Lactobacillus* preparations, see the section above on prevention; don't rely on them as a cure.

General care and recovery Apart from any antibiotic or other drug treatment that's needed, the keys to recovery from travellers' diarrhoea are rest and plenty of fluids (*see box*). Food is less important so long as you take sweetened drinks, but it *is* important to start eating with the right types of food. Avoid anything rich, spicy or fatty (including all fried foods). Bland soups are a good start. For the first solids, try easily digested starchy things like potatoes, rice, pasta (without a rich sauce), bread (without butter) or dry salt biscuits (crackers). Bananas are good – and safe in areas with dodgy food hygiene so long as you peel them carefully. After that, you can graduate to fish or chicken (both either steamed, boiled or grilled), beans and lentils. Keep off dairy products and alcohol until your bowels are back to normal.

Aftereffects Diarrhoeal illness injures your intestines, and in a few cases diarrhoea lasts for weeks or even months after the infection is eliminated. Often the cause is lactose intolerance – an inability to digest and absorb lactose, a sugar found in milk and dairy products. Abstaining from all dairy products for a week or two may restore normality. Other possibilities are irritable bowel syndrome or a little-understood condition called tropical sprue. In either case, it's best to get medical help in a major city or academic centre as soon as you can, and meanwhile keep to a bland diet.

AMOEBIC DYSENTERY

Sometimes this version of travellers' diarrhoea, caused by a protozoan called *Entamoeba* (*see p.36*), is quite mild; but in other cases it causes severe dysentery (diarrhoea containing blood) and a fever. Worldwide, it's estimated to affect nearly 50 million people, causing 70 000 deaths, each year. You can get it anywhere, but it's most prevalent in the tropics – especially in Latin America, southern Africa, and southern and south-east Asia.

The diarrhoea usually starts about eight to ten days after infection, often beginning quite gradually and with no fever at the start. But it can drag on for weeks if it's not treated successfully. Diagnosis depends on examining a stool sample under a microscope for the living amoebas. (If only the cysts are found, these may be from the more common and harmless *Entamoeba dispar* rather than *Entamoeba histolytica*, the cause of amoebic dysentery.) It's usually treated with metronidazole ('Flagyl'; *see p.41*), often followed by a second course of a different drug to prevent a relapse. Avoid alcohol.

CRYPTOSPORIDIUM

Another protozoal parasite (*see p.36*) often simply known as 'crypto', this is a very resistant bug that can survive in water treated with chlorine or iodine (so you can catch it from swimming pools); only boiling water makes it safe. It occurs worldwide, and is often spread by farm and domestic animals.

It causes abrupt watery diarrhoea, with stomach cramps, that lasts for six to ten days in most people. But in those with a weakened immune system (from HIV, drug treatments or some other reason) it can drag on much longer and even threaten life. (It and related infections are a major cause of AIDS-related wasting disease in Africa and other tropical regions.) Unfortunately, there's no effective treatment, although early evidence suggests that a new antibiotic, rifaximin, may help.

CYCLOSPORA

This and some related protozoans (*see p.36*) are also widespread, but have been particular problems in Latin America and Nepal. Like *Cryptosporidium* it survives chemical sterilization of water, which has to be boiled. It causes even more severe diarrhoea – similar to giardiasis (*see below*) – that may last as long as three months if it's not treated; but fortunately co-trimoxazole ('Bactrim'; 'Septrin') is an effective treatment.

GIARDIASIS

This is one of the more unpleasant forms of travellers' diarrhoea, caused by another protozoan (*see p.36*), called *Giardia*. It can be picked up almost anywhere, from Canadian ski resorts and Russian cities to the tropics; it's carried and spread by humans and by wild and domesticated animals, who contaminate surface water supplies. Normal chemical treatment of water doesn't always eliminate it, and water is best boiled to kill the *Giardia* bugs. It can, like *Cryptosporidium*, be picked up from swimming pools

The symptoms usually begin one to three weeks after infection, with nausea and a feeling of a bloated stomach, a poor appetite and foul-smelling ('eggy') wind, often from both ends. There's diarrhoea, often watery at first but then with pale-coloured, fatty, foul-smelling loose stools that float. If you're lucky, giardiasis clears up in a week or so, but in some people it drags on for months and can cause vitamin deficiencies and weight loss. If a stool sample shows that you have *Giardia*, treatment with metronidazole ('Flagyl') or tinidazole ('Fasigyn'; *see p.41*) is usually effective, but two courses of treatment may be needed. Avoid alcohol, and reduce the unpleasant effects of the infection by sticking to a low-fat, bland diet until you're better.

CHOLERA

A nasty version of diarrhoea, but no longer a terror disease.

Cholera is one of those diseases whose name is enough to give you an anxiety attack – but the terror is almost completely unjustified as far as today's travellers are concerned. In the 19th century, huge numbers died of it around the world, but that was before modern public hygiene measures, antibiotics, and understanding of the need for oral rehydration therapy. What's more, the bugs causing cholera at that time may have been more virulent than the main strain found today. Without wanting to sound callous, cholera is still a serious danger to people living in poverty in the developing world, but the risk to most travellers is very low. (Even when there's an epidemic on, cholera is reckoned to account for only 1 in 20 cases of diarrhoea among local populations.)

This could be changing, however; a new strain – 'Bengal' cholera, officially known as the O-139 type – appeared in Bangladesh in 1992, and caused more than 100 000 deaths. It seems to have more in common with the old 'Classic' strain – including the ability to attack adults – than the 'El Tor' (O-1) strain responsible for most recent cholera epidemics. 'El Tor' emerged in Indonesia in 1961 and spread to Latin America 30 years later. Cholera has always taken decades to spread around the world; who knows how far O-139 has to go?

What it is There's nothing inherently different between cholera and most other diarrhoeal diseases (*see p.34*). It's caused by bacteria called *Vibrio cholerae*, which are mostly spread in food and water contaminated by infected people's faeces – either directly or via hands, contaminated utensils and so on. In fact, they're not very hardy little bugs, and in a healthy adult who's not taking a course of antacids or other drugs for heartburn or a stomach ulcer, they may be killed straight off by stomach acids. If they do get through this line of defence, they act in much the same way as other bacteria that cause travellers' diarrhoea – only sometimes more so.

Where you can get it Cholera is essentially a disease of poor conditions in developing countries; you're only at serious risk if you work as a professional or volunteer in health facilities, refugee camps or slums, or travel far beyond where you can get safe water – *and* fail to take the precautions mentioned below. Geographically, the main risk areas are sub-Saharan Africa, Latin America and southern and south-east Asia; there have also been cholera outbreaks in the Pacific, particularly in Fiji and Micronesia.

How you can avoid it As with other types of travellers' diarrhoea, the most important precautions concern food hygiene (*see p.28*) and clean water (*see p.32*). Shellfish are a particular danger, and you should avoid eating undercooked or raw seafood. (In response to the South American epidemic in the 1990s, the Chilean authorities insisted on thorough cooking of all shellfish and even ceviche, the traditional dish of raw marinated fish.) Boiling or treating water with chlorine or iodine quickly kills cholera bacteria.

Cholera vaccinations used to be compulsory for travellers entering many countries, but they were largely ineffective, both in preventing the disease on an individual level and in halting its spread around the world. The ineffective vaccine has now been withdrawn in most places, and it's officially forbidden to demand a cholera vaccination certificate from travellers anywhere in the world. Nevertheless, border officials in some places may still do so (perhaps as a means of small-scale extortion?); if you're concerned, ask your doctor for an exemption certificate before you travel.

Having said all that, there are now new – and, by most reports, much more effective – cholera vaccines available in some places. (At the time of writing, for example, you can get them in Canada and Australia but not in the UK or USA.) They are taken orally, and give protection for at least a year (longer if you travel frequently in a cholera zone, so that your immunity is topped up by exposure to the bug) against the 'Classic' and 0-1 cholera strains; they're not effective against 0-139. Among them is the 'Dukoral' vaccine, mentioned on page 38, that also gives some protection against another common cause of travellers' diarrhoea, enterotoxigenic *Escherichia coli*. Another ('Colertif') gives protection against both cholera and typhoid. If you're planning a long stay in a risky environment, discuss vaccination with a travel doctor.

What it does to you 'El Tor' cholera is very much the same as most other types of travellers' diarrhoea (*see p.38*), beginning quite abruptly and often accompanied by vomiting, but generally quite mild. However, in rare cases of the 'El Tor' type, and in 'Classic' and 0-139 cholera, the diarrhoea may be dramatic and extreme. It's quite possible to lose 5 or 10 litres (up to 2 *gallons* or more) of body fluids in a matter of hours, leading to extreme dehydration and death if they're not very quickly replaced. (The diarrhoea is often described as 'rice-water' – watery, with white bits in it.)

How it's treated Follow the same rules for getting immediate medical help as in other kinds of travellers' diarrhoea (*see pp.39–40*). With or without a doctor, the first priority is to replace lost fluids by drinking lots of rehydration solution – a sugar and salt mixture in clean water (*see pp.40–41*). In most cases, this is all that's needed to ensure recovery within three to five days or so. (The introduction of proper oral rehydration therapy is reckoned to have reduced the cholera death rate from 80 per cent to below 1 per cent.) The only problem is likely to be getting enough fluid down if the diarrhoea is extreme; **if in doubt, seek medical help**.

A doctor may suggest a course of antibiotics such as azithromycin or erythromycin. These can shorten a bout of cholera if begun soon after the symptoms appear, but they're usually justified only in severe cases or where someone's obviously at risk in an epidemic.

TYPHOID

One of the great 19th-century killers that's still a serious travel risk.

Typhoid – sometimes known by the rather Victorian-sounding name enteric fever – is one of the most serious 'dirt and mouth' diseases, transmitted by contaminated food or water, that's still a threat to travellers. It's not common, but outbreaks occur in most developing countries, where it affects as many as 16 million people each year, causing 600 000 deaths.

Even if you've been vaccinated (*see below*), you're at risk if you visit these regions; among travellers to India, for example, there are more than 800 cases for every million visitors. One big problem is that 'carriers' can pass on the disease without showing any symptoms – or even suspecting themselves that they are infected. If you do catch typhoid fever, the symptoms can be confused with those of malaria, and prompt medical tests and care are vital.

What it is The bacteria that cause typhoid, called *Salmonella typhi*, are closely related to other varieties of *Salmonella* that cause travellers' diarrhoea (*see p.36*). They're spread from person to person in the same way, by infected faeces or urine (or sometimes vomit) contaminating food or water supplies – either directly or indirectly, via hands or utensils. Shellfish growing in polluted waters are a common souce of typhoid bacteria, but other foods and drinking water are a risk too. Carriers who prepare or serve food are often the source of outbreaks.

The bugs multiply in the intestines, but unlike most other 'food poisoning' bacteria they quickly spread to other parts of the body, causing generalised illness. They're also unusual among such bugs in causing constipation more often than diarrhoea – especially in adults and older children. Related bacteria called *Salmonella paratyphi* cause a similar but milder disease known as paratyphoid.

Where you can get it Typhoid exists worldwide, but it's rare in the developed, industrialised world and is most common where there are poor sanitary and water-purification facilities, and where standards of food hygiene are low. It's widespread in Africa, much of Asia (especially the Indian subcontinent and

Tajikistan), and Latin America (notably in Peru). The risk is generally low in resort areas and most capital cities.

How you can avoid it Typhoid injections used to be one of the more unpleasant travel vaccinations, but modern vaccines cause far fewer side-effects than the old version. There are now both oral types – taken as a course of three or four capsules every other day – and injections (including combined typhoid and hepatitis-A vaccines). None of them give total protection – they're reckoned to be about 75 or 80 per cent effective – but they do reduce the disease's severity if you succumb. Also, the heavier the infection – ie, the more typhoid organisms you take in – the more likely they are to cause the disease. So it's still important to keep to the same strict food and drink guidelines as for avoiding travellers' diarrhoea (*see pp.28–34*).

What it does to you The incubation period of typhoid fever varies from about one to two weeks – the higher the dose of bacteria you receive, the quicker the symptoms are likely to appear. You may suddenly develop a high fever – 39–40°C (102–104°F) is typical – or it may build up gradually over a period of a week or so. Other symptoms are stomach pains, a headache, a raw tongue, aching limbs, tiredness and weakness, and loss of appetite. As already mentioned, most adults and older children with typhoid are constipated, but sometimes there's diarrhoea – particularly after the second week. Unlike in most fevers, the pulse rate isn't raised. A red skin rash – 'rose spots' – may (rarely) develop in the second week.

If your immune system is weak (through HIV, drug treatment or for other reasons) or if you're being treated for a stomach or duodenal ulcer, the risk of serious illness is increased. Untreated, typhoid causes perforation of the intestines and internal bleeding from about the third week. About one in five people who don't get treatment die of the disease or its complications.

How it's treated It's vital to get professional medical attention quickly if you suspect a typhoid infection – not only because the disease is so serious if it's not treated, but also because malaria (*see p.107*) has similar symptoms and is just as serious. Blood (or sometimes bone-marrow or stool) tests are needed to establish that typhoid is the cause of the symptoms; then antibiotics will usually bring an improvement in five to seven days. Chloramphenicol used to be the main treatment, and it's still effective in some regions, but elsewhere resistance has developed, and ciprofloxacin or another antibiotic may be needed. If you've had significant diarrhoea, you'll need oral rehydration therapy (*see p.40*) to replace lost body fluids.

During treatment for typhoid you continue to excrete the bacteria – and in some cases do so for weeks or months afterwards. In other words, you may become a carrier. Strict toilet hygiene is essential during this time: scrub your hands thoroughly every time you go to the loo. Avoid handling or preparing food. It's important to have stool samples tested to check whether you're still shedding the bugs – you can relax only when two successive tests are clear.

POISONS IN FOOD

Danger on your plate from plant and animal toxins.

Much rarer than 'food poisoning', these are true poisons in what you eat. The dangers of some toxic plants are well known – from deadly nightshade to poisonous fungi – but poisoning by them mostly results from mistaken identity when collecting in the wild. More insidious poisons can lurk in apparently safe food – often with no suspicious taste or smell to alert you.

Danger vegetables and fruits

Local people usually know far better than you the risks of toxic plants growing in their area. Except perhaps in droughts or famines, you can rely on locals to prepare them properly for eating by treating them to remove the toxins. Some examples:–

→ Cassava (manioc) tubers, a staple crop in sub-Saharan Africa and other parts of the tropics – must be grated, soaked and pounded to remove cyanide and yield safe-to-eat tapioca.

→ Cycad flour – must be made in a similar way, from seeds of the false sago palm (different from true sago, from the stems of a different plant), to remove nerve toxins. It grows in the Far East and parts of the Pacific.

→ Dried beans (eg, red kidney beans) – need soaking and proper cooking.

→ Ackee, known in Nigeria as isin and also popular in Jamaica – mustn't be eaten unripe, and has to be boiled properly and the water thrown out.

If you're tempted to forage for wild food, my advice is a firm *don't*. Certainly don't eat any colourful fruits or berries unless you know they're safe, and don't eat anything that looks like a tomato unless you're certain it *is* a tomato. Most members of the tomato family are highly toxic. And immediately spit out anything that tastes bitter or unpleasant, or stings your tongue.

Scombroid poisoning

A kind of allergy, this is the most common type of poisoning by seafood. It can happen anywhere, but especially in hot climates where fish spoils quickly. It mostly affects tuna and mackerel (the scombroid fish family) but also herring, sardines, ancovies, mahi-mahi, amberjack, bluefish and others. If they're not processed or chilled properly, high levels of histamine can build up in the flesh. The fish may taste bitter or peppery, or may make your mouth tingle; then, within two hours, there's nausea, vomiting and/or diarrhoea, together with a headache, hot flushes, an itchy rash and other symptoms. These usually go in 8–12 hours or so without treatment, but antihistamine drugs may help. If you have difficulty breathing, get immediate medical help; you may need an injection of adrenaline (epinephrine).

Ciguatera poisoning

Nothing warns you if the fish you eat contains this toxin, which comes from tiny algae eaten by the fish. It affects reef-living fish in warms waters of the

Caribbean (including Florida) and the Indian and Pacific oceans – especially surgeon fish, trigger fish and parrot fish, and big fish that feed on these, such as moray eels, grouper, snapper and barracuda. This last is banned in Florida, but it's worth asking locals if there have been any outbreaks of ciguatera in the area before you eat any local reef fish.

The toxin is most concentrated in the internal organs of the fish (including the roe), so make sure that any fish you eat is thoroughly cleaned. If you are poisoned, the symptoms begin within one to six hours, usually with diarrhoea and vomiting, often followed by pins-and-needles, weakness or dizziness. Sometimes, the senses of hot and cold are reversed. But it is very variable: Symptoms may disappear within two days, or may continue for months; very rarely, it causes death through respiratory failure. There's no specific treatment, but anyone suspecting ciguatera poisoning should see a doctor.

Other seafood risks

There's the deadly-poisonous (if incorrectly prepared) but supposedly delicious Japanese puffer fish, or fugu – which has all the appeal of Russian roulette, I reckon. Otherwise, most seafood poisoning comes from shellfish (which are also a potent cause of diarrhoea; *see p.34*). One of the most dangerous is called paralytic shellfish poisoning, and is often (but not always) caused by a 'bloom', or burgeoning, of plankton called a 'red tide'. Fishermen usually know when to avoid collecting shellfish, but if you eat affected mussels, clams, scallops or other species, the effects are immediate and dramatic: numbness and paralysis within half an hour. One toxic clam is enough to cause mild poisoning, four heart failure.

WORMS AND FLUKES

You'd rather not think about them, but they affect billions of people.

It's estimated that at least one in every three people in the world has a worm of one kind or another inside them. They're often the result of poor sanitation, and get into your intestines by the same route as diarrhoea bacteria – via contaminated food. But some, such as hookworms, get in directly through your skin (*see p.91*), and others have to pass through an animal host before they can infest people, and can be picked up if you eat undercooked meat or fish. Threadworms (pinworms in the USA), however, occur wherever there are children – ie, everywhere; almost every parent knows them well. (Incidentally, 'ringworm' is a fungal infection; *see p.156*).

The main types of worms and flukes (flatworms) that may affect travellers are covered below. If you keep to tourist resorts and better-class hotels, and eat well-prepared and properly cooked food (*see p.28*), you're unlikely to be bothered by them. The greatest risk faces backpackers using more primitive facilities, people travelling a lot in rural areas, and 'ecotourists' and others who stay (and share food) with local people. Many worms cause few symptoms apart perhaps from stomach discomfort, and you may not suspect any problem until you spot something unexpected in the loo!

Roundworms

These come from contaminated foods, and grow 30cm (12in) or more long. (Finding one in the toilet can be pretty traumatic.) They're very common in the tropical and subtropical developing world, but travellers rarely pick up more than one or two. In this case, you'll probably feel no symptoms. If you do find the signs, a doctor can prescribe an antiworm treatment (usually mebendazole, or piperazine for young children) that will soon get rid of any worms that may remain. (A heavy infestation, common among local children in the developing world, is more serious.)

Whipworms

Much smaller than roundworms, growing up to about 5cm (2in), these are equally widespread. They may cause no symptoms at all, or varying degrees of diarrhoea. Stool samples need to be checked to confirm the diagnosis, but then the treatment is the same as for roundworms.

Tapeworms

These are rarer, but occasionally result from eating undercooked or raw fish (especially from Canada, northern Europe and the Far East), pork (most common in Africa, South America, Asia and eastern Europe), or beef (including underdone burgers and steak; most common in the same areas as the pork tapeworm, plus Mexico). Again, tapeworms often cause few symptoms, in spite of growing as long as 4m (13ft) in the case of the beef type. Segments of the worm break off, and may be found in your stools. A drug treatment usually eliminates the worm quickly.

Dog tapeworms are also occasionally a problem. They can be picked up from food contaminated by dog faeces, or by stroking or being licked by a dog with eggs on its coat and then transferring the eggs to your mouth. It's mainly a problem in cattle- and sheep-rearing areas of Africa, South America, Australia, eastern Europe and the Middle East. Always wash your hands thoroughly after any contact with a dog in such an environment, because any infection can be quite nasty. The worm larva forms a fluid-filled sac called a hydatid cyst, more or less anywhere in the body – often in the liver, but sometimes elsewhere in the abdomen, in a lung or even in the brain. It can develop for years before damaging the organs, causing pain or other symptoms; you may need surgery to remove it.

Others

Toxocariasis, caused by a dog roundworm, is picked up in the same way as the dog tapeworm, mostly by children in the tropics. The worm usually ends up in the liver and may cause abdominal tenderness. It often disappears by itself, but drug treatments are available if necessary.

Liver flukes can be caught by eating undercooked fish in east and south-east Asia, or from contaminated watercress from rivers near sheep pastures in Europe and South America. They also result in tenderness and other vague symptoms. Lung flukes can be picked up, usually from freshwater shellfish, in parts of Africa, Asia and South America; they cause coughing, wheezing and breathlessness. Both can be eliminated with drug treatments.

HEPATITIS A AND E

The commonest cause of jaundice, but easily prevented by vaccination.

The term 'hepatitis' simply means inflammation of the liver. Its most obvious symptom – your skin and particularly the whites of your eyes turning yellow – is known as jaundice. Other things can also cause jaundice, including drug and alcohol abuse, glandular fever (mononucleosis), sometimes malaria or yellow fever, but a virus infection is by far the most common cause.

Viral hepatitis used to be divided into two types: infectious or epidemic hepatitis (so called because it can be caught like other infectious diseases) and serum hepatitis (which is transferred directly via blood – 'serum' – and also by sexual contact). Now a whole series of hepatitis viruses are known; they're lettered from A to E, and there's at least one other type that's not very well understood and is known as 'non-A, non-E' hepatitis. (It's basically what you've got if they know you have hepatitis but can't find any of the A to E viruses – but it could consist of two or more further viruses.) Hepatitis B is what used to be called serum hepatitis, and C, D and the non-A, non-E type are spread in the same way, so I've covered them all separately on page 148.

Hepatitis A (sometimes nicknamed 'hep-A') is the old infectious hepatitis. It's very common all around the world, and is a real risk to travellers outside the developed, industrial regions. In fact, it's the commonest travellers' infection that can be prevented by a vaccine. If you travel widely and aren't already immune (catching the disease usually gives lifelong immunity), it's well worth getting vaccinated. Hepatitis E is much rarer.

What it is Both viruses attack the liver, and can be spread by close personal contact (I don't just mean sex). But the most common route – especially in less-developed countries – is contaminated food and water, because people with (or simply incubating) the disease excrete them in their faeces. Cooks with poor hygiene habits can pass on the viruses, but common sources are poorly cooked shellfish from polluted waters and vegetables fertilised with 'night soil' and not adequately cleaned and cooked.

Where you can get it Anywhere, but you're at greatest risk in places where sanitary and hygiene standards aren't as good as they might be. That means especially developing countries in Africa, the Americas and Asia, and also parts of central and eastern Europe, the Mediterranean region and the Middle East. The longer you spend in such areas, the greater the risk. One survey suggested that backpackers and trekkers have a 1 in 50 chance of getting hepatitis A for each month spent in a risk area, while in tourist resorts the risk is only one-sixth as high. Returning travellers may infect their family.

How you can avoid it There are several hepatitis A vaccines (including combined ones against hepatatis A and B, or hepatitis A and typhoid). For best protection, they need to be given two to four weeks before you set off; a second dose 6 to 12 months later will protect you for about ten years. At one time, the only protection was with gamma-globulin, a blood product that gives short-term (two to six months) 'passive' immunity. It's now rarely used unless you're travelling at short notice. There's no generally available hepatitis E vaccine at the time of writing, but at least one type is being tested.

Because of this (and because of the many other possible infections from contaminated food and water), take care with personal hygiene and what you eat and drink (see p.28) even if you are vaccinated. This is particularly important for pregnant women – hepatitis E is a serious threat to them.

What it does to you There's an incubation period of three to five weeks between picking up the virus and the first symptoms (during which time, as mentioned above, you're already infectious). Hepatitis usually begins with a fever with chills and a headache, general aches and pains, and a feeling of weakness and fatigue. After a few days, there's often nausea, vomiting and/or a loss of appetite. The upper right-hand side of your abdomen often starts to feel tender, and your urine turns much darker than normal (but your faeces pale), as jaundice sets in. On the other hand, sometimes the illness is very mild (especially in children) and may never be diagnosed as hepatitis.

Hepatitis A rarely has serious long-term effects, but it can lay you low for several weeks. However, hepatitis E may be life-threatening for a pregnant woman and her baby, by causing liver failure.

How it's treated There's no specific treatment other than rest and plenty of fluids, but it's important to get professional medical advice to confirm the diagnosis and rule out other types of hepatitis. (You'll need a blood test.) Call a doctor immediately if symptoms get suddenly worse. Meanwhile, keep to a bland, low-fat diet and avoid all alcohol – perhaps for as long as six months. Don't take painkillers or any other drugs unless specifically prescribed – they put an extra load on your liver – but women on the Pill can continue to take it.

BRUCELLOSIS

This is basically a disease of cattle and other farm animals that can spread to people. Efficient animal vaccination means it's a very low risk in northern Europe, North America and Australasia, but elsewhere brucellosis can be caught by eating unpasteurised dairy products (particularly goat's cheese) – always avoid these – and a number of travellers catch it every year. The symptoms are rather vague and slow-developing, and include a headache, fever with chills, sweating, aches and pains, and weight loss. Once it's diagnosed, treatment involves taking antibiotics for several weeks.

HEAT, COLD AND OTHER ENVIRONMENTAL HAZARDS

If you travel far beyond your comfortable, temperate home environment, you're bound to encounter physical conditions that you're not accustomed to, and you and your body may have trouble adapting. It may be much stronger sunshine than at home, sheer heat (with or without high humidity), cold (again with or without damp) or the lower air pressure (and particularly oxygen levels) at high altitudes. In many cases, you'll face no more than temporary discomfort, eased by commonsense precautions. But in some cases environmental conditions can cause serious problems and even become life-threatening.

This chapter deals with a variety of conditions, but in almost all cases the byword is caution: Don't rush in; don't underestimate the problem(s); and allow your body ample time to adapt to the new conditions – particularly before you undertake any strenuous activity that will stress your body further.

SUNBURN AND SKIN CANCER

Have fun in the sun – but don't underestimate its strength.

Some doctors – particularly dermatologists – are a bit purist about the sun. They see every ultra-violet ray as an enemy, and can think only of the damage that sunbathing does to you. Today's sun-bronzed gods and goddesses, they say, are tomorrow's wrinklies; basking in the sun is a recipe for skin cancer.

It's all true, at least in part, but the words fall largely on deaf ears – certainly in parts of the world where sunshine is less than plentiful and a deep tan is at worst a sign that you've had a happy, sunny holiday and at best is attractive to the opposite sex. I ignore the dermatologists to an extent myself, so I won't preach what I don't practise – which is care and moderation, without becoming a hermit. But I certainly have a healthy respect for the sun in places where it's much stronger than where I live in gloomy England, so I'll lay out a few facts and leave the rest to you.

What it is Ultra-violet (or UV) is the invisible part of the light spectrum, or rainbow, that's deeper than the deepest blue. It's produced in abundance by the sun, has a very short wavelength, and is very powerful – penetrating parts that other light waves can't reach. In particular, it penetrates skin, with several distinct effects: It burns; it makes the tough outer skin layer thicker; it can cause mutations in skin cells, sometimes eventually resulting in skin cancer; it breaks down elastic skin fibres and causes other changes that we recognise as ageing; and it makes certain skin cells produce more of the brown-black pigment melanin. Only the last of these – tanning – is generally considered desirable, but it's quite tricky to get one without the others. UV can also damage the cornea of your eyes (*see p.71*) or cause cataracts.

To understand how to tip the odds, you need to realise that all UV isn't equal. In fact it spans a far wider wavelength range than the visible spectrum, but rather than colours it's named by rather mundane initials:–

→ *UVC* The very shortest-wavelength, most powerful UV. Fortunately, it's all absorbed in the atmosphere – the ozone hole permitting – or it would kill a lot of simple organisms and cause widespread sunburn and skin cancers.

→ *UVB* The medium-wavelength type; it's partly blocked by the atmosphere, and is the main cause of sunburn. It also usually produces tanning – although not before it has burned you – and skin thickening, and with repeated or long-term exposure may trigger skin cancers.

→ *UVA* The third, longest-wavelength and weakest type; ironically, it easily gets through the atmosphere and is all round us all day and all year. At a big enough dose it also burns, but it tans skin (so long as the skin is tannable; *see below*) before this stage. But all's not sweetness and light: One of the lesser-known sun facts is that UVA also causes skin ageing and cancers. And it can continue to do so even when the sun's rays seem too weak to worry about, so you don't bother to top up your sunscreen lotion.

Who is most at risk Fair-skinned people are certainly more likely to burn that those with dark skin – especially brown or black. But it's not quite as simple as that. Everyone burns if they get enough UV – even black people – but tanning and thickening of the skin do give some protection. (But it may not be as much as you think; a 'good' tan is equivalent to using a sunscreen with a sun protection factor [*see below*] of only about 4.) Luckiest are those whose skin tans readily – including fair 'Nordic' types. Those most prone to burning are albinos (who have no skin pigment at all) and 'Celtic' types, often with reddish hair and freckles, who tan only with difficulty. These are gross generalisations, of course – you best know your own skin, so act accordingly.

A special word of warning to travellers: Certain drugs can make your skin unusually sensitive to the sun. They include tetracycline antibiotics (among them the widely used antimalarial drug doxycycline; *see pp.115–116*), ciprofloxacin (often prescribed for serious diarrhoeal illness; *see p.40*), and others. Always check for side-effects with your doctor or pharmacist, and use extra sun protection if advised.

So much for the short-term effects. The same people who are most prone to burning are also probably most at risk from skin cancer, because tanning also offers some protection here. But even black- and brown-skinned people get skin cancers, so the protection is far from absolute. The same is true of

---

TYPES OF SKIN CANCER

Skin cancers take years to develop, mostly affecting people in the 40–60 age-group, so they're not something that's likely to crop up suddenly on even a year-long world trip. But they increasingly occur in young people (often apparently linked to excessive sun exposure in childhood), so everyone should be aware of the danger signs; the sooner they're detected, the sooner they can be removed and the less likely they are to spell long-term trouble. Apart from Kaposi's sarcoma (almost solely an AIDS-related condition), there are three main types:–

→ *Basal cell carcinoma* is slow-growing and almost always curable. A small pink or greyish lump slowly grows and forms a central scab.

→ *Squamous cell carcinoma* is also slow-growing and usually curable, but sometimes spreads. It forms a non-healing sore or ulcer (a so-called 'rodent ulcer').

→ *Malignant melanoma* is by far the most dangerous type, and can be fatal if it's not caught early. The danger signs are a rapidly enlarging dark spot, or a mole that grows bigger, often with an irregular edge, a crusty surface, bleeding, itching or inflammation, or with variable colouring. Always tell a doctor if you (or your partner) notice *any* of these changes in a mole.

skin ageing; if you're young the problem may seem an lifetime away, but taking care needn't deprive you of fun and beauty in the short term!

Where you can get it The simple answer of course is anywhere in the sun – but some UV penetrates cloud, so it's quite possible to get sunburned on an overcast day. The slightly more complex answer is that the higher the sun is in the sky, or the higher you are above sea level, the stronger the UV is (simply because there's less air in the way to absorb it). This is particularly true of fast-burning UVB, so the more easily and quickly you can burn.

The sun is highest and strongest for about two hours either side of midday – but that's midday by *solar* time. If the clocks are moved forward for 'daylight saving', the period of strongest sunshine moves later in the day, so in many places the riskiest time is 11am to 3pm. But in Spain, for example, clocks in summer are two hours ahead of solar time, so the sun is highest at 2pm and the danger period is from about 12 noon to 4pm. The sun also, of course, rises higher in the sky the nearer you are to the equator, extending the danger period. If you travel long-distance this is a very important factor – and not just in the tropics. To give one example, the midday midsummer sun in Sydney is only about 10 degrees away from vertically above you.

As for altitude, there's about 5 per cent more UV for every 300m (1000ft) you are above sea level, so at 3000m (10 000ft) the radiation is about 50 per cent stronger. Your surroundings affect your exposure, too. Snow in particular – but sand, rocks and water too – all reflect UV; it's quite possible to get badly burnt under a sun-umbrella. (And don't be lulled by the cooling effect of a sea-breeze, either.) Finally, clear blue sky scatters a lot of UV, so it's more dangerous than partial cloud even if the sun's no stronger.

How you can avoid it It was the Australian Cancer Council, in the 1980s, that originated the slogan 'Slip! Slop! Slap! – Slip on a shirt. Slop on sunscreen. Slap on a hat.' They know what they're talking about; more than quarter of a million Aussies get skin cancer every year, and about 1200 die of it. Apart from keeping out of the sun altogether in the middle of the day – a good rule of thumb is not to sunbathe when your shadow is shorter than you are – it's still the best advice for enjoying the sun safely. It applies even if you're determined to ignore the long-term risk and think only of tomorrow.

Most people know about sun protection factors (SPFs) of sunscreens. But not everyone knows that they apply only to UVB absorption – ie, primary burn-prevention. UVA, as already explained, also causes damage (as well as tanning), and in the medium term can also burn. Many sunscreen brands (but not all) indicate UVA screening by stars; four stars protects the most. Some clothes – especially protective clothing designed for hot-climate travel or for children – nowadays carry similar protection-factor information, and are well worth using if you have to spend long periods in strong sunshine.

The SPF indicates (roughly) how much longer you can stay in the sun without getting burnt; so if you'd burn in 30 minutes without protection, a factor-8

> ### Cold sores
>
> If you're prone to cold sores (*Herpes simplex*), strong sunshine will very likely bring them out – as can the stress of travel itself. So be particularly careful to apply a high-factor sunscreen to your face and a sunblock to your lips. Also pack some aciclovir (acyclovir; 'Zovirax') cream, and apply it as soon as you get the tell-tale tingling sensation.

sunscreen is meant to put it off to four hours. But for proper protection, you need to apply the cream or lotion thoroughly and adequately, then re-apply it every two hours or so – or more often if you swim, shower, or sweat a lot. 'Waterproof' sunscreens are supposed to last longer, but still need regular top-ups; creams and lotions do, however, certainly stay on better than oils.

If you have to travel in strong sun (eg, when trekking at high altitude) then all exposed skin should be protected by a sunscreen with the highest-possible SPF (30 or more). Use a broad-brimmed hat, and put a sunblock such as zinc cream or a cosmetic containing titanium oxide (which reflect rather than absorb UV) on vulnerable bits such as your nose, ears and lips. But most experts feel that an ultra-high SPF is unnecessary or even undesirable for simply hanging about on the beach. It may lull you into a false sense of security while the sun does long-term damage to your skin. And you pay a lot more for very little extra UV adsorption. (Factor-16 absorbs about 94 per cent of UVB, factor-25 about 95½ per cent, and factor-30 about 97 per cent.)

It's far better to start off using a sunscreen with an SPF between 15 and 20 for fair skins (perhaps 10 to 15 if you tan easily or have a dark skin), and limit your sunbathing to 20–30 minutes at first. (And, to repeat, don't go out in the middle of the day, and do chose a product with good UVA protection.) You can then gradually increase your time in the sun as you build up a tan, but you'd be well advised not to reduce the SPF you use until the second or third week at least.

If you want to look brown before you go out in the sun, fake-tan products may suit, *but most types give no sun protection*. You'll still need to use a good sunscreen and limit your exposure as above. Experts agree that so-called pretanning preparations, together with vitamin pills that are supposed to protect you from the sun, do little or no good. Using a sunbed before you travel can give you a tan, but you need to take the same precautions as in the sun. The marginally safer type emits only UVA, and tans without thickening the skin – but this means that it doesn't give you so much sun protection. Newer types of sunbed that also emit some UVB give better protection in the long term, but you need to be even more careful using them. If you spend too much time on them, they'll do just as much damage as the sun itself.

How it's treated If, despite all, you do get sunburnt, stay out of the sun for at least two or three days. Calamine or after-sun lotions may soothe the soreness, but a mild painkiller such as aspirin, paracetamol (known in the

USA as acetaminophen; eg, 'Tylenol') or ibuprofen can relieve the pain and also reduce inflammation (redness). An ibuprofen gel can be applied to the burnt skin to give more direct relief.

Severe sunburn – with blistering – needs to be treated like any other burn (see p.179) if it covers only a small area; don't deliberately prick blisters, but protect them if they burst. But if burning is extensive, you need professional medical care, while resting in bed with plenty of fluids to drink, painkillers, and possibly steroid drugs to speed up healing and antibiotics against infection. In the very worst cases, hospital treatment is needed.

HEAT ILLNESS

Dehydration and mild heat exhaustion to life-threatening heat-stroke.

Landing in a hot, dry climate like the Arizona desert, even in summer, is not usually too much of a problem, so long as you stay in the shade as much as possible, protect your skin from the sun (see p.54) and drink plenty of fluids. You sweat a lot but hardly notice it, as the sweat evaporates quickly and cools you. Landing in hot, humid conditions such as the south-east Asian or Amazonian rainforest is quite another matter. Your body tries the same trick to keep cool; the sweat pours off you, but it doesn't do much good. The humidity's so high that little of it evaporates, and the high air temperature means there's little or no direct cooling effect. If you've just got off a long-haul flight, with its dry, dehydrating atmosphere – exacerbated if you've been tackling the duty-frees – that can only increase the problem. You'll certainly feel the heat, and may be in line for worse.

This is a fancy way of saying that heat is subjective. There's rarely a serious problem below about 30°C (86°F), but above that level your body depends on evaporating sweat to get rid of excess heat. If it struggles to do so, the body's temperature-maintaining system may become unstable. It can take up to two or three weeks for your body to acclimatise to a hot climate, and in the meantime you should take things very easy. Too much heat and especially humidity, too little (non-alcoholic) drink and too much exertion spells trouble. The relatively mild (but still debilitating) first stage of heat illness is called

---

FAINTING AND SWOLLEN ANKLES

It's quite common, when you first arrive in a hot climate, to feel dizzy and even faint if you stand up suddenly, or stand still for a long time. The reason is that blood tends to pool in your legs, because your circulation is still adjusting to the heat, and this deprives your brain of oxygen. Anyone who faints should be lain down with feet raised, or sat down with head between legs. S/he should rest, sip a drink, and take it easy for a day or two. Swollen ankles –known medically as heat oedema – have the same cause, and the same rest and acclimatisation will cure them in a few days.

heat exhaustion. The rare but far more serious second stage – heat-stroke – may develop from heat exhaustion but occasionally strikes without warning.

Who is most at risk Young children and unfit people – particularly if they're also elderly – are more prone to heat illness than others. So are those who are overweight, or have a heart or lung problem, and pregnant women. Anyone who does strenuous exercise – whether fit or not – anyone wearing waterproof clothing, and anyone with certain skin conditions that cut down their sweating ability is also at greater risk. If you take some drugs, both prescription (such as diuretics) and recreational (eg, 'Ecstasy'), or alcohol you're also more likely to get ill in the heat.

How you can avoid it Apart from avoiding the situations just mentioned and spending time acclimatising, the most important precaution in a hot climate is to keep up your fluid intake. Your sense of thirst may be a poor guide, but you do need to drink an awful lot: at least 3 litres (5 pints) of fluid a day, or 1 litre (1¾ pints) per hour exposed to a temperature over 35°C (95°F) – and even more if you're involved in sporting or other strenuous activities. Children need a bit less, but are much less tolerant of fluid loss. For all ages the best gauge is the colour and amount of urine produced; dark, smelly and sparse urine is a sign of dehydration, and more drink is needed. (For guidance on safe water and other drinks, see pages 31–33.)

Lack of salt is not usually as big a problem as many people believe, although some people do suffer from excessive salt loss in their first few days in a hot climate. This may lead to heat exhaustion with muscular cramps (*see below*). Most doctors today don't advise people to take salt tablets, but you should make sure that you eat enough savoury, naturally salty food – particularly in those first few days – or simply add a *little* salt to your normal diet. And adding rehydration salts to water (*see box, p.40*) helps your body to absorb it.

What it does to you With simple dehydration – as with the more serious heat illnesses – you may or may not feel thirsty, but you will usually at least have a somewhat dry mouth. Other common symptoms include...

→ Drowsiness, listlessness or mild confusion; dizziness.
→ Loss of skin elasticity, so that it feels flabby and flaccid when pinched.
→ Reduced output of concentrated (dark and smelly) urine.

Early signs of heat exhaustion are usually excessive sweating and flushing, as the body pumps blood nearer the skin surface to try to cool it. Other symptoms, some due to the dehydration resulting from sweating, include...

→ Dizziness, restlessness and a pounding headache.
→ Weakness and exhaustion; if salt is deficient, muscle cramps.
→ Nausea and possibly vomiting.
→ Rapid pulse and breathing; temperature of up to 39–40°C (102–104°F).
→ In a few cases, palpitations and an urgent need to urinate.
→ With extreme dehydration, the mouth becomes very dry.

In true *heat stroke* (which used to be called sunstroke, and as I've said is much rarer), body temperature usually (but not always) rises above 40°C (104°F), and if untreated may reach 44°C (111°F) – at which point death is likely. Other symptoms before that extreme stage may include...

→ Confused or irrational behaviour; possibly lack of coordination.
→ Decreased sweating; skin may feel hot and dry.
→ Sometimes shivering and complaints of feeling cold.
→ High pulse rate (over 100 per minute) and breathing (over 30 per minute).
→ Delirium; eventually possibly convulsions and unconsciousness.

Warning: You might confuse heat illness with fever-inducing illnesses such as malaria (*see p.107*) or dengue fever (*see p.125*), although the pattern of symptoms and onset are usually different. (Note that neither of these is likely within the first week of arriving in a hot climate, however.) If in any doubt, get urgent medical help – but meanwhile don't delay treatment, especially if you suspect heat stroke.

How it's treated Any victim of heat illness needs to be placed in as cool and shady a position as possible – in air conditioning if feasible – and kept still; s/he shouldn't undertake any physical exercise until fully recovered (a day at the very least). S/he should drink plenty of cool fluids – as much as 2.5 litres (4½ pints) in the first hour – even if s/he resists. If available, ready-mixed or home-made rehydration salts dissolved in clean water (*see p.40*) are best, but otherwise plain water, diluted fruit juice or any other non-alcoholic drink will do fine. (It's best to shake fizzy drinks to get rid of some of the fiz.) If the symptoms include muscle cramps, add a pinch of salt to water or soft drinks.

Meanwhile, cool the victim by loosening or removing his/her clothing, fanning and (if body temperature is 39°C or more) sponging down with cool but not ice-cold water. This cooling is particularly important if body temperature goes above 40°C, but should be stopped when it drops below 38°C (100.4°F). **If the victim is unconscious, delirious, or shows any other signs of heat stroke, get him/her to hospital urgently, while working to bring body temperature down.** Lay any unconscious patient in the 'recovery position' (*see p.173*) to prevent choking on vomit, while sponging with cool water.

Any heat-stroke victim will need hospital care for several days, but even those recovering from the milder heat exhaustion should stay out of the sun, in as cool an environment as possible, for at least two days. Be sure to keep up fluid intake – you'll be prone to another attack for some time.

PRICKLY HEAT

A common reaction to a hot, sticky climate is to develop an itchy, prickly rash of tiny red blisters, probably due to blocked sweat glands. They're often worst on the chest, around the waist, in the armpits and at the front of the elbows – anywhere where clothing, bedclothes or skin rubs, or where skin is constantly damp and becomes waterlogged.

A cold shower, followed by very careful drying with a soft towel, may bring some relief; so may applying calamine lotion or hydrocortisone cream (eg, 'HC45') to the affected areas. Wear loosely fitting cotton clothing, and if possible sleep in an air-conditioned room or under a slow ceiling fan – but don't risk doing without a mosquito net in areas prone to malaria or other mosquito-borne diseases (see p.75).

COLD EXPOSURE

Hypothermia is a serious threat at temperatures well above freezing.

Cold is an insidious danger that can creep up on you far more stealthily than excess heat. Of course, if you fall into ice-cold water – or even water that's cold but significantly above freezing – you'll know all about it in an instant. Below 5°C (41°F), the very shock can sometimes cause heart failure and death, but if it doesn't you're at risk of severe acute (sudden) hypothermia – cooling of the body – even if you escape drowning (see box).

Chronic hypothermia – defined by doctors as a gradual lowering of the body's core (internal) temperature below 35°C (95°F) – can develop unnoticed and while you're still feeling remarkably well; it can kill without you realising that you're in trouble. (Some seriously hypothermic people behave in dangerously irrational ways, even trying to pull their clothes off.) And you don't need to be a polar explorer, skier or mountain climber to develop it – although such

---

IN COLD WATER

Falling into a cold sea, lake or river is a real emergency. Your first reaction is usually to gasp and curl up, almost guaranteeing lungs full of water and drowning within minutes – even if the initial shock doesn't bring on cardiac arrest. Or your muscles may tense up so much that swimming is impossible. Your best chance of survival is if you're wearing a good life jacket and insulating clothing, and keep *still* – a tall order unless you've had special training. People with survival training can last an hour after falling overboard even in ice-cold water, and much longer at higher temperatures.

Someone pulled from the water who is unconscious has probably breathed in water, and needs urgent heart and lung resuscitation (see pp.173–174). A conscious but incoherent person is probably suffering from serious hypothermia. Take care; violent action may provoke collapse. But, as with chronic hypothermia on land, the priorities are to prevent further cooling and gradually warm the victim. The same methods can be used (see p.64), but on a boat it may be feasible to use a warm bath – at no more than 40–42°C (104–108°F), tested as for a baby's bath, with the elbow – or to sit the person in a warm shower.

people are certainly are at risk if they're not properly equipped. If it's windy, and particularly if your clothing is also wet, you can lose body heat rapidly even if the air temperature (without taking account of wind-chill) is 10° or as much as 15°C above freezing (ie, at 50 to about 60°F).

What it is The body's internal mechanisms usually keep its temperature close to 37°C (98.6°F) – so-called 'normal'. But, just as it may have difficulty in preventing overheating in some conditions (*see p.58*), the body has only a limited ability to stop its temperature falling in the cold. In biological terms, we have to take steps to reduce heat loss by 'behavioural' means – in other words, by putting on warm clothes, getting out of the cold and doing other things to warm up. If we don't, the body doesn't just slow down; its systems become unstable and threaten life itself.

The body's own automatic mechanism for creating warmth in cold conditions is shivering. All muscular contractions – exercise – generate heat, and shivering is simply the body's involuntary way of doing this. It can boost heat output to as much as five times the level when you're at rest, but this is still a good deal less than if you're doing strenuous exercise.

As a general rule, uncontrollable shivering (together with other symptoms; *see below*) begins at a body temperature of about 35°C (95°F) – as already said, the 'official' threshold of hypothermia. If the temperature drops even more, shivering dies down around 32°C (89–90°F), and the victim may fall into a coma. Below 28°C (about 82°F), breathing usually stops. The person may now suddenly die, usually because of irregular heart rhythms, but people have been known to survive after their body temperature has reached 10°C (50°F) or below. (It's a well-known medical saying that no one's dead unless they're *warm* and dead.)

Where you can get it As already emphasised, conditions don't have to be ice-cold for you to suffer from hypothermia, although it's rare if the air temperature is above about 15°C (59°F). So, while climbers, high-altitude trekkers and travellers in freezing conditions anywhere need to beware of hypothermia (including downhill skiers, who create wind chill by their own movement), it's also a risk in relatively temperate regions.

The alternative name 'exposure' gives the clue: You're most at risk on hills or in other open country where there's no shelter from the wind (which can rob your body of its protective layer of warm air next to the skin) and rain (which rapidly conducts body heat away if it saturates clothing, reducing effective air temperature by another 6°C [by about 11°F]). Hail and sleet are even worse, of course. The sun – or rather its absence – can make a big difference, too; a pleasant walk or trek on a sunny day can change into a danger situation if clouds come over. And bear in mind the risk if you're travelling in a vehicle in winter far from civilisation or in heavy snow; if you break down or get snowbound, hypothermia is a real danger unless you're carrying protective clothing and survival gear.

Who is most at risk Elderly and thin people are more likely to develop hypothermia than fit, young people with a good covering of fat to slow down heat loss. So are those who are hungry, tired or injured, and those without proper clothing (including spare dry things), shelter and a sleeping bag. Children are particularly vulnerable, because they have a greater surface area in relation to body weight than adults; they're even more at risk if they're being carried in a back-pack or pulled on a sledge rather than doing heat-generating exercise.

How you can avoid it The keys to preventing hypothermia lie in planning and preparation: wearing the proper clothing and footwear, taking the proper equipment, and being prepared for the worst the weather can throw at you. If you're expecting to travel on foot in harsh conditions, it's worth discussing your needs with specialist outdoor activities suppliers. Their equipment won't come cheap, but it could save your life in extremes.

Wear layered clothing so you can adjust to varying conditions. Each layer should be well-fitting but slightly larger than the one beneath, so that layers of warm air are trapped and not squeezed out. If possible choose materials that keep you warm even when damp – such as synthetic fleece and pile fabrics. You need to allow the clothes to 'breathe' so that they don't get saturated with sweat, so loose fittings at the neck and wrists are useful. In the same way, your outer 'shell' needs to be water- and wind-proof while allowing sweat vapour to escape; don't go for totally impermeable garments. On the other hand, in rain without too much wind, a fully waterproof poncho, umbrella or even a big plastic bag will keep you dry while allowing ventiltion. Don't forget good headgear; at least a quarter of your body heat can be lost through the head and ears. Mittens are warmer than fingered gloves

Other points to watch if you're walking in cold conditions:–

→ Food supplies energy, so eat plenty of calorie-rich snacks (eg, chocolate).
→ Don't drink any alcohol; it reduces blood sugar and increases heat loss.
→ Do drink plenty of non-alcoholic fluids – preferably hot.
→ Keep moving; when you do stop, do so in natural or self-made shelter.
→ Take a change of clothing and footwear, and keep them dry.
→ Change into dry things at night; next day, wear your day clothes and boots, even if damp, so that you still have a dry set to change into again at night.
→ Take spare mittens and a hat; they're easily lost.
→ Carry a sleeping bag for emergencies even if not planning to sleep out.
→ A silvered 'space blanket' is no better – perhaps worse – for emergency protection than a large, sturdy plastic bag or sheeting.
→ Operate a 'buddy' system (see p.68).
→ If you're stranded in the cold (eg, in a vehicle or on a chair lift), try to keep exercising your leg and arm muscles to generate heat.

What it does to you Unless you've got a special low-reading clinical thermometer (normal ones stop at 35°C [95°F]) and use it rectally or in a good stream of urine (mouth and armpit measurements are useless in the cold), you'll have to gauge hypothermia by touch, appearance and behaviour. Remember in particular that children may not even realise that they're feeling cold, let alone able tell you. An adult should frequently check their body warmth by touch; the danger sign is cold hands, feet *and* trunk.

The early stages of hypothermia are when the cold is felt worst and shivering starts. As shivering lessens, the real danger begins; judgement becomes clouded and people begin to lose the will to look after themselves. This is when an observant 'buddy' can save a life, by noticing listlessness, slurred ('drunken') speech, poor physical coordination – stumbling or falling over – or mental deterioration (eg, repeated failure to respond to questions, or possibly responding with uncharacteristic aggression). As already mentioned, a hypothermic person may act irrationally, in a way that puts him or her in greater danger, because s/he doesn't *feel* ill. Or s/he might have hallucinations, before collapsing into a coma. The pulse may be irregular.

How it's treated A difficult decision has to be made between pressing on to warmth and shelter (on the basis that continued exercise will generate extra body heat) and opting for immediate shelter and treatment. If the victim is only just starting to show signs of hypothermia, is still coherent and physically coordinated, and proper shelter is not far away, many experts advise pressing on. But if there is any doubt about quickly reaching shelter, or if the victim is deteriorating, then you'd best stop immediately. Then:–

→ Choose or make a dry, wind-proof shelter with a tent, poncho, etc.
→ Lay the victim down on a waterproof sheet, insulated from the ground.
→ Strip off his/her wet clothes and put him/her in a sleeping bag if possible.
→ If you have no sleeping bag, improvise with blankets, dry clothes, etc.
→ Keep the victim's head, neck and entire body covered.
→ If s/he is conscious, give a hot sweet drink (*not* alcoholic) and hot food.
→ If not, a companion should strip, get in the bag or bed and warm him/her with body heat (but without putting him/herself at risk).
→ Reheating should be slow but steady.
→ Be ready to give resuscitation (*see p. 173*) if breathing and/or pulse stop.
→ Call for help (making sure messengers are warm and well equipped) and/or carry the warmed victim (well insulated) to safety on a stretcher.

TRENCH FOOT

So called because it was first recognised in the trenches of World War I, this is also known as immersion foot. You're liable to get it if your feet are continually immersed in cold, but not freezing, water – especially if they're inside tight waterproof boots that restrict blood flow. It's rare and involves a bacterial infection, but can affect anyone wearing tight rubberised boots that don't 'breathe', from yachtsmen and white-water rafters to walkers in cold, muddy conditions and people attending outdoor music events in cold rain. The best preventive is to wear well-fitting, ventilated footwear and warm, dry socks that you change regularly.

As with frostbite (*see below*), you're liable to feel only numbness – although there may also be pain and itching. Although your feet don't freeze, the effects and treatment are much as for mild frostbite. If you remove your boots, the skin of your feet looks blotchy and swollen. As your feet warm up, they become red, painful and even more swollen, often with blisters. They need professional medical attention, possibly with painkillers and antibiotics, and should be kept warm, dry and clean for a couple of days. As with frostbite, rubbing can result in more serious damage.

CHILBLAINS

Although the mildest form of cold damage, and very common, chilblains cause a lot of discomfort. They're more common in women than men, and usually occur when the skin is repeatedly cooled to near freezing and rapidly warmed again. Wet conditions make them worse. The result is swollen, tender (or sometimes numb), inflamed (red) areas with an itchy rash or blisters. The fingers, toes and ankles are most affected. There's no specific treatment for chilblains, but if you keep them clean, warm and dry they usually clear up in a week or two. Whenever possible, keep the affected limb(s) raised above the rest of the body.

FROSTBITE

A risk to skiers and others below freezing, but not to most travellers.

Frostbite is literally freezing of bodily tissues. It's most likely to affect the extremities – hands, feet, ears, nose, cheeks and so on – or small areas that are accidentally exposed by gaps between clothing. Like hypothermia (*see p.61*), it's more likely in windy conditions – if the temperature is below freezing – and downhill skiers and people riding skidoos and the like are among those at risk. If you trek above about 3500–4000m (11 500–13 000ft) you may be affected if you emerge onto an exposed, windy ridge. (In a strong wind at –30°C [–22°F], exposed skin is said to freeze in less than a minute.) Other risk factors are poorly fitting (or simply inadequate) boots or clothing that restricts blood flow, smoking (which constricts blood vessels), and direct contact with metal (such as glasses frames, a watch strap, or jewellery).

As with other types of cold hazard, it's best avoided by being properly clothed and equipped. Chemical hand-warmers (activated by crushing) are useful to keep your hands and possibly feet warm. Wear mittens, not gloves.

Mild frostbite

Also known as frostnip, this involves numbness – often, but not always, combined with initial sharp pain from the affected area – and superficial freezing. Of course, your extremities may well feel numb in cold conditions that are well short of the frostbite zone, but in frostnip the skin may become white or greyish, and leathery or waxy. (In black- or brown-skinned people, the skin loses some underlying colour, but texture and pain are the main clues.) Only the surface layer is frozen, so the skin is still soft if pressed.

The affected part should be gently rewarmed as quickly as possible – by blowing warm breath on it, covering it with warm hands, or putting it in a warm place (eg, hands under the armpits or between the legs; feet on the body under the clothes of a willing companion). Warm water – not more than 40°C (104°F) – can be used if available, but *don't* try the Hollywood method of rubbing the area with snow (or anything else); it's liable to do damage. Meanwhile keep moving, to encourage circulation. If it's working, thawing should cause pain as blood returns to the affected area. (This is one occasion when an alcoholic drink may help, by encouraging blood flow to the surface, but not if there's any associated hypothermia.) Keep the damaged area well protected, as it's liable to freeze again, and head for shelter.

Severe frostbite

If you don't treat frostnip quickly, it can progress to severe, deep frostbite, as flesh and other tissues under the skin freeze solid and hard, like a chicken leg from the freezer. Unfortunately, you get no more warning, as you'll feel nothing from the affected limb (it's usually a foot or hand that's frozen). Medical attention is always needed, and weeks of treatment may be needed to minimise permanent damage. (Stories of frostbitten toes or fingers falling off are only too true.) However, only a very small number of intrepid travellers – mainly in high mountains or polar regions – face this prospect.

What to do depends on how far from professional medical help you are. If you can warm the affected area and evacuate the victim quickly by stretcher – *and make sure that the limb doesn't refreeze during evacuation* – this is the best option. Water at 40°C (104°F; *see above*) can be used; there'll be considerable pain, needing strong painkillers if available, plus antibiotics if possible to prevent infection of the tissues. Otherwise, it's best not to try to thaw the frostbitten part until it can be done by a doctor. If possible, very carefully remove the boot and sock, or glove, and wrap the affected area loosely with cotton wool or padding and wrap gently. Keep the victim as warm as possible, giving warm drinks and food, while evacuating. If absolutely essential, s/he can walk or ski on a frozen limb, *so long as it hasn't been thawed.*

ALTITUDE SICKNESS

Heed the warning signs if you go above 2600m (8500ft), or even less.

A friend of mine, Charles Allen, was trekking in Tibet some years ago, doing research for his book on the sacred Mount Kailas. One of his companions suffered serious altitude sickness, despite their taking time to acclimatise before gradually going higher, and had to be evacuated to a lower altitude. But on the way Charles met up with a group of middle-aged Indian pilgrims who'd flown to Kathmandu, driven up to Lhasa and immediately set off on their trek without acclimatising. All of them suffered from the altitude to some degree, but they pressed on regardless. Two died. They were educated, professional men – some were dentists – who should have known better.

Altitude sickness is not just a problem for mountaineers and intrepid travellers any more. It can strike anyone, however young and fit they are, if they go too high too quickly. Tour companies make it possible to start trekking in the Himalayas or Andes just hours after leaving a comfortable home close to sea-level. Altitude sickness – caused by the body's inability to cope with (or inappropriate response to) reduced air pressure and oxygen availablity – can affect you at a height of as little as 2000m (6500ft), becomes significant from about 2600m (8500ft), and can be serious from 3000m (10 000ft). That puts several favourite tourists' and backpackers' destinations – cities as well as other attractions – well in the danger zone.

Apart from Lhasa (3600m; 11 800ft), major cities over 3000m include La Paz in Bolivia and Cuzco in Peru; many others are in the caution zone between 2000 and 3000m, so check before you go. Cuzco is, of course, the starting point of the 'Inca Trail' to Machu Picchu, which rises to 4200m (13 800ft) before reaching the Inca ruins at 2350m (7700ft). Lake Titicaca, on the Peru–Bolivia border, is 3810m (12 500ft) above sea level. And several 'real' mountains are targets for travellers as well as mountaineers, including Mt Kilimanjaro (5895m; 19 340ft) and Mt Kenya (5199m; 17 058ft) in Africa, and Mt Fuji (3776m; 12 388ft) in Japan. They can all be done, in relative comfort and safety, by most reasonably fit people; the key is acclimatisation.

What it is Air contains the same proportion of oxygen – just over 20 per cent – wherever and whatever altitude you are. But the air pressure at 3000m is less than 70 per cent of that at sea level, so there's actually less air (so less oxygen) around, and less pressure to 'push' it through your lungs and into your blood. It's this lack that underlies the symptoms of altitude sickness – known more formally, especially in its less serious form, as acute mountain sickness, or AMS – although exactly why isn't properly understood.

One effect of the low oxygen level is that you tend at first to breathe faster and more deeply than normal (like you do after exercise), to compensate. In fact, you're hyperventilating, and one effect of this is that you breathe out more carbon dioxide as well as taking in more oxygen. As a result, your blood becomes more alkaline (less acid); this has just the opposite effect of what you need – it slows down your breathing. So it can lead to fatigue, light-headedness and other early symptoms of AMS. Fluid balance is also upset. After two or three days, your kidneys usually wake up to the situation and start to adjust your acid and fluid balance; this is the basis of acclimatisation.

If, however, you don't give your body enough time to adjust – or in some cases (for reasons that aren't understood) even if you do – the advanced and much more serious stages of altitude sickness may kick in. It can go two ways. If a headache becomes crippling and lethargy progresses to coma, the cause is probably an accumulation of fluid in your brain, known as high-altitude cerebral (ie, brain) oedema, or HACE. Or fluid and blood may ooze into your lungs, 'waterlogging' them and reducing even further the amount of oxygen you can take in. This is a real crisis, which can come on without warning as well as following the milder symptoms of AMS; it's called high-altitude pulmonary (ie, lung) oedema, or HAPE.

Who is most at risk Anyone can get AMS, as I've said, but no one can predict who will. However, in some people it's likely to be more serious than in others. Anyone with a heart or lung condition (especially bronchitis or emphysema) should get specialist advice before tackling high altitudes – even over 2000m – as should anyone taking beta-blocker drugs (eg, for high blood pressure). There may very well be no reason to worry, but it's best to check it out. The same applies to anyone who's elderly or has diabetes or anaemia. Children don't seem to be at any more risk than adults, but adults with them should keep a close watch – they may not be able to say if they're beginning to feel ill. Most experts suggest an absolute limit of 2000m for very young children, and 3000m for under-eights.

It goes without saying that you should make sure you're fit enough to undertake a high-altitude trek or climb. In one respect, however, fitness can put you *more* at risk – very fit people tend to push themselves, and climb farther and faster than they should. If you've had AMS before, you may be at higher risk again and should take special care – but you might be perfectly OK the second time. (Statistics show that a person who's had HAPE once has a 60 per cent risk of getting it again.) One group, as already mentioned, are at special risk: those who start off trekking from a high-altitude starting point that they've reached by plane, train, bus or car.

One final word before actually setting off: **Make sure that your travel health insurance covers you for trekking or climbing,** *including helicopter search and rescue*. If you're not covered, it could be very expensive indeed.

How you can avoid it To repeat again, the basic rule for avoiding all forms of altitude sickness is to give yourself plenty of time to acclimatise. Plan your schedule to allow for basic acclimatisation if you have a high-altitude starting point, for easy daily stages (especially at the start), and for appropriate (and also for unplanned) pauses on the way. Don't travel alone; if you're in a pair or threesome, look out for each other, and if you're in a larger group operate a 'buddy' system whose pairs keep watch on, and are ready to help, the other. Learn the danger signs (*see below*) – you may not realise if you yourself are becoming ill – and intervene if your buddy shows signs of AMS. Don't be impatient; travel at the pace of the slowest member of the group (and if you are that slowest member, don't let the others push you beyond what's comfortable – least of all the trek leader, who should know better). Here are some specific points to keep in mind:–

→ If you start from a height of 3000m or more, allow at least three days to acclimatise at that height before starting your trek or climb. Don't start if you're still feeling any symptoms (however mild) of AMS.

→ If you've trekked up to 3000m, stop for one or two full days at or just below that height to acclimatise before going higher.

→ 'Climb high but sleep low.' Don't take this as a carte blanche to go as high as you can during the day, but *do* ensure that, from 3000m, you sleep no more than 300m (1000ft) higher than you slept the night before. (You're more likely to develop AMS at night, when your blood-oxygen level naturally drops, and the symptoms may be masked by tiredness.)

→ The above can be a particular problem on 'trekker's' (as against climber's) mountains, such as Mt Kenya, where the established refuges are widely spaced; if you feel at all unwell, it's far better to go back to the next-lowest refuge for the night and only continue after an acclimatisation break.

→ Take one or two rest days every three days or 1000m (3300ft) altitude.

→ Don't carry on if you're unwell; rest and if there's no improvement descend by at least 300m (*see more below*). Always keep in mind an 'escape route'; if you become unwell and the only way down is first to climb up, over a ridge, you're in a real crisis situation.

→ Keep up your fluid intake; you need at least 3 litres (6½ pints) a day in the mountains to avoid dehydration. Eat a high-carbohydrate diet.

→ Avoid alcohol; it causes dehydration and depresses breathing, making AMS and its complications more likely.

→ There are drugs that can help you to avoid AMS (and treat it; *see below*), but they're controversial as preventives. They can be particularly useful if you fly into a high-altitude city and/or you have to climb at a greater rate than 300m per day, but they're *not* a substitute for acclimatisation. The one most commonly used is acetazolamide ('Diamox'), but it's a sulphonamide (sulpha drug), and some people are allergic these. Alternatives are dexamethasone (eg, 'Decadron') or possibly nifedipine (also sold as 'Adalat' and under other trade names). They aren't generally licensed for this purpose, so you'll have to get a prescription from a specialist doctor, who will advise which, when and how much to take, on using them in emergency, and on side-effects. They may be available over the counter in some countries, but I suggest you consult a doctor anyway.

→ Local people in the Andes routinely drink coca maté (tea made from coca leaves, which are even reportedly sold in the form of tea bags) to prevent altitude sickness. I haven't been able to find any authoritative scientific evidence of its effectiveness, so you're on your own if you want to try it. But I wouldn't advise using coca instead of more conventional methods.

What it does to you *Caution*: Some of the symptoms of AMS are similar to those of other conditions such as dehyration and exhaustion. They may also be mimicked by side-effects of the antimalarial drug mefloquine ('Lariam'; *see p.116*); if you're taking this drug, get special advice from your travel doctor. But otherwise always play safe, assume AMS is the cause, and move to a lower altitude. If the symptoms then quickly improve, AMS is almost certainly the cause; if not, get medical help anyway.

The first symptoms of mild (or 'benign') AMS are vague, so anyone on a trek or climb should be alert to unusual or out-of-character behaviour in their 'buddy', or any other companion. Early symptoms include...

→ Mild to moderate headache; dizziness or lightheadedness.
→ Loss of appetite; nausea; possibly vomiting.
→ Fatigue and poor performance; irritability.
→ Breathlessness with only slight exercise; possibly discomfort in the chest.
→ Sleeping difficulties, often with irregular breathing and deep intakes.
→ Maybe slight swelling of the face or limbs (especially fingers and ankles).

With more serious forms of altitude sickness, some of these symptoms may worsen (or they may kick straight in at a serious level, without any warning). Danger signs of the serious pulmonary (lung) form, HAPE, include...

→ Breathlessness even when sitting down.
→ A dry, persistent cough; but especially...
→ Coughing up frothy, bloodstained, watery phlegm.

Specific symptoms of the rarer cerebral (brain) form, HACE, include...

→ Severe, throbbing headache that painkillers don't relieve.
→ Loss of balance; a stumbling, 'drunken' gait.
→ Confusion; memory loss; double vision; hallucinations; unusual or irrational behaviour.
→ Drowsiness and difficulty in waking, leading to coma.

Note: In all cases, there may be all or only one or a few of these symptoms.

How it's treated Serious altitude sickness is always an emergency. Either HACE or HAPE can kill quickly if untreated, so act promptly. Get medical help if possible, but don't wait for it to arrive. *The key in all cases is to descend to a lower altitude, until the symptoms reduce and disappear* – which they generally do, quickly and dramatically. Go by walking (gently) with a companion's support, by being carried on a makeshift stretcher, by helicopter, or by any other means available.

However, if the symptoms are clearly only of the benign form (*see above*), it is worth taking a mild painkiller – aspirin, paracetamol (acetaminophen; eg, 'Tylenol') or ibuprofen – for the headache, drinking plenty of fluids, and resting for a couple of days to acclimatise. Better still, take acetazolamide ('Diamox'; see above) if it's available; it's the most widely used drug for treating AMS, and is usually very effective against mild symptoms in adults. However, children shouldn't take it, and it can cause side-effects such as tingling of the extremities. Sleep at a lower altitude if possible, and don't go any higher until your headache gets permanently better (ie, without drugs).

If acetazolamide or painkillers don't relieve the headache in a few hours, if the symptoms get worse, or if specific symptoms of HAPE or HACE (*see above*) develop, then **you must descend without delay**. Meanwhile, other treatments can be used to buy time (eg, if it's night-time or if weather conditions are bad) – *but not as an alternative to descent*. Dexamethasone (eg, 'Decadron') can save the life of someone with HACE, by reducing (temporarily) the swelling inside the skull. Nifedipine (eg, 'Adalat' etc) can similarly help people with HAPE, but is not so effective.

Few trekking expeditions carry oxygen, but it'll help if it's available. Similarly, putting the victim in a hyperbaric (eg, 'Gamow') bag – a sealed nylon bag that is then kept pumped up – can bring a dramatic improvement. But beware: the improvement may be short-lived, and the victim must still get down to a lower altitude as soon as possible. S/he should then soon feel much better.

OTHER HIGH-ALTITUDE PROBLEMS

Apart from sunburn, dehydration and the effects of cold (see pp.54–66), a few other conditions can be troublesome at high altitudes.

Sleep disturbances

These may be part of altitude sickness (*see article above*), but can occur on their own. As with AMS, you may have irregular, slow breathing – which seems to stop altogether until you take a deep breath and often then wake up, anxious. (The technical term for it is Cheyne-Stokes respiration.) Acetazolamide ('Diamox') – as used to treat AMS – is a good remedy, but normal sleeping tablets are best avoided unless you suffer genuine sleeplessness.

Snow blindness

This is caused by ultra-violet light, which is much more intense at high altitudes than at sea level (especially if it's reflected off snow or ice) and also causes sunburn (*see p.54*). The ultra-violet damages the cornea (the transparent front of the eyes), resulting in temporary blindness, or at least blurred vision, with watery, painful eyes.

If you're affected, rest with your eyes completely covered, and take a painkiller for the grittiness and pain; some doctors recommend hydrocortisone eye drops if available. Prevention, of course, is the best cure: Wear proper UV-blocking mountain or skier's goggles that protect the sides as well as the front of your eyes.

THINGS THAT BITE, STING AND BURROW

Personally, the things that spook me most when I go travelling long-distance aren't the disease organisms I can't see, but the creatures that I can – just: the buzzing, creepy-crawling, scuttling things (spiders most of all, if I'm being truthful). Well, you'll find plenty of all those in most parts of the world – particularly in its warmer places – and in the pages of this chapter. But there are bigger things, too, from snakes to sharks, from bears to jellyfish. Yes, lots of creatures in the world are quite happy to take a bite at you, or sting you – including plants – even if they don't literally make a meal of you.

As if that wasn't enough, many creatures carry disease organisms that they're liable to pass on to you while they're taking a nibble. In fact, diseases carried by insects and other animals are among the most important health threats you face overseas; but this chapter would be too unwieldy if I tried to cover all those diseases alongside the things that transmit them – not least because many biting creatures can pass on several types of disease. So here you'll find the biters and stingers themselves, while the following chapter, starting on page 106, deals with the ailments they carry.

You'll also find hookworms, bilharzia and a few similar conditions where the disease organisms or parasites burrow directly through your skin; they're covered in these pages because they are in a sense biters too.

MOSQUITOES

The most deadly wild creatures on Earth?

Forget (for the moment) sharks, venomous snakes and spiders, man-eating tigers and rabid dogs. Mosquitoes are far more dangerous to far more people – at least the females, which are definitely deadlier than the male. They're bloodthirsty little critters, and are by far the most important vectors (carriers of disease), transmitting disease organisms when they bite human skin in order to feed on blood. Most male mosquitoes don't bite.

Mosquitoes live everywhere except Antarctica, but fortunately most are merely a nuisance. Even the nuisance factor is serious in places such as the sub-Arctic tundra, however, where you'll find them in plague proportions in summer. And even if they don't pass on any specific disease, mosquito bites can itch badly, and can pave the way for unpleasant skin infections if you scratch them – especially in hot, humid regions. Fortunately, after a few months of suffering from bites, you'll probably become immune – until you move somewhere with a different mosquito population, when the torment begins all over again. The related but even smaller biting midges (Americans call them 'no-see-ems') are equally tormenting, but don't pass on disease.

What they are and what they do Mosquitoes (sometimes called gnats) are insects – small flies, mostly around 6–8mm (¼–⅜in) long. Some, but by no means all, make a humming or whining noise with their wings as they fly. The males feed mainly on nectar from flowers, but female mosquitoes need a meal of blood (from various warm-blooded animals, not just people) for their eggs to mature. When they bite, they inject saliva containing substances to prevent the blood clotting, and it's an allergy to this saliva that makes your skin itch. As with other allergies, some people are much more sensitive to the bites than others, but most people become desensitised after a while.

A serious word of warning: **Just because your skin isn't covered with red, itchy bites doesn't mean that the mosquitoes aren't biting you – and possibly infecting you with a serious disease.**

It's while they're injecting their saliva that mosquitoes can infect you. The most important and dangerous mosquito-borne disease is malaria (*see p.107*), which kills 2 million or more people worldwide each year, including a small but increasing number of travellers and tourists from developed countries who return home with the disease from malarial areas. Yellow fever (*see p.123*) and Japanese encephalitis (*see p.128*) are rarer, but can also be fatal – although vaccines are available in both cases. Filariasis (*see p.131*) is unpleasant but easily treatable in early stages. Dengue fever (*see p.125*) has reached epidemic proportions and can be fatal, but in the great majority of cases is no worse than a very bad dose of flu. This is also usually true of Rift Valley and Ross River fevers (*see p.128*) and most kinds of mosquito-borne encephalitis other than the Japanese variety (*see p.133*) – but in some cases there may be serious complications.

Only certain mosquito species carry particular diseases, and it pays to know where you might meet them and to learn to recognise them. (But don't let such knowledge make you complacent about preventing bites; *see pp.75–78*.) The three most important mosquito vectors are called *Aedes*, *Anopheles* and *Culex* (*see box, below*). When resting – usually on a wall – or feeding, *Culex* (the common house mosquito) and *Aedes* hold their body parallel with the surface; *Anopheles* (the malaria-carrier) holds its rear end up or away at a sharp angle. *Aedes* (which carries yellow fever and dengue) has black-and-white striped legs, while both *Culex* and the harmless male *Anopheles* have bushy antennae. A fourth type, *Mansonia*, is somewhat similar to *Culex*, but with stripy wings and legs; it transmits filariasis in Asia.

Treating mosquito bites There's no sure way to get the itch out of a mosquito bite – at least, I've never found one that works long for me. Some people swear by tea-tree oil, others by calamine lotion, tiger balm or crotamiton crean (sold as 'Eurax') – or even toothpaste. Most of these are soothing, but tiger balm is a so-called counter-irritant, which distracts you from the itching by causing a different kind of irritation.

There are also various aerosol sprays and creams that contain a mild local anaesthetic (eg, 'Lanacane'), an antihistamine (eg, 'Anthisan') or both (eg, 'Wasp-Eze' spray). But these can themselves cause an allergic reaction, and many doctors advise against them; you certainly shouldn't use them for more than about three days. You may need a prescription to buy them in some countries, but those mentioned can be bought over the counter in the UK at the time of writing. The same applies to some mild hydrocortisone (steroid) creams, such as 'Eurax HC', 'Lanacort' and 'HC45'; these are useful if you have lots of persistent, very itchy bites – but be sure to keep these creams well away from broken or infected skin, the eyes (in fact the face as a whole), and the genital/anal region; don't use them for more than a week.

Otherwise, the most important thing is to wash the bite and the area around it carefully with soapy water, and try not to scratch it. Resist the temptation to puncture watery blisters if you get them. If you do scratch the top off a bite, it's even more important to keep it clean – especially in a tropical climate – so clean it with antiseptic (*see p.96*) and cover it with a small sticky dressing.

Danger species of Mosquitoes				
Species	*Aedes*	*Anopheles*	*Culex*	*Mansonia*
Habits	Day biter (esp. early morning & evening); breeds in fresh water	Evening/night biter; breeds in stagnant water	Evening/night biter; breeds in stagnant water, rice paddies, etc	Night biter; breeds on roots of aquatic weeds
Diseases; areas found	Dengue (most tropics and subtropics); yellow fever (tropical Africa and the Americas)	Filariasis (Africa and SW Pacific); malaria (wide areas, *see p.107*) other viruses (tropics)	Filariasis (all tropics); Japanese encephalitis (S, SE and E Asia; SW Pacific)	Filariasis (SE Asia)

AVOIDING MOSQUITOES AND OTHER FLYING INSECTS

First rule: Don't rely on vaccines and drugs to prevent diseases carried by mosquitoes and other insects; try to stop them biting you in the first place.

This is a war, and it demands a three-way strategy: Kill or prevent the mosquitoes breeding in the first place (the strategic bombing approach); keep them out of your room, hut, tent, bed or wherever you happen to be (the Maginot Line strategy – but a bit better thought out, I trust); and, as the final line of defence, protect your body itself from attack (how does a biowarfare suit sound?). No, anti-mosquito warfare isn't quite as drastic as that, but the comparisons aren't entirely fanciful.

Controlling mosquitoes Draining swamps and spraying whole regions with insecticide is a bit out of your range, but there are things you can do to help keep mosquito numbers down in your immediate vicinity – or, just as important, *keep yourself out of their vicinity*. It helps to know their habits. They all need water to breed, so wet places and wet seasons are to be avoided – not entirely practicable, of course, but it's an indication of when and where to be most on your guard and where to choose or not choose your accommodation.

Anopheles and *Culex* tend to breed in stagnant water – not necessarily putrid except in the case of some *Culex* species, but certainly still, so that includes swamps, ponds and rice paddies. *Aedes* and some *Anopheles* breed in standing fresh water, including rainwater collecting in pots, buckets, old tyres and puddles, as well as in water tanks, troughs and so on. If you have any say in the matter, tanks and troughs should be covered with mosquito-proof netting (a legal requirement in some tropical cities), or have a layer of expanded polystyrene beads floating on the top. (The vents of drains, septic tanks and so on should be similarly screened.) You can certainly do your bit by not leaving out any containers where rainwater can collect – and emptying any that there are.

Protecting your personal space If you have any choice or say in the matter, find accommodation where solid walls, floor and ceiling keep the mosquitoes and other flying insects out; almost any kind of woven material or thatch is like an open window to them. And talking of windows, of course you'll want the maximum ventilation by day if you're in a hot climate and don't have air conditioning, but do make sure that both doors and windows have effective screens. If they don't, you may be able to improvise with mosquito netting – preferably insecticide-impregnated (*see below*) – but remember that mosquitoes and particularly sandflies (which carry leishmaniasis; *see p.118*) can get through a *very* narrow gap. An air conditioned room is usually well mosquito-proofed, but perhaps you can't afford or find such a luxury – or, indeed, may not want to stay in such decadent 'tourist' accommodation.

Again, a knowledge of mosquitoes' habits will help you to plan your defences and when you can afford to drop them. *Anopheles* and *Culex* generally bite in the evening and at night. *Aedes* bites in the daytime, but especially in the morning and late afternoon (except in shady places when it may bite at any time). So in a sunny spot – especially one that's also breezy – you can afford to leave the windows open by day; but do close up well before dusk.

The next step is to knock out any insects that have got in during the day. Ozone-friendly aerosol insecticide sprays are the easiest solution. (Purists may prefer a mechanical pump spray.) The best and safest contain pyrethroids – synthetic versions of pyrethrins, which are natural insecticides produced by pyrethrum flowers (close relatives of chrysanthemums). (You may or may not see the name pyrethroid on the label; look for such names as allethrin, deltamethrin, permethrin, resmethrin, sumithrin or tetramethrin.) No insecticide is 100 per cent safe, but these do little or no harm to people (including children and pregnant women), pets or domesticated animals; but they are very toxic to fish (which do an extremely useful job in ponds and rice paddies by eating mosquito larvae). Also keep them off food. Follow the instructions, and don't forget crevices and corners, toilets and showers.

But what about insects that get in through cracks or gaps in window-frames during the night? Your next line of defence should be slow-burning mosquito coils that release pyrethroid smoke, or a small electrical device that slowly vaporises pyrethoids into the air. The latter, of course, needs a reliable electricity supply, but versions using a methylated spirit burner are also available. If you use mosquito coils, make sure they're pyrethroid-based, and don't just contain incense. (Joss-sticks are no substitute.) An insecticide vaporiser is effective in a room up to about 3.5m (11ft) square and 2.5m (8ft) high – about 30m³ (1000 cu ft) – a coil rather less. A word of warning: **An electric buzzer is useless for deterring mosquitoes**. A fan helps to disperse insecticide, but isn't much use on its own.

Protecting your bed A mosquito-proof bed net is an essential accessory if you are travelling anywhere where mosquitoes are a danger – whether or not you have screened windows and doors, and whether or not you also use a vaporiser or mosquito coils. You may or may not find a mosquito net installed in your room, but if you do it may well have tears or holes (even cigarette burns are big enough to let insects through) and it may or may not have been treated with insecticide. So it's best to take your own – it won't take up much room or add much weight to your luggage.

Various designs are available, supported from one point (like a bell tent), from a hoop, or from two or four corners. The latter give you more space – and more air – above the bed and, more importantly, mean that you're less likely to sleep against the net and get bitten through it. Make sure that the net is big enough to hang right to the floor (and tuck in) around a single or double bed, and that it's not too difficult to rig up. (There may or may not be a hook in your room – if necessary ask for one, or improvise.) Some nets even come with a collapsible self-supporting frame.

But the most important precaution is to soak it in a pyrethroid insecticide such as permethrin or deltamethrin to kill mosquitoes (and give a measure of protection in the rest of the room – helping, along with a coil or vaporiser, to protect you when you get up in the night to use the loo). Whether or not your net comes ready-treated, re-soak it (then hang or lay it out to dry) every six months or every five washes. *Note:* Some mosquitoes, especially in west Africa, are becoming resistant to permethrin, but the evidence so far is that treated bed nets are still effective. However, alternative soaking agents may soon become available – seek up-to-date advice from a specialist supplier.

Protecting your body The last line of defence – but the first and only one when you're outdoors, particularly at night – is yourself and your clothing. It's easy enough to say on an English autumn day, but a lot less easy to do when humidity and the thermometer are both heading for 100, but the key really is to cover up as much as you can stand. Then apply an effective insect-repellent to every inch of the rest.

At night, wear long-sleeved and long-legged clothes – choose baggy, lightweight cotton for maximum comfort – tucked in and done up at the ankles, wrists and neck. Pale colours are often advised, but they don't make much difference to mosquitoes, which home in on smell, warmth and possibly carbon dioxide more than on colour. (Smelly feet are said to be particularly attractive!) However, pale is cool in the temperature sense, and in the tsetse fly belt of Africa (*see p.78*) dark colours – especially, it's said, blue – attract these big biting flies (carriers of sleeping sickness). Soaking or spraying your clothes with permethrin or deltamethrin, just like your bed net, is very effective – especially when combined with an insect-repellent on your skin.

There are various insect-repelling chemicals, but a favourite and probably the best is diethyl meta-toluamide (sometimes written as one word, sometimes without the 'meta', and sometimes prefixed 'N,N-'). It's best known simply as DEET or DET, and it's pretty effective against ticks, leeches and other nasties as well as insects. It comes in various concentrations, but 30 to 50 per cent is recommended for adults, or up to 30 per cent for children. (Recommendations for using it for young childen vary, but it should always be applied with caution.) Always note the precautions on the container. Avoid getting it in your eyes, mouth or any cut or broken skin; don't breathe it in. It can damage plastics (eg, watch straps and 'glasses') and some synthetic fabrics. Lemon eucalyptus oil and citronella are less damaging but usually less effective. You should re-apply DEET every four hours. Pay particular attention to the wrists and ankles; DEET-impregnated ankle and wrist bands are useful, or you can improvise by spraying or soaking sweat bands. A DEET-impregnated cotton scarf or cravat can be worn around your neck.

A final word Vitamin tablets (especially B-12) and garlic are claimed to deter mosquitoes. Don't believe it; there's not a shred of hard evidence to back up the claims, and mosquito-borne diseases are far too serious to rely on myths for protection.

OTHER BITING AND STINGING INSECTS

They can vary from a nuisance to carriers of serious diseases.

Lots of insects apart from mosquitoes can bite or sting you. Like mosquitoes, most of them are simply a nuisance, or cause a sting that's painful but not life-threatening. Others (again like some mosquitoes) are a serious danger, passing on a nasty infection. Still others can take up residence on or inside your body in a way that's at the very least unpleasant and irritating.

Particularly in hot countries, you're liable to encounter a much wider selection of these malign six-legged beasties than at home. In many cases, the precautions you take against mosquitoes to avoid catching malaria and other diseases will also protect you from their cousins. But beware: some have their own ways of getting at you that need specialised defences. And some of their antics don't make pleasant reading for the squeamish.

Biting flies

Tstetse (pronounced *tset-si* or *tet-si*) flies and horseflies (also called gad-flies, mangrove flies or red flies) are big African flies that transmit African sleeping sickness (*see p.119*) and loiasis or African eyeworm (*see p.132*) respectively. The former is extremely serious, and you should do all you can to avoid being bitten by tsetse flies in the areas where they're found (much of tropical Africa, including most game parks – ask for local advice); precautions include wearing pale, sandy-coloured clothing that doesn't attract the flies. Loiasis, a form of filariasis, is less serious, and you can take protective doses of a drug called diethylcarbamazine if you're travelling in the west or central African jungle where it mainly occurs.

Blackflies and sandflies are much smaller. The former are stout, hump-backed flies, up to 4mm (less than ¼in) long, that transmit another form of filariasis called onchocerciasis or river blindness (*see p.132*) in tropical parts of Africa and the Americas, and also in Yemen. Despite its name, this disease usually results in no more than an extremely irritating skin condition; it very rarely causes blindness unless it's left untreated for a long time.

Sandflies are smaller still, hairy and sandy-coloured (not sand-living), and are found in the Americas, the Mediterranean area, through the Middle East to the Indian subcontinent, and in sub-Saharan Africa. They spread a disease called leishmaniasis or leishmania (*see p.118*), which again is rare but far from unknown among travellers. Again, it usually causes a skin disorder, but can develop into the much more serious kala-azar. Other basic facts:–

→ Blackflies are daytime biters, whereas sandflies attack at night.

→ For both, take similar precautions to those advised against mosquitoes (*see p.75*), but in blackfly country cover up and protect *all* exposed skin all day, using an insect-repellent such as DEET.

→ It's particularly important to use an insecticide-treated bed net against sandflies, as they're small enough to get through the mesh of most nets.

Tumbu flies and botflies

Both these flies can cause an infestation of larvae (maggots) within your skin, known medically as myiasis. (I said it wasn't a pleasant read!) But these two types of flies differ in where they live and the way they get into your skin.

Tumbu flies – known in some parts of Africa as *putsi* – are found over a wide area of sub-Saharan Africa, especially where the humidity and temperature are high. You can pick up their eggs or larvae directly from the ground (if you walk with bare feet), or from your clothing; the female flies often lay their eggs on drying laundry, or the eggs or larvae can be picked up if clothes are left on the ground. However they get there, their next stop is your skin, where they burrow themselves a cosy hole in which to feed (on you!) and grow.

Botflies live in the tropical Americas, and hitch a ride on mosquitoes. Female flies lay their eggs on the mosquitoes, which introduce them to their next (human) host when they bite. The tiny larva gets into your skin via the mosquito bite itself or through a hair follicle.

The result in both cases is an abcess- or boil-like inflamed swelling that oozes fluid. You may get just one of these or (especially in the case of tumbu flies) a whole crop – often around the waist, in the crotch, or on the buttocks or legs. They're uncomfortable and unnerving at best (especially if the larvae crawl around under your skin), and the boils are liable to get infected with bacteria, causing a fever as well as pain and pus. Tumbu fly larvae mature more quickly – in a week to ten days, reaching 10–15mm (about ½in) long – than those of botflies, which grow twice as big over two or three months.

Once mature, the larvae exit the way they came, to pupate and mature on the ground – but you'll probably want to be rid of them long before then. Trained medical personnel – *so long as, most importantly, sterile surgical instruments are available* – may be able to use surgical methods. At the other extreme, there are 'patent' remedies ranging from tempting the larva out of its hole with raw meat or bacon to poisoning it with nicotine from a cigarette stub, then grabbing it – again with tweezers. Or try suffocating it by putting a thick blob of petroleum jelly ('Vaseline') on the boil to cover the larva's breathing hole(s) and covering it with a sticky dressing overnight. You should then be able to squeeze the pest gently from its burrow, or ease it out with tweezers.

Whatever method you use, do it carefully so you don't leave part of the larva behind to go septic and cause more trouble. Clean the wound thoroughly afterwards with antiseptic (see p. 96) and cover it with a dressing. (Always take these same precautions with all wounds, however minor, in the tropics to prevent 'wound myiasis' – maggot infestation from flies laying their eggs on the wound. Sometimes these maggots are in fact beneficial in cleaning the wound, but others can cause problems by invading living tissues.)

Both flies are best avoided in the first place. Keep out botflies by avoiding mosquito bites (see p. 75). In Africa, don't leave washing out to dry on the ground, and press laundered clothes with a hot iron to kill tumbu fly eggs.

Jiggers

Also known as chigoes or sand-fleas (and different from chiggers; see p. 88), these are smaller but have similar habits to tumbu flies and botflies (see above). They are tiny, weakly jumping fleas called Tunga that live in sandy soil throughout the African and American tropics. You're likely to pick them up by walking barefoot or wearing open sandals or flip-flops. They burrow into your skin, usually on the feet or toes, and form an abcess the size of a pea with a black spot in the middle. They cause intense itching, and almost inevitably get infected with bacteria. You may be able to remove them with a sterilised needle (make it red-hot in a candle flame), but again make sure you get all of the insect! Then carefully clean and dress the wound as before (see p. 96).

Other body-biters

Fleas, bed-bugs and lice are usually more of an nuisance and irritation than a danger to health (although rat fleas can, rarely, transmit plague and a few other diseases; see p. 130). You're liable to pick up both bed-bugs and fleas in cheap hotels, hostels and other substandard accommodation. Fleas are sprightly jumpers, and are difficult to catch, but squashing is the surest way of killing them. Or try simply turning your bedding out and leaving it open to the sun and air during the day – fleas prefer dark, sheltered places. If this doesn't work, try an insecticide spray – though an extensive infestation in carpets and so on will need a more drastic insecticide 'bomb'. You might be better off moving on, making sure that your own clothes are disinfested.

Bed-bugs hide by day in cracks, crevices, dark corners, walls, mattresses, carpets and even folds of mosquito nets, crawling out at night to bite for a blood meal. The bites themselves and the itching they cause can be enough to keep you awake. Again, the answer is to use an insecticide or move on. For both flea and bed-bug bites, calamine lotion may give relief, but a 1 per cent hydrocortisone cream (see p. 74) may be more effective. The related assassin bugs also give painful bites, and some are important as the carriers of Chagas' disease, or American trypanosomiasis (see p. 121).

Body and head lice are usually passed on by close personal contact (or a shared hair-brush or comb) rather than via bedding; pubic lice ('crabs') are caught by sexual contact. Lice are common anywhere that's crowded, from schools in the developed world to hostels and refugee camps. They have nothing to do with dirt as such, and are said to prefer clean hair. Again, they cause intense itching, and although they're big enough to be seen, it's often easier to spot the little white eggs ('nits') stuck to body or head hair. They are best killed by direct treatment with a lotion containing an insecticide such as carbaryl, malathion or permethrin. Follow the instructions on the packaging strictly, treating the head in the case of head lice and the whole body if you have body or pubic lice. Friends, partners and family should be treated at the same time, to stop the infestation being passed back and forth.

Stingers

Bees, wasps, hornets and ants exist – and may sting you – all over the world. They vary from the familiar yellow, brown and/or black wasps and bees to red or black ants, tiny (4mm; ⅙in) black 'sweat' bees (which are attracted to perspiration), and both blue and orange varieties of wasps. No insect-repellent is sure to keep them away, but remember that they're often attracted by bright colours (even perhaps mistaking a floral-print dress for real flowers!), by anything sweet and sugary (especially if it smells of fruit or flowers), and by perfume. The best defence is simply to keep out of their way as much as you can. If you meet a swarm, beat a calm retreat without creating too much fuss or waving your arms around, and you may be OK.

But stings do happen. They're usually painful but – even on children – normally do no lasting harm. If you get stung, this is what to do:–

→ If the sting is still embedded in the skin – common with bee strings, which have a barb, but not usually with wasp stings – *gently* remove it by scraping with a fingernail, blunt knife or needle. **Don't squeeze it with tweezers, or you'll pump more venom into the skin.**

→ Relieve the immediate pain with an ice pack or cold water. If you have it, a sting-relief spray (eg, 'Wasp-Eze', which contains a local anaesthetic and an antihistamine) will cool as well as numb the pain and reduce swelling. Or calamine lotion or cream, tea-tree oil or lavender oil may help. So may a simple painkiller such as paracetamol (acetaminophen) or aspirin.

Sometimes, however, a bee or wasp sting is more serious:–

→ If there's rapid extensive swelling.
→ If there's a more generalised reaction – eg, itching all over; difficulties in breathing; and especially signs of shock, such as a weak and rapid pulse, a pale, cold and clammy skin, and/or a feeling of dizziness or faintness.
→ If the sting is inside the mouth or throat and causes swelling. (Rarely, this can result in suffocation and death.)

These are emergency situations; get immediate medical help. With a sting in the throat, try to remove it, then give an ice cube to suck or a very cold drink to sip to try to reduced the swelling. Give an antihistamine tablet if you have one to hand, and be ready to assist breathing.

The generalised symptoms metioned above are signs of anaphylactic shock – an extreme allergic reaction to the sting – which affects about 1 in 200 people (more adults than children) and can kill in minutes. In this case...

→ Lay the victim down, with legs and feet above body and head level.

→ If available *and if no doctor arrives quickly*, give an injection of adrenaline (epinephrine) into the muscle of the upper arm or thigh; it can be life-saving. Adrenaline comes in various concentrations; for 1:1000 adrenaline (0.1 per cent, or 1mg/ml), the correct dose is 0.25ml for a child aged 6–12, or 0.5ml for an adult. Otherwise, if available, give an antihistamine tablet; but neither will work if the victim's airway is obstructed.

→ Be ready to give mouth-to-mouth resuscitation and heart massage (*see pp.173–174*) if necessary, but this won't work without adrenaline.

There's always a first time, but often people know if they are prone to an extreme allergic reaction to a sting. In that case, they should discuss their problem with their doctor before travelling, always wear a medical alert bracelet or tag, and carry a self-injection adrenaline kit.

SPIDERS AND SCORPIONS

Death – or a nasty bite or sting – on eight legs.

The stuff of nightmares, these are not to be confused with six-legged insects (*see pp.73–82*). The danger – and it's serious in some cases – comes from their venom, rather than from any diseases they might pass on to you.

Spiders

Love 'em or hate 'em, the truth is that most of the world's spiders are quite harmless, despite the fact that they virtually all have venom glands and fangs. (In fact, they're positively beneficial in gobbling up insect pests.) They're geared to stunning or killing their natural prey – usually insects and other small creatures – and most just don't have strong enough fangs or potent enough venom to be a danger to people.

About 100 spider species around the world can inflict a nasty or even life-threatening bite, however, and you need to be on guard in many regions. But remember that they usually bite something as big as you only if they are provoked or disturbed, so don't go rummaging around in dark corners and other spider haunts. (A notable exception is the Australian funnelweb [*see below*], whose male is particularly aggressive in the breeding season.)

Danger zones and species Only a handful of spider species are likely to pose a serious threat – and they're not always the big ones. The greatest variety live in the Americas (especially South America) and Australia. It's worth getting *authoritative* local advice – although local people themselves may tell hair-raising stories of danger that bear little relation to reality.

In Africa The so-called tarantula of north Africa is a large hairy spider whose bite is painful but rarely lethal. (The name is given to a number of different spiders worldwide variously supposed to cause their victim to dance the tarantella, or whose sting is supposedly cured only by performing this dance.) Not so the black widow; the 25mm (1in) long female – black with a red marking on the underside – is a dangerous spider related to other 'widow' species (*Latrodectus*) around the world. It lives in many parts of the continent, including South Africa. Species of brown recluse or fiddle (violin) spiders (*Loxosceles*) are also found widely in Africa and elsewhere; they have a violin-shaped pattern on their back. A rarely seen but highly venomous spider of southern Africa is the sand-living crab spider (*Sicarius*).

In the Americas Brown recluses or fiddle spiders (*Loxosceles*) are long-legged brown spiders that live throughout much of the Americas. (There are stories – echoed in Australia about redbacks – of people being bitten on the bottom or genitals when sitting on an outside loo.) Species of black widows (*Latrodectus*) also live in North and South America; their bite is extremely painful but only rarely fatal. The venomous and very large wolf spiders (*Lycosa*) and huntsman spiders (*Phoneutria*; also called wandering or banana spiders) are mostly found in South America, but there are also North American wolf spiders which are night-time hunters.

In Asia Apart from black widows (*Latrodectus*; *see above*), which live in most warm parts of the continent, and species of brown recluses (fiddle spiders) in the Middle East, there aren't many venomous spiders in Asia. Scorpions (*see below*) and snakes (*see p.97*) are a far bigger problem.

In Australasia The island continent has a number of venomous spiders – many of them poorly understood. Most famous are the funnelwebs (*Atrax*) – best known around Sydney, but also found across a wide area of eastern and southern Australia – and the redback (*Lactrodectus*), the Australian member of the widow group, with red markings on its back rather than undersides. As already mentioned, male funnelwebs may attack if you simply get too close, especially in summer and autumn. (Sydneysiders know not to do gardening or search in a wood pile without wearing strong gloves and shoes). Redbacks are rather timid and generally bite only when provoked – despite stories of bites on trips to the dunny (outside toilet). Close relatives of the Australian redback live in New Guinea, New Zealand and islands of the western Pacific.

In Europe There are very few venomous spiders, but a species of black widow (*Latrodectus*) lives in southern Europe (*see above*).

What they do to you Spider venom can act in two quite different ways, apart from causing immediate pain – often severe – in the area of the bite. Brown recluse or fiddle spiders (*Loxosceles*), wolf spiders (*Lycosa*), the Australian white-tailed spider (*Lampona*) and some others mainly cause severe swelling and tissue necrosis – literally the death of body tissues – in the area bitten, and sometimes more widely. Areas of skin become blistered or are 'eaten away' to leave ulcers that may last months or even years.

The second group – generally the most dangerous species, including funnelwebs (*Atrax*), black widows and redbacks (*Lactrodectus*), and huntsmen (*Phoneutria*) – produce neurotoxins that directly attack the victim's nervous system. As well as severe pain, the symptoms may include:–

→ Headache; sweating and goose flesh.
→ Numbness and twitching around the mouth.
→ Nausea and vomiting.
→ Muscular spasms.
→ Sometimes breathing difficulties.

Widow spiders and huntsmen rarely cause worse symptoms than these, but in some cases of severe untreated bites, especially by a funnelweb, the victim may eventually become confused, fall into a coma, and die.

How it's treated Most spider bites are no worse than a bee sting, but if in doubt or there are any of the above symptoms, treat it as an emergency and get professional medical help as quickly as possible. If you can do so safely, catch the spider (alive or dead) or note its appearance to help identification – but don't risk another bite. Meanwhile, if there is significant pain…

→ Reassure the victim, and keep him/her as calm as possible.
→ Keep the victim immobile – particularly the bitten limb, with a splint.
→ Apply a firm pressure bandage directly to the bitten area, and the parts above and below it, to slow the spread of venom; don't use a tourniquet.
→ Don't cut or try to suck out venom, clean the wound or apply ice *directly* to it, but do use a melting ice pack (or very cold water) to soothe the pain.

Specific antivenom is available for most dangerously venomous spider bites in areas where they occur, but it has to be administered under professional medical supervision. If given quickly, the correct antivenom can bring recovery in a matter of hours. But some cases of tissue necrosis persist for a long time, and surgery – or even, very rarely, amputation of the affected area – may be unavoidable to remove dead tissues.

Scorpions

These are stingers rather than biters, looking a bit like a miniature lobster with a hooked sting at the end of their tail; this they arch over the body to strike at prey held in their pincers. (They generally lie in wait for their prey to come to them rather than aggressively hunting for it, so you're most likely to get stung as a result of accidental contact.) There are around 1500 species of scorpions worldwide, but only about 50 of them are dangerous to people; the sting of the others is no worse than a bee sting, or even a pinprick. Yet medical authorities record more than 100 000 cases of people being stung each year, and more than 1000 – possibly over 2000 – deaths. (The statistics, often from parts of the world with poor infrastructure, vary widely.)

Many scorpions are small, but some in Africa and Asia grow 18–20cm (7–8in) long. However, size is not a reliable danger sign – some big scorpions are less dangerous than some of their smaller bretheren. As a very general rule, be most cautious of scorpions with rather small, slender pincers, a thin body, but a thick, powerful tail. However, some with a long, slender sting are also highly venomous, so don't rely on this rule.

Where you can get stung Scorpions live in all kinds of environments, but the most dangerous types generally like warm, dry places – especially desert and semi-desert country. There are venomous scorpions in the south-western USA (mainly in Arizona, but also parts of California and Utah), but the greatest danger is 'south of the border'. Mexico probably has more scorpion-sting deaths than any other country – running at more than 1000 a year (mostly children), far more than from snake bites, until antivenom became more widely available in recent years. Central and South America, Trinidad and southern Africa also have venomous scorpions, but many of the most dangerous species live in north Africa, the Middle East and the Indian subcontinent. Serious scorpion stings are rare in Europe and Australasia.

How you can avoid them Remember two basic facts: Scorpions tend to hide in nooks, crevices and vegetation, or under logs, rocks, clothes or other objects left on the ground. And they are nocturnal. So, in scorpion country...

→ Don't wander around at night without shoes.
→ Avoid poking in dark crevices or under rocks, logs, etc.
→ Take care when lifting a rucksack, groundsheet, clothes and so on from the ground; clear all rocks and debris from a camping area.

And, as you'll know from Western films, you should check your shoes before putting them on, and shake out clothes and sleeping-bags, especially if you're camping outdoors.

What they do to you The immediate effect of almost any scorpion sting is severe pain where you were stung. If you are lucky, that's all you'll suffer, and it'll begin to die down after about half an hour. But the most dangerous scorpions produce powerful neurotoxins which cause similar effects to the most venomous spiders (see above). In some, the heart is directly affected, causing palpitations and sometimes death from cardiac arrest. Children and old people are generally the most severely affected, but healthy adults may be at risk, too – notably from the sting of the south Indian red scorpion. The danger is greatest if the sting penetrates deeply enough to inject venom directly into a vein; then general symptoms may begin within minutes and death can follow in less than an hour. But, as a rule, they develop at least half an hour and sometimes as long as 4 to 12 hours after the sting.

How stings are treated Having read the above, I hope you'll be more determined than ever not to get stung. But if you do, and if the pain is severe, get immediate medical help – particularly if general symptoms similar to those described above for spider stings develop:–

→ Profuse sweating
→ Involutary muscular spasms ('the shakes').
→ Rapid heartbeat or palpitations; breathing difficulties.
→ A general feeling of serious malaise – feeling very unwell.

Antivenom is available in most places where scorpion stings are a serious danger, but it must be given professionally and only if there are general symptoms. Otherwise, aspirin or paracetamol (acetaminophen; eg, 'Tylenol') may relieve the pain – or, if it's prolonged, an injection of local anesthetic. Sometimes morphine or a similar strong painkiller may be needed, but this can be dangerous if there's any risk of nervous or breathing complications. There's also a dispute as to whether an ice pack or cold compress is effective in reducing the pain – some say yes, others that they only make it worse, but I'm glad to say I can't speak from personal experience! Certainly it makes sense to keep the stung limb immobile and as comfortable as possible.

TICKS AND MITES

Tiny eight-legged relatives of spiders and scorpions.

Both ticks and mites live in long grass, scrub and woodland, and mainly affect hikers, campers and hunters, but in some areas are also found in gardens and parks. They live on every continent except Antarctica.

Ticks

You may never know when one of these tiny creatures – only few millimetres (¼in or less) long – first bites you. In fact, if you're not on the lookout you may only notice a tick several days later – often tucked away in an obscure corner such as the crotch or under your waistband or even in your hair – when it's gorged on your blood, blown itself up to several times its original size and perhaps caused an inflamed red swelling on your skin. But the real danger lies in the diseases that some ticks carry.

What they are and what they do An unfed tick has been described as looking like a sesame seed on legs, yet when it's had its fill of blood it can be as big as a large bean and dark red in colour. But ticks feed slowly – over a period of several days – and are only likely to pass on infections towards the end of this time; so removing them quickly (*see below*) can prevent trouble.

The best-known tick-borne disease is Lyme disease (*see p. 135*), which can have serious consequences, although anything worse than arthritis is rare. Potentially even more serious is tick-borne encephalitis (*see p. 133*). Tick typhus (*see p. 137*) is usually relatively mild, but Rocky Mountain spotted fever is a more serious form. Finally, tick paralysis (*see p. 138*) – which mainly affects young children – can be devastating, but in many areas often cures itself as soon as the offending tick is removed.

How you can avoid them Ticks are most likely to trouble you in long grass, scrubland, woods and jungle – particularly where there are wild or domesticated animals, which are their main hosts – and in garden shrubbery in some areas. It's worth seeking reliable advice on the risk, from a local farmer or doctor, before walking or camping in such country. If you do...

→ Wear long-sleeved and long-legged clothes, done up at the wrists and tucked into your socks and waist, with proper boots. If you're trekking for a long distance or time, spray or soak your clothing in permethrin or one of the other pyrethroid insecticides (*see p.76*). Apply an insect-repellent containing DEET (*see p.77*) to your skin, and wear DEET-soaked wristbands. (Ticks are arachnids like spiders, not insects, but both DEET and permethrin are effective against them.) Keep away from animals.

→ If you sleep in the open, use a sleeping bag slung in a hammock – not flat on the ground – and protected by a permethrin-soaked bed net.

How to deal with them Check your clothing and body every day for ticks, paying particular attention to crevices and remembering that they may look very small and insignificant. Get a companion to check your back.

Ticks hold on tenaciously with their jaws once they've started to feed, although you may be able to simply brush them off before they get a hold. If they're attached, **don't just try to pull or scrape them off**, or the body will come away, leaving the jaws behind – leading to a septic wound. **And be careful not to squeeze the tick's body**, as this risks pumping toxins or infectious organisms into your skin. What's more, if its body should burst, the contents may infect you *through* your skin.

The key is to get hold of the tick by its head – not its body – and pull it gently but firmly, with a slight twist, until it lets go. If you have them, a pair of tweezers is the ideal tool; otherwise, finger and thumb nails will do – the longer and sharper the better, and preferably protected by surgical gloves (or failing that a plastic bag). Then wash and disinfect the bite and your fingers, preferably with povidone-iodine (*see p.96*) or simply diluted tincture of iodine – or, failing that, with surgical spirit or even neat vodka, gin or whisky. And do be aware of the symptoms of the various tick-borne diseases mentioned above, and seek medical help if any of them develop later.

Mites

Mites are even smaller than ticks – usually less than a millimetre long – and tend to be more of a nuisance than a danger. Some mites (transmitted by personal contact) may burrow into your skin and become apparent only a month or more later with a bout of the intense itching known as scabies. Known as 'the itch', this used to be an everyday fact of life in less fastidious ages, but travellers today are only likely to catch it by prolonged contact with infected people in unhygienic conditions. Scabies mites usually attack between the fingers or toes, or at the wrists, but sometimes in the groin, armpits or other skin folds, often causing small watery blisters. Other mites simply bite the skin and make you itch because you're allergic to their saliva. But some grassland mites (known as chiggers – not to be confused with jiggers; *see p.80*) – transmit scrub typhus (*see p.138*), which can be serious.

The same general precautions need to be taken against mites as against ticks (*see above*), but they're so small that it's impracticable to pick them off individually. The best bet is to brush or wash them off, or use sticky tape (medical or stationery) to collect them up. Chiggers generally fall off after a few hours or days (although they may have infected you by then), but scabies mites that have got into your skin need to be killed with an insecticidal lotion.

Apply this lotion to the whole body after thorough bathing and drying. One containing permethrin or malathion (as also used for head lice; *see p.81*) is safest. Lindane lotion is also suitable, but it shouldn't be used on young children (who are the most likely to have scabies) or pregnant women. Benzyl benzoate is irritant and less effective; it's also not to be used on children. Avoid washing the lotion off hands after treatment. Crotamiton cream ('Eurax') will relieve the itching (which can persist for up to two weeks), but calamine lotion is safer if the skin is scratched and broken. The mites aren't usually transferred on clothing, bedding or towels, but it's a sensible precaution to wash these in hot water – as it is to treat close companions.

LEECHES AND OTHER CREEPY-CRAWLIES

Land leeches

These bloodsucking worms are strong on the 'Ugh!' factor, but they don't transmit disease and are usually harmless unless the wounds they cause get infected. They're a great nuisance, though, and are hard to avoid in wet forests (and in other wooded or scrubby habitats during rainy seasons) through all the tropics and subtropics. (Aquatic leeches are similar but even more tanacious – *see box*.) Land leeches are particularly a problem in Madagascar, Asia, eastern Australia (where they're found as far south as the temperate rainforests of Tasmania) and many Pacific islands. They may drop down on you from tree branches, but are more likely to attach themselves to your legs and feet as you push through the undergrowth.

Leeches are said to be able to take up to ten times their own weight of blood in half an hour – probably without you knowing anything about it unless you spot them or the bloodstains, because they inject you with a local anaesthetic. Before they've fed, they're as thin as a bootlace, and can easily squeeze through tiny holes to get under your clothes. After feeding, they look like fat black slugs. They drop off spontaneously once they've had their fill, but you'll keep on bleeding because the leech's saliva also contains an anticoagulant that stops your blood clotting. In any case, unless you've got nerves of steel (or a strong masochistic bent), you won't want to wait for them to let go. So you need a strategy for repelling and dealing with them.

AQUATIC LEECHES

There's no fundamental difference between land and aquatic leeches, except that the latter live in fresh water, especially in forest pools and streams. You could encounter them in southern Europe, north Africa, the Middle East and other parts of Asia and Africa, and in parts of South America; they're probably most troublesome in south-east Asia. They mainly attack swimmers, and have the nasty habit of crawling into body crevices and orifices, including the nose and mouth. (Stories of them entering more intimate places are probably exaggerated.)

The other big snag is that they hold on tenaciously much longer than land leeches, so leaving them to fall off of their own accord may not be an option (even if you do have nerves of steel). A strong salt solution (in purified water) will usually dislodge them from the mouth or nose, but in other awkward places they may have to be removed surgically. Far better to avoid them by not swimming in rivers and pools.

How you can avoid them Leeches aren't insects, but insecticides and insect-repellents do help. So, even if it's hot and sticky...

→ Wear long-legged and long-sleeved clothes, tucked into socks.

→ Apply an insect-repellent containing DEET to exposed skin, and especially ankles and legs *even if your trousers are tucked in as above*. Apply DEET to your boots and socks (but remember, it dissolves some plastics).

→ It's a good idea – particularly in hot and sweaty conditions when any insect-repellent is liable to be washed off in an hour – to treat your clothes with permethrin or one of the similar pyrethroid insecticides (*see p. 77*).

How to deal with them If you've been walking in a leech-infested area, check all over yourself regularly – or at least at the end of each day. If you have leeches still clinging do you, don't try to pull them off or you'll leave their jaws still attached, encouraging a nasty infection. You can encourage them to let go by putting salt, vinegar, chilli, or alcoholic spirit on them, or by applying a lighted cigarette or match to their tail – but not with the alcohol!

Clean the wound carefully with antiseptic (*see p. 96*) – or with neat vodka, gin or whisky if you've got nothing else. To stop the bleeding, you could use a styptic pencil if you have access to such a thing. Otherwise, apply a clean dressing and maintain steady pressure on it for as long as necessary – which may be some hours, so a firm bandage is best.

Centipedes and millipedes

No, you don't have to count the legs to tell them apart – and they don't have a hundred or a thousand legs anyway! The main difference is that millipedes have two pairs of legs on each segment, under the body, as opposed to a single pair per segment at the sides in centipedes. Millipedes are slower, more sedate, snake-like movers, and are rarely more than a nuisance, although they sometimes squirt a noxious fluid that will irritate your skin and harm your eyes if you happen to get some on your hands and transfer it to your face.

Centipedes are a different matter – they're venomous little (and not so little) critters. Their legs are much longer than millipedes' legs, and the creatures run much faster. They live all around the world, with some in the tropics growing as long as 25cm (10in) or more; less than 15cm (6in) is more usual, however. They have a pair of vicious-looking claws at the rear, but the dangerous ones are the fangs at the front. They can inflict a painful bite – particularly the bigger species – but there's only one confirmed case of a person (a child) ever being killed by a centipede.

There's no specific antidote, so by far the best advice is to avoid them – they mainly live in leaf litter, under stones and so on, so take care when camping or simply sitting on the ground. If you do get bitten, very weak ammonia solution is said to help, but the best bet is to use a regular over-the-counter painkiller such as aspirin or paracetamol (acetaminophen; eg, 'Tylenol') for slight bites, or consult a doctor for an injected local anaesthetic if the pain is severe. You may even need a morphine jab.

Caterpillars and beetles

Be particularly wary of hairy and spiny caterpillars: the hairs and spines are often toxic. Some may have bold 'warning coloration' – provided by evolution to warn off predators – but others look positively cuddly with their furry brown hairs. Don't be fooled; at the very least they may cause itching or discomfort, but some inflict considerable pain or cause more deep-seated problems. Some of the worst offenders live in South American forests – their toxins can cause arthritis or blood-clotting problems. But even the less dangerous types can cause extreme discomfort if the hairs get in your eyes. And some beetles – most notoriously the ill-named 'Spanish fly' of Europe – also emit powerful substances that cause painful blisters if they are threatened (or squashed!).

The best way to remove caterpillar hairs is with fine-pointed tweezers and a magnifying glass – but avoid squeezing any remaining toxin into the skin. If you don't have any tweezers, try using sticky tape to pull them out. A soothing skin cream (as advised for serious mosquito stings; see p.74) – possibly combined with an over-the-counter painkiller such as aspirin or paracetamol (acetaminophen; eg, 'Tylenol') – should relieve the irritation. But in more serious cases consult a doctor.

If caterpillar hairs get in your eyes, resist the temptation to rub, but use an eyebath or plain clean water to wash them out as best you can; get prompt medical help if the irritation persists.

HOOKWORMS AND LARVA MIGRANS

Risks from contaminated soil and beaches.

There's something pretty revolting about the idea of worms living in your intestines – partly because you know they must have got there through your mouth, via contaminated food, water or fingers. Not necessarily. Most worms do get into a new host that way, and they're covered in the chapter dealing with food and drink (*see p.49*). But hookworms – and a similar but unrelated and rarer worm called strongyloides – are more cunning: Their larvae get in through the skin of your feet or legs from soil or sand contaminated with animal or human faeces.

That means you're at risk not only anywhere with inadequate sanitary facilities but also on beaches where dogs roam. It also explains why hookworm infestations are one of the most widespread medical conditions in the world, affecting almost 1.3 *billion* people. The good news is that, unless the infestation is heavy – which it hardly ever is among tourists and travellers – the ill-effects may well go unnoticed, and the worms will die out once you're back home. And if you do need treatment, it's usually quick and easy.

What they are The adult worms are tiny – 1cm (less than ½in) or less long. Hookworms have hook-like teeth; they use these to attach themselves inside the intestines so they can suck blood. Strongyloides aren't bloodsuckers, but live in the intestinal lining. Both shed thousands of eggs, and these or the larvae pass in the faeces. The larvae can penetrate the next victim's skin (usually causing a transient itchy red wheal where they do so) and reach the bloodstream, which takes them to the lungs. Larvae in phlegm are swallowed, taking them to their long-term home in the intestines. All this can happen in people or, with some hookworm species, in animals such as dogs.

However, non-human (eg, dog) hookworm larvae that penetrate human skin don't usually get any farther – they cause a condition called *larva migrans*, in which they crawl around just under the skin's surface, sometimes for weeks, causing itchy red lines and blisters. But there's at least one type of dog hookworm that can get as far as the intestines and cause serious enteritis, with pain and vomiting.

Where you can get them The greatest risk of picking up a hookworm is in rural villages, farms, slums and beaches in the developing world – anywhere with poor sanitation. But that's not all. Anywhere where 'night soil' (human waste) is used as fertiliser can be infected. And *larva migrans* hookworms can be picked up from the ground and beaches wherever dogs are allowed to roam or defecate – but mainly in the tropics and subtropics. (On beaches the risk is greatest above the high-tide mark and under buildings on stilts.) The dog hookworm that causes intestinal problems is a particular risk on the north-eastern coast of Australia, but it's also found elsewhere.

How you can avoid them Apart from avoiding obvious contact with human or animal faeces, you can reduce the risk by wearing good shoes or boots in areas that might be contaminated. Not that these will help much in monsoon rains – and who wants to wear boots on a beach? But do protect your feet and legs especially on parts of the beach not washed by the tide.

What they do to you Apart from the obvious symptoms of larva migrans, the greatest danger of most hookworm infestations is anaemia. And that probably won't show up unless your doctor gives you a blood test, possibly for something completely unrelated. There may also have been a spell of coughing and wheezing during the lung infestation stage, and possibly abdominal pain. But strongyloides can be a serious threat to people whose immune system is suppressed (whether from HIV or by steroid or other immunosuppressive drugs). In such people, the worms may invade the body tissues in large numbers; doctors guard against the problem by checking that there's no infestation before treatment starts. In this and other cases, diagnosis depends on finding eggs and/or larvae in a stool sample.

How they're treated Anti-worm drugs generally clear up any hookworm infestation in a matter of days, although strongyloides may prove a bit more persistent. *Larva migrans* is treated with a special ointment or by drugs.

STINGING AND IRRITATING PLANTS

Poison ivy, poison oak and poison sumach – scrambling or bushy American plants – are probably the best known plants to cause marked dermatitis; merely brushing against them, or even second-hand contact via clothes or pets, is enough to give you a rash and intense itching. If you're hiking or just taking a walk in the woods almost anywhere in North America, you'd be well advised to ask a local to show you how to recognise them. (For the record, poison ivy and poison oak have shiny green leaflets – small leaves – in threes; poison sumach has them in twin rows.)

But these are far from the only irritating plants. The closely related garden sumach, or Japanese wax tree, and other members of the same family such as the cashew-nut tree, the mango tree and the tar tree of northern Australia, also give skin problems. In the last case, it's the resin or sap that irritates. The same is true of many members of the euphorbia family, such as the poinsettia (you probably know it as a Christmas pot-plant, but it's grown outdoors as a large garden shrub in many warm countries, including Australia) and the manchineel tree, which grows behind many Caribbean beaches (don't use them to shelter from the sun or rain – or eat their fruits, which are poisonous). The sap from this family is particularly harmful if it gets in your eyes, and may cause temporary blindness. Stinging plants and trees are also a danger – ranging from the ubiquitous stinging nettles to Queensland's gympie bush, whose sting can be painful on and off for weeks.

Such plants are so varied that, as already indicated, local advice is the best protection if you're hiking or trekking. (Manchineel trees in the Caribbean often have a red warning mark painted on them.) The same applies to relieving the pain or irritation, but as a general rule antihistamine tablets and/or applying a 1 per cent hydrocortisone cream (eg, 'Eurax HC', 'Lanacort' or 'HC45') are the best bets for reducing the symptoms. (But beware: If something else is causing the itching, hydrocortisone could make it worse, so if in doubt consult a doctor.)

BIG BITING ANIMALS

Mammals, reptiles, fish and others may all attack – if you're not careful.

You'd do well to forget what you've seen on TV wildlife documentaries about fraternising with wild animals. Whether on land or in the sea, give wild creatures space and respect, and they'll usually reciprocate. Very few, unless they're ill or deperate for food, will attack you without provocation.

Dogs are probably far worse culprits, in fact, than tigers, bears, bison, sharks or crocodiles because they're the single most common source of the most deadly disease transmitted by four-legged creatures: rabies. For more information, see the article on page 139; but it bears repeating here that, unless you're *certain* that they're safe and healthy, treat every dog as you would any other wild animal – keep well clear. In many parts of the world, most dogs are not pets as we know them.

Quite apart from the danger of rabies or being trampled or eaten alive, a major threat from animal bites comes from the bacteria they have in their mouth. (In this respect, people are just as dangerous as other living creatures, and monkeys as bad as wolves.) This means that any bite should be taken seriously and cleaned properly (*see box, p.96*).

There's no room here to cover all the animal threats you might encounter around the world, so be sure to inquire of responsible authorities at your destination of any specific dangers. (That doesn't mean hotels or tourist offices, who in some places may unfortunately be less interested in your welfare than in making sure you aren't scared away; however, national parks and similar authorities can usually be relied upon.) But a basic truth is that, unless you act stupidly, you're far less likely to be a victim of an attack than local people who have to work in fields close to forests or travel through bush country unprotected. Especially in parts of Asia, the pressure on land usage makes confrontation between people and wild animals inevitable.

Note the separate articles on snakebite (*p.97*), marine stingers (*p.99*), and insects and other small biting and stinging creatures (*pp.73–90*).

On land

Setting aside rabid dogs, the greatest risk from large land animals is in Asia, sub-Saharan Africa and parts of the Americas – particularly in Central and South American scrubland and forest, and in the wilder parts of North America. National parks and the like, where wild animals are protected, are often the most dangerous places. As national parks authorities will tell you,

FACE TO FACE

However unlikely the situation may seem, what should you do if you're confronted at close range by a large predator (or any large animal)? The last thing to do – excuse the joke, but it's perhaps the last thing you *will* do – is run. Predators expect their prey to run away, and they're much faster and better runners than you. (Of course, if there's a good tree to climb, and you're fit, that may be the best escape route – unless the animal, as with some big cats, is a good climber too.)

In most cases, your best chance is to stand your ground, facing your adversary, and back *slowly* away while waving your arms slowly above your head to make yourself look big. If the animal shows interest in attacking, stand still until (you hope) it veers away. If it makes contact, play dead by curling up face-down with your hands linked behind your head and your arms protecting your neck; if you're wearing a backpack, keep it on for protection. If it persists in attacking you, the best bet is to change tack and fight back – wave your arms or a big stick at it, or throw stones if they're available.

Aerosol pepper sprays are said to be effective against bears up to about 6m (20ft) away, but I don't know how well they repel other animals. If you do take one into the bush, be sure you know how to use it safely; if let off upwind or in a confined space, it could disable you yourself.

it's unwise in many regions to venture far from established camps and other facilities without an experienced (and officially accredited) guide.

Don't walk through long grass or dense scrubland where you could stumble across big game animals unexpectedly – they'll be as surprised as you, and their first reaction is likely to be to attack. (Give them a chance to get away by making plenty of noise as you walk.) Even near camp, don't stray far on dusk or night-time strolls without a good torch and preferably a guide; this is often feeding time, and many wild creatures approach campsites for scraps. In some areas such as North American national parks, curious bears that have got used to a diet of food scraps can be a serious hassle in campgrounds. Whether camping there or in the wild, be sure to keep food and other fragrant items – fresh and waste – well away from your tent.

Big carnivores are often not the most dangerous animals. In North America, bison are responsible for more attacks than bears. In Africa, hippos, buffaloes, chimps and baboons are regarded as the greatest threats, together with crocodiles beside waterways (*see below*). Elephants are dangerous if you get too close to a family group – especially if there are young ones around – but are rarely a threat if you keep your distance. Old male buffaloes, on the other hand, are notoriously aggressive; professional guides know that a rifle bullet is occasionally the only solution.

In Asia, rhinos and wild elephants can and do attack people. The big cats tend to be more aggressive than in Africa – largely because their territory has long been eroded for farmland, so they have little space to live in peace. They often live close to villages, whose inhabitants are just slightly larger versions of the monkeys and apes they like to eat. The saltwater or estuarine crocodile of southern and south-east Asia and northern Australia grows even bigger than African crocodiles, and can attack well up onto a river bank.

In the water

It's not just sharks that can get you if you're unwary about where and when you swim. Quite apart from stinging creatures (see p.99) and sea snakes (see p.97) in warm waters, many other large species attack people from time to time – barracudas, groupers, moray and conger eels, rays, garfish (which have a long, sharp snout) and crocodiles among them. And, in any case, by far the most common cause of death in the water is none of these; it's drowning. Think before you swim.

Nile crocodiles – which live in fresh and brackish water throughout much of Africa, including Madagascar – are said to kill more than 1000 people each year. Overall figures aren't available for the caimans and crocodiles of the Americas (where they live from Florida and Louisiana to tropical South America, and are said to be less dangerous) or for the Asian and Australian estuarine crocodile, but there are regular reports of people being attacked by what they mistook for a floating log. (Despite its name, the estuarine or saltwater croc is often found many miles from the sea.) Compare that with the typical year's tally, worldwide, of a dozen or so fatal shark attacks.

This isn't to belittle the danger from sharks. The point is that the danger is so well known that most people take precautions where they know sharks are a risk, and many beaches in popular but risky areas (such as around Sydney, Australia) are protected by nets. (I've seen for myself how big some of the holes are in those nets, but that's another story...) Take your lead from those precautions: Ask the locals where the danger is, and don't swim where there's no protection and no shark patrol or lifeguard, especially at dusk or after dark. And don't swim if you have an open cut or where fishermen are throwing waste into the sea – as everyone who's seen sharks on TV or has watched Jaws knows, blood attracts sharks.

One warm-sea hazard that doesn't actually bite, but has much the same effect, is coral. Some corals sting, but almost all are extremely sharp, and

A WORD TO WOMEN TRAVELLERS

You may, without realising it, be more attractive to wild predators, both on land and in the water, if you're having your period. It's as well to time your visit to a game park accordingly, and to avoid swimming in waters where there may be sharks when menstruating, even if using a tampon.

FIRST AID FOR ANIMAL BITES AND CORAL SCRATCHES

→ Remove any obvious dirt or other particles, then scrub the wound with soap and clean running water (bottled if nothing else is available) for at least five minutes. (You usually don't need to be quite so thorough with small insect and similar bites.)

→ Disinfect it, preferably with an antiseptic such as providone-iodine (eg, 'Betadine' or 'Videne'); alternatively with tincture of iodine, or surgical spirit or any other neat alcohol – vodka, gin or whisky will do.

→ Apply a clean sterile dressing.

→ If there's significant bleeding, apply direct pressure to the wound to stop or slow it; raise a bleeding limb above the rest of the body.

→ Get (or get to) professional medical attention ASAP. You'll need a tetanus vaccination if you're not already protected (which you should be; see p.166) plus, in many areas, rabies jabs (see p.139).

→ Coral cuts may need antibiotic treatment (cream, powder or pills).

---

you can get nasty scratches just by scraping against them. And unless the cuts are cleaned thoroughly and treated with antiseptic, just as for a bite (see box), they're very likely to go septic and cause throuble for weeks.

Fresh water can also be dangerous, and here South America is in the lead. You'll have heard about piranhas, flesh-eaters with teeth like razors that inhabit wide, slow-flowing rivers such as the Amazon. Stories of them eating people are almost certainly hugely exaggerated, though no doubt they do sometimes bite – and perhaps remove toes or other appendages. Even more exaggerated, it seems, are the antics of the candiru, or carnero or urethra fish; it's a small – barely more than 50mm (1in) long – parasitic catfish that lives in the gills of other fish, feeding on their blood. Stories are lovingly told of it swimming up (and lodging itself inside) the urethra (urine passage) of swimmers. There are remarkably few – if any – autheticated accounts of this actually happening, and it probably rates as the Amazon jungle version of an urban myth; but it makes a good scare story for the folks back home! Nevertheless the candiru almost certainly would attach itself to body crevices or cuts if it got the chance, so it's not to be messed with.

Much more serious, if rare, are various electric fish. The South American electric eel is again the most dangerous, able to generate large charges at several hundred volts – quite enough to kill a person or stun a large animal (which is of course their purpose). The electric catfish of African rivers has a weaker electric organ, but the seagoing torpedo ray can be dangerous if you get too close. The main danger is from drowning if you are stunned, but anyone hit by a large electric charge may need resuscitation (see p.173).

Avoiding trouble A few general rules will minimise your risk of bites or other wounds – or worse – in the water:–

→ Check and follow local advice on where it's safe to swim or dive.

→ Wear protective footwear – sports sandals stay on better than flip-flops, but canvas shoes with strong rubber soles are best of all – in reef areas, shallow waters and on the beach in the tropics and subtropics.

→ Don't be tempted to touch any underwater creatures.

→ Don't venture into murky water on or under the surface – it could harbour predators such as sharks or crocodiles.

→ Don't poke your fingers or feet into underwater crevices – or even near them; you don't know whose home you're invading!

→ As already said, don't swim at night, or from a deserted beach, or if you're bleeding or there's fish blood or guts in the water.

VENOMOUS SNAKES

High on people's spook list, but they pose little danger if you're careful.

Let's get it in perspective: Only one in five snake species in the world is venomous, and fewer than half of those are ever likely to cause serious poisoning. They rarely bite unless you provoke them – deliberately or accidentally. And even if you are bitten, there's estimated to be a 50 to 80 per cent chance that no venom will be injected into you – the bite is 'dry'.

Even if you are poisoned (the correct term is 'envenomed'), the effects usually take hours, rather than minutes (as many believe), to have an effect. And a high proportion those bitten 'successfully' (from the snake's point of view) have no long-term ill-effects. However, to come down to earth, more than 50 000 people every year do die from snakebites – the majority in the Indian subcontinent and Brazil. It may sound heartless, but most of those are local rural people, who often have to work or hunt (and walk) barefoot in fields, scrubland and forests. Very few travellers suffer serious snakebites.

That's not much comfort if you are one of the bitten, of course, so every traveller in rough country where venomous snakes exist should be prepared and know how to avoid and deal with bites. This is covered below; but, first, you should be aware that there are two main groups of venomous snakes, and the first-aid treatment of the two is slightly different. The first group, the elapids, includes cobras, coral snakes, kraits, mambas, all the snakes of Australia, and all sea snakes; their venom mostly acts systemically – on general body systems – so the priority is to stop it spreading. The second group, the viper family, includes vipers, pit-vipers, rattlesnakes and moccasins, and the bushmaster of South America; they generally have a distinct, triangular head, and produce less potent venom (but more of it), which mainly acts close to the site of the bite and also slows the clotting of blood. There are other venomous snakes, but these are the main danger.

Where you can encounter them Very few parts of the world – notably the islands of Crete, Iceland, Ireland, Madagascar, New Zealand and some Caribbean and Pacific islands – have no venomous snakes. They are found almost everywhere else below about 5000m (16 500ft), but are mostly a problem in tropical, subtropical and warm temperate regions – forests, scrubland, grasslands and deserts. Sea snakes live in warm parts of the Indian and Pacific oceans, not in the Atlantic, Mediterranean or Red Sea.

How you can avoid them As always, the first rule is to take local advice on what snakes you may encounter, and where. Then follow some basic rules:–

→ Don't disturb, prod or handle any snake you may come across. If you do come face to face with a snake, keep still and wait for it to retreat; it's more likely to strike if you move.

→ When walking in snake country, especially in long grass or sand, wear strong boots and socks, with trousers tucked in. Carry a heavy stick, and make plenty of noise; snakes respond to vibrations, usually by slithering away. At night, use a torch.

→ Don't poke your hand or anything else into holes, crevices or thick foliage – or into dark corners indoors; don't move boulders or logs barehanded. Take care walking through dense foliage, particulary if it hangs over you.

→ If sleeping out, use a hammock and net or a zipped-up tent with a sewn-in groundsheet; a snake may seek your body heat, then bite if rolled upon.

→ If you encounter a sea snake, simply swim gently away; although its venom is the most potent of all, it will almost never bite unless provoked.

What snakebite does to you It's perhaps flippant, but true, to say that the first effect of a snakebite is anxiety verging on panic. Other symptoms are divided into local (near the bite) and systemic (general). Local swelling and pain is particularly common with viper and some cobra bites, and begins soon after the bite. General symptoms are usually slower (sometimes appearing days later), and include bleeding (particularly from the gums, nose, stomach or intestines), especially with vipers and Australian snakes; paralysis (usually first causing drooping of the eyelids, later difficulty in swallowing and breathing), especially with elapids and some vipers; sometimes shock (causing faintness due to a drop in blood pressure) after a bite from one of the viper family; and in some cases kidney failure. It's usually the paralysis that is most dangerous in the short term.

How snakebite is treated The priorities are to keep the bitten person calm and still, and get him/her to professional medical help. (If you yourself are bitten, try to keep calm and sit down, and ask a companion to do all the necessaries.) The aim is to prevent the venom spreading until you can get proper help. Panicking and running around are the worst things to do.

Cut clothing if necessary to expose the bite, and wash it gently with clean soapy water, if available. If a limb starts to swell, remove anything that constricts it (such as a watch strap, ring or shoes). Forget what you've seen in films: **Don't cut the skin (even with a gadget supposedly made for the purpose), or try to suck out the venom, or apply ice packs or potassium permanganate crystals**; such 'remedies' do more harm than good.

The most important thing is to immobilise the bitten part: an arm by tying it against the body with a sling, a leg with a splint or by tying it to the other leg. Keep the bitten part below the level of the heart if possible while transporting the patient to a clinic or hospital, and be ready to resuscitate the victim (*see p.173*) if breathing fails. If you're *certain* that the bite is by one of the elapids (*see above*) – but *not* an African spitting cobra – then pressure-bandaging the bitten limb will slow the spread of venom. This is not the same as a tourniquet (which is dangerous – it prevents all blood flow, and can lead to the loss of a healthy limb if done inexpertly), but firm bandaging – preferably with a stretchy crepe bandage – of the whole limb. But beware: *With bites by the viper group, this can make things worse; leave them unbandaged.*

Paracetamol (acetaminophen; eg, 'Tylenol') or codeine can be given to reduce pain – but *not aspirin*, which may make bleeding worse. Don't try to catch the snake, but if it is dead take it – with care; even dead snakes can bite by reflex action – to the hospital for identification. (Or try to give a good description.) Then the doctor will be able if necessary to administer a specific antivenom (which is more effective than a multi-purpose 'polyvalent' antivenom).

Note: Giving antivenom is dangerous; it's a job for professionals, who will only administer it if there are clear signs of envenoming. The only circumstances when it's justified for travellers to carry antivenom is on expeditions in snake country far from professional medical facilities; then expert instruction and training in its use is needed before setting off.

MARINE STINGERS

Perils of beaches and reefs, whether you paddle, swim or dive.

The sea's a hostile place, and not just for humans: Sea creatures are involved in a constant fight for survival, and many of them use offensive weapons or behaviour that they'll turn on you just as much as the next fish, particularly if you threaten them. Apart from biting creatures, from sharks (*see p.95*) to sea snakes (*see p.97*), there are lots that are armed with stings that can cause pain at best and sometimes death at worst.

Stinging fish

These usually have venom glands associated with one or more needle-sharp spines. If you disturb or tread on the fish, it may stab you, then automatically pump venom into the wound from glands at the base of the spines. Stingrays have tail spines; they often rest half-buried on the bottom, and if you tread accidentally on one the tail whips round to sting you. It's painful, but rarely fatal. Stingrays live almost worldwide in tropical and subtropical waters.

The stonefish – an ugly, warty brute that (as the name says) looks like a half-buried stone – has its venomous spines on its back, ready to pop up and stab the sole of your foot. It has the most potent of all fish venoms, which stings agonisingly and can cause collapse and even death. Like its relative the beautifully patterned lionfish (or butterfly cod) – a reef-dweller with a painful but not quite so dangerous sting – it's found in warm waters of the Indian and Pacific oceans (both are well known in Australia, for example). Both fish are members of the scorpionfish family (and may be referred to by that name), which includes lots of other venomous types. And they're not the only ones; weevers, for example, live almost everywhere, even in cold waters, but their sting is usually nasty rather than life-threatening.

How to avoid and treat fish stings Reef-dwelling fish are easily avoided if you treat them as you should when diving or snorkelling – by keeping your distance and not poking into holes and crevices. Sand-living species such as stonefish and stingrays are very difficult to see, so in warm beach and reef waters always wear protective footwear. Canvas shoes with tough rubber soles are best, but rubber sports sandals or flip-flops (thongs) are better than nothing. Try to resist running about in the shallows in warm waters – stonefish spines can even penetrate rubber if you land heavily. It's best to shuffle, disturbing the sand to warn any lurking stingray to get out of the way.

Severe fish stinging is potentially serious; always get medical help. Fish venom is neutralised by heat, so in the meantime the best move – if possible – is to plunge the stung limb (or bathe it) in water that's as hot as you can stand without scalding; continue for up to an hour and a half, until the pain subsides. Otherwise use a hot compress. Try to remove (safely) any spines that are still embedded. Rest the victim – but be ready to give resuscitation (*see p.173*) if the sting is severe and breathing or even the pulse stops. Stonefish antivenom is made in Australia, and weever antivenom in Europe. A doctor may also be able to relieve the pain with a local anaesthetic.

Jellyfish and relatives

These creatures – together with sea anemones and corals – have tentacles with stinging cells, whose effects range from an itchy rash to painful stings. You'll know about it when most jellyfish sting you, but only two types are really dangerous. They're the box jellyfishes, which live mainly in the tropical waters of the Indian and Pacific oceans, and the Portuguese man o'war, which is more widespread (sometimes sailing on the Gulf Stream to Europe)

The most notorious of the box jellyfishes, or sea wasps (which have a rather box-shaped, colourless medusa, or bell-like body), is the common species of northern Australia, called *Chironex*. Its sting is extremely painful, and has caused the death of a number of swimmers – mostly children. A related species, *Chiropsalmus*, has killed people from southern India to the

Philippines, and also extends to Australia. The irukandji, yet another north Australian type, is smaller. Its sting is weaker (and the pain is delayed by 20–30 minutes), but multiple stings by a swarm of them can be dangerous.

The Portuguese man o'war (known in some areas as the bluebottle) isn't a true jellyfish at all – not that that stops it stinging you painfully. Its sting is rarely fatal. Partly that's because the creature's body is a gas-filled bladder – unlike a true jellyfish's – that floats on the surface and can be seen for some distance. However, the blue tentacles are extremely long, so keep well clear. These creatures are often washed up on beaches, and even if dead their tentacles can sting. The same is true of other jellyfish.

Among those that irritate rather than endanger life are 'sea lice', which cause a red itchy or stinging rash – often under a swimming costume as well as on bare skin. They are believed to be the larvae of small jellyfish species that live in warm waters in many parts of the world.

How to avoid and treat jellyfish stings The simplest way is to keep out of the water when jellyfish are around. Beaches in northern Australia have signs warning you not to swim in the stinger season, October to May (the southern summer), and they mean it. (The season reverses north of the Equator – eg, in the Philippines.) Not that it's impossible to be stung at other times; as ever, take the advice of knowledgeable locals. If you *must* swim, protect yourself with an elasticated 'stinger suit'; they're expensive, so some people improvise with two pairs of heavy-duty women's tights (pantyhose) – one worn normally, the other (with a hole cut in the crotch for the head) on the upper body. It's worth looking ridiculous to avoid a dangerous sting!

With any severe jellyfish sting, call medical help or a lifeguard urgently; lifeguards in the risk areas of Australia can usually administer an injection of box jellyfish antivenom on the spot. Meanwhile, if you get stung by one of the box jellyfishes, pour vinegar onto the affected area if you have any – it inactivates the stinging cells, although it doesn't help the stings you already have. (Tests have shown that Coca-Cola is the next-best substitute, while alcohol or urine may actually make the stinging feel worse.) But don't use vinegar for Portuguese man o'war stings – it can make them worse. Instead, rinse the area thoroughly with water (sea or fresh), or apply an ice pack.

Then (with any type of jellyfish sting) use a blunt knife or piece of plastic (a credit card will do) to carefully scrape off any remaining bits of tentacle. Be ready to give resuscitation (possibly including cardiac massage; *see p.174*) if needed. Antihistamines may help. The best cure for sea lice seems to be a vigorous shower (after removing your swimsuit), preferably in salt water. Wash your costume in a washing machine to rid it of any remaining larvae.

Other stingers

Cone shells – as the name suggests, cone-shaped shellfish varying from less than 2.5cm (1in) up to 25cm (10in) long – and the blue-ringed octopus (which is only the size of your hand) both produce a powerful venom that can kill by causing breathing failure. Cone shells are pretty collectors' items, but their poisonous barb can sting through clothing – so don't collect live specimens, and certainly never put them in your pocket. The blue-ringed octopus is common in rock pools and shallows in warm waters of the Indian and Pacific oceans; it's normally a dingy brown, but shows bright blue ring-shaped markings when it's angry. Take this as a warning to keep clear unless you want a life-threatening bite. In both cases, treat any sting or bite as you should a bite from an elapid snake (*see p.99*), with pressure bandaging and immobilisation of the affected limb. **Get medical help**, and be ready to give resuscitation (*see p.173*) if breathing is affected.

The crown of thorns – a big, spiny, coral-reef starfish – and sea urchins are among the many other sea creatures that can cause painful stings if you tread on them. In both cases, remove as many spines as you can, carefully, apply hot water (as with fish stings), and get medical help.

BILHARZIA (SCHISTOSOMIASIS)

Danger lurking in fresh water – in most of Africa and places beyond.

You're hot and dusty, and at the end of the day a cooling swim in a river or pool – or maybe a dowsing under the makeshift camp shower – beckons. While you're cooling off, something in the water that's too small to see gets in through your skin, unnoticed, and you're infected with a parasitic worm that may take weeks or months to show its presence. Or perhaps you go skin-diving in a freshwater lake, assured by the diving instructor that the water's perfectly safe, and the same thing happens. Or it can even happen simply paddling in shallow water, or through falling into the water while windsurfing or rafting. It's not perhaps quite as revolting as the idea of swallowing worm larvae or eggs (or faecal bacteria) in your food, but I find it pretty spooky.

It's known medically as schistosomiasis – sometimes abbreviated 'schisto' – but I'm sticking to the alternative name bilharzia (after the 19th-century German who discovered the parasite), which is a bit less of a mouthful. The WHO (the UN health agency) reckons that more than 200 million people, in 76 countries, are infected with it – 20 million of them seriously – making bilharzia the second most common tropical disease after malaria.

Fortunately, the disease is associated with a relatively modest 20 000 deaths each year, but it seriously affects general health among people who are exposed to it long term and are repeatedly infected. By far the biggest problem is in Africa, but there's also bilharzia in other continents, from Brazil to the Philippines.

What it is Several different but closely related bilharzia parasites are found in various parts of the world. They're small blood flukes or flatworms, called *Schistosoma*, which as adults live in veins mainly around the intestine or the bladder and genitals of the 'host' – a person or, with some species, another warm-blooded creature. They can live there as long as 15 years, shedding eggs which pass out in the host's urine or faeces. In most areas where bilharzia is widespread, the sanitary arrangements are primitive, and the eggs easily reach a river or lake. Larvae hatch out and next infect freshwater snails; they multiply and develop into huge numbers of tiny, free-swimming microscopic larvae called *cercariae*, which have a forked tail. It's these minute larvae that penetrate your skin (or, of course, get an even easier ride if you drink contaminated water).

Lesson one: Bilharzia can only exist in fresh water where snails live; without the snails there's no bilharzia. Snail-free water – in a tank or even a swimming pool – is safe after standing for at least two days, so long as no snails get in (and no more water that's infested with the larvae is added), because cercariae don't live long if they can't find a host. They can't survive at all in salt water. The greatest risk is in still or slowly-moving water near sources of infection – ie, villages and towns without proper (or any) sewage-treatment facilities.

Where you can get it Bilharzia is often thought of as an African problem – which it is, very seriously. But the disease also exists in fresh water in many other tropical and subtropical areas. *Beware false reassurance from tour operators and guides, diving instructors, guide books and even official government tourist boards that lakes and rivers in risk areas are bilharzia-free.* In sub-Saharan Africa particularly, this is simply untrue.

In Africa Africa has more than 80 per cent of the world's 200 million bilharzia-infected people. Most of sub-Saharan Africa, south of a line from Mauritania to Sudan, as far south as eastern South Africa, is a bilharzia-risk area, plus Madagascar and Mauritius, the Nile valley, and parts of Algeria and Libya. (*Parts* of Cameroon, Equatorial Guinea, Gabon and the two Congoes are bilharzia-free, as are parts of east Africa, most of Namibia and western Botswana. The risk is now zero in Tunisia and very low in Morocco – both formerly risky.) Artificial irrigation lakes, such as Lake Kariba in Zimbabwe, Lake Volta in Ghana and the Diama reservoir on the Senegal river, are heavily infested. Lake Malawi, once claimed to be bilharzia-free, is now known to be an important source of the disease – particularly the popular water-sports area of Cape Maclear. (True, the risk is lower in deep water well away from the shore, but it still exists there.)

Elsewhere In the Middle East, the Tigris and Euphrates valleys and parts of the Arabian penisular have bilharzia (although it's greatly reduced in Saudi Arabia itself). The main areas of risk elsewhere in Asia are marshes and lakes in China; it also exists – but with much lower risk – in parts of Laos, Cambodia, the Mekong delta and southern Thailand, in central Sulawesi (Celebes) in Indonesia, and in the southern Philippines. (Japan is now bilharzia-free.) In the Americas, the main bilharzia infestation is in eastern Brazil (where is exists around cities in the north-east), Surinam, Venezuela (low risk), and some islands in the Caribbean (including Antigua, Dominican Republic, Guadeloupe, Martinique, Montserrat, Puerto Rico and St Lucia).

How you can avoid it There's no vaccine (although work is going on to develop one) and no preventive drugs that can kill the bilharzia larvae. The only sure way of avoiding bilharzia is to avoid contact with contaminated water. However hot and sweaty you are, however tempting the water looks, *don't swim, bathe or even paddle in fresh water (even under a waterfall) in regions where there's schistosomiasis; and don't shower or bath in river or lake water unless the water has been filtered (a simple paper filter is enough for washing water), treated with chlorine or iodine, or is snail-free and has been left to stand for at least two days.* As already mentioned, properly maintained and chlorinated swimming pools are safe.

The greatest risk, as already said, is in shallow, still or slow-moving water, especially where there are reeds or water-weeds where snails live, and especially close to villages or places where people wash in the water. If you accidentally get a dipping, rub yourself down vigorously straight away with a towel; it can help to stop the parasites getting under your skin.

What it does to you A few hours, or up to a day or two, after that cooling swim or shower, you may notice a itchy rash – known as swimmer's itch (*see also box*) – where the bilharzia larvae invaded; it usually fades in a few days. Several weeks may pass before any more symptoms develop, when the parasites have found their permanent home and started to shed eggs.

The symptoms are very variable. Many people have none at all until – perhaps – serious liver, bladder or other problems develop much later. Others develop a high fever (sometimes called Katayama fever) weeks after infection, with itching, muscular pain, swollen lymph nodes ('glands'), diarrhoea, coughing and wheezing. A doctor may be able to feel enlargement of the liver and spleen.

In the longer term, there may be abdominal pain, and you may notice blood in your urine or faeces – or (rarely) in your semen if you're a man. If it's untreated, bilharzia can go on to cause serious liver damage, bladder cancer

---

SWIMMER'S ITCH

Known medically as cercarial dermatitis, this skin rash can also be caused by parasites similar to those responsible for bilharzia but living well outside the normal bilharzia zone – even as far north as Scotland and Long Island, New York. The parasites' normal warm-blooded host is usually a bird or small mammal, and they can't permanently infect humans. They trigger an allergic reaction when they penetrate your skin, but soon die, and the rash usually disappears within a week. If the itching is bad, you could try bathing in warm water with baking soda dissolved in it, or apply a soothing lotion such as calamine or a cream containing 1 per cent hydrocortisone (eg, 'Lanacort' or 'HC45'). In an extreme, you may need to take antihistamine tablets.

or (by obstructing the flow of urine to the bladder) kidney failure. The eggs can also lodge in other organs and cause damage. But these serious complications take a long time to develop, and it's very unlikely that you wouldn't be diagnosed and treated long before that stage.

Many experts advise having a routine check for bilharzia at least six weeks (to allow for the incubation time) after visiting a risk area.

How it's treated If you have the pattern of symptoms described, get expert medical attention immediately – especially because they could be caused by malaria (*see p.107*) or typhoid (*see p.46*). Blood and/or urine or stool-sample tests can confirm if you do have bilharzia – but often not for several weeks. However, doctors outside areas where bilharzia is common may not be fully aware of the risk, so if the symptoms develop later in your trip or after you return home, mention if you might have been exposed to the parasite – ie, if you have been in fresh water, however briefly, in a bilharzia area.

Once diagnosed, treatment is quick and safe, with a drug called praziquantel ('Cysticide') – usually a single dose. However, this can't cure scarring caused by a long-term infestation of the worms. Nor is it effective until the bilharzia parasites have matured, so it shouldn't be taken until six weeks after the last possible date of infection.

LEPTOSPIROSIS

Also known as Weil's disease, this is an infection caused by spiral-shaped bacteria called leptospires; but I'm covering it here rather than with other infections because it's spread in much the same way as bilharzia (*see above*). The bacteria spend part of their life-cycle in animals such as rats and bats, and get into waterways via these creatures' urine. You can be infected by drinking contaminated water, through scratches, or via the membranes of the eyes and nose when swimming or diving (including sump-diving in bat caves). Unlike bilharzia larvae, they can't penetrate unbroken skin.

Leptospirosis can be caught almost anywhere in the world, but it's most common in warm tropical and subtropical regions – including many popular holiday spots. The symptoms develop about one to two weeks later: usually a flu-like fever with a headache and muscular pains (especially in your thighs and lower back); often there's nausea and vomiting. Usually the disease clears up more or less unaided, but in rare serious cases there's jaundice or kidney failure; a few patients need kidney dialysis for a time. For this reason, a doctor should be consulted promptly – and told if you think you may have been exposed to the bacteria. Antibiotics normally bring a quick recovery.

If you're already taking doxycycline as protection against malaria (*see pp.115–116*), this may also prevent leptospirosis infection. In any case, you should cover any cuts or scratches with waterproof plasters before swimming in areas where rats or bats live.

DISEASES FROM INSECTS AND OTHER BITERS

They may not be quite the most common medical conditions that you face on your travels, but diseases transmitted by the bites of insects, ticks and other wild creatures are probably the most important and potentially dangerous. Malaria is undoubtedly top of the list, and on its own makes the mosquito worldwide public health enemy number one. But there are many other diseases spread by the bites of mosquitoes, flies and other insects.

The second-biggest group (after insect-borne diseases) consists of those carried by ticks – tiny eight-legged relatives of spiders that may cling to you unnoticed until they have gorged themselves on your blood. In the process, they may be passing disease organisms to you – although, fortunately, they usually have to cling on for quite a long time in order to do so. Finally, not only mini-creatures can be deadly; the deadliest animal-borne disease of all – if you don't do anything about it – is rabies. It's probably either non-existent or very rare in the country you live in; not so in many of the places you may visit, so be aware of the danger and be prepared in case you should encounter it.

The previous chapter (*pp. 72–105*) deals with the carriers themselves, and how to protect yourself from them; here the emphasis is on the diseases...

MALARIA

The most serious health risk to travellers in the tropics and subtropics.

The explorer, planter or colonial administrator heroically fighting bouts of malaria in a hut in the jungle with a cocktail of quinine and gin may make good Hollywood drama, but it's not a drama you want to take any part in. Malaria is deadly serious – literally. It afflicts between 300 and 500 million people worldwide and kills 1 to 2 million (some estimates suggest even more), many of them children. It's a threat to 40 per cent of the world's population – and to you, if you travel to any of the 100-odd countries where malaria exists. There's no vaccine (yet), and the situation is getting worse rather than better in many places, as strains of malaria parasites develop increasing resistance to antimalarial drugs.

The World Health Organisation (WHO) estimates that, each year, around 125 million travellers throughout the world visit countries where there's malaria. Of those, as many as 50 000 return home infected with it, according to some estimates, including up to 20 000 in Europe. The UK figure is between 2000 and 2500, with up to 16 malaria deaths each year since 1990. France has a similar number of cases, but the figures for Australia, Germany and the USA are somewhat lower. You can add to that deaths among travellers and tourists while still overseas – and there are some of those almost every year.

You can't completely eliminate the risk of catching malaria, but you can greatly reduce it if you strictly follow sensible guidelines.

It's astonishing (at least to doctors involved with malaria, and to me) that an estimated one in every three travellers going to malaria-risk areas – which include very many backpacker destinations – don't take the recommended doses of antimalarial preventive drugs ('malaria prophylaxis' in doctors' jargon). In one survey, at least half of the travellers who died of malaria either took no antimalarial drugs at all, or took them for too short a time, or didn't follow the recommended drug regime. And as many as 96 per cent of travellers fail to combine these drugs properly with other protective measures (such as using bed nets and repellents to deter mosquito bites).

No doubt the bad press given to some antimalarial drugs – mefloquine ('Lariam') in particular – is partly responsible for people failing to take their pills. It's true that mefloquine does have unpleasant side-effects in some people. But, unless you are a woman who is pregnant or breast-feeding and you are visiting areas where the malaria bugs are resistant to other drugs, there are effective alternatives (*see p.115*). (The options are fewer, too, for children under 8 or 12.) Believe me, catching malaria is much worse.

Special warning: Many people who live in areas where malaria is a part of everyday life build up resistance or even immunity to the disease over many years. But this doesn't last if they leave the area and move for a while to a part of the world where there's no malaria, or where there's a different type of malaria parasite. Their resistance needs to be constantly 'topped up'.

Every year, there are many cases of malaria – sometimes extremely serious – among people who revisit their country of birth after living for as little as two or three years in Europe, North America or Australasia. This is particularly true of people from Africa and from south and south-east Asia. They think they're still immune to malaria – and they may be told by people back home (who *are* resistant) that there's no malaria risk. But they're not immune. They don't bother to take antimalarial drugs, they don't take enough care about being bitten by mosquitoes, and they become ill.

Another group at particular risk is pregnant women – particularly during their first pregnancy. They can also lose their immunity and catch malaria when they would normally be resistant to it.

What it is Malaria is an infectious disease carried from person to person by female mosquitoes of a particular type, known as *Anopheles*. You can read more about mosquitoes and how to stop them biting you on pages 73–78, but a few key facts about *Anopheles* are worth remembering:–

→ They bite mainly from dusk to dawn.

→ You can recognise them because they rest in a distinctive posture, with the rear end of their body held up (or away from the wall).

→ There are species of *Anopheles* that live well outside the current malarial zone – which used to extend as far north as the British Isles and New York – and they could (and occasionally do) become infected again. The risk isn't usually widespread or prolonged, but such local malaria outbreaks have occurred in California and New York. (This is a separate phenomenon from so-called 'airport malaria', where somebody gets infected by the bite of a mosquito imported in the cabin of a plane.)

The cause of malaria is a microscopic, single-celled parasitic animal – ie, a protozoan, not a bacterium or virus – called *Plasmodium*. More than 100 species of *Plasmodium* are known, but only four of them cause human malaria. By far the worst is *Plasmodium falciparum*, which is responsible for virtually all fatal cases of malaria. (As a shorthand, the variety of malaria this bug causes is referred to simply as '*falciparum* malaria'.) The others are *P.* (that's an abbreviation for *Plasmodium*) vivax, *P. ovale* and *P. malariae*.

Plasmodium go through a complicated life-history in mosquitoes and people. You don't need to know all the details, but if you know the outline it'll help you to understand why malaria symptoms may crop up when they do, and why it has to be treated at different stages in the way it is:–

→ When an infected female *Anopheles* feeds on your blood, it injects malaria parasites into you.

→ The bloodstream carries the parasites to your liver, where they stay a while, maturing and multiplying. Meanwhile, you feel perfectly well.

→ About one to three weeks later (depending on the species of *Plasmodium* you've got – the process is fastest with *P. falciparum*), the parasites return to the bloodstream in a different form.

→ There they invade red blood cells (corpuscles), and grow and mature some more inside these blood cells. After a while they grow so big that they burst the red blood cells, scattering more parasites into the blood. These can invade more red blood cells, prolonging the infection, but they can't re-invade your liver.

→ *P. falciparum* multiplies much faster than the other types of parasite, and can invade the brain and other vital organs; that's why it's so dangerous.

→ At the same time, certain parasite cells that have grown inside red blood cells themselves burst. This releases malaria toxins (poisons) into your bloodstream; it's the toxins that cause the sudden and violent fever, chills and other classic symptoms of malaria (*see below*). Important fact: The very shortest time between being infected by a mosquito bite and these symptoms appearing is seven days; nine days is more usual, and often it's considerably longer.

→ Meanwhile, in the case of *P. ovale* and *P. vivax* only, some of the parasites remain in your liver in a dormant or resting state. Not only do these 'wake up' from time to time, releasing parasites into the bloodstream to cause recurring attacks of malaria after months or even years without symptoms, but also they are protected (inside liver cells) from most antimalarial drugs.

→ *P. malariae* parasites behave differently again. They don't rest in the liver, but they may stay in the bloodstream for a long time without invading red blood cells – but then do so and cause repeated malarial attacks.

→ Towards the end of the various stages in your body, separate male and female forms of malaria parasites develop in your bloodstream, ready to be taken up by another blood-sucking mosquito. But even then the cycle isn't quite complete, because the males and females have to get together inside the mosquito's gut before a new victim can be infected.

Where you can get it Malaria is today almost entirely a disease of the tropics and subtropics. Thanks to eradication campaigns, it disappeared from Europe and most of the Caribbean in the second half of the 20th century. Its impact was also enormously reduced in the Indian subcontinent, but it has since returned in much of the southern half of Asia.

You are highly unlikely to catch malaria above 3000m (10 000ft), and it's rare – but certainly not impossible – to get it above 2000m (6500ft). There are seasonal factors too: in many regions, you are only likely to catch malaria during or just after the rains, when the mosquitoes are rampant.

The picture is also complicated by the fact that the four different types of malaria are not all equally common in different places. (As explained above, it's the *falciparum* type that's most dangerous, accounting for most malaria deaths.) What is more, strains of malaria parasite that resist particular antimalarial drugs have cropped up in a number of places.

And the raw level of risk – how common malaria is – also varies. Detailed information for the most popular destinations is given in Part three of this book (*pp.182–273*), but remember that the situation can change with time, so *check before you go*. In outline you can (at the time of writing) get malaria...

In Africa A small area of Egypt, plus everywhere south of about 20°N (including most of Sudan, Chad, Niger, Mali and Mauritania), south to about 20–25°S. (Only the extreme north of Namibia and Botswana, and the north-east of South Africa – including Kruger National Park, and down to within 100km (60 miles) of Durban – have malaria, but you can catch it throughout Mozambique, Madagascar and the Comoros, in parts of Mauritius and in the lowland areas of Swaziland.) In most of Africa, *P. falciparum* is the main cause, and in some areas it accounts for up to a half of all deaths of children under five (I'm talking about in the local population, of course). Many strains are resistant to common drugs.

In the Americas From the Pacific coast of northern Mexico and the Yucatan Peninsula through most of Central America and Colombia to parts of Venezuela, Guyana and the whole Amazon Basin. In the Caribbean, only parts of Haiti and the Dominican Republic have malaria, mainly due to *P. falciparum*. Elsewhere, *P. vivax* is the main parasite in most areas, but there's good deal of *P. falciparum* in the Amazon region and it's the main type in Guyana, Surinam and French Guiana. Some strains are drug-resistant.

In Asia In the western (Red Sea) and southern parts of the Arabian peninsula, and from the extreme south of Turkey through parts of the Middle East (especially in northern Iraq and along the Gulf coast of Iran); throughout virtually all of the Indian subcontinent and south-east Asia (both mainland and islands, except in small areas); and China (Yunnan and Hainan, plus some other isolated areas). *P. falciparum* is the main malaria parasite in Burma, Cambodia, Laos, Sabah and Vienam, and it also exists in many other areas except in extreme western Asia. There are drug-resistant strains in many regions.

In Australasia and the Pacific In the lowland areas of Papua New Guinea (and Indonesian New Guinea), and south-eastwards through the Solomon Islands and Vanuatu – mainly caused by *P. falciparum*. At the time of writing there's no malaria in other Pacific islands or in Australia.

How you can avoid it Basic facts: There's not yet any malaria vaccine, nor likely to be one for some years. And antimalarial prophylaxis – taking preventive drugs (to most travellers, simply 'malaria pills') – is no panacea. It's essential, but it's only one part of the battle against malaria. You also need to do all you can to avoid getting bitten by mosquitoes, especially between dusk and dawn. But even if you're careful and take your pills, you still *may* catch malaria. In that case, you need to get medical attention quickly. (In the case of *falciparum* malaria, 24 hours can make all the difference.) So it pays not only to understand the risks of catching malaria, but also its incubation period and its main symptoms (*see below*).

For full advice on protecting yourself from mosquitoes, see page 75, but...

→ Wear baggy clothes done up at the neck, ankles and wrists.
→ Use an insect-repellent such as DEET on all exposed skin.
→ Spray rooms with insecticide every evening.
→ Make sure there's a mosquito-proof screen on doors and windows.
→ Use a mosquito net (preferably soaked in permethrin or a related insecticide such as deltamethrin; *see p.77*) over your bed.

However much these precautions help, you're still at risk unless you back them up with effective antimalarial drugs, which aim to prevent malaria parasites getting established in your body if a mosquito does get through and infect you. For more information on the main individual antimalarial drugs and drug combinations you may be prescribed, see the listing that starts on page 115, but with all of them, there are a number of general principles:–

→ Strictly follow your doctor's or travel clinic's advice on the dosage, frequency and period for which you should take the tablets. Pay particular attention to dosage and frequency for children, which will be different from the general guidelines mentioned in the listing.

→ In a few cases of tablets that are taken daily, you can start taking them only one or two days before you reach an area where there's a risk of malaria.

→ As a rule, however, and particularly with tablets taken weekly, start taking them one week in advance. An exception is mefloquine ('Lariam'); this is best started at least three weeks beforehand in case you suffer any side-effects – in which case, there's still time to switch to an alternative medication before you need to start the main course of protection.

→ While you're in the malaria-risk area, take the prophlyactic drug(s) at the same time each day – ie, every 24 hours, allowing for any changes of time zone – or on the same day each week, as appropriate.

→ If you forget to take a dose, take it as soon as you remember, followed by the next dose at the normal time or day. Meanwhile, take special precautions not to get bitten.

→ If you have vomiting within about an hour of taking a malaria pill, take another one *unless your doctor advises otherwise*. If you have diarrhoea or prolonged vomiting, or if you are being treated for another illness, ask the advice of the doctor who's treating you.

→ Take your malaria pills with food and plenty of water.

→ As a rule, *continue to take your malaria pills for four weeks after the last possible date when you could have been infected*. This is because malaria parasites remain hidden inside your liver cells (*see above*) for that time, and most prophylactic drugs can attack them only in the bloodstream. The only exception to this advice is if you are prescribed atovaquone plus proguanil (combined in 'Malorone'); this can kill malaria parasites in the liver as well as the blood, so it needs to be continued for only one week.

Which pills? The particular drug or combination of drugs you need to protect you from malaria depends on the type(s) of malaria parasite you're likely to encounter, and whether they're resistant to certain antimalarial drugs. This is mainly a matter of geography, so the recommended medication depends on your planned route, including stopovers, and in some cases on the precise area of a country you plan to visit. So tell your doctor as fully as you can where you plan to go.

It's vital to take the right malaria pills. National and international bodies keep track of changes in drug resistance, and issue new recommendations from time to time. The information given on pages 182–273 is correct at the time of writing, but it could have changed by the time you read it. So **get the up-to-date advice of an experienced doctor – preferably at a specialist travel clinic – on which malaria pills you should take**, or consult an official travel health information line. In some countries you can buy certain malaria pills over the counter from a pharmacist, without a prescription, but these may not be suitable for your intinerary, and could leave you unprotected.

The doctor you consult should prompt you, but do be sure to tell him/her of any existing medical condition or allergy (including any drug allergy) you may have, any medication you're currently taking, or if you're a woman who is or might be (or plans to be) pregnant. As with all medicines, antimalarial drugs can interact badly with certain drugs or conditions. Also tell your doctor how long you intend to be away; some drugs are suitable only for a short trip. It's worth getting a clear written prescription to take with you in case you need to get more pills while you are travelling.

At the same time, if you're going to a seriously inaccessible spot where, if an emergency should arise, it would be impossible to get professional medical help within 24 hours, discuss with the doctor the need to take emergency standby treatment (*see below*).

What it does to you As already explained, the first symptoms of malaria can't appear until at least a week after infection, and the delay could be a year or more – especially with *vivax* malaria. However, the *falciparum* type generally shows up within a month and usually much less.

The start is almost always abrupt, and resembles severe flu without the sore throat or runny nose. You begin to feel unwell and feverish, with aches and pains, a bad headache and nausea. As your temperature soars – possibly above 40°C (104°F) – you sweat profusely, are seized by chills and severe, uncontrollable shivering fits; you feel utterly exhausted. You probably won't feel like getting up, but if you do you are liable to feel dizzy or faint. You may well vomit and/or have diarrhoea. A companion may notice pallid skin and

> **WARNING**
>
> The most important rule with malaria is: **Immediately seek expert diagnosis and treatment if you develop a fever a week or more after you enter an area where there's a risk of catching malaria.** This still applies for at least a year after you return home, but especially during the first three months. However, as explained in the main text, the incubation period means that *a fever developing less than a week after you arrive in a malarial area is highly unlikely to be malaria.*

tongue, and possibly jaundice (yellowing of the whites of the eyes) caused by liver damage. If s/he presses under the left side of your rib-cage, the spleen may feel enlarged and tender.

If the infection isn't too severe, the worst symptoms are likely to die down after a day or so, but then return after about three days. This is because the next generation of malaria parasites (from red blood cells invaded during the first attack) burst out. (In the case of a *P. malariae* infection the delay is a bit longer – four days on average.)

If you're unlucky enough to be infected with *P. falciparum*, much more severe symptoms *may* set in within a further few days (although sometimes in as little as 24 hours). As the malaria parasites block small blood vessels in the brain, you may have convulsions and fall into a coma; or unconsciousness may set in more slowly after a period of confusion and increasing delirium. Even if you eventually recover, you may be unconscious for several days. Other complications can include severe anaemia, shock, very low blood pressure, kidney damage, and more. If haemoglobin from the blood gets into your urine after lots of red blood cells are destroyed, it turns the urine brown or black – a rare complication known as 'blackwater fever'.

Such complications are by no means inevitable even in *falciparum* malaria, and are almost unknown in other types. But if they do occur, the grim news is that there is about a one in ten chance of dying, even with the best treatment. That's why it's so important act quckly, *before* complications set in.

How it's treated Speed is vital. If you or a companion develop the malaria symptoms described above, get (or get to) immediate medical help – within 24 hours at the very most. **(If help is more than 24 hours away, see the following section, *Emergency treatment*.)**

Of course, lots of things – especially in the tropics – can cause a fever, aches and pains, headache, vomiting and so on, and blood tests are needed to find out whether or not malaria is the cause. Doctors in malarial areas should be used to diagnosing the disease, usually by examining a blood sample under a microscope or possibly using an instant 'dipstick' test (a bit like a pregnancy test kit, but used with blood rather than urine). But if you've already returned home when you get ill, emphasise to your doctor where you've been, as s/he may not have seen many cases of malaria before.

Once it's diagnosed, there are a range of antimalarial drugs the doctor can give – by tablet, injection, intravenous drip or even suppository – to attack the malaria parasites, while at the same time treating the fever and other symptoms. The choice of drug will depend on the type of malaria prophylaxis you have been taking, the type of malaria parasite found, and whether the particular parasites in that area are resistant to certain remedies.

Some treatments are the same drugs as those used (generally in smaller doses) for malaria prophylaxis. Some are brand-new, but others (such as quinine) have been used to fight malaria for hundreds of years – or even longer in the case of drugs derived from wormwood, which is a traditional Chinese medicinal herb. (I'd like to emphasise, however, that malaria is too serious to leave to herbal practitioners, without denying that some of their remedies may contain valuable drugs.) Finally, remember that malaria can recur – you may need treatment from time to time for many years.

Emergency treatment Rapid diagnosis is important, but treatment is even more so. (At the time of writing, 'dipstick' tests are not really suitable for self-diagnosis by travellers, because they need to be stored in a fridge – but this may change.) So, if you seriously think that you may have a case of malaria on your hands, and can't get to a doctor – or get a doctor to you – within 24 hours, then you'll need to give (or take) a course of emergency malaria treatment. It could be life-saving.

As mentioned above, you should have discussed this with a specialist travel doctor before departure, and he or she should have prescribed emergency 'standby' treatment and given you instructions on when and how to use it. The drugs supplied will depend on where you're travelling, and what routine malaria prophylaxis you're taking. (Clearly if malaria parasites have broken through the protective barrier of a particular drug, there's not much point in trying more of the same.) You're most likely to be prescribed a course of one of the following for such emergency treatment (listed alphabetically, not in any order of preference or effectiveness):–

→ Artemether plus lumefantrine (combined as co-artemether or 'Riamet').
→ Atovaquone plus proguanil (combined as 'Malarone').
→ Chloroquine (also sold as 'Avlochlor' and 'Nivaquine'); only for areas with non-resistant strains of malaria parasites.
→ Mefloquine ('Lariam').
→ Pyrimethamine plus sulphoxidine (combined as 'Fansidar').
→ Quinine.
→ Quinine plus either doxycycline or tetracycline (antibiotics, both also supplied under trade names).
→ Quinine plus 'Fansidar'

But remember: **it's still vital to get professional medical help ASAP.**

DRUGS FOR PREVENTING MALARIA

As explained in the main text, advice on the best drugs to take for malaria prophylaxis – ie, routine 'malaria pills' – changes quite often. It depends on the changing pattern of the disease in different parts of the world, and with the development of drug resistance and new drugs. At the time of writing, these (in alphabetical order; with some trade names in brackets) are the main drugs prescribed to travellers – **but always check with your doctor for updates**. Alternatives are drugs that give equivalent protection, but they may not be suitable for all people. (Note that 'arrival' and 'departure' refer to period in the malaria-risk area.)

Atovaquone plus proguanil (combined in 'Malarone') Effective against chloroquine- and mefloquine-resistant malaria (especially *falciparum* type), and a good alternative to mefloquine ('Lariam') or doxycycline for people who can't (or don't want to) take either of those drugs. Quite new and expensive, but short dosage period means the cost is reasonable for short trips. Other facts:–

→ Recommended for short-term use only (currently licensed in the UK as prophylaxis for trips of up to 28 days, but may be prescribed by clinics for up to three months).
→ Normal dosage: One tablet a day, starting one or two days before arrival and continuing for only seven days after departure.
→ Not recommended for pregnant or breast-feeding women.
→ Not suitable for babies and small children under 11kg (24lb).
→ Not suitable for people with severe kidney problems (consult doctor).
→ Side-effects: Few known so far; occasional nausea or headaches.

Chloroquine (also sold as 'Avlochlor' and 'Nivaquine') Long used and safe, but *P. falciparum* is resistant to it in many areas. (At the time of writing it's recommended for use alone only in Turkey, Syria, Iraq and Egypt; Azerbaijan and Turkestan; Mexico and Central America north of Panama; Haiti and Dominican Republic; and Paraguay.) In some other areas, can be combined with proguanil (*see below*). Cheap. Other facts:–

→ Normal dosage: One or two tablets once a week (or smaller daily doses), from a week before arrival until four weeks after departure.
→ Suitable for pregnant and breast-feeding women, and children.
→ Not suitable for people with a history of epilepsy or chronic psoriasis.
→ May cause itching in people with dark skin.
→ Can interfere with rabies vaccine if given at the same time (*see p.139*).
→ Hydroxychloroquine ('Plaquenil') is similar but more expensive; not normally used for malaria prophylaxis in the UK.

Doxycycline (also sold as 'Nordox' and 'Vibramycin') An antibiotic related to tetracycline that is highly effective against chloroquine- and

DRUGS FOR PREVENTING MALARIA (*continued*)

mefloquine-resistant malaria, and is also a good alternative for those who can't (or don't want to) take mefloquine ('Lariam'). In sub-Saharan Africa it has been shown to give as good protection as mefloquine, and is particularly recommended in the border areas of Burma (Myanmar), Cambodia and Thailand, and in New Guinea, Solomon Islands and Vanuatu. It also gives protection against some forms of traveller's diarrhoea (*see p.34*), despite sometimes itself causing mild diarrhoea. Cost is mid-way between that of mefloquine and atovaquone plus proguanil. Other facts:–

→ Normal dosage: One capsule a day, starting one or two days before arrival and continuing for four weeks after departure. Take on a full stomach with plenty of water while standing upright.
→ Not suitable for pregnant or breast-feeding women.
→ Not suitable for children under eight years old (not licensed in UK for children under 12).
→ Not suitable for people who are hypersensitive ('allergic') to tetracycline antibiotics, or for those with liver problems.
→ May cause nausea and possibly transient diarrhoea (but see above).
→ May increase risk of vaginal thrush (*see p.157*) in women.
→ In some people, makes skin more susceptible to sunburn; if you have sensitive skin, use extra-high-protection sunscreen (*see p.56*), cover up and avoid prolonged exposure to strong sunshine.
→ Alternative: atovaquone plus proguanil (*see above*).

Mefloquine ('Lariam') Has earned a bad reputation for psychiatric and other side-effects (*see below*), but it's highly effective in most areas (except parts of south-east Asia) against chloroquine-resistant *falciparum* malaria. The great majority of side-effects show up within three weeks, so you're advised to start taking it at least three weeks before leaving home, to allow time to switch to an alternative if necessary. Relatively cheap (about double the cost of chloroquine plus proguanil, but cheaper than listed alternatives). Other facts:–

→ Normal dosage: One tablet once a week, starting at least two weeks before arrival (but preferably three; *see above*) and continuing for four weeks after departure.
→ Not to be taken within 12 hours of treatment with quinine.
→ Not suitable for young babies (under 5kg [11lb]).
→ Not suitable for people who have had epilepsy or a psychiatric disorder (including depression).
→ Not suitable for people with certain heart problems.
→ Side-effects (more common in women than men) include dizziness, headaches, insomnia, vivid nightmares, anxiety, depression, panic attacks and sometimes hallucinations. In a very few cases there may

be convulsions or disorders so severe as to need psychiatric treatment.
→ May also cause irregular heart-beat and other heart disorders.
→ Transient effects include nausea and possibly vomiting and diarrhoea.
→ Alternatives: doxycycline; atovaquone plus proguanil (*see above*).

Proguanil ('Paludrine') **plus chloroquine** Proguanil not used alone. The combination has long been used in areas with drug-resistant malaria, but is much less effective than mefloquine ('Lariam') and its alternatives, particularly in sub-Saharan Africa. But the combination is still suitable in many areas of Asia. Usually taken as separate tablets, but in some countries (eg, France), a combined chloroquine–proguanil tablet ('Savarine') is available. Quite cheap. Other facts (in addition to those applying to chloroquine; *see above*):–

→ Normal dosage (in addition to chloroquine): Two tablets a day, starting one week before arrival and continuing for four weeks after departure.
→ 'Savarine' combination tablet to be taken daily, starting one or two days before arrival and continuing for four weeks after departure. (*Note*: Tablet is big and suitable only for adults.)
→ Suitable for pregnant and breast-feeding women, and children.
→ Not suitable for people with liver or kidney problems.
→ May cause mouth ulcers.
→ Alternative for some areas: pyrimethamine plus dapsone (see below); except as noted above, mefloquine ('Lariam') or its alternatives.

Pyrimethamine plus dapsone (combined in 'Maloprim') Don't confuse with the similarly-named 'Malarone', especially as the latter is taken daily whereas 'Maloprim' must only be taken once a week. Long used in southern Africa and the south-western Pacific, but not very much today (and no longer available in Europe). However, can be a useful alternative in some places to chloroquine (or proguanil plus chloroquine; *see above*) in people – especially children – who can't take chloroquine because they've had epilepsy. Other facts:–

→ Normal dosage: One tablet a week, starting one week before arrival and continuing for four weeks after departure.
→ May cause serious side-effects if dose is exceeded.
→ Not suitable during early pregnancy.
→ May cause blue-grey colour in nails (due to changes in blood).

Tafenoquine A new and still experimental drug that has so far been tested mainly on military personnel but may be more generally available in the future. For short visits to malarial areas, it may only be necessary to take a short course of three tablets before departure. It seems (so far) to have few side-effects, but can't be used by people with a genetic disorder called G6PD deficiency.

LEISHMANIASIS AND KALA-AZAR

Unpleasant, unslightly – and spread by sandfies that don't live in sand.

The bad news is that, every year, up to ten million people around the world catch leismaniasis (also known as leishmania). The relatively good news is that less than half a million of them get the potentially fatal internal form, called visceral leishmaniasis or kala-azar. Almost all the rest have the cutaneous (skin) form of the disease. This is unpleasant and disfiguring, causing long-lasting lumps or ulcers on the face, arms or legs, but it's not usually life-threatening. Rarely, it may gradually destroy the nose and lips.

Although cutaneous leishmaniasis occurs more often than many other travellers' diseases, no type is particularly common in travellers. Partly for this reason – and because it can be slow to develop, and in the visceral, kala-azar form can resemble leukaemia or lymphoma (a type of cancer) – your doctor back home may overlook it.

What it is Leishmaniasis is an infection caused by parasites known as Leishmania – single-celled protozoans like those that cause malaria (*see p.108*). They are carried by a wide range of wild and domestic animals, including foxes, jackals, rodents and dogs, but you can't catch it directly from them. (It's said that, around the Mediterranean, thousands of dogs carry it for every person who's infected.) Sandflies transfer the infection to people by biting an infected animal and then a person.

Sandflies are tiny – only about 2mm (less than 1/10in) long – sandy-coloured flies that live in cracks in masonry, in animals' burrows, and in forests and undergrowth. Other facts about them:–

→ Sandflies bite mostly from dusk until dawn. They're most numerous during and after the rainy season.
→ They're small enough to get through most mosquito nets, but are deterred if the net is treated with insecticide (eg, permethrin; *see p.77*).

Where you can get it Over a surprisingly wide area, mostly in rural areas or town outskirts: It exists from Bangladesh, India and Pakistan, through much of the Middle East (where there's an urban form in Baghdad, Damascus, Teheran and some other cities) to both coasts of the Mediterranean (ie, southern Europe and north Africa), parts of sub-Saharan Africa, and parts of the Americas in Texas (rarely) and from southern Mexico to Bolivia, Paraguay and Brazil. In most of these places, only the cutaneous form is at all common, but there's kala-azar in parts of eastern India, Bangladesh and Nepal, and in east Africa from Sudan and Eritrea to Kenya; also in Brazil. There have been big epidemics, particularly in India and Sudan.

How you can avoid it There's no vaccine or preventive drug, so it comes down to avoiding sandfly bites (along with mosquitoes and so on carrying other diseases in most of these places). Sleep under a insecticide-treated net if you're not in a well-screened, air-conditioned room. Spray the room, too.

When you go out at night, cover up and put an insect-repellent such as DEET on every inch of exposed skin (see p. 77). It's said that, should you happen to be camping in semi-desert country in the Middle East, you should avoid gerbils' burrows – a favourite sandfly haunt. I'm not sure how practicable this advice is, but at least now you know!

What it does to you A sandfly bite may itch, but it doesn't sting and often goes unnoticed. A few weeks later, nodules (lumps) or ulcers form where you were bitten. They don't usually make much puss unless they get infected with bacteria, and often heal without treatment in a few months – but may leave unsightly scars. In kala-azar, the parasites spread to the liver, spleen, bone marrow and other internal organs. Sometimes as long as two years after the original infection, it causes fever, loss of weight, anaemia and enlargement of the spleen and liver. Unless treated, it may eventually be fatal.

How it's treated There are effective drug treatments, but they may have side-effects and have to be given under close medical supervision. And some are very expensive, and may not be available in certain areas. So it's important to consult a doctor with experience of leishmaniasis if you do catch it – and to tell any doctor of your travels if you develop slow-healing sores or if you should ever be investigated for leukaemia or lymphoma (cancer of the lymphatic system). A skin and/or blood test can establish if you in fact have leismaniasis or kala-azar.

SLEEPING SICKNESS (AFRICAN TRYPANOSOMIASIS)

Danger in game parks and rural areas in much of sub-Saharan Africa.

It doesn't always cause sleepiness, but it *is* always deadly serious – literally: if you get it and don't treat it, it'll probably kill you in anything from a matter of weeks to a few years. It's not a common condition in travellers or tourists, but the seriousness of the disease means that anyone who visits tropical Africa should be aware of it.

There are two related forms of sleeping sickness, caused by slightly different bugs but both transmitted by the bite of tsetse flies. The west and central African form develops much more slowly and insidiously than the east African type, which usually causes severe symptoms within a few weeks. There are normally about 20 000 new cases of sleeping sickness a year in Africa, but the WHO (the UN health agency) reckons that civil wars and disturbances have resulted in half a million people catching it since 1990.

What it is Both types of African sleeping sickness are caused by tiny single-celled parasites called *Trypanosoma*, or trypanosomes – hence the name trypanosomiasis. (They are protozoans, as are malaria parasites; see p. 108.) The parasites are carried by domestic cattle and game animals in east Africa, but the west and central African trypanosome lives mostly in people.

The tsetse (pronounced *tset-si* or *tet-si*) flies that transmit them are quite big, blood-sucking greyish-brown flies, 6–15mm (up to just over half an inch) long, or to up to twice the size of a housefly. Other facts about them:–

→ They live in woodland, in thickets on the savannah plains, and in trees and dense undergrowth along streams or by waterholes. They're particularly common near domestic and game animals in east Africa.

→ They fold their wings along their back when they rest.

→ They bite mostly during the day, aren't put off by insect-repellents, and can bite through thin clothing.

→ They're attracted to moving vehicles and the dust that they and game animals stir up, and also to bright or dark contrasting colours (especially dark blue, according to some reports).

Where you can get it Only in Africa – broadly, rural parts of the tropics from about 15°N to 20°S. That takes in more than 35 countries, from Senegal, Mali, Chad, Sudan and Ethiopia in the north to Namibia, Botswana, Zimbabwe and Mozambique in the south (although the risk is normally quite low in Senegal, Gambia, Ethiopia, Namibia, Botswana and Zimbabwe). There have been no recent cases in Eritrea, Djibouti or Somalia, and South Africa and Madagascar are also free of the disease. You don't get it in cities.

East African trypanosomiasis is a risk from Ethiopia, Kenya and Uganda through Tanzania, Malawi, Zambia and Congo (Zaire) to Mozambique, Zimbabwe and Botswana. The disease exists in the popular game parks and lodges of these areas, although the risk isn't high.

West and central African trypanosomiasis is found throughout west Africa and parts of central Africa – especially in Congo (Zaire), northern Uganda and southern Sudan. Because it's a disease of forests and other wooded areas, aid workers and other long-term visitors are more at risk than short-term tourists and travellers.

How you can avoid it Number one fact: There's no vaccine and no protective drugs to stop you catching sleeping sickness. Number two: If you recover from one dose of sleeping sickness it gives you no immunity to a second. So it all comes down to avoidance and personal protection.

Take reliable local advice on tsetse-infested areas, and avoid them. Keep out of dense undergrowth, bushes and other thick vegetation. However tempting it may be, it's best to avoid travelling on the open back of a jeep or pick-up truck through tsetse country. You should be using insect-repellents against mosquitoes, but protect yourself against tsetse flies in other ways:–

→ Wear long-sleeved and long-legged clothes made of fairly thick material, as tsetse flies can bite through thin cloth. Choose pale-coloured clothing – tan, or a pale khaki or olive-green shade (classic safari gear, in fact!).

→ Make sure rooms and tents have effective screens (as well as a bed net), and spray them – and inside vehicles, if necessary – with insecticide.

What it does to you You'll probably know if you've been bitten by a tsetse fly – it's usually quite painful. Otherwise, the first sign of trouble, especially in the east African form of sleeping sickness, may be a swollen red sore, or chancre, where you were bitten. This usually develops within a week or two, but after that west African trypanosomiasis develops much more mildly and slowly – as a chronic illness over months or even years – than the east African type. Not that the symptoms aren't basically similar:–

→ Fever, severe headaches, weakness and fatigue.
→ Painful joints, and often swollen lymph nodes ('glands') in the neck.
→ Sometimes a rash.

Later (depending on the type caught) there are behavioural changes:–

→ Irritability, lack of concentratrion, slurred speech and confusion.
→ Seizures.
→ Difficulty in walking and talking.
→ Sometimes insomnia at night while sleeping for long periods by day.

These are signs that the brain is affected, and without treatment they gradually worsen until death follows – usually within weeks or months with east African trypanosomiasis, or in a matter of months to years in the west African form of the disease.

How it's treated If the above hasn't frightened you enough to **get immediate medical attention if you get a fever or other symptoms after being bitten by a tsetse fly,** let me just add that it could also be malaria (see p.107), as well as more benign ailments such as dengue fever, glandular fever (mononucleosis) or flu. The point is to get expert help as soon as possible. Your blood, lymph and/or possibly cerebrospinal fluid – fluid from your spine, withdrawn via a lumbar puncture – or skin need to be tested to identify the bug that's reponsible, and that normally needs to be done in hospital. The same applies to treatment with a course of anti-trypanosomal drugs, and follow-up tests which may be needed for up to two years. Luckily, the treatment is usually effective.

If symptoms develop after you return home – even months or years later – and you have been in an area where tsetse flies live, it's vital to tell your doctor and consult or get referred to a specialist in tropical diseases.

CHAGAS' DISEASE (AMERICAN TRYPANOSOMIASIS)

Mostly a risk to trekkers or campers, or if you sleep in huts or shacks.

In theory, you can catch this relative of African sleeping sickness through most of the Americas, from the northern USA to southern Argentina. However, thanks to campaigns to control the bugs that spread it, it's a significant problem only in certain areas (see below). Even there, you need to be travelling in rough country and/or sleeping in huts or poorly built houses – *and* unlucky – to be at much risk. You can also catch it from contaminated food or poorly cooked small game such as opossums, and from unscreened blood transfusions, but this is hardly a wide-scale problem among travellers. However, an estimated 16–18 million local people in Latin America have it.

What it is Like sleeping sickness, Chagas' disease is caused by a single-celled parasite, a trypanosome called *Trypanosoma cruzi*. It's spread by the rather unpleasant habits of a type of assassin bug known as a kissing bug or cone-nosed bug (and locally by such names as *vinchuca, chipo, pito, chinchorro* or *chirimacha* in Spanish-speaking countries, or *barbeiro* in Brazil). They're pretty big insects – up to 45mm (1¾in) long, but usually less – with a pointed head. They may drop on you at night from a thatched roof or crawl from cracks in the walls, or fly to you in forests.

They bite (often painlessly, and often near the lips – hence their name) to suck blood, and at the same time defecate; it's the (liquid) faeces getting into the bite or your mouth or eyes – not the actual bite – that infects you. However revolting this sounds, it isn't a very efficient method of infection; experts say the odds are 1000 to 1 in your favour even if you are bitten.

Where you can get it The risk of Chagas' disease is significant only in rural areas from southern Mexico to Colombia and Venezuela, then south down the Andes through Peru and into Bolivia and Paraguay; also in eastern Brazil. There's a lower level of risk in central Mexico, northern Chile, and from the southern half of Brazil to central Argentina.

How you can avoid it There's no vaccine or preventive drug. The direct risk is nil in tourist-class hotels, but if you sleep in rough accommodation...

→ Use an insecticide spray, if available, on cracks and crevices. Use an insect-repellent such as DEET on all exposed skin. Sleep under an insecticide-impregnated bed net (*see p.77*). A hammock is safer than sleeping on the floor.

→ If you get bitten and/or notice brown spots of insect faeces, wash them off thoroughly (away from your mouth, eyes or broken skin) using alcohol if possible, otherwise lots of soapy water.

Whatever your accommodation, avoid possibly contaminated cold food and drink, and unscreened blood transfusions.

What it does to you Many infected people have no initial symptoms, but in some cases there's swelling around one eye, or swollen lymph nodes ('glands'), with or without fever. After that, you may feel fine for as long as 10 or 20 years before the more serious effects of Chagas' disease crop up:–

→ Most often heart problems (enlargement; irregular rhythm; heart failure).
→ In some cases enlargement of the oesophagus (gullet) or intestine, causing constipation or difficulty in swallowing.

Many infected people develop no symptoms at all – ever.

How it's treated If you have any reason to suspect a Chagas' infection (or, if you're being ultra-cautious, if you've had to have a blood transfusion in Latin America and want reassurance), consult a tropical disease specialist. Blood tests are needed to check for the parasites, and prolonged drug treatment (often for up to two months) if you are infected. The drugs used may have side-effects such as itching or peeling of the skin, or may make you feel generally unwell, but they're effective in the earlier stages of the disease and for children.

Unfortunately, there's not a lot that can be done specifically for an adult who has been infected for many years, other than treat or relieve the long-term effects themselves.

YELLOW FEVER

One of the big killers, but easily preventable with a safe vaccine.

If fact, a yellow fever vaccination is the only jab widely demanded by international regulations if you're going anywhere where it could occur. That means most of tropical America and Africa. It used to be a huge health threat in these areas, and tracing its mosquito 'vector' – the critter that carries and spreads the yellow fever virus – was a heroic effort by doctors working alongside the engineers who built the Panama Canal.

What it is Since it's carried and transmitted by mosquitoes, the yellow fever virus is known as an 'arbovirus' – an arthropod-borne virus. For more details about mosquitoes, see page 73, but the key facts about those that spread yellow fever are:–

→ In the South American jungle, *Haemogogus* mosquitoes spread yellow fever between monkeys, but among people in cities the vector is an *Aedes* mosquito similar to the one that spreads dengue fever (*see p.125*).

→ In Africa, *Aedes* spreads both jungle and urban yellow fever.

→ These mosquitoes are particularly active in the evening, and breed in the rainy season in standing fresh water – puddles, water lying in old tyres, water jars and tanks open to the air. So that's when the risk is highest.

Where you can get it See the country-specific information on pages 182–273 for the current risk and vaccination requirements, but yellow fever exists, or has existed in the relatively recent past:–

In Africa Everywhere south of a line from Senegal to northern Ethiopia (including the southern parts of Mali, Niger, Chad and Sudan) as far south as Angola and parts of Zambia (but excluding Malawi, Zimbabwe, Mozambique and Madagascar).

In the Americas From Panama south to southern Brazil, including the parts of Colombia, Ecuador, Peru and Bolivia east of the Andes; also in parts of Trinidad and Tobago.

Note: It's advisable to get a yellow fever vaccination (and a certificate) if you're travelling to or through anywhere listed as a yellow fever area, whether or not it has an outbreak at present, to avoid delays (and maybe compulsory vaccination) at borders of those or other countries.

Note that the need for vaccination may have nothing to do with there being a current yellow fever outbreak in a country; if the right species of mosquitoes live there, plus monkeys or apes that can carry the disease, then just one infected traveller could result in yellow fever getting established.

How you can avoid it In theory, you could try to avoid getting bitten or reckon that the risk is lower in town, but it's not worth *any* risk: **Get a yellow fever jab** unless you're in the small group specifically advised against:–

→ Children under 9 months old.

→ People *seriously* allergic to eggs. (If you can eat eggs, you should be OK.)

→ Pregnant women – who are advised by some doctors not to travel to yellow fever areas until after the baby is born. (If you're pregnant and have to travel to a high-risk area, the advice is to get vaccinated anyway – the risk of the vaccination is regarded as less than that of the disease.)

→ People with a weak immune system due to HIV, cancer treatment, corticosteroid drugs or certain other drug treatments – consult your doctor.

Vaccination involves a single jab, which gives immunity for ten years, starting ten days after it's given. Only approved doctors or clinics are allowed to give it and issue (or officially stamp) the certificate that you've had the jab, so check in advance with your doctor or travel clinic. If you belong in the group advised against it, make sure you get an official waiver or doctor's letter, stamped by the health department or authorised vaccination centre – and preferably also by the relevant consulates – before departure.

What it does to you If you've taken my advice, you shouldn't need to know this, but yellow fever causes a sudden high fever – 40°C (104°F) or more – headache, muscular and back pain, stomach pain and nausea, and vomiting. In more serious cases, there's liver damage causing jaundice (with yellowing of the whites of the eyes that gives the disease its name), gastrointestinal bleeding (resulting in black vomit and stools), maybe bleeding from the eyes, nose, anus and bladder, and kidney failure. It's a thoroughly unpleasant disease that kills about one in five sufferers – as it did one of the doctors who discovered how it was spread by deliberately allowing himself to be bitten.

How it's treated There's no specific treatment other than general hospital care in the hope of relieving the symptoms and tiding the patient over. Remember, there are a lot of other fevers in the areas where yellow fever occurs, so it's vital to have blood tests to make sure exactly what is the cause: **Never delay seeking medical advice.**

DENGUE FEVER

Like a very nasty bout of flu, and it can sometimes be fatal.

It's very rarely that serious among travellers; sadly, it's mostly children and some adults in countries where dengue occurs all the time who get the deadly form, called dengue haemorrhagic fever, or DHF (*see p. 127*).

Dengue is spread by mosquitoes and it's getting to be almost as common as flu through almost all the tropics and subtropics, and especially in towns and cities. A lot of travellers' favourite destinations have it, particularly in south and south-east Asia, the Pacific, parts of Africa, Central and South America and the Caribbean. An example: an epidemic in Rio de Janeiro during the summer of 2001-02 struck more than 300 000 people, and killed 50. The WHO – the UN health agency – reckons that, worldwide, there are 50 to 100 million cases of dengue every year, and calls it 'the most serious mosquito-borne disease affecting humans'. You can avoid it if you're careful, but you can't get vaccinated against it.

What it is Dengue – pronounced *den-gy*, with a hard G – is a virus disease. It's transmitted by mosquito bites, like malaria and yellow fever. You can read more about mosquitoes on page 73, but the key facts about the ones that can give you dengue are:–

→ They're called *Aedes*. They live mostly in urban areas and love to feed on people. They bite in the daytime, especially in early mornings and late afternoons.

→ They breed in fresh standing water – rainwater puddles, water lying in old tyres, water jars and tanks open to the air, and so on. So dengue is commonest during rainy seasons.

In fact, there are four different strains of dengue virus. If you catch dengue, it'll give you immunity to that particular strain, so you probably won't get it again – but you can still catch any of the other three.

Where you can get it In a phrase, most tropical and subtropical regions below about 1200m (4000ft); *Aedes* mosquitoes don't like heights. It's more common in cities – especially in crowded slums – than in country areas. Look up the country-specific information on pages 182–273, but to summarise:–

In Africa Most of Africa south of of the Sahara is dengue country, except for the parts of South Africa west of the Drakensberg. There have been epidemics in many areas, from Senegal and Gambia to Eritrea and Egypt, and from Angola to Lesotho and Mozambique – and most places in between.

In the Americas Mexico south through all of Central America to Ecuador, Colombia, Venezuela and Guyana; eastern Brazil (including Recife, Salvador, Rio and São Paulo); parts of Bolivia and Paraguay; much of the Caribbean. There have been a few cases along the US Gulf coast and in Florida; *Aedes* live there, so an epidemic could just be waiting to happen.

In the Asia-Pacific region More or less everywhere from Pakistan and India east and south to Malaysia, Indonesia and the Philippines; Thailand, Cambodia, Vietnam, Laos and southern China; New Guinea, many islands of the south-western Pacific, and Hawaii; northern Queensland in Australia.

How you can avoid it Scientists have been working on vaccines for years, but nothing is yet available. So it comes down to avoiding mosquito bites – particularly in early morning and late afternoon, but at other times of day too if it's shady or overcast. For fuller advice, see page 75, but...

→ Wear baggy clothes done up at the neck, ankles and wrists.
→ Use DEET on exposed parts.
→ Spray rooms with insecticide.
→ Make sure there's a mosquito-proof screen on doors and windows.
→ Use a mosquito net.
→ Do your bit to stop *Aedes* breeding by not leaving out containers where rainwater can collect.

In many dengue areas you should take similar precautions against malaria, but there are lots of malaria-free places where you can catch dengue.

What it does to you The symptoms begin five to eight days after you are bitten. The first symptoms are:–

→ A sudden high fever – 40°C (104°F) or more.
→ A really bad headache. Pain behind the eyes (especially if you press or move them from side to side).
→ Pain in your back, joints and muscles – hence the old nickname 'breakbone fever'.
→ Perhaps also nausea, vomiting and/or a rash almost anywhere.
→ You basically feel terrible – and I'm speaking from experience of a dose of dengue I caught once in the Caribbean.

Often, the symptoms wain after a few days, you feel a lot better, and you think, 'Aha, I'm well again' – then it all comes back for another few days. If you get intense itching on your hands and feet, that's usually a sign that you're over the worst. But the bad news is that you probably won't feel 100 per cent for two or three weeks after all the major symptoms have gone.

Note: Early symptoms of DHF are the same as for 'simple' dengue. **Look out for signs of haemorrhaging or shock** (*see pp.127 & 175*); **prompt medical attention could save your or a companion's life.**

How it's treated Get medical help whether you are in the middle of your trip or have just returned home, as dengue can be confused with malaria or other more serious conditions, but rest as much as possible (in a dimly lit room – the light will probably hurt your eyes). If necessary, a blood test will show whether or not you do actually have dengue. If you do, there's in fact no specific treatment. But do...

→Take plenty of fluids (in a safe form, with rehydration salts if you've really sweated a lot; *see pp.40–41*). Take paracetamol (acetaminophen; eg, 'Tylenol') to relieve the aches and pains.

→ **Don't take any painkillers containing aspirin or ibuprofen** – these can thin the blood, encouraging internal bleeding and increasing the risk of DHF, or cause other complications.

DENGUE HAEMORRHAGIC FEVER (DHF)

Although DHF is rare, it's quite often fatal if it's not treated. However, with prompt and proper treatment the death rate is less than 1 per cent. So be aware of the symptoms. DHF mostly affects people – particularly children under 15 – who live permanently in places where dengue is endemic (ie, always around, causing epidemics).

What it is A complication of dengue fever (*see p.125*) that causes haemorrhaging (internal and external bleeding). The result is what doctors call circulatory failure and shock – hence an alternative name for the severest form, dengue shock syndrome, or DSS. The bottom line is death in about 1 in 20 cases (5 per cent) on average, but a much lower death rate with proper rehydration therapy (*see below*). The experts think that DHF is more likely if one dengue infection is followed by a second *caused by a different strain of dengue virus* (there are four types), usually in a subsequent year.

Where you can get it In theory, anywhere that has 'simple' dengue fever, but it's most common where two or more of the four dengue virus strains both occur. It's endemic in Brazil, Venezuela, parts of the Caribbean, the Indian subcontinent, south-east Asia, southern China and the western Pacific.

How you can avoid it Take the same precautions as for dengue fever.

What it does to you Initial symptoms are the same as for dengue fever (although sometimes without the muscular pain), but watch for:–

→ Petechiae – lots of tiny blood spots (like a rash) under the skin; they sometimes merge into a larger red patch. If you press on the rash with a glass (so you can still see it), the spots *don't* disappear.
→ Easy bruising.
→ Bleeding from gums, nose or internally (causing black vomit and/or stools).
→ Discomfort or tenderness of the abdomen.
→ Shock – weak pulse; weakness or fainting; often with cold, clammy skin.

How it's treated Uncontrolled shock kills, so **it's absolutely vital to get prompt medical help.** Proper rehydration therapy – which means a drip or transfusion to replace lost blood and body fluids, not simply drinking water with rehydration salts – has to be given in a hospital or clinic, possibly with oxygen. In a mild case the doctor may decide that drink is enough – but even then close monitoring is needed. Raise the alarm immediately if you're with a patient who seems to be deteriorating.

RIFT VALLEY AND OTHER FEVERS

Rift Valley fever

Another virus disease that is spread mostly by mosquito bites, this was – as the name suggests – originally found in Great Rift Valley in Kenya, in 1930. But it's now known to occur in many parts of Africa and recently in the Arabian peninsula. It mainly infects cattle, sheep and other domesticated animals, but often spreads to humans when swarms of mosquitoes follow heavy rains. There have been big outbreaks recently in Egypt, Mauritania, Saudi Arabia and Yemen, and parts of southern Africa also have it.

The usual symptoms are a fever, and aches and pains rather like those of dengue fever (*see p. 125*). Most people recover within a week with bed-rest and painkillers (but **not aspirin**). In up to one in ten cases, however, there are serious complications – haemorrhaging, a brain infection, or impaired vision. An antiviral drug called ribavirin is a promising treatment for such serious cases, but it's unlikely to be available locally.

Ross River fever

Also a virus disease and also spread by mosquitoes, this occurs mainly in Australia, where there are around 5000 cases a year. (Kangaroos are among the carriers.) But there was a much bigger epidemic in some of the Pacific islands when it spread there at the end of the 1970s. Again, it's seasonal in some areas, coinciding with the 'wet', but elsewhere can strike all year round.

Like flu, it's 'self-limiting' – in other words, it burns itself out without specific treatment – but it can be pretty unpleasant while it lasts. There's not by any means always a fever. A lot of people don't get any symptoms at all; only the antibodies in their blood prove that they've had it. But the main symptoms are painful muscles and joints – wrists, fingers, knees, ankles and toes. The pain may last up to six weeks, but usually less. Recovery can be quite slow in some people, and it may leave you with arthritis for nine months or more.

As with similar fevers, the best cure for Ross River and Rift Valley fevers is prevention, using mosquito nets and insect-repellents to avoid getting bitten by infected mosquitoes. (This is particularly important in the case of Rift Valley fever, as there's malaria in most of the areas where it you can get it.)

JAPANESE ENCEPHALITIS

Not just in Japan, it's an increasingly serious virus disease.

The symptoms can range from nothing or a flu-like fever to convulsions, unconsciousness, paralysis and even death, so it's not something to take lightly. There are an estimated 50 000 cases a year – perhaps many more – and at least 15 000 deaths. Almost all adults living in the affected areas are reckoned to have caught it at some time, because they have the antibodies in their blood. There's an effective vaccine with few side-effects

What it is Japanese encephalitis (sometimes called Japanese 'B' encephalitis) is a virus disease that's spread by mosquitoes. You can read more about mosquitoes on page 73, but the key facts in this case are:–

➔ Japanese encephalitis is carried by chickens, pigs, wild birds and other animals. It mostly occurs in rural areas.

➔ Its most important vector (transmitter) is a *Culex* mosquito that breeds in rice paddies.

Where you can get it Look up the country-specific information on pages 182–273, but you can catch Japanese encephalitis everywhere from eastern and southern India and Sri Lanka through Bangladesh to much of China, all of Korea and Japan, and throughout south-east Asia (mainland and islands, to Papua New Guinea). It has also cropped up in the Kathmandu Valley and in far northern Australia. In the more temperate areas, it occurs mainly in summertime epidemics, but in the tropics it's a year-round problem.

How you can avoid it The current vaccine is highly effective, and has far fewer side-effects than the one used in the 1970s; only about 1 in 40 000 people get a serious reaction, although more may have itching or swelling at the site of the jab. You need two injections a week apart, and another a month later (without which protection is incomplete and lasts only about a month). You may need a booster a year later, then every three years for long-term protection. A promising and cheaper new vaccine is being developed in Asia.

The official advice is to get Japanese encephalitis jabs only if you expect to...

➔ Spend at least three months in an affected area;
➔ Go for a shorter trip during an epidemic; or
➔ Do a lot of outdoor activities (eg, trekking, cycling or camping).

However, a few experts suggest that all visitors to rural parts of affected areas should be vaccinated, because the illness can be so serious and the serious side-effects of vaccination are rare. I'd advise you to talk it over with your doctor or travel clinic. Otherwise, the key is to avoid mosquito bites (*see p. 75*) – a wise precaution anyway, given the prevalence of malaria, dengue fever and other nasties in many of the same areas.

What it does to you A mild infection – by far the most common – may go unnoticed or be no worse than flu, with a headache, fever, nausea and vomiting. But in more serious cases there may be, after a few days:–

➔ Tremors; convulsions (especially in children); semi-consciousness; disorientation.
➔ Coma; sometimes paralysis.

The death rate can be 30 per cent or more in such serious cases.

How it's treated There's no specific treatment, but with such a potentially serious disease **it's vital to seek immediate medical attention if you develop serious symptoms.** You'll need intensive care in a hospital or clinic.

PLAGUE

Black Death still exists – but isn't so dangerous thanks to antibiotics.

Plague hasn't changed its habits – it's still spread from rats and other rodents to people by flea-bites, just as it was in the Middle Ages – and it's still endemic in wild animals over wide areas of the world. But it's very unlikely to infect travellers unless they visit an area where there's an epidemic. What's more, provided it's caught early and treated, it can be cured – unlike in the Middle Ages. Epidemics still occur – there was one in Vietnam in the 1960s and early 70s, largely as a result of the war, and in parts of Africa in the late 1990s. However, they are on nothing like the scale of the great pandemics of the past, with a few thousand cases rather than the millions who died in the 6th and 14th centuries or in the last pandemic a century ago.

What it is Plague is a bacterial infection (the bug's called *Yersinia pestis*). The main way you can catch it is by being bitten by an infected rat flea. These prefer rat blood to yours – there's no accounting for taste – but if/when the rat dies of plague they'll jump for any source of blood they can find, and if there are no more rats around, they may turn to you. That's why dead rats – particularly in large numbers – have been seen for centuries as an omen of the plague. Pneumonic plague (*see below*) can be caught directly by breathing in infected droplets or by contact with an infected person's clothes, bedding or other belongings.

Where you can get it In the past, infected domestic and ship-borne rats brought plague to cities, but today it's usually caught in rural areas from wild-animal fleas. There are natural 'reservoirs' of the disease in most continents except Australia and Europe. See the country-specific information on pages 182–273, but in recent years most cases have been in rural parts of Africa, especially in Madagascar, Tanzania and Malawi. A few cases occur each year in the western USA.

How you can avoid it Plague vaccine is available only for laboratory and other workers at high risk. If you travel in areas where plague exists, it makes sense to avoid contact with rats (dead or alive) or their fleas. (Insect-repellents such as DEET on the skin are not very effective, but soaking your clothes in an insecticide such as permethrin is.) If, however, you have to travel to a place with a current or recent plage epidemic – and you'd be pretty daft not to avoid it if you can – consult your doctor or travel clinic about taking a supply of protective or emergency antibiotics, especially if you will be a long way from expert medical care.

What it does to you If you do get infected, and are not treated, the disease may develop through three stages:–

→ *Bubonic plague* After an incubation period of two to seven days, you get a high fever with rigors (shivering), headache and painfully swollen lymph nodes ('buboes') in the groin, or sometimes the neck or armpits. This stage is treatable.

→ **Septicaemic plague** If the infection gets into the bloodstream, causing septicaemia (blood poisoning) – with severe fever, malaise, and a drop in blood pressure leading to shock – death is almost inevitable.

→ **Pneumonic plague** The infection reaches the lungs, adding pneumonia to the other effects and causing coughing that spreads plague germs through the air. That's why this form is directly catching, without needing fleas to carry it, so anyone with pneumonic plague needs to be isolated. It can be treated in the early stages.

How it's treated Plague is quite easily treated with strong antibiotics such as tetracycline, streptomycin or chloramphenicol, but treatment needs to start as soon as possible. So get medical help urgently if you develop a fever – especially if there are painful swellings in the groin or elsewhere – when travelling in a plague area. In some cases, antibiotics or other antibacterial drugs may need to be given by intravenous drip.

LYMPHATIC FILARIASIS

A low risk, but it's widespread and can cause grotesque deformities.

The extreme version of this disease can lead to the gross swelling of the legs known as elephantiasis, or in men a similar gross swelling of the scrotum. Even in areas with poor medical facilities, permanent symptoms like that are rare, but it's reckoned that more than 125 million people worldwide have lymphatic filariasis, and it's a leading cause of long-term disability.

It mainly affects permanent or long-stay residents, but visitors can catch it, too – though that's highly unlikely without being in an infested area for several months. It's caused by thread-like worms up to 10cm (4in) long that live in (and are liable to obstruct) the vessels that carry watery lymph (which is like blood plasma – blood without the red blood cells) in the sufferer's body. Not a nice thought.

What it is The microcopic larvae of two filarial worm species – *Wuchereria* and *Brugia* – are carried by mosquitoes, and infect a person when s/he is bitten. However, it usually takes many bites over a prolonged period for the disease to get established.

Where you can get it Several different species of mosquitoes spread lymphatic filariasis throughout most of the tropics, but more than 40 per cent of all cases are in India and almost as many in Africa. The rest are mainly in south-east Asia, the western Pacific and South America.

How you can avoid it There's no vaccine and no proven preventive drugs (unlike for the related loiasis; *see p.132*). So the motto, as ever, is to avoid mosquito bites – with bed nets, cover-up clothing and an insect-repellent such as DEET applied to all exposed skin. Note that one of the mosquitoes that transmit lymphatic filariasis in Africa also carries malaria, so it's doubly important to protect yourself.

What it does to you If lympatic filiariasis becomes established, the worms develop into adults, grow and eventually (sometimes after a few months, sometimes longer) block the lymph vessels. The result: painful swelling of the lymph nodes ('glands'), especially in the groin and scrotum, or in the armpits or breasts, together with a fever and general illness. After years of such attacks, permanent elephantiasis (with thickening and hardening of the skin) may develop.

However, some people with lymphatic filariasis have little or no lymph node swelling, but instead develop a cough, wheezing and breathlessness.

How it's treated You'll need specialist blood tests to confirm a filarial worm infection, and the devastating long-term effects mean that this should be done as soon as possible. If it's confirmed, it can be treated with drugs.

OTHER FILARIAL INFECTIONS

Similar worms – some of them even longer than those that cause lymphatic filiariasis – can cause other tropical diseases. They're generally spread in a similar way by fly or midge bites. Although one type can cause blindness, skin problems are more common.

River blindness (onchocerciasis)

This is caused by a worm called *Onchocera* that's spread by small blackflies, mainly in tropical Africa but also in Yemen and Central and South America. It affects nearly 20 million people altogether, and can cause blindness if the microscopic young worms – called microfilariae – get into the eyes. But more often it infects the skin, causing extreme itching, lumps (when they've grown into adults) and loss of skin pigment.

If confirmed by a skin test, onchocerciasis can be treated with an effective drug – but treatment must be repeated every six months to entirely get rid of it, and sometimes surgery is needed to remove skin nodules (lumps) containing the worms. Widepread spraying has managed to wipe out the disease (by killing the blackflies) in some areas, including most of Kenya.

Loiasis

Also called loa loa or African eyeworm, this also mostly infects the skin, causing painful, itchy lumps called Calabar swellings, after a town in Nigeria. (The disease mainly crops up in the west and central African forests.) Sometimes a worm reaches the eye, and can even be seen crawling across it; it causes itching but does no permanent harm.

Loiasis is spread by the bite of large horseflies. It can be treated with a drug called diethylcarbamazine, possibly with minor surgery. If you're visiting a high-risk area for loiasis, a 300mg dose of the same drug, taken once a week, can protect you from the disease; it's the only form of filariasis that can be prevented in this way.

TICK-BORNE ENCEPHALITIS

Danger from tick bites in the forests of central and eastern Europe.

In Russia, it's sometimes called 'spring–summer encephalitis', as that's when it's most common. In fact, there are two closely related types of virus found in Europe and Asia – the Eastern and Western forms – with an overlap in central and eastern Europe (*see below*). Both affect your body generally, like flu, but they can cause inflammation of the brain (which is what encephalitis means) – in which case it's pretty serious, with an estimated 10 per cent risk of death or disability. It's mostly a danger to hikers and campers in woodland. A vaccine is available.

What it is A virus disease that's carried mainly by small animals such as rodents, but also infects goats, sheep or other domestic animals – and people. It's transmittted by the bite of a tick called *Ixodes*, and sometimes in unpasteurised milk (especially goat's milk).

Where you can get it The two forms of tick-borne encephalitis occur mostly in forests and farmland across a wide band from the North Sea and Baltic to the Pacific. In Europe, it's endemic from Germany and the Baltic states through Austria, Switzerland, the Czech Republic, Slovakia and the northern Balkans, eastwards to most of the former Soviet Union up to the Urals. There are sporadic infections in a wider area, including southern Scandinavia (Norway, Sweden, Denmark and Finland) and France. The eastern form occurs in much of Russia and in northern China, Korea and Japan.

How you can avoid it For advice on avoiding tick bites and removing ticks from your skin, see page 86. However, lots of people who get the disease can't recall being bitten, so it's wise for anyone going on a spring or summer camping, hiking or cycling trip in the high-risk areas to get vaccinated. You'll need two jabs, four to six weeks apart. Avoid unpasteurised goat's milk.

What it does to you There's an incubation period of up to two weeks after infection, so you could be back home before symptoms develop – in which case tell your doctor where you've been. Then you get a sudden fever, headache and nausea, and bright light hurts your eyes. If you're lucky, you'll feel better after about a week, but in some cases there's a second, much more serious phase: paralysis of the shoulders and arms, and sometimes difficulty in breathing and even death.

How it's treated There's no specific treatment, but the serious possible complications mean *it's vital to get expert medical help* – and hospitalisation if necessary, where a ventilator can be used to aid breathing.

OTHER TYPES OF ENCEPHALITIS

Apart from Japanese and tick-borne encephalitis (*see p.128 & above*), there are lots of other mosquito- and tick-borne encephatitis viruses lurking in various parts of the world. They usually don't cause anything worse than a bad dose of flu, but if they infect the brain – the meaning of encephalitis – it can be much more serious, needing hospital or clinic care. So, as a general rule, *get expert medical help urgently* if there is any reason to suspect a mosquito- or tick-borne infection, or if there are any of the following symptoms, alone or especially in combination:–

→ A fever of 40°C (104°F) or above.
→ A persistent severe headache.
→ Stiffness in the neck or limbs.
→ Vomiting.
→ Signs of delirium, confusion, convulsions, tremors, drowsiness, partial consciousness or paralysis.

These symptoms can also indicate other serious conditions, so don't delay getting help. There are no vaccines against any of these viruses (though some are being developed), and no specific treatments, so this is another good reason to avoid mosquito and tick bites (*see pp. 75–78 & 86–87*).

These are some of the most important types:–

Colorado tick fever

A virus disease carried by chipmunks, ground squirrels and other small animals in the US Rocky Mountain states. Humans are infected by tick bites, and usually have a mild illness, but it's more serious in about one in ten cases, mainly in children.

Equine encephalitis

Every few years in Venezuela and neighbouring parts of South and Central America there's an outbreak of encephalitis in horses and people caused by mosquito-borne viruses. The 1995 epidemic affected 100 000 people – most only mildly, but 300 died. *Check before you go*, especially to rural areas.

Murray Valley encephalitis

One of several mosquito-borne virus diseases found in Australia – mainly in the Outback, but increasingly near towns. It also occurs in New Guinea. The main carriers are water birds, and outbreaks tend to occur in late summer. They don't generally affect many people.

St Louis encephalitis

Another mosquito-borne virus disease carried by birds. Outbreaks occur from time to time in the USA – mostly in the Midwest, the South and California, but there has been at least one case in every state except Alaska since 1964. It also crops up in south-eastern Canada and in most of South America. It's another usually mild illness, but is sometimes serious.

West Nile fever

This first caused a stir in the USA in 1999, when there was an outbreak in New York City. Sporadic cases cropped up in many other parts of the States after that (including some possibly spread by blood transfusions). The number of confirmed cases increased rapidly during 2002, until by the end of January 2003 there had been more than 4000 human cases in 40 states. (Apart from one case in California, none of these were west of the Rockies.) Before that, West Nile fever had been confined to the southern half of Europe, much of Africa, the Middle East, and Asia as far west as India.

Another worry is that the West Nile virus is tending to cause more cases of serious encephalitis, whereas it originally almost always simply caused a flu-like fever. As of the end of January 2003, more than 260 people had died in the American outbreak. Again mosquitoes are the cuprits, spreading the disease between birds (such as crows, jays and pigeons) and people. Authorities warned people to avoid mosquito bites (see p.75) and report unusual numbers of dead birds.

LYME DISEASE

An infection spread by ticks, sometimes with serious complications.

People (especially Americans!) tend to think of the USA – the East Coast in particular – as the home of Lyme disease, but in fact it's found all around the Northern Hemisphere outside the tropics, and perhaps also in south-eastern Australia. Over the last 20 years there have been at least 150 000 confirmed cases in the USA, and some estimates put the true figure at two million or more. If the the figures are so uncertain it's clear that in most cases the symptoms are non-existent or very mild. Yet Lyme disease affects some people quite seriously, causing nerve damage, arthritis or heart problems. Fortunately it can be treated and usually prevented.

What it is Lyme disease is a bacterial infection caused by various related bacteria called *Borrelia*. These are carried by wild animals including rodents, badgers, deer and birds, and are transferred to people (and their pets) by *Ixodes* and other kinds of ticks (including hedgehog, sheep and deer ticks). The bacteria live in the ticks' salivary glands, and are injected when the ticks attach themselves to the skin to suck blood.

Where you can get it Lyme disease exists in all the temperate zones of the Northern Hemisphere (North America, Europe and Asia); experts are still arguing over whether it exists in Australia. In the USA in 1999, over 90 per cent of the 16 300 cases were in nine states: on the East Coast in Massachusetts, Rhode Island, Connecticut, New York, New Jersey, Pennsylvania, Delaware and Maryland, and in the northern Midwest in Wisconsin. There's a lower level of risk in other parts of the East Coast, some other parts of the Midwest and a small bit of northern California, but elsewhere the risk is very low or nil.

You can catch Lyme disease wherever its natural hosts and vectors (ie, the animals that carry it and the ticks that spread it) live – that is, mostly in scrubland, woods, forests (especially glades, paths and clearings) and similar country (including gardens with bushes and other undergrowth in high-risk areas). The prime Lyme disease seasons are late spring and summer, when the ticks are biting. The good news is that a tick needs to hang on to you for at least 24 hours to infect you.

How you can avoid it A vaccine against Lyme disease used to be available in the USA but was withdrawn in 2002 following claims of serious side-effects. Experts doubted how useful it would be in Europe and elsewhere, since the Lyme disease bacteria there are slightly different, and in any case was reckoned to be only about 75 per cent effective. It was recommended only for people at high risk, meaning:–

→ Those working in forestry, landscaping or other outdoor activities in high-risk areas (which could include work at some summer camps); or
→ Those hiking, camping, fishing and so on in high-risk areas.

At the time of writing, there's no telling if or when it (or another Lyme disease vaccine) will become available again. Meanwhile, whether vaccinated or not, you should take sensible precautions to prevent tick bites. See the detailed recommendations on page 87, but...

→ Wear long-sleeved, long-legged, light-coloured clothing done up at the wrists and tucked into your socks.

→ Apply DEET insect-repellent to exposed skin and clothing (and/or permethrin to clothing only).

Also, inspect yourself carefully every day, carefully removing any ticks with tweezers (*see p.87*).

What it does to you The first sign of Lyme disease comes anything from three days to a month (but usually about two weeks) after being bitten – and since the ticks are pretty small until they start feeding on your blood, and they don't cause any itching, this may be the first you know about it. Your skin turns red around the bite, but there's usually no pain or itching. Over the following days and weeks, the red area expands while the skin in the middle returns to its normal colour – making a characteristic ring-shaped or 'bull's-eye' pattern. If you're bitten more than once, you can get several bull's-eyes. After a few weeks the ring may disappear, or it might go on expanding for months until it's several feet across.

In less than one in five cases there are one or more more serious symptoms, such as:–

→ A mild flu-like fever.
→ Partial paralysis, often on just one side of the face – known as Bell's palsy.
→ Nerve pain (neuralgia) in certain parts of the body.
→ Muscular and joint pain (sometimes with swelling in a major joint such as the knee) – in a few cases developing into long-term arthritis.
→ Rarely, a stiff neck (a sign of meningitis), and sometimes unsteadiness.
→ In up to 1 in 30 people, an irregular heartbeat.

These last two are particularly serious, but don't be too alarmed – prompt treatment can usually prevent these and other complications.

How it's treated If you get a rash like that described above after being in a tick-infested area, be sure to get medical attention, as prompt treatment can virtually eliminate the risk of long-term complications. The usual treatment is a course of antibiotics, usually for 10 to 14 days, although some doctors recommend a longer, three-week course.

EPIDEMIC TYPHUS

There are various types of typhus, all caused by rickettsias – small bacteria with some of the characteristrics of viruses. They vary in severity, the most serious being epidemic or louse typhus, which is spread by the faeces of body lice (*see p.81*). People are infected when these are inhaled or rubbed into the broken skin caused by the louse bites. It was a scourge mainly associated with wars and social upheaval during the 20th century, and in recent years has been a problem in the refugee camps, prisons and shantytowns of Africa (especially at relatively high altitudes in the tropics – notably in Burundi, Ethiopia and Nigeria).

Volunteer workers in such environments are the only travellers from the developed world who are likely to be at risk from it. The main symptoms are a high fever, severe headache and muscular pains, and a body rash. Fortunately, rickettsias can usually be countered with doxycycline or other tetracycline antibiotics, and protective doses of doxycycline (also a malaria preventive; *see p.115*) can be taken by people at risk. Travellers are more likely to encounter tick typhus (*see below*) or scrub typhus (*see p.138*).

TICK TYPHUS

Ticks don't spread quite as many nasty diseases as mosquitoes, but tick typhus needs to be taken seriously in some areas. Unlike viruses, they usually respond to antibiotic treatment, so most forms of the disease (including those caught from wild game ticks in African game parks) are relatively mild if treated promptly. The main symptoms are usually a rash, fever, and often a headache and vomiting.

Rocky Mountain spotted fever

This is one of the most dangerous forms of tick typhus, with a few deaths in spite of antibiotic treatment. It's completely misnamed, as it's quite rare in the Rockies and more than half of all cases in the USA are in the south-east, from Delaware to Florida. But in fact you can catch it in tick-infested parts of almost all of North America, and through Central and South America too.

As with other tick-borne diseases, prevention is the best cure, so follow the advice on personal protection and tick-removal on page 87. If you do develop symptoms, get prompt medical help.

SCRUB TYPHUS

It's less dangerous than tick typhus, but you still need to beware of this disease in the area where it occurs – southern and south-east Asia, the islands of the Indian Ocean, Japan, and through the south-western Pacific (especially New Guinea) to north-eastern Australia. (In some parts of Asia it's called tsutsugamushi disease.)

Like other types of typhus, it's caused by small, virus-like bacteria called rickettsias, whose main hosts are rats and mice. The bugs are transferred to people by tiny mites (see p.87), known in Australia as chiggers; you're most likely to encounter these in tall grass – either in open country or in jungle clearings. They're so small that you may well have had them clinging to your skin, biting and infecting you (and falling off again after a few hours), without even knowing it.

After an incubation period of a week to ten days, sores with black scabs appear where you were bitten, followed by a severe headache and a few days later by a fever and a more general rash. Without treatment, you're likely be be knocked out for two or three weeks, but prompt treatment with tetracycline antibiotics can reduce this significantly. (Rickettsias, unlike viruses, respond to these drugs.) So it pays to get medical attention as soon as you notice the symptoms.

OTHER TICK-BORNE DISEASES

Tick paralysis

This is a fairly rare condition, but it occurs on virtually all continents and sometimes causes the death of young children – who are those mostly affected. You need to be aware of it if you take a toddler travelling, particularly to north-western North America or to bushland areas of eastern Australia, where most of the serious cases have been recorded.

A few days after being bitten by a tick, the victim's hands and feet start to become paralysed. Then coordination begins to be lost, speech slurred and eye movements uncontrolled. There's general weakness and a loss of appetite, and unless action is taken breathing starts to be affected about a week after the bite; it may stop entirely.

Before the condition was properly understood, the death of most young victims was put down to 'infantile paralysis'. It's now known that recovery usually begins almost immediately the tick is removed (see p.87), cutting off the secretion of toxins into the victim's body. However, the Australian form of the disease tends to be longer-lasting, and intensive care and an injection of antitoxin – available at major hospitals in the affected area – may be needed.

Prevention is of course much better; parents should check their offspring frequently for ticks clinging to the skin and for unexplained lumps (including in skin folds and under the hair).

Crimean–Congo haemorrhagic fever (CCHF)

In spite of its name, this is a widespread (but uncommon) virus disease. It causes a sudden severe headache, fever and pains, and then in some cases internal haemorrhaging. The virus is carried by herd animals, and is generally transferred by a tick bite; the symptoms begin as little as three days after the bite. Unusually for such a disease, it's also transferred directly between people and from infected animals – especially by blood contact. It can be fatal, but is treatable with an expensive antiviral drug called ribaflavin.

It's possible to catch CCHF in wide areas of Africa, parts of southern and eastern Europe, the Middle East and Asia. Avoid tick bites in such areas (*see p.87*) and don't sleep on the ground in grazing country.

RABIES

Deadly danger from the bite of a wild or domestic animal.

It nowhere near approaches the seriousness of, say, malaria on a global scale, but rabies is undoubtedly a serious, and potentially fatal, health risk to travellers in certain parts of the world. And it's possible to catch it through simple carelessness. That's why this article is so long – stick with it and you might save your (or your companion's) life.

Consider this stark fact: If you get bitten by a rabid animal, and do nothing about it, you have virtually written your own death warrant. Sorry to be so melodramatic, but at least 35 000 people die every year from rabies – and that's just the official figure. Even the WHO – the UN health authority – says that the true figure could be as much as double that.

And what's the chance of surviving the disease? Virtually nil once symptoms appear. There has been just one proven case in more than 20 years of a person with rabies symptoms surviving, plus a small handful of others who probably had the disease – and they all needed prolonged intensive care. If you need scaring any more, be aware that it is a very unpleasant way to die, by all eyewitness reports and by records made by victims themselves. But let me reassure you that rabies *is* avoidable and preventable – so long as you act sensibly and promptly if you're bitten. The point is that symptoms take some time to develop – and that's the window for action.

What it is Rabies is a virus disease. The viruses are found in the saliva of infected animals (and people, for that matter), and can get into your body if you're bitten – or even if the animal licks broken (eg, scratched) skin. They can also penetrate mucous membranes – such as in your mouth, nose, eyes or lungs – but they can't normally get through healthy, unbroken skin. There have been a few cases of cave-explorers getting rabies by breathing in viruses in dust from infected bats' droppings. Once inside your body, the rabies viruses travel via nerves to the central nervous system (spinal cord and brain); it's at that point that the nasty symptoms begin.

Any warm-blooded animal can catch, carry and pass on the rabies virus, but in the developing world, where rabies is commonest, the main culprits are those that are in constant human contact – cats and especially dogs. But wild animal bites can give you rabies too; they're the main source of the few rabies cases that occur in Europe, North America and Australasia. They include especially foxes, wolves and bats (both insect-eating and vampire) in many parts of the world; also skunks and raccoons in North America, and jackals, mongooses and civets in Africa and Asia. Vegetarians (eg, horses, cattle, deer and fruit bats) can get rabies but only rarely pass it on to people.

Where you can (or can't) get it Frankly, it's easier to say where you're *not* likely to get rabies. These are the major countries which, at the time of writing, had been **rabies-free in recent years**:–

In Africa and the western Indian Ocean Libya; Cape Verde; Mauritius, Réunion and Seychelles.

In the Americas Uruguay; Barbados, Jamaica and most of the smaller Caribbean islands (but there is rabies in Cuba, Dominican Republic, Grenada, Haiti, Puerto Rico, and Trinidad and Tobago).

In Asia Bahrain, Kuwait, Qatar and the UAE; Brunei, Sabah, Sarawak and Singapore (but there is rabies in peninsular Malaysia); Hong Kong island (but it does exist in the New Territories); Taiwan; Japan.

In Australasia and the Pacific Papua New Guinea (and also the Indonesian part of New Guinea); New Zealand; most (possibly all) Pacific islands including Hawaii (but no confirmation on some). Australia has had a few cases of bat rabies, but has otherwise been rabies-free.

In Europe Ireland; Iceland, Norway (except Svalbard), Sweden and Finland; Italy and Switzerland; Albania and Greece; Cyprus; Malta; Portugal. Britain and Spain have had a few cases of bat rabies, but have otherwise been rabies-free. It's been pretty rare elsewhere.

Of course, there's no guarantee that rabies won't crop up sometime in any of these countries, despite their usually stringent controls on imported pets. *But everywhere else in the world has had at least some rabies cases in recent years.* By far the biggest human rabies problem is in India, where 30 000 people are reported to die of it every year. There are no complete figures, but other areas where it's been a significant problem include the rest of the Indian subcontinent, much of south-east Asia, most of Africa, and many parts of Latin America. However, the situation is improving in China, Thailand, Sri Lanka and some parts of Latin America, thanks to the vaccination of dogs and of people who have been bitten, but it still exists in those places.

How you can avoid it The most obvious advice is: **Don't get bitten!** If you're travelling in an area where rabies is common...

→ Avoid contact with wild and domestic animals – keep your distance from wild animals of all sizes, and particularly from dogs, domestic or feral.

→ Treat any abnormal animal behaviour with the greatest suspicion. Forget what you may have heard about 'mad dogs'; a rabid animal *may* act aggressively, rushing around drooling and biting at random, but *it may also seem abnormally tame, or may act perfectly normally.*

→ Beware scratches, sprayed saliva and licks, as well as bites.

Vaccines are available, but it's not as simple as getting a jab and you're safe. **If you are bitten by a possibly rabid animal, you will still need booster vaccinations** (*see below*) **whether or not you have previously had rabies jabs.** But it'll be less urgent and you won't need so many injections. The official advice is to get so-called pre-exposure vaccination before you leave home...

→ If you will inevitably come into contact with animals that could be infected (eg, in agricultural, veterinary or biological work, or by caving or hunting).

→ If you're going to a rabies-endemic area far from reliable medical facilities (eg, travelling through remote villages where there'll inevitably be dogs).

→ If you stay longer than a month in an area where dog rabies is common (on the basis that the longer you stay the more likely you are to be bitten).

However, take into account not only the risk of rabies where you're intending to go but also the standard of health care you can expect. In some places, modern vaccines may be very expensive or unavailable. (Some developing countries still use the old rabies vaccine that entails daily injections into the abdomen over 14 days, plus boosters.) In particular, it may be difficult or impossible to get rabies immunoglobulin ('RIG') – ready-made antibodies that should be given immediately after a suspect bite to give some protection while the vaccine proper swings into action and gets your own defences moving. If you have been vaccinated before you travel, you don't need an RIG injection, only the booster vaccine jabs (*see below*); these aren't so urgent, so you may have time to reach a modern hospital.

The best advice is to talk it over with an experienced travel doctor. (This is particularly true if your immune system is damaged by HIV, cancer or certain drug treatments; vaccination may be ineffective in these cases.)

Bear in mind that modern rabies vaccines are not cheap, but in some parts of the world you can save money by planning well ahead. You need three doses: two a week apart and then a third, three weeks after the second. (Further boosters are given every two years if necessary.) If you have intramuscular injections – ie, deep into a muscle – you need a full 1ml dose of vaccine each time. But with one type (known as human diploid cell vaccine, or HDCV), you can have intradermal injections – into the skin – in which case a 1ml dose can be shared between up to ten people, saving money. (If you're travelling as a group, you can organise a mass jab-in; what fun! Or some travel clinics may be able to arrange shared vaccinations – I don't mean shared needles, of course – between strangers.)

However, there are a couple of snags. Firstly, this type of vaccine isn't available everywhere. (It's not currently licensed for use in Europe, for instance.) Secondly, *intradermal vaccination isn't effective if you're taking chloroquine or mefloquine ('Lariam') against malaria*. You need to start taking these antimalarial drugs two or more weeks before travelling, so make sure you leave plenty of time to fit in all three rabies jabs well before that.

What it does to you Remember that rabies viruses usually get into the skin through a bite or cut, and then make for the nervous system. As a general rule, the closer the bite is to the head or trunk, the faster the symptoms are likely to begin, since the viruses don't have to travel so far to reach the spinal cord and brain. (So, for example, a child bitten on the face is likely to get symptoms within a few days, but in an adult bitten on the foot there could be a delay of weeks, months or even years.)

The early symptoms of true rabies are often vague: a general sense of apprehension, malaise, headache and/or fever, sometimes with diarrhoea and/or difficulty in breathing. There's usually itching, tingling, irritation or pain where the person was bitten.

From that point it usually progresses rapidly:–

→ In so-called 'dumb' rabies, paralysis is the main symptom, with weakness, pain and loss of sensation.

→ In 'furious' rabies – more common than the dumb type – the victim becomes confused, hyperactive and aggressive, with hallucinations.

→ The most infamous symptom is hydrophobia, in which the neck muscles and those involved in swallowing and breathing go into uncontrollable spasm at any attempt to drink. The patient seems to be literally terrified of water.

After this, delirium, convulsions, paralysis and coma lead to death, usually within a few days and usually from respiratory failure.

How it's treated As I've said, once symptoms appear there's nothing that can be done other than prolonged intensive care – and the odds against that being effective are many thousands to one against. So let's move on to...

How to treat a bite by a possibly rabid animal – ie, to prevent symptoms developing in the first place. First of all, don't panic but do act quickly:–

→ Clean the wound as thoroughly as possible with clean soapy water. Rinse it thoroughly with antiseptic solution; povidone-iodine (eg, 'Betadine' or 'Videne') is ideal, or use tincture of iodine. If you have nothing else, use strong alcohol – surgical spirit, or even vodka, gin or whisky.

→ Don't try to stitch up the wound.

→ *If (and only if) it can be done safely*, confine or tie up the suspect animal. If a dog is still healthy after ten days, you can be confident it hasn't got rabies. Meanwhile, however, don't wait before you...

→ **Get expert medical help** – the more modern and Western-orientated the better. **Don't** rely on traditional folk practitioners; a life is at stake, and they don't 'know best how to treat rabies'. If you're near (or within a day or so's journey) of a big-city hospital or university medical department, go there; they are the most likely to have the vaccine needed. Otherwise, seek advice from your own or a friendly consulate (*see pp. 182–273*) or from the local health authorities or an expat organisation – even from the medical staff of a Western mining or other company if there's one nearby.

This second stage is to ensure that you get what doctors call 'post-exposure vaccination'. As I've already implied, the nearer the bite is to your head, the more urgent this is. In any case, **don't wait until you return home**. If you haven't been vaccinated before, you will need an immediate injection – partly into and around the wound itself – of the rabies immunoglobulin (RIG) mentioned above. The human type is best, as it's less likely to cause side-effects than the type extracted from horses. But both are in short supply worldwide – a good reason to get vaccinated before you travel.

You'll also need several injections of vaccine proper, *whether or not you've had a course of rabies vaccine before.* They will be spread over a number of days. The number of jabs will depend on whether you've had a previous vaccination and on the type of vaccine – again try to get imported modern human vaccine if possible. But *one injection is never enough*, whatever the local medical staff may tell you. Treatment should only stop on completion of the course, or when the animal that bit you is proved to be rabies-free.

Finally, remember that animals carry a lot of nasty bugs in their mouths apart from rabies, so you'll also need antibiotics and possibly a tetanus booster (*see p. 166*) if you're not up to schedule.

SEXUALLY-TRANSMITTED INFECTIONS

To paraphrase the old song, it's not so much what you do – or where or with whom you do it – as *how*. Travel often presents the opportunities and stimulates the inclination. The *where* only becomes a factor because sexually-transmitted infections (STIs) are much more common in some parts of the world than others. If, like many travellers, you meet new sexual partners on your travels, it's vital to make sure they don't pass on to you any nasty germs that they have picked up on the way – or vice-versa.

Of course, HIV/AIDS is the first threat that comes to mind when talking or thinking of the dangers of unprotected sex, but it's by no means the only one. Sexually-transmitted hepatitis (mainly hepatitis B, but there are other types) is less dangerous but far more easily caught. And the whole range of 'traditional' STIs, which are much older than human history, flourish all around the world. The only preaching I'll do is to suggest that you do your bit to stop them spreading any farther.

It's a pretty simple and straightforward cautionary tale, summarised on the page opposite, but it's as well to know something of the details of the varied risks, and how to recognise and deal with them if you do become infected.

SAFER SEX

It's deadly serious, literally – so don't live to regret the fun you had.

A moonlit tropical beach, an attractive stranger, a bit of booze, the cares and inhibitions of home far away, the excitement of travel...you know the rest.

Fact no. 1: There's no such thing as safe sex, only saf*er* sex. Fact no. 2: Sexually-transmitted diseases are almost as common, worldwide, as malaria. Fact no. 3: Although certain groups of people are more likely to give you an infection than others – sex workers or people who inject drugs, for instance – you can't tell by appearances (and s/he may not even know) if a person is HIV-positive (*see p. 146*), is a hepatitis-B carrier (*see p. 148*), or even in many cases has one of the more traditional sexual infections (*see p. 149*). (Men who are gay or bisexual are often included in the higher-risk group; it may be true statistically, but HIV is no 'respecter' of sexual orientation – and the same is certainly true of other STDs.)

Perhaps even more to the point for travellers, having multiple sex partners is a risk factor, and so is having sex with anyone who him/herself has had sex with someone in one of the risk categories. I'm not suggesting you can't trust anyone you meet on your travels, but you can't tell by looking and you may or may not be able to tell by asking...

Safer sex basically means no penetrative sex without a condom (male or female – eg, 'Femidom'), and no oral sex without ditto or using dental dams. Most people don't like using them, but there's no better alternative, so I'd advise all travellers – male and female – to carry a supply with them, get replacements whenever necessary (preferably in major cities), and use them, every time. No condoms or dental dams? There are other ways of having fun! A few further points about condom use:–

→ Condom sizes vary: often bigger in Africa, smaller in Asia. (Don't ask!)

→ Buy what seems like a reliable brand from a reliable source (eg, a pharmacy rather than a village store, if possible); check the expiry date.

→ Be aware that, in some countries, condoms may be difficult to get; you could try inquiring of health centres, expat organisations or consulates.

→ Sun and heat can perish rubber, causing tiny holes, so store them carefully and check them before use.

→ Anything oily or greasy – including petroleum jelly ('Vaseline'), sun-tan oils and lotions, and insect-repellents – also perishes rubber; use only a water-based lubricant (eg, 'KY Jelly'). Better still, use a spermicidal lubricant, pessary or cream (which is toxic to viruses as well as sperm).

→ Diaphragms, caps, coils and Pills don't protect you from STDs.

Want more information on safer sex? Log in to *www.sexhealth.org/safersex*; *www.sexuality.org/safesex.html*; or *www.safersex.org*.

HIV AND AIDS

The most common fatal disease people bring back from their travels.

The last thing you want, I'm sure, is another lecture on the dangers of HIV and the ultimately fatal collection of diseases the virus causes (or, rather, *allows* to develop) – AIDS. So I'll take at least some of the basics as read and concentrate on putting HIV/AIDS in a travel context, with some plain facts...

→ Forget the 'gay plague' label; in most parts of the world, HIV is passed on mainly by straight sex – vaginal, anal or oral – from men to women and (somewhat less often) from women to men. (This isn't to say that male gay sex is less risky than straight; I'm talking global statistics here.)

→ Despite the difference in infectivity, almost as many men as women are HIV-positive – perhaps because men still tend to sleep around more.

→ Globally, after sex of all varieties, the second most important route is from infected mother to new-born child, with shared use of needles and infected blood products significant but coming well down the percentage scale.

→ Even in such countries as Britain, the number of new straight cases of HIV has overtaken the number from gay sex. The vast majority of straight HIV-positive people in Britain (and probably also other industrialised countries) in recent years were infected overseas. One London survey of straight men having post-travel screening (admittedly therefore probably biased towards long-term travellers) found that 1 in 80 were HIV-positive.

→ The longer you travel, the more sexual partners you have, and the more often you have sex, statistically the more likely you are to get HIV – whatever your sexual orientation. (The exception is gay women who don't have sex with men; they have the lowest HIV rate of all.)

→ You can't pick up HIV from a mosquito or other insect bite, a loo seat, a swimming pool, shared cooking or eating utensils, social hugging or kissing, or any other casual contact.

→ You can catch it through any 'invasive' procedure that involves non-sterile instruments – and that includes body- and ear-piercing, tattooing, acupuncture and even wet shaving, as well as injections, blood transfusions, surgery and dentistry. (*See also pp. 16 & 172.*)

→ Having one of the 'classic' STDs (*see p. 149*) increases your chance of both catching and passing on HIV through sex.

→ The incidence of HIV/AIDS varies enormously around the world (for more information, see the individual regional articles on pp. 182–273), but almost everywhere the trend is up. Currently the highest figures are in sub-Saharan Africa, where in some countries more than 30 per cent of the adult population is HIV-positive. But infection rates are also increasing particularly fast in parts of Asia, the Americas and eastern Europe.

→ In truth, however, the risk of catching HIV/AIDS is a matter of behaviour rather than geography...

→ In many places, sex workers have the highest rates of infection (in some places up to 90 per cent) – so sex tourists should particularly beware.

→ In areas where HIV-infection rates are high, there's an increased risk that another traveller you meet and have sex with has picked up an infection en route – think about it!

→ The only *sure* way to avoid HIV is total abstinence or a constant, faithful (on both sides) relationship with an uninfected person. Otherwise, at all times, practise safer sex (*see p.145*).

→ There's not yet any HIV vaccine – not for want of trying – and none on the near horizon. There's no cure, but cocktails of (expensive) drugs can keep AIDS at bay – often for many years, but no one's yet sure just how long.

If you think you may be infected Overt AIDS symptoms probably wouldn't show up for years if you were to be infected with HIV, although you might have a brief flu-like illness early on. Blood tests don't show anything for about three months. Meanwhile, if you're worried, my first advice is to share your worries with an experienced counsellor on an AIDS helpline. They exist in many major cities, so there may be no need to wait until you get home unless you're already on your way. Remember (and this isn't meant to be a carte blanche for gung-ho behaviour), the risk of catching HIV from a single sexual encounter with an infected person is usually well under 1 in 100.

Then the priority – on reaching home, or on reaching a city preferably in a major industrialised country – is to have a proper consultation with a sexual health clinic, with further counselling, a blood test and, if appropriate, discussion of a treatment plan. Meanwhile, it's more important than ever to practise safer sex with any new partners you may have.

There's a lot of controversy about emergency treatment for HIV exposure – what doctors call post-exposure prophylaxis – to prevent the virus getting a hold. It's an established procedure for 'needle-stick' accidents in hospitals (ie, accidental infection with an HIV-positive patient's blood or other body fluids from a needle, scalpel, etc), but there are doubts and enormous problems in other situations. It involves taking a 'cocktail' of anti-AIDS drugs for several weeks, starting within hours of possible infection (and thus long, long before any blood test is possible). One currently recommended regime includes zidovudine (AZT; 'Retrovir') plus lamivudine ('Epivir'; or combined with zidovudine in 'Combivir') and either indinavir ('Crixivan') or nelfinavir ('Viracept'), but the recommendations change from time to time.

These drugs all tend to have unpleasant side-effects, but the bigger problems are practical ones. The drugs may or may not be available locally on your travels, and if you're thinking of taking a supply 'just in case', think in terms of £200 or more (or its equivalent) for just a five-day 'starter pack'; is that realistic in relation to the scale of the risk? But who's to say that a rape victim, for instance, shouldn't receive such treatment – just in case? And why stop there? In such an extreme emergency involving a friend or relative, could I say that I wouldn't move heaven and earth to try to get treatment from a local AIDS centre or university hospital?

HEPATITIS B, C, D AND OTHERS

Types of hepatitis transmitted by sex, dirty needles and blood products.

As explained in the article on types A and E (*see p.51*), hepatitis is a liver disease, mainly caused by viruses of various types, whose main symptom is jaundice (yellowing). Hepatitis A and the much less common type E are spread mainly by contaminated food and drink, so they're sometimes called infectious hepatitis. The other types are infectious, too, but they aren't passed on by food or everyday contact, only by direct contact with contaminated blood or blood products (or 'serum' – hence the old name serum hepatitis), by sexual contact, or by using a hypodermic, acupuncture or other needle contaminated with an infected person's blood.

Sound familiar? You've got it (the idea, that is, not the disease I hope): You can catch it in exactly the same way as HIV/AIDS. The big difference is that hepatitis B (the commonest type of serum hepatitis), although not usually fatal like HIV is, is about 100 times more infectious. It can also, at least in theory, be transferred by bed-bugs (although that's pretty rare). And after recovering from an acute hepatitis B infection, you may have chronic (long-term) hepatitis for years and perhaps become a carrier, able to pass on the virus even though you're symptom-free. It's reckoned that there are at least 350 million hepatatitis B carriers around the world.

What it is There are at least four types of virus that cause serum heptatitis, named (as you'll realise from the above) by letters of the alphabet. The main one transmitted by sexual contact – vaginal, anal or oral – is hepatitis (or 'hep') B. Hepatitis C, the next most common type, is transmitted via blood transfusions and blood products, and by contaminated needles; sexual transmission is reckoned to be possible but not proven. Hepatitis D is an oddball; you can't get it on its own, but only if you already have hepatitis B. It's sometimes called delta hepatitis (it makes for some variety!).

But that's not the end of the list; there's at least one other virus – probably several – that can cause hepatitis after a blood transfusion. Doctors haven't yet pinned it (or them) down, so they use an even more distinctive name: 'non-A, non-E' hepatitis. (They mean non-B, non-C and non-D as well.)

Where you can get it Hepatitis viruses are more or less common everywhere, but the highest risk of catching the B type is in sub-Saharan Africa, south-east and central Asia, China (where 60 per cent of the people have the hepatitis B virus), the Pacific islands and parts of South America. As many as 1 in 5 people – perhaps more – are carriers in parts of Africa, Asia and the Pacific; up to 1 in 10 in parts of Central and South America and in countries bordering the Mediterranean; about 1 in 20 in eastern Europe; but only 1 in 1000 in North America, Australia and northern Europe. Hepatitis D is most common in parts of Africa and South America, and in southern Europe and the Middle East. The risk of contracting any type of hepatitis from blood products is greatest in developing countries where blood for transfusion isn't always screened properly.

How you can avoid it The precautions against catching serum hepatitis, particularly type B, are the same as for avoiding HIV: Practise safer sex (*see p.145*) and avoid any contact with possibly contaminated needles – whether for acupuncture, tattooing or self-injection, or for receiving a prescription drug from a doctor (*see p.16*). However, unlike HIV, there's an effective vaccine against hepatitis B (and one against hepatitis C is on the way). The one snag is that the vaccine is relatively expensive – especially if you go for the combined hepatitis A and B vaccine, which can protect you for 10 years from type A and for a long time against type B. In fact, many countries around the world (including Australia and the USA, but not yet Britain) include hepatitis B vaccination in the routine childhood immunisation schedule.

If you're going on a prolonged trip in an area where the risk is high, you'd be well advised to get vaccinated. For others, it's your call. The official advice is that for a short trip you don't need it, unless you're in one of the statistically high-risk groups (much the same as for HIV):–

→ You're a gay or bisexual man.
→ You inject drugs.
→ You may have intimate contact with any of the above or with sex workers.
→ You'll be taking part in activities with a high risk of injury.
→ You need blood transfusions, dialysis or other 'invasive' procedures.

What it does and how it's treated Acute (sudden-onset) viral hepatitis is much the same whatever type of virus causes it; see the notes on the symptoms and treatment on page 52. The big difference is in the long term. Apart from the chance of becoming a carrier (reckoned to be about 1 in 10 to 1 in 20 for hepatitis B, and meaning that you should practise safer sex for the rest of your life), both B and C hepatitis bring the risk of serious long-term, or chronic, effects. These can include permanent liver damage and in some cases liver cancer – even better reasons to avoid the disease. And remember that getting one type gives you no protection against the others.

OTHER SEXUALLY-TRANSMITTED DISEASES

Syphilis, gonorrhoea and others are increasingly common worldwide.

Travellers have no monopoly of STDs, also known as STIs (sexually-transmitted infections) and sometimes still called venereal diseases (VD). But there are lots of reasons why you may have a higher risk of picking up an infection on your travels – particularly the opportunity and inclination to meet new sex partners, and the temptation to have sex without physical protection. (As explained on page 145, methods of contraception such as the Pill, coil, diaphragm and cap give no protection against STDs; only using a condom or femidom can do that, and they're not 100 per cent effective. This applies to the long-established 'classic' STDs as much as to the new threat of HIV/AIDS.) So here I'll briefly outline the various diseases that you might encounter, and advise on how to get effective treatment.

Warning signs But, first, what are the signs that you might have picked up an infection from a sexual partner? The truth is that there may be no symptoms – especially in women – so you'd be well advised to have a routine check-up after (or even during) your trip if you think you could have been exposed. (In one Swedish survey, one in four apparently healthy women travellers were found to be infected.) Certainly you and also your partner should have any of the following symptoms looked at:–

→ A discharge from your penis or vagina (in the case of women, one that's thicker or smellier than normal, or is discoloured).
→ Itchy genitals (although this may be due to thrush; *see p.157*).
→ Spots, warts or an ulcer on or around your genitals.
→ Pain when you urinate (although, especially in women, this is usually due to cystitis; *see p.158*).
→ Pain during sex or, at any time, in a man's testicles or a woman's lower abdomen.
→ Abnormal or unusually painful menstrual bleeding in women (although women travellers often have irregular periods).

The main STDs Most of the 'classic' STDs occur everywhere, but a few are mainly found in warmer regions. Almost all are much more common in developing countries – because of poorer control programmes and treatment – than in the industrialised world. (For the incidence of HIV/AIDS worldwide, see page 146 and the regional articles on pages 182–273.)

Gonorrhoea An estimated 250 million people are infected worldwide. It's a bacterial infection that usually causes a discharge and (in men) pain on urination. It can lead to complications such as pelvic inflammatory disease (PID) – a cause of infertility – in women if not treated. It's often resistant to antibiotics (including penicillin, which used to be effective), so powerful new antibiotics are needed, with follow-up checks that they've worked.

Chlamydia Sometimes called the 'silent' STD because there may be no symptoms at all, it's also sometimes grouped with certain other bacterial infections as nonspecific urethritis or non-gonococcal urethritis (NSU or NGU). There's been a massive increase recently. It's like a milder version of gonorrhoea caused by different bacteria, and is usually treated with antibiotics. Untreated, it can lead to PID and often infertility in women.

Lymphogranuloma venereum This is related to chlamydia, but causes small genital ulcers or blisters, or tenderness and swelling of the lymph nodes ('glands') in the groin. It occurs patchily worldwide, but mostly in the tropics and subtropics, and is treated in the same way as chlamydia.

Syphilis There are around 50 million new cases of this ancient disease every year. Its first symptoms are usually relatively mild – a painless ulcer on the genitals and a rash – but if untreated it can lead to much worse things, including brain damage decades later. You'll need a blood test for confirmation, and usually injections of a penicillin derivative to cure it.

Chancroid This is even more common than syphilis, worldwide, but mostly affects people in the tropics and subtropics. It causes painful genital ulcers and often swollen lymph nodes in the groin. It can be cured with antibiotics.

Trichomoniasis Said to be the commonest STD of all worldwide, with at least 170 000 new cases every year, it's caused by a protozoan (a single-celled animal parasite). Most infected men and many women have no symptoms, but in others it may cause a foul-smelling yellowish vaginal discharge, and pain or discomfort in both sexes when having sex or passing urine. It may only show up during a routine smear test. It's quite easily treated with drugs.

Genital warts Basically the same as any other skin warts, they're caused by a virus (the human papilloma virus) and are painless and usually harmless – if not very pleasant. However, in women this virus is the main cause of cervical cancer, so any woman who's been infected should have regular smear tests. (A vaccine is being developed.) The warts can be painted with a chemical that dries them up, so that they drop off, but they may have to be removed by freezing, laser burning or surgery.

Genital herpes A close cousin to the type of herpes that causes cold sores, it's a common cause of multiple painful ulcers on and around the genitals. A person with cold sores can give his/her partner the virus during oral sex, but this slightly different type of virus can be passed on during vaginal or anal intercourse. In some people, it disappears after one attack, but more often (like cold sores) it comes back from time to time. There's no cure, but antiviral drugs can reduce the severity of attacks. A vaccine is on the way.

Pubic lice ('crabs') Not really an STD, but transmitted by sex; see page 81.

Getting treatment One 'advantage' of the worldwide spread of STDs is that there is no shortage of specialist doctors – although there are plenty of quacks and pedlars of useless patent 'cures' out there, too, in some parts of the world. If you can't find a sexual diseases specialist or clinic, make inquiries of skin specialists; many are also experts in STDs.

Whatever you do, don't try to diagnose or treat yourself. Proper diagnosis may need lab tests, and many STD bugs are resistant to certain drugs. Only a specialist will know (or can test for) the most effective antibiotic or other drug treatment to cure your condition. Always complete the full course of drugs, even if the symptoms seem to disappear, and abstain from sex – altogether if possible, and certainly without protection – until you're cured.

SKIN AND OTHER INFECTIONS

In most of the developed world, we've all but eliminated many infectious diseases carried by insects or other creatures (*see pp. 106–143*), but this isn't so true of illnesses spread by droplets in the air or by direct contact with an infected person – just think of colds, flu and the common diseases of childhood such as chickenpox, measles, whooping cough and so on. If you go travelling, particularly in less developed regions, you could well come up against infections in both categories, including quite a few that have become rarities on your own home patch.

This chapter deals with things in the second, 'contagious' category. I've ignored conditions (such as colds, flu and the childhood diseases) that occur more or less equally all over the world and aren't a special risk if you travel. But I have included tuberculosis (TB), polio, diphtheria and others that were once scourges everywhere, have been brought more or less under control in many places, but are still rampant in regions you might visit on your travels. And there are still others that are specific risks in certain outlandish places.

However, it's often much more mundane things that are the real everyday bain of travellers' lives – a flare-up of thrush or cystitis (especially likely if you're a woman), or problems with your skin, feet, eyes or ears. Especially in hot, humid climates, or if you go trekking or do other strenuous activity, skin and foot problems are among the most common travellers' complaints. Even the simplest scratch can often go septic and lead to serious trouble, so you can't do better than start off with the advice opposite on keeping your skin and feet healthy...

HEALTHY SKIN AND FEET

Skin conditions are among the most common troubles on your travels.

Skin's just there; beyond pampering it with cosmetics, most people take it for granted. But it's your body's front-line defence to the world, so it's no real surprise that skin is liable to give problems as soon as you venture out of your comfortable, temperate environment into somewhere harsher. Sometimes the effects are direct, immediate and clear: The sun may attack it directly (*see p.54*) or bring out a rash of cold sores (*see p.57*); heat or extreme cold may cause acute problems (*see p.60 & pp.64–66*); and biting, stinging or parasitic creatures of various kinds may assault it (*see pp.72–105*). But in hot, humid climates particularly, and in conditions where it's difficult to keep clean, small skin injuries and infections that would normally cause little trouble can grow into major causes of discomfort – if rarely anything more serious.

Avoiding trouble Many skin problems can be prevented by wearing loose, well-ventilated cotton clothes and by simple, basic hygiene. If it's hot, you'll no doubt want to shower at least once and probably several times each day; but don't over-do the soap, or it'll denude your skin of natural protective oils. Make sure you dry yourself thoroughly (but gently) afterwards; using a non-greasy moisturising cream helps to restore protection to the skin in both sexes. And get into the habit of checking for cuts, sores, blisters or other signs of trouble to come.

In heat and humidity even the smallest skin break can go septic and cause a skin infection that may be difficult to clear up (*see p.155*), so try hard to avoid scratching bites, and use a soothing cream to reduce the temptation (*see p.74*). The same applies to rashes, but the best treatment for them depends on the type of rash (always remembering that a rash is a common symptom of many illnesses that have very little basically to do with the skin).

If a rash is dry and scaly (like some forms of eczema), use a moist cream or ointment. If you're prone to atopic eczema – which usually improves in the sun, but may well get worse in hot, humid conditions – be sure to moisturise your skin regularly, and also take with you a supply of any special treatment, such as steroid cream, that your doctor recommends. But if the rash is moist and oozing – and also for a minor cut or scratch after you've cleaned it thoroughly (*see p.178*) – use an antiseptic skin wash that dries rather than moisturises, dabbed on with cotton wool.

Among the best such antiseptics is povidone-iodine (eg, 'Betadine' or 'Videne'), which is available in liquid or dry aerosol-spray form. Or you could use tincture of iodine, a chlorhexidine solution (sold under various brand names), or some brands of antiseptic wipes. However, the easiest and cheapest antiseptic to obtain in developing countries is often potassium permanganate. You need only a very weak solution – a few crystals dissolved in a glass of clean water, or a quarter-teasponful in a litre; just enough to turn it deep pink colour. But beware: the solution and the wet crystals can stain both your skin and your clothes – as can iodine. And iodine and antiseptic wipes containing alcohol will both sting broken skin.

Other pre-existing conditions Psoriasis usually improves in the sun or with sea bathing, but sunburn may trigger a flareup; discuss the best treatment with your doctor beforehand, and take a supply with you. Contact eczema – the type caused by irritating substances or an allergy to particular materials in contact with the skin – is also liable to get worse in hot and damp conditions; tight clothing, backpack straps, money belts and so on often cause trouble. This kind of rash is best treated with an antiseptic skin-wash, followed by moisurising cream and, if the itching is bad and the skin inflamed and red, cream containing 1 per cent hydrocortisone (eg, 'HC45').

Any condition or treatment that suppresses your immune system is likely to make skin conditions more troublesome. These include not only HIV/AIDS but also some kinds of cancer, alcohol or drug abuse, and long-term treatment with steroids and certain other drugs. Anyone in these categories should consult a medical specialist before travelling to hot climates.

Caring for feet Your feet don't have such a good blood supply as the rest of your body, so any trouble is likely to be slower-healing – which is all the more reason for keeping them clean and healthy in the first place. The basic rules are to keep your feet moisturised and to remove dead skin. (If you're diabetic, you'll know about the special problems you could face, and should take special advice before setting off on your travels.)

If you're trekking or doing much ordinary walking, make sure that your footwear is up to the job, fits properly and is well worn in. Wear two layers of soft, well-fitting socks. Most people advise socks with a high percentage of natural fibres (wool or cotton), but some prefer certain soft synthetic fibres for their 'wicking' effect, which draws moisture away from the skin. Change your shoes and socks at the end of the day – and if possible take them off during a midday break too – to give your feet a chance to 'breathe' and dry, making them less vulnerable to blisters. Rubbing them with surgical spirit

---

TREATING BLISTERS

Drain any large unbroken blister (after cleaning the area) by puncturing it with a sterile needle (hold it in a flame for a few seconds, then let it cool) and gently squeezing out the fluid. Then cover it with a non-adherent dressing (eg, 'Melonin') with the perforated plastic film side next to your skin, and fix it firmly with sticky plaster – or, if available, use a self-adhesive non-adherent dressing (eg, 'Medipore' or 'Primapore'). If the blister has already burst and the skin rubbed off, wash the area carefully and coat it with antiseptic cream; then apply a suitable clean and soft dressing. In any event, if at all possible avoid wearing the shoes or boots that caused the problem until the blister has healed.

(rubbing alcohol) before and during your trek will also toughen the skin, while blister dressings (*see below*) can be used to prevent as well as treat blisters on your heels and elsewhere.

Soaking your feet in hot, salty water (or, again, weak permanganate; *see above*) at the end of the day isn't only soothing; it also cuts the risk of infection from small abrasions and blisters. If you notice red but not yet blistered skin, or small blisters, clean and dry the affected area, then stick on a special blister dressing – preferably the 'hydrocolloid' type, which acts like a flexible second skin. You can get these from adventure travel stores and pharmacies, but if you don't have any, use low-allergy or regular sticky plaster instead.

SKIN INFECTIONS

Bacteria and fungi flourish in tropical and subtropical conditions.

It doesn't take much to start a skin infection – a fall, an argument with a hard object or prickly plant, a minor accident with a knife or other sharp implement, or even scratching an insect bite or a patch of eczema, and the skin is broken, letting bacteria or other germs get in.

Back home, most such 'wounds' would hardly warrant a second thought after washing them, perhaps putting on a bit of antiseptic cream and, if they're more than very trivial, applying a sticky plaster. In a hot climate – especially if it's also humid – it's a different matter. Sweating, particularly if combined with chafing by folds of skin, can quickly encourage bacteria to invade, and hot, sweaty corners are also prime breeding grounds for fungal infections. Both types of infection are very common and sometimes persistent in the tropics, and wide-scale infected eczema (*see below*) can be especially dangerous. Remember too that any deep wound that gets dirty is also at risk of infection with tetantus bacteria – which can be life-threatening (*see p.166*).

Bacterial infections Bacteria may stay in one small area of the skin, forming a pimple or boil; they may spread over the skin surface to form the weeping, encrusted rash and reddening of impetigo; or, in cellulitis, may spread further to affect slightly deeper tissues, causing raised, inflamed skin that is red and hot. Skin ulcers or sores may have various causes, but these also can include bacterial infections.

Boils and pimples are particularly common in the tropics, and may need antibiotic treatment if they're very large or you have lots of them. But normal boils are best allowed to come to a 'head' and burst naturally; don't squeeze them, or the infection may spread. Meanwhile, simply wash them frequently with hot soapy water, and apply antiseptic cream. Hot compresses may ease the discomfort. A large boil may need lancing with a sterile (flame-heated) needle or scalpel, especially if it's in an awkward place such as the armpit or groin. Wipe and wash away the pus carefully, to avoid spreading the infection, rinse with an antiseptic wash (*see p.153*), apply antiseptic cream, and cover with a non-adherent dressing or sticky plaster.

A rash of pimples – known as folliculitis, because it's caused by infection of the hair follicles – may develop after swimming in dirty water. Treat such pimples in the same way as small boils, using an antiseptic wash or cream.

Note: Some parasites, such as tumbu flies (*see p.79*) cause swellings that resemble boils, so it's best to consult a doctor if possible.

Impetigo more often affects children, but it can strike adults too and is very common in hot, humid climates. It's easily recognised by the yellowish crusty sores, and is very infectious – so anyone with the infection shouldn't share face cloths or towels with anyone else until it's cured. Wash the area with an antiseptic solution (*see p.153*) to remove the crusts, and then apply an antibiotic ointment or cream – eg, fucidic acid ('Fucidin') or neomycin ('Cicatrin' or 'Neosporin') – three or four times a day for five to seven days. These are prescription drugs in the UK and elsewhere, but may be available over the counter in some countries; you should in any case see a doctor if the impetigo continues to spread, as antibiotic tablets may be needed.

Cellulitis is the most serious of common bacterial skin infections, because it can spread rapidly and may – rarely – result in septicaemia (blood poisoning) if it's not treated promptly. The first sign is often reddening and throbbing of an area of skin, which begins to feel hot. It's usually also tender and painful, and as the infection spreads the nearby lymph nodes ('glands') may swell. You may start to feel feverish, with chills.

Cellulitis needs urgent medical treatment. A one-week course of antibiotic tablets – eg, a penicillin derivative such as flucloxacillin, or (for people allergic to penicillin) erythromycin – will usually clear it up; but you may also need to take painkillers such as aspirin or paracetamol (acetaminophen; eg, 'Tylenol') to relieve aches and pains in the early stages. Keep the infected part raised as much as possible to reduce swelling and pain.

Ulcers can develop very quickly in the tropics; they're often painless, so check your skin – legs particularly – each day. In many regions they may be caused by leishmaniasis (in which case they'll appear in various places on your body; *see p.118*). One form of skin cancer also forms a slow-developing ulcer (*see p.55*). In none of these cases will they respond to direct skin treatment, so any ulcer or sore that won't heal should be seen by a doctor. If s/he finds that it's caused by a bacterial skin infection – an infected cut or scratch developing into a so-called 'tropical ulcer' – you'll need a course of antibiotics. In the meantime, it should be carefully cleaned with an antiseptic wash (*see p.153*) and dressed, and the affected part kept raised.

Fungal infections Just as food goes mouldy quickly in warm, wet weather, the same applies to your skin: Fungal infections love damp, warm nooks and crannies where air doesn't circulate – especially in hot, humid climates. To avoid them, it's best to wear loose, airy clothing, especially underwear.

The microscopic fungi that infect skin often spread outwards from the original point of infection, forming a red, flaky ring with a clear area in the middle. (The process is much the same as toadstools forming a 'fairy ring' in grass.) So such skin infections (known medically as *tinea*) are commonly called ringworm – although they've got nothing to do with worms.

Depending on the part of the body involved, they're also given names such as athlete's foot (medically *tinea pedis*, or tinea of the foot) and 'jock itch' (*tinea cruris*; tinea of the crotch) – which can affect women as well as men. A scalp infection (*tinea capitis*; tinea of the head) is also common, but in fact the fungi can infect any part of your body, including the nails (which become discoloured and brittle). A type of fungal skin infection known as pityriasis – which is also very common in the tropics – causes scaly patches that are darker or lighter in colour than the surrounding skin, rather than reddened.

In all fungal skin infections, the skin is itchy, and the infection is often transferred by scratching the affected area and then touching a new victim. But it's common knowledge that you can also pick it up from showers and other damp places.

Most of these infections can be treated with an antifungal cream, powder or spray, such as clotrimazole (eg, 'Canesten'), used several times a day. There are also effective treatments in tablet form (usually on prescription) that are especially good for persistent infections or those of the scalp or nails. Avoid using a steroid skin cream (eg, one containing hydrocortisone, such as 'Eurax HC', 'Lanacort' or 'HC45'), which helps many itchy skin conditions, including dermatitis; in the case of fungal infections it'll only make things worse. Always keep the affected area clean and dry.

THRUSH

A common women's complaint that's likely to flare up in the heat.

Women are much more prone to this fungal infection (together with cystitis; see p.158) than men – although men can also be infected, often with few if any symptoms. Special factors add to the likelihood of getting it when you're travelling: As with other fungal infections (see p.156), hot, humid, tropical conditions encourage the thrush fungi to grow – especially if you wear tight clothing, and also if you spend a long time sitting on a hot train or bus. You may also have more opportunity for sex when away from home, and frequent lovemaking may encourage thrush (as well as cystitis) to develop. Other factors can include diabetes, taking the contraceptive Pill or certain antibiotics – including the antimalarial drug doxycycline (see p.115) – and, ironically, using too much soapy water on your genital area.

What it is Medically, thrush is known as vaginal candidiasis; it's an infection of the vagina with a yeast organism called *Candida albicans*. In fact, this very commonly lives in the vagina without causing problems; trouble begins when it grows too rapidly, forming a cheesy (but not foul-smelling), whitish, itchy discharge. Sometimes, there are white deposits around the vaginal opening. Sex may cause discomfort or soreness – and more importantly may pass on the infection to your partner, who (as I've said) may show no symptoms but may possibly pass it back to you after you've been cured.

How it's treated The over-growth of thrush organisms is often due to the vagina becoming too alkaline. (This is why soap, which is alkaline, can encourage it.) So the only treatment needed to counter it may be to return the vagina to its normal (slightly acid) state by douching with very dilute vinegar (30ml – 2 tablespoons – in a litre or 1¾ pints of water). Or try plain yoghurt.

But if this doesn't clear up the itching and discharge, you'll need an antifungal cream or pessary containing a drug such as clotrimazole (eg, 'Canesten') in either a single large dose or a week-long course. (If your partner shows symptoms, the same cream should be applied to his penis. *Warning*: It can perish the latex of a condom or diaphragm.) Or, in many countries including the UK, you can get a single-dose treatment of fluconazole ('Diflucan') in tablet form without prescription; but you shouldn't take this if you may be pregnant. (If you're prone to thrush, you'd be well advised to take one or other of these treatments with you on your travels.)

Other commonsense measures include keeping your genital area clean, dry and airy. (Wear a long skirt and loose or no underwear.) If the thrush doesn't clear up, or if the discharge smells bad, get medical advice; there may be the possibility of a more serious sexually-transmitted disease (*see pp. 144–151*).

CYSTITIS

The positioning and shortness of a woman's urethra (urine passage) means that they're much more likely to get cystitis – a bacterial infection of the urethra – than men. (Men can also get it, however, and with them it may be even more serious and so should always be investigated by a doctor.) Moreover, because the distance is less, the infection in women is more likely to spread upwards to the bladder or even the kidneys, making it more difficult to eliminate. It's also quite likely to recur if you've had it once.

As well as poor personal hygiene, many of the same things encourage cystitis as they do thrush (*see p. 157*) – including wearing tight clothing and frequent vigorous sex. (That's of course why it's sometimes called 'holiday cystitis' or 'honeymoon cystitis'.) One tip for reducing the risk is always to urinate after having sex. This last point is one clue as to why it's much more common in hot climates – if you pass less urine, cystitis is more likely to develop: one more good reason (*see also p. 58*) to keep up your fluid intake.

Ironically, the main symptom of cystitis is a feeling that you need to urinate frequently, but you usually pass only a small amount, and feel a burning or stinging pain when you do. (If you feel pain when you urinate without any increase in frequency, the cause may be a sexually-transmitted disease; *see pp. 144–151*.) As a first measure, try drinking plenty of cranberry juice, if you can get it, to reduce the acidity of your urine. Otherwise drink (safe) water with a teaspoonful of baking soda (sodium bicarbonate) dissolved in a glassful, and alternate this with a glass of plain water every 20–30 minutes. After a few hours the pain and urgency may begin to subside as your urine washes out the bacteria and its acidity reduces.

But if things don't improve – and particularly if you develop a fever or notice blood in your urine – you should see a doctor to get antibiotic treatment. Various antibiotics can be used, and if possible a urine sample should be sent to a laboratory for testing, as identifying the precise bacterial infection you have will make treatment much more certain. As already mentioned, such investigations are particularly important for men, and also children.

EAR AND EYE PROBLEMS

Hot and either humid or dusty conditions may mean you get more frequent ear and eye problems on your travels than at home, but few are specifically associated with travel.

Ear problems

Ear trouble is most likely to begin on your flight, due to changes in air pressure; if your ears or eustachian tubes (which link the inner ear on each side with the throat) are partly blocked, you may get earache. It's easily remedied with wax-dissolving ear drops or a decongestant such as pseudoephedrine (eg, 'Sudfed') respectively, plus a mild painkiller such as aspirin or paracetamol (acetaminophen; eg, 'Tylenol'). If at any time you have persistent earache on one side, or one ear that becomes itchy and inflamed, it's probably caused by an infection that should be checked by a doctor; antibiotic drops or tablets will normally cure it in a few days.

Eye problems

The most important specific travellers' eye condition is snow blindness due to excessive ultra-violet (UV) light at high altitudes (see p.71). However, lower-intensity UV over long periods can eventually damage the light-sensitive retina and, in some cases, cause cataracts. Even if you think you're used to bright sunlight, always wear good UV-blocking sunglasses.

The commonest eye infection, at home or even more so in the tropics, is conjunctivitis – inflammation of the thin membrane covering the front of the eye. It causes reddening, a feeling of grittiness, and pus that may stick your eyelids together in the morning. It's highly contagious, so don't rub your eyes! Antibiotic drops will usually clear it up, combined with soothing eye-baths if necessary. But avoid drops containing steroids such as hydrocortisone; these can make the condition worse if it happens to be caused by viruses rather than the more common bacteria. Viral conjuctivitis won't respond to antibiotics, and sometimes needs specialist treatment, but it often clears up on its own if it's associated with a cold-like illness.

Trachoma is a type of conjunctivitis that's a common cause of blindness in hot, dry climates where medical facilities are poor, but it needn't worry you too much at a personal level. It's spread by direct contact or by flies, but the infection takes many years to do its worst; a three-week course of antibiotic eye-drops can eliminate it while it's little worse than other types of conjuctivitis. If you spend a long period in an area where trachoma is common, however, you should have regular eye checks by a specialist.

Apart from these, the most common problems come from getting dust in your eyes – particularly if you wear contact lenses. Avoidance measures are pretty obvious – wear good sunglasses or goggles when necessary, and simply close your eyes if the dust's blowing. If a dust particle gets under the eyelid – when it can feel more like a rock! – a companion should 'roll' the eyelid back over a cotton bud (or improvise with a pencil etc), and gently brush the particle away with the corner of a tissue or a moistened cotton bud.

If you wear contact lenses, take at least one spare pair (plus ample solution) and a pair of glasses with you. Take your lenses out during long flights, and also give your eyes a rest from time to time – especially in hot, dry weather.

TUBERCULOSIS

A 'disease of poverty' that's making a comeback in many places.

Tuberculosis, or TB, is far from the 'romantic' disease of the starving artist in his garret, and far from a disease of the past. For decades it seemed to be in decline in developed countries, but it has come back with a vengeance in many parts of the developing world, and the WHO – the UN health agency – declared it a world emergency in 1993.

Even in industrialised countries, cases of TB are on the rise, but the biggest increases coincide with areas where HIV/AIDS is rampant, for being HIV-positive increases the risk of TB infection by 100 times. One-third of the world's population – around 3 billion people – are reckoned to be infected with it, and there are 8–10 million new cases every year. About 3 million people a year die of TB – a figure that could almost double in the next 50 years – making it the world's biggest killer among diseases caused by bacteria.

Having said that, TB isn't very infectious, and fairly prolonged contact with an infected person is needed to catch it. On holiday trips staying in reasonable hotels or other accommodation, you face little risk – certainly not from casual contacts in markets and the like. But if you have to share crowded living or working conditions in poor areas, or have long-term contact with people who live in such conditions, you're at risk.

What it is Tuberculosis is a bacterial infection caused by bugs known as *Mycobacterium tuberculosis*. These are spread through the air in droplets when an infected person coughs – coughing is one of the first symptoms (*see below*) – but it's less infectious than, say, the common cold. In this form, TB first infects the lungs, but as many as 90 per cent of those who catch it never develop the disease. If they do – and this can take months or even years – it first causes a form of pneumonia, gradually destroying lung tissues and causing the endless hacking cough of the 'classic' TB patient.

However, the bugs can also travel to other parts of the body, to many of the internal organs, including the brain, joints and abdominal organs. In fact, one form of TB first shows up in the intestines, and is caused by drinking or eating infected, unpasteurised milk or dairy products. (Cows can get TB.)

As already said, you're highly unlikely to catch TB from casual contact, and certainly not from simply touching someone with the disease. Nor can you catch it from drinking water, cooking or eating utensils, or insect bites. It's possible, but rare, to become infected during an air, train or bus journey; the risk is greatest if you sit in a closed carriage close to someone with TB who coughs throughout a long journey. (Air filters in modern aircraft *should* trap TB bacteria, but it's possible to catch them from people sitting nearby.) Most cases in travellers returning to developed countries are among people who have been visiting their family home in a poor region.

Where you can get it In theory, anywhere; but you're most at risk in poor, overcrowded areas in parts of the world where rates of infection among local people are highest. As already mentioned, these include areas with high rates of HIV infection, but also some others: Africa (especially south of the Sahara), parts of Central and South America, southern and south-east Asia, and parts of eastern Europe, including the former Soviet Union.

How you can avoid it There's a vaccine (known as BCG) against TB, but it's no more than 80 per cent effective (less in most areas). For this reason, it's not often used in North America, but in many other countries (including parts of the UK) it's part of the normal childhood vaccination schedule, given at the age of 10–14. It leaves a small scar on your arm as evidence that you've been vaccinated, and lasts at least 15 years. The effectiveness of a booster jab is doubtful, and there's little evidence that BCG is effective if given to an adult.

Official British guidelines suggest vaccinating several groups of travellers and other people *who haven't previously had a BCG vaccination*. They include:–

→ Contacts of known TB sufferers.
→ People immigrating from areas where TB is rife.
→ Medical and veterinary personnel and others likely to be working with people or animals infected with TB.
→ People intending to stay for more than a month in areas with a high rate of TB infection.

You need to allow a week for a preliminary skin test (which reveals any present or past TB infection, or existing immunity), then six weeks before the vaccine becomes effective, so plan well ahead of travelling.

The American approach is different. There, people expecting to come into prolonged contact with TB sufferers are advised to have a skin test before and after travel, followed by treatment if these tests show that they've become infected. (Anyone having such a skin test should warn the doctor if they've ever had a BCG vaccination, as it can cause a 'false positive' result.)

Apart from these precautions, the only way to avoid infection is to take sensible measures to avoid risky situations – eg, crowded slums and similar places – especially for long periods. This is particularly important if you're HIV-positive, but in this case your doctor may advise taking anti-TB drugs as a preventive measure while you're at risk (although their effectiveness is uncertain). Medical workers treating TB patients are advised to use special face masks, and volunteers in refugee camps and the like should get special advice. It makes sense for everyone to avoid consuming unpasteurised milk, cheese and other dairy products in developing countries.

What it does to you As already mentioned, the symptoms of TB can take a long time to develop, and the disease may be detected by a skin test before they appear. If they do, the first symptom is usually a dry, irritating cough that gradually worsens over a period of weeks or months, eventually producing a lot of phlegm – sometimes bloodstained. Other symptoms include general malaise; a fever, often worse at night, with copious sweating; and gradual loss of body weight (the origin of the old name 'consumption').

How it's treated Anyone with a persistent cough, especially if they're in or recently returned from an area where there's a lot of TB, and especially if they have any of the other symptoms listed above, should get it checked out. A positive skin test isn't conclusive; chest X-rays and tests to detect TB bacteria in phlegm are needed for confirmation. The disease can then usually be treated quite easily, but a combination of antibiotics is generally needed, because many strains of TB bugs are immune to individual drugs. It's important to keep taking the drugs for six months, or until cleared by the doctor – even if the symptoms subside – to be sure of eliminating the infection. All family members and other close contacts need to be checked.

LEGIONNAIRES' DISEASE

Although a headline-maker when outbreaks occur, legionnaires' disease is simply a form of pneumonia caused by small bacteria known as *Legionella pneumophila* (so it's also sometimes called legionellosis). Forget any link you may imagine with the French Foreign Legion; the name comes from a meeting of the American Legion – an ex-servicemen's group – in a hotel in Philadelphia 1976, when the first recognised outbreak took place. (It's since been realised that similar outbreaks occurred long before that.) And far from being a desert disease, you're most likely to get it from a modern building's (or cruise liner's) air conditioning or hot-water system, or sometimes from a hot tub or steam room. (To get infected, you need to breathe in the bugs in a mist – eg, in the shower.) As a result, there are probably more cases in the USA – between 8000 and 18 000 a year – than anywhere else. (The UK has around 200 cases annually.) Individual cases crop up here and there, but the headlines appear when a group of people catch it in one place.

Only about one person in 20 who's infected with *Legionalla* shows any symptoms, and when s/he does – a few days after infection – they're usually little different from the symptoms of other types of pneumonia: a cough and fever, with shortness of breath and chest pain. There may be diarrhoea or vomiting, and some victims become confused. The big problem is that the bacteria may not show up in normal lab tests, unless *Legionella* is suspected and specifically looked for.

There used to be a similar problem with treatment; it was labelled a 'killer' because the usual antibiotics given for pneumonia don't affect these bugs. But now it's known that erythromycin, rifampicin and some other antibiotics can cure it, and doctors often include one of these drugs in a regime for treating any case of pneumonia whose cause is unclear. As a result, the only people at serious danger from legionnaires' disease tend to be heavy smokers, people who are elderly and infirm, and those with a suppressed immune system (from HIV/AIDS or another cause).

There's not much you can or should do to avoid the disease, since it's pretty rare and sporadic. However, it makes sense to avoid staying in any hotel or other building where's there's been a recent case, as the bugs can linger in the water or cooling system for a long time if it's not thoroughly cleaned.

MENINGITIS

A low but serious risk – vaccination is vital for some travellers.

It's one of those 'dread' diseases whose very name is enough to make you feel frightened – and not without reason, as some forms of meningitis can, in a few cases, be fatal in a matter of hours. But it's rare and pretty well down the order of risks for travellers. However, people going to certain regions should take it seriously, as epidemics do occur, and it can have devastating effects if you're far from medical help. Fortunately, there are safe and effective vaccines against most of the common types of the disease.

What it is The name means inflammation of the meninges, the membranes around the brain. Several types of bacteria and viruses can cause it. Viral meningitis is usually relatively mild and not life-threatening. The type that sometimes strikes young children – known as *Haemophilus influenzae* type b (or 'Hib') – is very rare among anyone over five years old, and almost all youngsters in the developed world are vaccinated against it as routine. A form of meningitis caused by fungal organisms may attack people with AIDS.

Many other cases belong to the type that regularly makes headlines when it strikes small groups of older childen or young adults, especially in schools or colleges. It's caused by bacteria called *Neisseria meningitidis*, but generally referred to (even by doctors) as meningococci; so the illness is known as meningococcal meningitis. It's the most important type for travellers to beware. The bugs are spread just like colds and flu – in droplets when someone coughs or sneezes – and in most cases they cause no more trouble than a cold or flu: a short-lived throat infection, or very often no symptoms at all. (Unfortunately, people with this form can pass the bugs on to others.) But in some people, for reasons that doctors don't understand, they get into the bloodstream and infect the brain. Or, even worse still, they cause general infection of the blood – septicaemia, or blood-poisoning. This last is the most often fatal form.

There are various strains of meningococci, known by letters of the alphabet; types A, B, C, W (or W-135) and Y are the main ones. Meningitis B is most common in Europe and the Americas, while types A and C occur mainly in Africa and elsewhere.

Where you can get it There have been sporadic outbreaks and epidemics of meningitis in various parts of the world since the 1980s, including India, Nepal, Mongolia and Brazil, but the most widespread and repeated outbreaks have been in Africa. The zone immediately south of the Sahara – stretching from Senegal and Guinea to Sudan and western Ethiopia – is known as the 'meningitis belt' because epidemics are so frequent there. This is the semi-arid Sahel, but outbreaks have also occurred farther south, in savannah country down to the forested regions of west and central Africa, and in the mid to late 1990s in Malawi, Mozambique and Zambia. Kenya and Tanzania have also had outbreaks, and there have been cases among Muslim pilgrims from places with meningitis to the holy sites in Saudi Arabia.

In the meningitis belt particularly, the outbreaks can be very big; in Nigeria in 1996, for example, there were about 80 000 cases. In this region, most outbreaks take place during the dry season, between December or January and May or June. They tend to die down as the rains come, often to return with the hot, dry weather the following year.

How you can avoid it There's no practicable way of avoiding meningitis on an individual level (and people with the disease are not particularly infectious anyway), so there's no need for most travellers to take specific precautions. But if you're visiting the African meningitis belt during the dry season, or any other area where an outbreak of meningitis is taking place (check with a travel clinic), you should be vaccinated at least ten days before you go.

There are three main types of vaccine. The type C vaccine is given as routine to children in Britain and many other countries, but is not enough for protection in Africa, where type A meningitis is more common. For most travellers the combined A & C vaccine is adequate; a single dose gives protection for at least three years (less in children). However, at the time of writing, the Saudi authorities require all hadj and umrah pilgrims to show a certificate that they've had a four-way vaccination against meningitis A, C, W-135 and Y; your doctor may also advise this for visits to some parts of Africa. There's no vaccine yet for meningitis B, although one is being developed.

What it does to you If you get any symptoms at all from meningococcal meningitis – and, to repeat, most people don't – they're usually very similar to a common cold or flu at first. But within a few hours much more serious symptoms may develop:–

→ Severe headache.
→ High fever – over 40°C (104°F).
→ A stiff neck (making it difficult to bend your head forward).
→ 'Photophobia' – discomfort in bright light.
→ Nausea and vomiting.

In many (but not all) cases, there's a characteristic purplish-red skin rash (sometimes merging into blotches); it can appear anywhere on the body, and if you press on it with a drinking glass (so you can see the rash as you press), the pressure *doesn't* make the rash fade. This isn't conclusive, but it's strong evidence for dangerously advanced meningitis that needs urgent treatment. Final confirmation involves a lumbar puncture – a needle inserted into the spine to draw a sample of cerebrospinal fluid for examination.

How it's treated It's vital to **get immediate medical help** for someone suspected of having meningitis, especially if they have the characteristic rash; a delay of only a few hours could prove fatal. The best treatment is an infusion or injection of benzyl penicillin, but many other antibiotics are effective if this isn't available. In some cases, doctors may want to give similar injections to close contacts, as a precaution.

POLIO

This is a feared disease of the past that really is – according to the WHO, the UN health agency – on the way out. There's been a long-standing campaign to eradicate it, through a global vaccination programme, and success is in sight. But, meanwhile, travellers to many regions are advised to have a booster vaccination – virtually all will have been vaccinated as children – if they haven't had one in the past ten years. (If they weren't vaccinated in childhood, a full course of three doses is needed.)

There's no need to bother if you're travelling *only* within western and northern Europe, North and South America, and Australia and New Zealand, but elsewhere polio remains a risk. (Most cases today are in west and central Africa and southern Asia, but some 30 countries in all had a total of 5000 polio cases in 1999.) The main vaccine used (the 'Sabin') is taken by mouth, on a sugar lump, but HIV-positive people may be given a different ('Salk') vaccine, by injection; the latter is also usually preferred for childhood vaccinations in North America.

Polio (in full, poliomyelitis) is a virus disease spread in the same way as flu – via droplets – and also, where hygiene is poor, by contaminated food and drink. Although regarded as a killer in its heyday, it's often in fact no worse than flu. In only about 1 in 500 cases does it spread to the nervous system, causing a fever, a severe headache, muscular pain and a stiff neck; and only a few of these result in 'floppy' paralysis (with muscular weakness).

TETANUS

Perhaps better known as lockjaw, tetanus isn't a risk only to travellers. You can get it in your back garden, and everyone should have an up-to-date vaccination (which is effective for about ten years); it's normally given as routine during childhood, usually in combination with diphtheria and pertussis (whooping cough) vaccines. But the risks of catching tetanus are increased by travel, and skilled treatment may be difficult or impossible to get in out-of-the-way places, so you'd be well advised to check with your doctor how long ago you last had a jab and if necessary get a booster (with diphtheria; *see below*) before you set off.

Tetanus is caused by soil bacteria called *Clostridium tetani*. Their spores are very tough, and exist almost everywhere, but they normally do harm only if they get directly into you through a cut, needle-prick or other injury. Any injury – particularly a deep puncture wound – that's contaminated by soil or any other form of dirt is a great danger (and not just the cut in the angle of the thumb and forefinger of playground folklore). The tetanus bugs multiply and produce a powerful neurotoxin (nerve poison), which travels to the nerves and causes painful muscular spasms, or at least stiffness. Lockjaw, when the mouth can't be opened, is one result; another is a characteristic (but very unfunny) 'smile' if the face is affected. If the toxin affects chest muscles, and no ventilator is available, death by suffocation is on the cards.

With skilled hospital treatment, involving antitoxin, antibiotics and other drugs, combined with intensive care, tetanus can be treated. But, as already said, it's far better prevented, by vaccination; this can be given as a precaution after an injury, but is best before you travel. However, don't take this as carte blanche to ignore cuts; deep ones in particular should always be cleaned thoroughly and dressed to prevent further infection (*see p.178*).

DIPHTHERIA

Often regarded in western Europe, North America and Australasia as a disease of the past, diphtheria is alive and a serious threat to health in many other parts of the world. (For example, there was a big outbreak in the former Soviet Union during the 1990s.) It's primarily an illness of the nose and throat, transmitted by droplets (like a cold or flu), and causes a leathery greyish 'pseudomembrane' to grow across the throat, making it difficult to swallow. But diphtheria can also infect the skin and be passed on by touch.

It's caused by bacteria called *Corynebacterium diphtheriae*, which produce a toxin (poison) that can be fatal, but the skin form of the disease is usually quite mild. As I've said, it occurs in many parts of the world, especially where (unlike in the developed world) there are no routine vaccination programmes. Most of the very few cases picked up by travellers are of the skin form, but even these are unnecessary. Most people in developed countries will have had a course of combined tetanus, diphtheria and pertussis (whooping cough) vaccines as children; if you haven't had a combined tetanus and diphtheria booster within the last ten years, you should have one before you travel, as both (see also above) are serious, safely preventable risks.

HANSEN'S DISEASE (LEPROSY)

It's in very bad taste to say so, but the greatest threat from Hansen's disease (as leprosy is nowadays more correctly termed) may be to your wallet. The disease is surrounded by myths and ingrained prejudice. It's quite easily treatable today, but never was as contagious as stories about 'lepers' ringing warning bells suggested. Simple everyday contact – even sex – with an infected person won't give you Hansen's disease; you need to live in close contact for a long time to catch it, and antibiotic treatment stops a person being infectious within days. So it's a completely negligible threat to most travellers. Nor does it directly cause damage to fingers and toes, or cause other deformities; what it does do is damage nerves, so that a sufferer can't feel repeated injury. So beggars and anyone else who has any of the deformities associated with Hansen's disease won't pass it on to you.

But this is not to belittle the disease as a serious public health issue in many parts of the world. It still exists throughout the tropics and subtropics, especially in parts of Africa, Asia and South America. About 70 per cent of all sufferers are in the Indian subcontinent, and more than 10 per cent in Brazil. There's no specific vaccine, but the BCG vaccine against tuberculosis (see p.160) also seems to give protection against Hansen's disease. (The bacteria that cause them – those of Hansen's are called Mycobacterium leprae – are closely related.) Treatment (with several antibiotics) needs to be continued for up to two years, depending on the precise type of the disease, and even this doesn't necessarily stop – let alone reverse – nerve damage. So people who've had the disease continue to suffer and to be on the receiving end of prejudice, from their own community as well as from travellers.

ANTHRAX

In spite of the uproar in the USA in 2001–02 about the use of anthrax spores as a terrorist weapon, it's highly unlikely that you'll come up against it in your travels. However, epidemics do sometimes occur in developing countries; for example, one in Zimbabwe in the 1990s infected some 10 000 people.

Anthrax is first and foremost an animal disease that can also be caught by humans, usually by close contact with dead stock animals or their products (such as hair, hide, bones or raw meat). It's not actually very infectious, but can be dangerous if not promptly treated with antibiotics. The most common form infects the skin, causing a red swelling which develops into a blister that forms a dark scabby ulcer; it's the easiest form to treat. Anthrax can also infect your intestines (from eating undercooked or raw infected meat) or lungs (from breathing the spores); these are the most dangerous forms.

Anthrax vaccine is available only to people at high risk through contact with possibly infected animals (which are themselves routinely vaccinated). It's sensible to avoid contact with animal products – especially folk handicrafts made of goat skin or hair, and the like – in developing countries, and not to eat undercooked or raw meat during epidemics.

LASSA, EBOLA AND SIMILAR FEVERS

Frightening headlines about exotic 'killer viruses' causing uncontrolled bleeding appear from time to time, but these occur almost entirely in remote rural areas well off the route of almost all travellers other than a few health and other aid workers. They are known as haemorrhagic fevers, and usually originate in animals – Lassa fever of west Africa, the hantaviruses of Asia and elsewhere, and some others in rats or other small mammals; Ebola and Marburg fevers of west and central Africa possibly in monkeys or bats (no one's quite sure). Human infection is, in a sense, accidental.

People are usually infected by contact with the animals' urine, or in a few cases – such as Crimean-Congo haemorrhagic fever (*see p.139*) and the similar Rift Valley (*see p.128*) and yellow fevers (*see p.123*) – the viruses are transferred to people by ticks or mosquitoes. However, the Crimean-Congo, Ebola, Lassa and Marburg viruses can also be caught by personal contact – but normally only with blood or other body fluids. ('Killer' outbreaks in bush hospitals have usually been due to a shortage of clean equipment, poor nursing techniques and a lack of simple disinfectants such as chlorine.)

Lassa fever is by far the most important, with an estimated 100 000 people infected and 3–5000 deaths each year in rural west Africa, from Senegal to Nigeria and Cameroon. It's usually a very general illness, often with a severe sore throat, and many sufferers recover without realising they've had it. But in some people it worsens, with diarrhoea, vomiting, bleeding and collapse of the circulatory system causing death. Lassa can be treated (and prevented in people who've had contact with sufferers) with the antiviral drug ribivirin.

There's no treatment for Ebola and Marburg virus. (The latter is sometimes called green monkey disease, because the first recognised cases were in laboratory workers in Marburg, Germany, who caught it from imported African green monkeys.) The diseases develop very quickly, after a few days' incubation, and up to 90 per cent of people with Ebola and 30 per cent of those with Marburg die within days. However, those who do survive (through no specific treatment other than good nursing) recover completely.

The hantaviruses are much more widespread around the world, including Asia (especially rural China) and parts of Europe and the Americas. Apart from a rare American form that affects the lungs, they have a much lower death rate than the African haemorrhagic fevers. One advantage of the bloodcurdling headlines the latter diseases generate is that you'll probably be well aware of any outbreak, and can change your plans if necessary.

ACCIDENTS, INJURIES AND EMERGENCIES

All the 'conditions' covered in this chapter can happen anywhere in the world, but statistics show that accidents – whether as serious as a car crash or as trivial as a cut finger – are more likely (often *much* more likely) when you're travelling than at home. Add to that the possibility of being far from any professional medical facilities (or certainly from facilities up to the standards you're used to) and it's clear that a working knowledge of first aid and what to do in an emergency is highly desirable.

As pointed out in the introduction to the section on first aid (*p. 172*), ideally one of your party, if you're travelling in a group, should attend an accredited first-aid course before you set off – particularly for 'adventure travel'. Whether or not you follow this advice, I hope you never need the information on these pages. But, if you do, the most important thing is not to panic – and a good grounding in what to do is the best antidote to panic I know. So please read what follows *before* you need it.

ACCIDENTS

Don't leave common sense behind when you venture far from home.

Now we get to the real nitty-gritty. You can forget – well, not literally, but on a strict risk-analysis basis – all those exotic tropical diseases that you may imagine lurk in faraway places, waiting to pounce on you. By far the most common cause of death or serious trouble among travellers – particularly in those below middle age – is an accident of one kind or another. The same is true on home turf, too. But unfamiliar surroundings, lower safety standards or habits in some places, and a carefree attitude that leads many travellers to take risks they wouldn't normally dream of taking mean that accident rates can be multiplied several times. Travel insurers say that almost a third of all the calls to their emergency helplines are to do with accidents, compared with less than one per cent for exotic infections. (Routine medical problems, often present before departure, are also well up the list; *see p.8*).

I'm not suggesting that you ignore the risks of those infections, or not know what to do if you confront them. Nor can you always avoid an accident. But a bit of common sense can greatly reduce your risk of becoming a victim.

On the road The UK has one of the lowest road-death rates in the world, in relation to both population and distance driven, yet well over 3000 people die on British roads each year. In some countries, the death rate per head or per mile driven is much higher – more than 20 times higher, for example, in Greece, Turkey, Korea and Sri Lanka; 40 times higher in Kenya and Egypt. So even if, like me, you're more afraid of an air crash (maybe due to the feeling of not being in control), it's the roads really you need to be wary of.

It's a bore to wear a seat belt or – if you're riding a motorbike or moped – a crash helmet, especially in the heat. But (without wanting to sound like a road-safety campaign) you do, I'm sure, know that it makes sense. The trouble is, laws in many countries don't insist on their use (or those laws aren't rigorously applied), so you may feel like a wimp if you're the only one around using them. Need I answer that? It's a bit more of a problem if a rental car or moped doesn't come with safety equipment, but personally I'd go elsewhere until I found one that was – and I'd make at least a quick check that the vehicle seemed roadworthy. (The same applies to taxis, although you may only have a few seconds to pretend to change your mind, and say that you don't want to hire it after all, if it looks really unsafe or if the driver seems to be drunk or drugged.) Make sure that a crash helmet fits properly.

And do you really know how to operate the vehicle properly? In some places, you may not need to show a driving licence (or you may get away with showing one for a different type of vehicle), but think about these statistics from a recent survey of motorbike and moped accidents overseas: Six out of ten were caused by the rider simply losing control, two involved colliding with an animal, and only two involved another road vehicle. Drink or drugs played a part in many of them.

On and in the water Much the same applies to wearing a life jacket, when canoeing, boating, water-skiing or doing other water sports, as to wearing a seat belt – but here you need to be doubly sure that the life jacket itself is up to the job of keeping you afloat. Remember, drowning is by far the main cause of death in or on the water.

Swimming accidents are common, so don't swim alone, or after dark, or when you've been drinking or taking recreational drugs. (Almost half of all drownings are alcohol-associated.) Ask the locals about safety issues, including dangerous currents, rocks or reefs, and dangerous creatures such as sharks (see p.95), sea snakes (see p.97), and stinging fish, jellyfish and other creatures (see p.99). But even if there are no specific hazards like these, you're at serious risk of spinal injury if you dive into shallow water or get 'dumped' by an unexpected big wave. The risks aren't quite so immediate or dramatic, but beware also of polluted water, and avoid swallowing any water in countries where hygiene standards aren't the best (see p.37).

There are special considerations if you want to go snorkelling or scuba diving. Both – but particularly the latter – need equipment up to international standards. You also need to be properly trained for scuba diving, so try to ensure that any school you attend, and its instructors, are fully accredited. What's more, you should be medically fit to dive. Some diving schools demand a medical certificate (perhaps including a chest X-ray), which you'd be well advised to get before leaving home. Others may only require you to sign a declaration that you are fit to dive.

Beware: If you sign knowing that you have a condition such as epilepsy, a heart or lung problem, or some others such as diabetes, you may unwittingly invalidate your travel health insurance – a potentially expensive mistake. Best get checked by a specialist doctor. You may also need to be cautious about diving if you're taking certain medications; check with your doctor.

In the wilds The same strictures about proper personal equipment and, in many circumstances, training apply to trekking and mountaineering. Here there are the special risks of high altitude (see p.66), the cold (see p.61) and perhaps wild animals (see p.93), but every year inexperienced people die or are seriously injured by falling from cliff paths or making other simple mistakes. The best insurance is to be or get fit before you set off, and to make sure that your group has an experienced guide who knows the terrain and also includes a properly equipped and trained first-aider. If possible, it should have a radio or satellite phone if venturing far from civilisation.

Everyday accidents But you don't need to go very far to run into accidental trouble. Backpackers' hostels and luxury hotels alike catch fire. People fall from balconies. Unsafe electrics give shocks. Gas heaters give off poisonous carbon monoxide. Cars hit people as they cross the road – particularly if they're looking the wrong way. Children, especially, may be so caught up in the excitement of travel that they're even more careless than usual. Look after them, keep your own wits about you, and have a safe trip.

BLOOD TRANSFUSIONS

These are always a risk, and in countries where there are no facilities for properly screening blood, the risk of getting a blood-borne disease such as HIV (*see p.146*) or hepatitis B (*see p.148*) can be thousands of times higher than in developed countries. As someone once quipped, the best blood transfusion is no blood transfusion. But sometimes a transfusion can be life-saving. The most common reason for needing one is a road accident – as a driver, passenger or pedestrian. But here are some points to note:–

→ If you're pregnant, or suffer from a blood-clotting disorder or any condition needing routine transfusions, you'd do well to avoid countries with poorly developed medical and transfusion facilities.

→ Know your blood group – A, B, AB or O *and* whether you're rhesus positive or negative – and note it clearly on the personal medical record on page 277. If you don't know it, why not donate blood (well before you set off), and find out that way rather than pay a fee?

→ Make sure your travel health insurance covers the delivery of safe blood within 24 hours. If not, and you're travelling to risky places, consider joining a blood-supply charity such as the Blood Care Foundation (**T** +44 [1403] 262652; **W** *www.bloodcare.org.uk*), which can supply safe blood anywhere in the world from regional depots.

→ Consider taking a sterile needle and transfusion kit, or 'AIDS kit', with you (*see p.16*). If you do, make sure it's used if/when needed.

→ A companion should make searching inquiries about blood safety and screening procedures, and the real necessity for a transfusion.

→ If safe blood isn't immediately available, it's often feasible to give a plasma-substitute or resuscitation fluid until safe blood can be couriered in. Some consulates hold stocks of such fluids.

FIRST AID

With major injuries, make sure that you don't do more harm than good.

You can't learn first aid properly from a book, but in some circumstances it can save someone's life. On the other hand, doing it incorrectly can make things worse. So if you're going on more than just a short tourist trip – and particularly if you're venturing far from medical facilities and emergency services – I'd strongly advise you or one of your group to attend an official first-aid course before you set out. The advice on these pages can then serve as reminders if you run into trouble. But bear in mind that recommended first-aid techniques sometimes change, so write notes in the margins if you're taught anything different from what's set out here.

Emergency – major trauma!

Faced with a serious accident or a major medical crisis, try not to panic, but, before rushing in to help, spend a few moments assessing the situation. Check if the person is wearing a medical alert bracelet or necklet that may give a clue as to why s/he is in trouble (eg, if s/he is diabetic or has epilepsy; *see below*). The first priority then is to **call – or send someone – for emergency assistance**. (See the following part of this book, pages 182–273, for emergency telephone numbers in popular destination countries.)

Make sure that you can intervene without yourself becoming a victim (eg, is the victim in contact with live electricity, in a gas-filled environment, threatened by a dangerous animal, etc?). If so, can you move him/her (or remove the source of danger) safely? If there's any risk of spinal (including neck) injury, or if the casualty complains of severe pain or paralysis anywhere, don't try to move him/her without expert help.

Assessment Once you and the casualty are safe from further harm, is s/he conscious? (Shout at or gently shake him/her if necessary.) If not, check...

→ *A for airway* Use your fingers to check the mouth and throat. If necessary, clear a swallowed tongue, dentures, vomit or other objects out of the way. (For choking, see below.)

→ *B for breathing* Is the victim's chest rising and falling? Can you feel his/her breath? If not, mouth-to-mouth resuscitation is needed (*see below*).

→ *C for circulation* Check for a heartbeat or pulse – easiest at the side of the neck (just below the jaw), in the groin, or on the left-hand side of the chest. (Practise on yourself or a companion.) If there's no pulse, you'll need to give cardiac massage as well. This is urgent, but also check...

→ *Major bleeding* Cardiac massage won't do much good if the casualty is losing a lot of blood, so get a companion to act on this (*see below*) while you try to resuscitate him/her.

Recovery position If you're satisfied that an unconscious victim's airway, breathing and pulse are OK, and that s/he can be moved, place him/her in this position to prevent choking if s/he vomits: Lay him/her on one side, head resting on the lower hand and lower leg straight; bend the upper leg and arm forward, and rest them on the ground to prevent him/her rolling right over.

Resuscitation This applies to drowning as well as to other cases where the pulse and/or breathing have stopped. If cardiopulmonary resuscitation (CPR – both heart massage *and* mouth-to-mouth resuscitation) is needed, it can be done by one person, but two are better if available. The aim is to keep blood and oxygen flowing to the brain (to stop brain damage or death) until professional help comes. **Never practise for real on someone whose heart and breathing are working normally.**

→ Lie the casualty on the ground on his/her back and gently tilt the head back to ensure a free airway. Kneel beside him/her.

→ *Mouth-to-mouth resuscitation* Use one hand to pinch the casualty's nose closed, the other to hold his/her mouth open. Take a deep breath, place your lips over the casualty's mouth, and breathe steadily into the mouth, counting slowly to three; watch for his/her chest to rise. Let go, counting to three again; the chest should fall. Repeat, aiming for about ten complete (in and out) breaths per minute. If a victim of near-drowning starts to bring up water, hold his/her head to one side to allow it to drain out.

With a child, be much more gentle – use puffs rather than full breaths.

→ *Cardiac massage* Place the heel of one of your hands on the middle of the casualty's breastbone, cover this hand with the heel of your second hand, and lock them together with your fingers. (For a baby just use two or three fingers, for a child only one hand.) With your arms straight and vertical, and your shoulders directly above the casualty, press straight down on the chest, enough to depress it about 4–5cm (1½–2in) – less for a child. Then release the pressure without removing your hands. (Don't press too hard, or you may break a rib; don't press too weakly, or you'll do no good.) Aim to press down once per second.

Count 15 cardiac compressions, then give two mouth-to-mouth breaths – each complete cycle about three times per minute. Check the victim's pulse every minute. Stop cardiac massage as soon as the heart restarts, but if not keep going until professional help comes; don't stop after just a few minutes, as near-drowning victims in particular may recover after a considerable time.

Once breathing and heartbeat are re-established, place the casualty in the recovery position (*see above*) until help arrives.

Choking

A slap on the back may be enough to dislodge something blocking a conscious person's windpipe and make him/her cough it up. If not, use the Heimlich manoeuvre: Stand behind the person (or kneel behind a child), with your arms around him/her under the arms and your hands linked to form a fist in the solar plexus, just below his/her ribs. Pull sharply upwards and towards you up to five times. If this doesn't work, try back-slapping again before repeating the Heimlich manoeuvre.

If the victim is unconscious, but believed choked, lay him/her on his/her back on the ground, and use your fist to apply repeated pressure as above, while straddling the victim. Or (particularly with a child and/or if s/he has choked on vomit) try holding the victim upside-down while slapping his/her back.

Major bleeding

Losing a lot of blood is of course life-threatening, and severe bleeding needs to be stopped urgently – but don't neglect resuscitation (*see above*) and do **call for professional help**. Wash your hands if possible, and put on surgical gloves if available (*see box, p.178*).

→ If the wound is clogged with flowing blood, quickly but gently wash or wipe it away so that you can see the source of bleeding. (*Note*: A crush wound very likely won't bleed a great deal because the blood vessels are sealed; in this case don't disturb it, but cover it with a clean cloth or dressing.)

→ If bright red blood spurts out in time with the pulse, an artery has been pierced. Apply immediate pressure (preferably with a clean cloth), pressing hard on the source of bleeding.

→ With more general or steady bleeding, similarly apply direct pressure via a cloth. Try to hold the edges of a gash together while you apply pressure. In a very big wound, you may have to apply pressure *within* the opening.

→ If there's something (eg, a nail or piece of glass) protruding from the wound, don't try to remove it unless it's very small. Use cloths to form a pad *around* the wound, and press on that, not directly on the object.

→ You'll need to press hard for at least ten minutes. If the cloth gets soaked through, apply another one on top; don't look to see if the bleeding has stopped. Once bleeding has slowed, you can apply a firm bandage.

→ If the bleeding is too fast to stop by direct pressure, press with your fingers or thumbs on the appropriate 'pressure point' between the site of the injury and the victim's heart, where a major artery feeding the wound passes over a bone – eg, the femoral artery in the groin for a leg wound, or the brachial artery under the biceps for a lower arm wound. *Don't* apply a tourniquet – it can make bleeding worse in the long term and can cause serious tissue damage.

→ Be alert to signs of shock (*see below*) and act accordingly.

Shock

Any severe loss of blood or other body fluids, or anything (such as a heart attack) that severely reduces blood circulation, can cause clinical shock. And that, if not treated promptly, can in turn lead to the failure of vital organs (heart, brain, etc) and death. The symptoms include...

→ A weak, rapid pulse.
→ A feeling of faintness.
→ Colourless or bluish skin, which is cold and clammy.
→ Rapid, shallow breathing; possibly breathlessness.
→ Possibly nausea and vomiting.

Anyone with shock needs urgent medical treatment. Meanwhile, treat any obvious cause (such as major bleeding; *see above*) and...

→ Subject to any injuries, etc, lay the casualty down comfortably and (unless a leg is broken) raise the legs slightly above the rest of the body.

→ Loosen any clothing around the neck and upper body, and keep the victim warm with a blanket or clothing.

→ Don't let him/her eat or drink anything, *except in the case of a person with diabetes who goes into hypoglycaemic shock*, who should be given a sugar lump, sweet food or a sweet drink immediately.

→ *Important*: A person with diabetes may go into a 'diabetic coma' – known medically as diabetic ketoacidosis – if s/he has too *little* insulin and/or too *much* sugar in his/her blood; in this case giving sugar will only make the condition worse – an insulin injection is needed instead. The symptoms of ketoacidosis include lethargy, nausea and/or vomiting, passing no urine, abdominal pain, confusion, and a fruity smell of acetone – like nail-varnish remover – on the breath. Most diabetics wear a medical alert tag or bracelet, and many carry an insulin applicator.

→ Stay with the victim; be ready to give resuscitation (*see above*) if needed.

Anaphylactic shock This resembles shock but is actually an allergic reaction to a sting, food or drug (eg, a vaccine injection). It usually comes on within seconds or a few minutes. Symptoms include puffy skin, swelling of the tongue and face, and itchiness; breathing may become laboured and wheezy, and the victim may become unconscious.

The remedy is an injection of adrenaline (epinephrine; *see p.82*); someone who's prone to such reactions may carry a self-injection kit, which should be used straight away. Otherwise, **call for medical help**, keep the victim warm and comfortable, and be ready to give resuscitation (*see above*) if necessary.

Convulsions (fits)

Except where there's a head injury (*see below*), fits in older children and adults are usually caused by epilepsy – abnormal electrical discharges in the brain – which may be signalled on a medical alert bracelet or necklet. But in young children (under-fives) and occasionally in adults, they may result from a high fever – over 40°C (104°F).

In either case, catch and lay the victim down carefully if s/he has not already fallen, and remove any nearby hard objects that s/he may hit. Then…

→ Loosen any tight clothing, especially around the neck, if possible. Use a cushion or folded clothing to pad the victim's head.

→ Don't put your finger *or anything else* into his/her mouth. If s/he bites his/her tongue, it will probably happen at the very beginning.

→ Place him/her in the recovery position (*see above*) – after the fit has subsided in the case of an adult. The victim will probably fall asleep.

→ In the case of a person (especially a child) with a high fever, remove clothing or bedclothes after the fit has subsided, and sponge down with tepid water – but don't let him/her get chilled.

→ Get medical help.

Fainting

This can be due to excess heat (*see p.58*) or various other causes. If someone faints, lie him/her down, with feet raised above the rest of the body. If unconsciousness is only partial, s/he can be sat down with head between knees. Check for a pulse or heartbeat; if there is none and the person is completely unconscious, start cardiopulmonary resuscitation (*see above*).

Head injury

Any head injury – including a blow to the head that may not leave any visible trace – is potentially serious, and **needs urgent medical checking and treatment**. Signs of trouble may show immediately, but can take up to 24 hours to develop. These are the main warning signs (apart from obvious damage) to look out for:–

→ Unconsciousness (immediate or delayed), especially if over a minute.
→ Confusion, drowsiness or abnormal behaviour (especially after a delay).
→ Slurred speech (which combined with above may resemble drunkenness).
→ Double vision; persistent headache (especially worsening); memory loss.
→ Nausea and/or vomiting (especially if prolonged).
→ Weakness or numbness.
→ Convulsions (fits).
→ Dilated or unequal pupils.
→ Laboured breathing; abnormally slow pulse.

There may be a fever, but if this is combined with unconsciousness, it may indicate a serious medical condition such as malaria (*see p.107*) or meningitis (*see p.163*) rather than an injury. In either case, **get a doctor fast**.

Spine or neck injury

This is possible in anyone who has fallen from a height, or who has fallen awkwardly. The victim may be unable to move, or may have numbness or pins and needles. **Call for help urgently, but don't try to move the victim unless s/he is in immediate danger where s/he is**. Safe movement involves keeping the head, neck and back stictly aligned and stretched, with special or makeshift splints; otherwise further (permanent) paralysis and even death may result. *Leave it to the professionals if at all possible!*

Broken bones and sprains

These may be obvious, but there may only be swelling and pain (although the victim may have heard or felt a break). Don't move the victim unless it's essential, but **call for medical help** and keep him/her comfortable until it arrives. Particularly in the case of a fracture, there may be a lot of internal bleeding, so watch out for the signs of shock (*see above*) and be ready to give treatment if necessary. If the broken end of the bone protrudes through the skin – ie, in a 'compound' fracture – keep it covered with a clean dressing to reduce the risk of infection. Don't give pankillers, as the victim may need to be given an anaesthetic when s/he reaches hospital.

If it's essential to move the casualty, avoid as much as possible moving the break itself – it'll cause a lot of pain. Immobilise a broken leg by strapping it – with plenty of cushioning – to the other leg; immobilise a broken arm or broken collarbone by bandaging the arm to the body. With any bandaging (or a plaster put on later), watch out for numbness or extremities turning blue due to the dressing being too tight and restricting blood flow.

Sprained ankles or wrists, or a strained muscle or joint, are best treated with cold (ice-cold if possible) compresses, firm (but not too firm) bandaging and rest, with the affected limb raised above the rest of the body. An anti-inflammatory painkiller such as aspirin or ibuprofen (eg, 'Brufen', 'Motrin' or 'Nurofen') is best for relieving the discomfort.

Cuts and grazes

The first priority, if or when severe bleeding has stopped (*see above*), is to clean the wound. In humid, tropical and unhygienic conditions in particular, even quite small cuts can become septic. Use plenty of clean water from a tap or jug to flush any dirt out of a wound; water pretreated with a sterilising agent such as iodine or chlorine (*see pp.32–33*) is best if available, but non-sterile water is much better than no water (and don't delay while you sterilise). If there's any mud, gravel, glass, bits of plants or any other foreign body, remove it using your clean fingers or a clean wet cloth (but don't try to remove the cause of a deep, severely bleeding wound; *see above*). Don't try to wash away blood clots, or heavy bleeding may start up again.

Once you have cleared away all visible dirt, treat the wound with antiseptic. Use whatever you have available; povidone-iodine solution (eg, 'Betadine' or 'Videne') 'painted' on (or a dry version sprayed from an aerosol can) is one of the best, or use diluted tincture of iodine. In developing countries, potassium permanganate is often the cheapest and most easily available antiseptic; dissolve enough crystals in clean water to turn it deep pink. If none of these is available, use a proprietary antiseptic cream.

Then dress the wound with a sticky plaster or bandage; if it's still bleeding or weeping, it's best to use a 'non-adherent' dressing with the perforated plastic side next to the skin. And seek professional care unless the cut is very minor. (Note that in tropical conditions it's usually best to leave even quite large cuts unstitched at first, as they are less likely to go septic.)

RISKS FROM BLOOD CONTACT

If you have cut or broken skin, you can become infected with the HIV virus (*see p.146*) or hepatitis B if you come into direct contact with an infected casualty's blood. (Remember that you can't tell by looking whether someone *is* infected.) So wear sugical gloves if possible; if none are available, improvise with plastic food bags if you have any.

For the dangers of tetanus, see page 166; for information on keeping skin healthy (including the dangers of minor cuts in the tropics and the treatment of friction blisters), see page 153.

Burns

Act as quickly as possible, removing the source of heat from the victim, or vice-versa. Put out any flames. Take particular care in the case of electrical burns. Then...

→ If possible, douse the burn with plenty of cold water.

→ Cut away any loose clothing or other material, but don't try to remove any cloth that's sticking to the burn.

→ Don't apply any cream, lotion or antiseptic,

→ Don't break or pierce any blisters.

→ Apply a dry dressing and bandage (or use sticky plaster for small burns). Give aspirin or ibuprofen (eg, 'Brufen', 'Motrin' or 'Nurofen') to reduce pain, and if possible raise the burned part above the rest of the body.

→ Watch for signs of shock (see above), and act accordingly. With deep or extensive burns, the main short-term danger is from loss of body fluids, so give water (preferably with rehydration salts added; see p.40) to sip.

→ **Get professional help** except in the case of the smallest burns. Severe burns need skilled attention and possibly evacuation to advanced hospital facilities back home or in a major city.

Bites

For the treatment of bites and stings – including those by mosquitoes and other insects, spiders and scorpions, larger animals, snakes, and sea creatures – see pages 72–105. For the dangers of rabies, see page 139.

SEXUAL EMERGENCIES

You'll need to make cool decisions at a time of severe emotional stress.

I hope it doesn't sound callous to say that I can't deal adequately here with the psychological and legal aspects of sex crimes and accidents. If you suffer a sexual assault or other emergency, you need on-the-spot help, perhaps first from trusted companions, then from sympathetic medical help.

So my first advice would be: Don't pretend that nothing has happened; confide in the best friend you have among your travelling companions. Failing that, contact your consulate (see pp.182–273) as soon as possible; staff there should be able to give advice and put you in touch with appropriate counselling, medical, legal and other assistance.

Rape

Quite apart from psychological counselling, women need practical medical help to deal with possible infection by sexually-transmitted diseases (STDs) and possible pregnancy (*see below*) after an assault. (Everything I say applies to men, too, although they are less frequently assaulted sexually.)

At the very least you should have an expert check-up. If you haven't already had a hepatitis B vaccination (*see p.148*), you may need one now. Some doctors are reluctant to give prophylactic (protective) antibiotics against other STDs without confirmation of infection, but others agree that it makes good sense; a combination of three or more injections and/or tablets may be needed. As discussed on page 147, HIV/AIDS prophylaxis is even more controversial; a test isn't possible for three months, but prophylactic treatment needs to start in a matter of hours. I suggest you should discuss the options with the most knowledgeable expert you can find (perhaps in a university hospital). Even if you don't have prophylaxis, be sure to get an HIV test after three months.

Pregnancy

If you are (or may be) pregnant but don't want to be – whether as the result of rape, a split condom or other contraceptive failure, or simply unprotected sex – your options (depending on your personal beliefs) are much wider if you considered the possibility before you left home. As well as regular contraception (*see p.14*) and condoms (as protection from HIV and other STDs), I'd advise women travellers to take one or two packs of emergency contraceptve pills (eg, 'Levonelle') with them. (In Britain, women over 16 can buy such treatments over the counter without presciption, but elsewhere you should check with a doctor, pharmacist or family-planning clinic.)

Commonly called the 'morning-after Pill', it in fact consists of two tablets, the first of which can be taken *up to 72 hours* after unprotected sex. In rare cases it causes vomiting; if this happens within three hours, you should take a second pill. In either case, you need to take a follow-up dose 12 hours later. (That's why it's best to take two double-dose packs, not just one, on your travels.) Another option – if you're somewhere that has good family-planning facilities – is to have a coil, or intrauterine device (IUD), inserted. This will prevent pregnancy if inserted up to five days after unprotected sex – or even slightly later, depending on how long it is since you had your last period.

If neither of these options is possible, or if you've gone past the point where they can be used, and you decide that the only way out is an abortion, then you face formidable obstacles – legal and/or practical – in many parts of the world. The most recent UN survey shows enormous variations in countries' attitudes to termination of pregnancy; some countries don't permit abortion in cases of rape or, in a few cases, even to save the mother's life. At the opposite extreme are countries where abortion is permitted on request, without specific reasons.

Where it's legal to get an abortion*		
Africa and the western Indian Ocean	Botswana (1); Cape Verde; Gambia (1); Ghana (1); Kenya (1); Morocco (1); Namibia (1); Nigeria (south only; 1);	Réunion; Seychelles (1); South Africa; Tanzania (1) ; Tunisia; Zambia (2).
The Americas and Caribbean	Argentina (1); Bahamas (1); Barbados (2); Belize (2); Canada; Costa Rica (1); Cuba; Ecuador (1); Grenada (1); Guadeloupe; Guyana; Jamaica (1); Martinique;	Mexico (varies with state; not Mexico City); Peru (1); Puerto Rico; St Lucia (1); St Vincent (2); Trinidad and Tobago (1); United States.
Asia	Bahrain; Cambodia; China; Hong Kong (1); India (2); Israel (1); Japan (2); Kuwait (1); Malaysia (1);	Pakistan (1); Qatar (1); Singapore; South Korea; Taiwan (2); Thailand (1); Vietnam.
Australasia and the Pacific	Australia (varies with state); Cook Is (1); Fiji (1); Hawaii; New Zealand (1); Papua New	Guinea (1); Samoa (1); Tahiti; Vanuatu (1).
Europe	All countries except Ireland and Malta. Northern Ireland, Poland, Portugal, Spain and Switzerland in category (1);	Cyprus, Finland, Iceland, Luxembourg and Great Britain in category (2). Others: any reason.

*On grounds other than preserving the life or physical health of the woman. Unless otherwise stated, abortion is allowed for any reason; otherwise, allowed (1) only on mental health or (2) also on socioeconomic grounds. In countries not listed, it may be allowed to preserve the mother's physical health and/or in cases of rape and/or foetal impairment. I have only included countries covered in Part three of this book (pp. 182–273).
Source: UN data published 2002.

Your consulate or a sexual health charity may be able to advise on the local position (including time limits, which also vary widely). But the table (*above*) lists popular destination countries that have the least restrictive policies at the time of writing. Of course, even if you can legally get an abortion, it may be very difficult or expensive – or both – to find modern facilities giving skilled and safe care. You may find that your only realistic option is to change your travel plans and fly to a developed country where you can get a safe abortion. (Note that, at the time of writing, the so-called 'abortion pill' – mifepristone or RU 486; also sold as 'Mifegyne' – which induces an abortion up to the ninth week of pregnancy, is cleared for use in only a few countries.)

AROUND THE WORLD

The risks to health and where to go for help in more than 100 popular destinations

This part of the book takes you on a world tour of major travel destinations. It explains the vaccinations and other precautions it's advisable to take in each region, points out other health hazards you may face, and then lists important contact details for each country covered.

Getting help

If you're ill overseas, your first priority is to find reliable medical help, preferably English-speaking. That's not usually too difficult in a developed English-speaking country, but it's much more so if there's a language barrier or if you're in the developing world. You might ask the manager of your hotel or hostel for a recommendation, but there have been occasional cases of hotels receiving 'commission' – you might call it a bribe – from doctors, clinics or hospitals. If your travel insurance company has a proper emergency assistance service rather than just a claims hotline (*see pp.13–14*) – and especially if it has a local branch or agent – that's probably your best bet, as it will usually sort out payment too. (Many doctors and hospitals around the world expect cash on the nail; not even a credit card will do.)

Next stop for unbiased information is your consulate, one of whose jobs is to help its own citizens. (Embassies and high commissions deal with governments, consulates with the hoi-polloi like you and me. If an address in the listings indicates an embassy or high commission, you'll have to ask for the consular section.) If your country doesn't have its own consulate, a 'friendly' consulate – eg, that of another Commonwealth country – may help, but may not be obliged to do so. (Australia and Canada, for example, do usually help each other's people in countries where only one of them has a consulate.) It's important to realise that consulates can offer only limited help; they can advise, help with messages to relatives at home, arrange the transfer of funds and so on, but they can't usually lend you money directly. If you stay a long time in a country, or if the security situation is volatile, it's worth registering your details with your consulate, in case of an emergency.

In the country listings, I've generally included all British consulates – both the main one (often called the consulate-general), and in most cases subsidiary offices and also part-time representatives (honorary consuls), who can usually provide only limited services. I've also listed the main Australian, Canadian, New Zealand, South African and US consulates (usually in the capital, if there are several). Many consulates have special numbers *for use in genuine emergencies only* out of hours. In other cases, the phone lines are manned 24/7, or you get a recorded message telling you where to call for emergency help. Where possible, local website addresses are given, for up-to-date information; some include on-line lists of doctors and hospitals.

If all else fails, there are emergency numbers you can call to reach a duty officer back home in your foreign ministry or equivalent – but this is unlikely to get such quick results or help as contacting your local consulate. The numbers for Britain and other major English-speaking countries are:–

→ *UK* **T** +44 (20) 7008 1500
→ *Australia* **T** +61 (2) 6261 3305; within Australia: 1 300 555135 (free)
→ *Canada* **T** +1 (613) 996 8885 (call collect)
→ *New Zealand* **T** +64 (4) 439 8000
→ *South Africa* **T** +27 (12) 351 1000
→ *USA* **T** +1 (202) 647 5225; +1 (202) 647 4000 (emergencies out of hours)

I've also usually listed the local health department or ministry – it may or may not be able to offer advice, but you'll certainly need it for information on any reciprocal health-care agreements – and a number of clinics and hospitals in many cases. **Don't take these listings as recommendations or endorsements**; the publishers and I can't take any responsibility for them. They're simply listed so that you have some point of contact in an emergency.

All telephone numbers are given in the international format, including the country's international access code. If you're calling from a fixed line within the country, substitute the access code for a local or long-distance call as appropriate (often 0 or 1). Finally, all the numbers have been carefully checked, but numbers do go out of date. If you find any incorrect or outdated information, please email *travelhealth@virgin-books.co.uk*.

Country by country

Regional chapters follow, in alphabetical order of the continents:–

NORTH AFRICA

Egypt, Morocco, Tunisia

Many reasons bring travellers to the northern edge of Africa (or the southern edge of the Mediterranean, whichever perspective you prefer): natural spectacles – the Nile, the coasts and seas, the Sahara – remains of ancient civilisations, a distinctive culture. In health terms, the region is a watershed, too: The vastness of the Sahara insulates it from many of the worst health hazards of Africa – the continent that probably presents the greatest health challenges to visitors from developed countries. And yet it's emphatically part of the developing world, often closer in spirit and practical facilities to the Middle East (*see p.226*) and other parts of Africa than to southern Europe just across the sea. There are good tourist facilities here and there, but the medical infrastructure – particularly for complex or emergency needs – doesn't usually match up. The best hospitals are probably in the major cities of Morocco. You'll need full medical insurance, including evacuation cover.

Everyday precautions Many visitors to north Africa – probably the majority – get travellers' diarrhoea (including sometimes giardiasis and, in Egypt, possibly cholera; *see pp.34–44*). Hepatitis A (*see p.51*) and brucellosis (*see p.52*) are also common; and typhoid (*see p.46*), especially in rural areas, and intestinal worms (*see p.49*) are a risk. So always **be very careful about what you eat and drink** throughout the region, but particularly in Egypt. Only in parts of Tunisia and perhaps major cities and resorts in Morocco is tap water safe to drink or make ice; it's not regarded as safe anywhere in Egypt, and must be boiled or otherwise treated (*see p.32*). But, wherever you are, you'd be well advised to play safe with reliable brands of bottled water for drinking and cleaning your teeth, and avoid putting ice in drinks. Use only pasteurised or sterilised milk and dairy products (or boil milk).

The sun is very strong, especially in summer, and you need to treat it with great respect; use a high-factor sunscreen (*see p.56*), wear a hat and sunbathe for only short periods at first. However, the Atlas Mountains and the Sahara can get very cold at night in winter. Sandstorms – mainly between March and June – can make it unpleasant to go outdoors and sometimes dangerous on roads, whether driving or on foot.

Most beaches are reasonably clean, but take care not to swallow seawater, especially near cities and towns. Avoid swimming in the Nile, in canals, or in any other freshwater pools or streams (other than well-chlorinated swimming pools), particularly in Egypt; they're likely to be infected with bilharzia (schistosomiasis; *see p.102*), and sometimes hepatitis and other infections. Jiggers (chigoes or sand-fleas; *see p.80*) are common, especially in Morocco and Tunisia, and may burrow into your feet if you walk barefoot on sandy soil. There are venomous scorpions and snakes (*see pp.84 & 97*) in rural areas, and the Nile crocodile is notoriously dangerous (*see p.95*).

Road accidents are a real risk to locals and visitors alike. Tunisia is probably the safest of the three countries, but Egypt has almost 50 times as many road deaths in relation to vehicle distance travelled as the UK.

Sex safety In one way north Africa is happily very different from most countries south of the Sahara: Adult rates of HIV infection are much lower – generally around the 0.1 per cent mark, which is similar to the level in Britain. As elsewhere, however, sex workers have a higher rate of infection, so it may be only a matter of time before the region catches up. A relatively high infection rate for other STDs (*see p.149*) is another danger signal. And the same low infection rate doesn't apply to heptatitis B (*see p.148*), which is also passed on by both unprotected sex and direct blood contact (including transfusions). So **practise safer sex** (*see p.145*) and consider having a hepatitis B vaccination (*see below*) before you go. Egypt demands an HIV test if you want a permit to work there.

Vaccinations etc There's no yellow fever (*see p.123*) in north Africa, but both Egypt and Tunisia demand a vaccination certificate for travellers over 12 months old arriving from 'infected' areas – almost all of sub-Saharan Africa as far south as Zambia, plus the Americas from Panama to Brazil. Egypt has particularly strict regulations: If you arrive from one of these areas without a certificate, you're liable to be detained at the airport until you depart.

There's a very low risk of malaria in summer in small areas of Egypt (around the El Faiyum oasis) and Morocco (Khourgiba province). The official WHO advice is that there's no need to bother with preventive pills, but if you're planning to spend a long time in either of these areas and are cautious, consult a travel doctor about taking chloroquine (*see p.115*). In any case, take precautions to prevent mosquito bites (*see p.75*).

Other vaccinations – or boosters if you were vaccinated some years ago – that you should have (or at least consider) before going to north Africa are:–

→ *Tetanus* and *diphtheria* (*see p.166*) – usually given together.
→ *Hepatitis A* (*see p.51*).
→ *Hepatitis B* (*see p.148*), especially if you might have sexual or blood contact with local people, or if you plan to stay for more than a short holiday or plan to travel extensively in the region by road.
→ *Typhoid* (*see p.46*), especially if you plan to visit rural areas.
→ *Cholera* (*see p.44*) – discuss getting one of the new vaccines if you are visiting Egypt, especially for an extended stay.
→ *Rabies* (*see p.139*), especially if you may have contact with animals.
→ *Polio* (*see p.165*), which still occurs – especially in Egypt – despite successes in eradicating the disease elsewhere.
→ *Tuberculosis* (*see p.160*), especially if you plan to stay with local people in crowded accommodation for extended periods in Morocco or Egypt.
→ *Flu* and possibly *pneumococcal disease* for older travellers and others who usually have a flu jab, especially for winter trips.

Other medical risks Apart from those mentioned above and common illnesses that occur everywhere, other diseases you may encounter in north Africa include dengue fever (see p.125), especially in Egypt, leishmaniasis (see p.118) and various types of filariasis (see p.131), especially in the Nile Delta region. Rarely and sporadically, there are outbreaks of such diseases as Rift Valley fever (see p.128), West Nile fever (see p.134), typhus (see p.137) and plague (see p.130). Blood supplies may not be safe for transfusion (see p.172)

EGYPT

Medical facilities OK for routine, non-emergency matters, but limited facilities for serious problems, especially outside Cairo. Evacuation (to Europe or Israel) may be needed.

Emergencies
Police **T** 112
Tourist police **T** 126
Ambulance **T** 123

Health ministry/dept
Magles Al Shaab, St Kasr Aaini, Cairo
T +20 (2) 355 7046; +20 (2) 354 1507

British consulates
British Embassy, 7 Ahmed Ragheb St, Garden City, Cairo
T +20 (2) 794 0850; +20 (2) 794 3065
W www.britishembassy.org.eg
Alexandria **T** +20 (3) 546 7001
Luxor **T** +20 (95) 382838; +20 (95) 374814
Suez **T** +20 (62) 334102

Other consulates
Australian **T** +20 (2) 575 0444

Canadian **T** +20 (2) 794 3110

New Zealand **T** +20 (2) 574 9360;
+20 (2) 579 9544

South African **T** +20 (2) 571 7234

US **T** +20 (2) 797 3300; +20 (2) 797 2301
W www. usembassy.egnet.net

Hospitals/clinics
Anglo-American Hospital, Zohoreya St (beside Cairo Tower), Zamalek, Cairo
T +20 (2) 340 6162; +20 (2) 341 8630

As Salam International Hospital, Corniche el-Nil, Maadi, Cairo
T +20 (2) 363 8050

Alexandria International Hospital
T +20 (3) 422 5017; +20 (3) 424 2454

Aswan General Hospital
T +20 (97) 322250

Luxor General Hospital
T +20 (95) 387192; +20 (95) 387193

MOROCCO

Medical care OK, particularly in Rabat and Casablanca, but not necessarily for serious problems that need specialised treatment. Facilities very limited or non-existent in mountain and desert areas.

Emergencies
Police **T** 19
Ambulance **T** 15

Health ministry/dept
335 Avenue Mohommed V, Rabat
T +212 (37) 761121

British consulates
British Embassy, 17 Boulevard de la Tour Hassan, Rabat
T +212 (37) 238600; +212 (61) 164335 (emergencies)
W www.britain.org.ma
Agadir **T** +212 (48) 823401; +212 (48) 823402; +212 (61) 164857 (emergencies)
Casablanca **T** +212 (22) 437700;
+212 (61) 13475 (emergencies)
Marrakech **T** +212 (44) 435095;
+212 (44) 436078; +212 (61) 148444 (emergencies)
Tangier **T** +212 (39) 941557

Other consulates
Canadian **T** +212 (37) 687400

South African **T** +212 (37) 706760;
+212 (37) 689160

US **T** +212 (37) 762265
W www.usembassy-morocco.org.ma

Hospitals/clinics
Hôpital Ibnou-sina (Avicenne), Rabat
T +212 (37) 772871; +212 (37 744275

Hôpital Hassan II, Agadir
T +212 (48) 846686; +212 (48) 841477

Centre Hospitalier Universitaire, Rue
des Hôpiteaux, Casablanca
T +212 (22) 224109

Hôpital Ibn Tofail, Menara, Marrakech
T +212 (44) 448011; +212 (44) 448585

Hôpital Al Kobbi, Tangier
T +212 (39) 934242; +212 (39) 932444

TUNISIA

Basic, only non-specialist medical
care available; immediate cash
payment required. Poor ambulance
service outside urban areas. Take
any prescription medicines needed.

Emergencies
Police **T** 197
Ambulance **T** 190; +216 (71) 341250

Health ministry/dept
Bab Saadoun, 1006 Tunis
T +216 (71) 560545

British consulates
British Embassy, 5 Place de la Victoire,
Tunis 1000
T +216 (71) 846184
W *www.british-emb.intl.tn*
Sfax **T** +216 (74) 223971

Other consulates
Canadian **T** +216 (71) 796577
W *www.dfait-maeci.gc.ca/tunisia*

South African **T** +216 (71) 803011
W *www.southafrica.intl.tn*

US **T** +216 (71) 107000
W *http://usembassy.state.gov/posts/ts1/*
wwwhcons.html

Hospitals/clinics
Polyclinique Taoufik, El Menzah, Tunis
T +26 (71) 848211

Polyclinique El Yesmine, 61 Ave.
Mohamed Badra, Houmt Souk, Djerba
T +26 (75) 652032; +26 (75) 652054

WEST AFRICA

Cape Verde, Gambia, Ghana, Nigeria, Senegal

There are, of course, many more countries than this in west Africa, but these
are probably the ones most visited by travellers from developed countries –
whether for tourism or to visit relations and family roots. Travel health risks
tend to vary less between individual countries than between the humid jungle
and coastal regions and the semidesert inland and to the north.

There are reasonable tourist facilities in a number of areas, particularly in
parts of the Cape Verde islands, Gambia, Ghana and Senegal, but the medical
infrastructure doesn't generally match up. The best care is probably to be
had in private clinics in Senegal's capital, Dakar; there are well-trained
doctors in other countries, especially Nigeria, but hospitals are often poorly
equipped and maintained. You may not be able to get prescription drugs or
even antimalarials in some places, so it's advisable to take anything you
know you'll need with you. You should certainly have full travel medical
insurance, including cover for emergency evacuation (to Dakar or Europe).

Everyday precautions Travellers' diarrhoea (*see p.34*), including giardiasis
(*see p.43*), is common throughout west Africa, and there's a risk of intestinal

worms (*see p.49*) and hepatitis A (*see p.51*). There have also been cholera outbreaks (*see p.44*) and typhoid (*see p.46*) – the latter particularly in rural areas. So **take great care with what and where you eat and drink**. Nowhere, except in Cape Verde and possibly Dakar, Senegal, is tap water safe to drink. All water elsewhere should be boiled or otherwise treated (*see p.32*), or use reliable bottled water in sealed bottles – preferably imported brands – for drinking, making ice and cleaning your teeth. Use only pasteurised or preferably sterilised milk and dairy products (or boil milk).

All these countries are in the tropics, and the sun is very strong. You need to treat it with great respect: Use a high-factor sunscreen (*see p.56*), wear a hat and sunbathe for only short periods at first. Humidity is also very high for all or most of the year in most of west Africa except in Cape Verde and the semidesert areas, and you should beware of heat exhaustion (*see p.58*), especially when you first arrive. Keep up your (safe) fluid intake, and don't over-exert yourself. In most of the region, skin infections (*see p.155*) are very common, especially in the rainy season(s), so make sure you clean and sterilise – and keep clean – any cuts, scratches, bites and so on.

Sea pollution varies from place to place, but a UN survey recently found that west Africa in general has some of the world's most sewage-polluted waters. Unless you can be sure that a particular area is safe, I'd suggest you be very cautious about swimming in the sea here, except in Cape Verde. There are dangerous waves and strong currents in some areas, too, so get reliable local advice on these and pollution. Bilharzia (schistosomiasis; *see p.102*) is common in fresh water throughout west Africa, but especially (out of the countries covered here) in parts of Nigeria, in Lake Volta and in the Diama reservoir in northern Senegal; so avoid swimming in lakes and rivers. (Well-chlorinated swimming pools are safe.) There are venomous scorpions and snakes (*see pp.84 & 97*), and road accidents are a real risk (*see p.170*).

Sex safety The sub-Saharan HIV/AIDs epidemic (*see p.146*) hasn't hit west Africa as hard as some areas farther south and east, but in all these countries except Senegal and probably Cape Verde (for which there aren't any official figures) at least 1 per cent of adults are HIV-positive. The figures are worst in Nigeria, where almost 6 per cent – 1 in every 17 people – have the virus, and in some parts of the country it's as high as 16½ per cent; up to 70 per cent of sex workers are HIV-positive in some places. There aren't precise numbers, but hepatitis B is also widespread in west Africa. Both viruses are mainly passed on by heterosexual contact, although infected blood and mother–child transmission are also significant. (More women than men have HIV here.) So it's vital to **always practise safer sex** (*see p.145*) and consider getting a hepatitis B vaccination (*see below*).

Vaccinations etc West Africa has many serious diseases that can be prevented if you're vaccinated. These are the vaccinations you should or must have – or at least consider – and precautions you should take:–

Cholera Vaccination isn't an international requirement any longer, and cholera in travellers is usually quite easily treated (*see p.44*), but some border posts may still demand a certificate of vaccination. The old vaccine isn't very effective, but newer ones are much more so; it's worth asking a travel clinic about these if you plan to travel extensively or an outbreak is in progress.

Hepatitis A All travellers to west Africa – indeed, any part of Africa – should have this vaccination (*see p.51*).

Hepatitis B Probably not necessary for short-term visitors, but if there's any chance of blood or sexual contact with local people, if you plan to take part in any hazardous activities that could cause injury, or if you're staying for an extended period (and so are more likely to need surgical or dental treatment, or even a blood transfusion), you should get vaccinated. (Blood supplies in west Africa can't be relied upon to be screened and safe; *see p.172*.)

Malaria There's a very high risk of catching malaria – mainly the sometimes dangerous falciparum type (*see p.107*) – all year round throughout almost all of west Africa, and certainly in all the countries covered here except most of Cape Verde. (In Cape Verde, there's a risk only on São Tiago island, and there only between September and November.) The risk is reduced (but not zero) in the central-western parts of Senegal from January to June.

Chloroquine-resistant strains of malaria parasites exist in most areas, so the currently recommended antimalarial drugs (*see p.115*) are mefloquine ('Lariam'), doxycycline (eg, 'Nordox' or 'Vibramycin'), or atovoquine plus proguanil (combined in 'Malarone'). (If none of these is suitable, you may be prescribed chloroquine plus proguanil, but this combination doesn't give complete protection.) In any case, also be sure to take strict precautions to prevent mosquito bites, including covering up as much as possible of your body, applying mosquito-repellent containing DEET to all exposed parts, and sleeping under a mosquito net (preferably one treated with permethrin or a similar insecticide; *see p.75*).

Meningitis Most of the region is within the sub-Saharan 'meningitis belt', where outbreaks of meningococcal meningitis (*see p.163*) are quite common – particularly in the drier northern areas, and particularly during the dry season (mostly December to June). If you're travelling in these parts at this season – and particularly if an epidemic is in progress – you'd be well advised to get vaccinated. If you're unsure, discuss it with a travel-clinic doctor.

Polio This still exists in west Africa – especially in Nigeria, among the countries listed – so you should get a vaccination or booster (*see p.165*).

Rabies You could encounter rabid animals – especially dogs – anywhere in west Africa except Cape Verde. As explained in the article on page 139, vaccination before you travel doesn't give complete protection, but it means that further jabs after a bite aren't so urgent. Given the poor medical facilities in most of this region (except perhaps Senegal), it's probably worthwhile unless you're only going on a short holiday to modern tourist centres and avoid all contact with animals. Discuss it with a travel-clinic doctor.

Tuberculosis It's widespread in west Africa and particularly common in Nigeria, so vaccination is generally recommended if you are likely to live in close proximity to local people during your stay. (American medical authorities prefer a system of testing for the disease before and after travel, followed by treatment if necessary; see p.160.)

Typhoid As this is common, especially in rural areas, it's a jab worth getting – although it doesn't give full protection, so you still need to take care with food and drink (see above). One plus point is that the newer vaccines have fewer side-effects than the old typhoid ('TAB') vaccine (see p.46).

Yellow fever This dangerous disease is a real risk in most of west Africa, especially in Gambia, Ghana, Nigeria and Senegal among the countries listed. Even if there hasn't been a recent outbreak where you've been, you may need a vaccination certificate to get into other countries in the region – or into other parts of Africa and tropical America. (The only exception is children under 9 or 12 months old.) The vaccination is safe, effective and long-lasting (see p.123), so everyone other than young children should have it before going anywhere in west Africa. A few people mustn't have the jab for medical reasons; in that case, take a doctor's letter to say so.

Others There are occasional outbreaks of plague, but vaccination isn't usually warranted (see p.130). If you're travelling in jungle areas where loiasis (African eyeworm) is prevalent, it's worth taking a weekly dose of diethylcarbamazine (see p.132) to prevent infection. Otherwise, you should make sure that all your childhood vaccinations are up to date, but especially tetanus and diphtheria (usually given as a combined jab; see p.166). Flu epidemics can occur at any time of year, so older travellers and anyone else whose doctor advises a regular flu jab should be vaccinated against both this and pneumococcal disease.

Other medical risks Frankly, most of the world's tropical and other diseases (including common everyday ones like measles that exist everywhere) crop up in west Africa. Apart from those mentioned above, other risks include...

→ **Myiasis** (maggot infestation of the skin; see p.79) caused by tumbu flies, mostly in rural areas, and **jiggers** (chigoes; see p.80).
→ **Dengue fever** (see p.125) in epidemics throughout the region, especially in urban areas.
→ **Leishmaniasis** (see p.118), mainly in dry seasons.
→ **Lymphatic filariasis**, and other filarial diseases (see p.131–132), except in Gambia in the case of river blindness (onchocerciasis).
→ The west African type of **sleeping sickness** (trypanosomiasis; see p.119) in rural areas of all countries, but especially in the south of the region.
→ All forms of **typhus** plus **Crimean–Congo haemorrhagic fever** (see pp.137–139).
→ **Lassa fever** and – much more rarely – **Ebola and Marburg viruses**, in rural areas (see p.168).
→ **Respiratory problems** in dry, dusty semidesert areas.

CAPE VERDE

Limited medical facilities. Some medicines in short supply; take any prescription medicines you need with you. Medical care expensive.

Emergencies
Police T 132
Ambulance T 130

Health ministry/dept
Palácio do Governo, Várzea, Praia, Santiago
T +238 610501

British honorary consul
Antonio A. Cabuto, c/o Shell Cabo Verde, Av Amilcar Cabral CP4, São Vincente
T +238 326625; +238 326626 (emergency help only)

Other consulates
US T +238 615616

Hospitals/clinics
Praia Central Hospital, Praia, Santiago
T +238 612142; +238 612234

Also small hospitals on other islands

GAMBIA

Medical facilities and treatments limited. Take any prescription medicines you may need with you, with copy of prescription. (Strict controls on import of some medications, including hydrocortisone – details from Gambian embassy or consulate.)

Emergencies
Police T 16
Ambulance T 17

Health ministry/dept
The Quadrangle, Banjul
T +220 227605; 220 228291

British consulates
British High Commission, 48 Atlantic Rd, Fajara, Banjul
T +220 495133; +220 495134

Other consulates
US T +220 392856; +220 391971

Hospitals/clinics
Royal Victoria Hospital, Independence Drive, Banjul
T +220 228223

Bansang Hospital, Bansang
T +220 674222

(UK) Medical Research Council, Fajara
T +220 495442; +220 494072

GHANA

Limited medical facilities, particularly outside Accra.

Emergencies T 999

Health ministry/dept
PO Box M44, Accra
T +233 (21) 662014

British consulate
British High Commission, Osu Link, off Gamel Abdul Nasser Ave, Accra
T +233 (21) 221665; +233 (21) 701 0650

Other consulates
Canadian T +233 (21) 288555;
+233 (21) 701 1593
W *www.dfait-maeci.gc.ca/accra*

South African T +233 (21) 762380;
+233 (21) 764480; +233 (21) 764500

US T +233 (21) 775347
W *http://usembassy.state.gov/ghana*

Hospitals/clinics
Korle-Bu Teaching Hospital, Korle-Bu, Accra
T +233 (21) 665401

North Ridge Hospital, Castle Rd, Accra
T +233 (21) 775341

Agogo Hospital, Agogo
T +233 (51) 20201; +233 (51)20202

Komfo Anokye Teaching Hospital, Kumasi
T +233 (51) 208119

Saltpond General Hospital, Saltpond
T +233 (42) 33850

NIGERIA

Many well-trained doctors, but poor medical infrastructure and care.

NIGERIA (*continued*)

Many medicines not available, and counterfeit preparations common, so take any prescription medicines you may need with you. Immediate cash payment often demanded.

Emergencies T 112
Police **T** +234 (1) 263 1913 (Lagos)
Ambulance St John Ambulance
T +234 (1) 263 5922
Air ambulance Global Medical Care
T +234 (1) 262 1910; +234 (1) 262 4571

Health ministry/dept
Block 4A (301-399) Third Floor, New Federal Secretariat Complex, Shehu Shagari Way, Anuja
T +234 (9) 523 4590

British consulates
British High Commission, Dangote House, Aguyi Ironsi St, Maitama, Abuja
T +234 (9) 413 4559; +234 (9) 413 0899
Ibadan **T** +234 (22) 810 4953
Kaduna **T** +234 (62) 233380
Kano **T** +234 (64) 631686
Lagos **T** +234 (1) 262 5930; +234 (1) 775 1651 or +234 (803) 402 2765 (emergencies)
Port Harcourt **T** +234 (84) 237173; +234 (84) 231776

Other consulates (Lagos unless stated)
Australian **T** +234 (1) 261 8875

Canadian **T** +234 (1) 262 2512; +234 (9) 413 9910 (Abuja)

South African **T** +234 (1) 267 1531

US **T** +234 (1) 261 1215; +234 (1) 261 0195 or +234 (1) 261 1414 (emergencies); +234 (9) 523 0916 (Abuja); +234 (803) 408 6000 (Abuja – emergencies)
W *http://usembassy.state.gov/nigeria*

Hospitals/clinics
Health Centre, Zone 3, Wuse, Abuja
T +234 (9) 523 1209

National Hospital, Abuja
T: +234 (9) 234 2686

International Clinic, 2A Airport Rd, Kano
T +234 (64) 649533; +234 (64) 633499

St Nicholas Hospital, 57 Campbell St, Lagos Island
T +234 (1) 263 5576; +234 (1) 263 1739

Kelu Clinic, 1004 Victoria Island, Lagos
T +234 (1) 261 6993; +234 (1) 262376

AEA International SOS Cinic, Intel Camp, Port Harcourt
T +234 (81) 611436

SENEGAL

Dakar has best medical facilities in west Africa, able to treat most conditions. Hospitals (especially private) approach European/North American standards. Facilities outside Dakar more limited.

Emergencies T 153
Police **T** 17
Ambulance **T** 18
SOS Médecin **T** +221 821 3213

Health ministry/dept
Building Administratif, Dakar
T + 221 823 1088

British consulate
British Embassy, 20 Rue du Docteur Guillet, Dakar
T + 221 823 7392; +221 823 2677

Other consulates
Canadian **T** +221 823 9290
W *www.dfait-maeci.gc.ca/dakar*

South African **T** +221 865 1959

US **T** +221 823 4296; +221 823 4606 (emergencies)

Hospitals/clinics
Hôpital Principal. Ave Nelson Mandela, Dakar
T +221 839 5050

Hôpital Aristide le Dantec, Ave Pasteur, Dakar
T +221 822 2420

Centre de Traumatologie, Dakar
T +221 827 7468; +221 825 0819

Clinique Internationale, 33 Boulevard Dial Dop, Dakar
T +221 824 4421; +221 824 2757

EAST AND CENTRAL AFRICA

Kenya, Malawi, Mozambique, Tanzania, Uganda, Zambia

Many of the most common travellers' destinations in east and central Africa are renowned for their stunning natural features, wildlife reserves and in some cases beaches. Standards of tourist and other facilities vary widely, with Nairobi in Kenya the most important regional centre for emergency medical care. (However, if you're in southern Zambia or Mozambique, South Africa may be a better bet for emergency evacuation.) Elsewhere, care is likely to be basic at best, and many medicines are in short supply – especially in Malawi, Mozambique, Tanzania and Uganda, and in rural areas everywhere. You'd be well advised to take with you any prescription drugs you know you'll need, plus malaria pills. You certainly need full travel health insurance, including evacuation cover.

Everyday precautions Travellers' diarrhoea (*see p.34*), including giardiasis (*see p.43*) and dysentery, is common throughout east and central Africa, and there's a risk of intestinal worms (*see p.49*) and hepatitis A and E (*see p.51*). Cholera (*see p.44*) and typhoid (*see p.46*) outbreaks are also common. So **take great care with what and where you eat and drink**. Nowhere, except possibly in Nairobi, is tap water safe to drink. All water elsewhere should be boiled or otherwise treated (*see p.32*), or use reliable bottled water in sealed bottles – imported brands if possible – for drinking, making ice and cleaning your teeth. (*Warning*: Bottled water may be scarce in some rural areas.) Use only pasteurised or sterilised milk and dairy products (or boil milk).

All these countries except the southern tip of Mozambique lie in the tropics, and many places visited by travellers (including several game parks) are well over 1000m (3300ft) above sea level. So the sun is very strong, and you need to treat it accordingly: Use a high-factor sunscreen (*see p.56*), wear a hat, and expose your skin for only short periods at first. Humidity isn't as high as in west Africa, but many areas have humid seasons when you should beware of heat exhaustion (*see p.58*), especially when you first arrive. Yet in some places you're high enough for it to freeze. Dry, dusty conditions are likely to be more of a general problem, often causing breathing troubles.

Sea pollution also isn't generally as bad as in west Africa, but beware of bilharzia (schistosomiasis; *see p.102*) in all freshwater lakes and rivers throughout the region. (To repeat the warning given elsewhere, Lake Malawi is *not* bilharzia-free, whatever local tourist offices may say.) Don't swim in any fresh water other than a well-chlorinated swimming pool, and take care using a camp shower. Also take heed of the warning in the article on page 66 about altitude sickness if you plan to trek to the summit of Mt Kenya or Mt Kilimanjaro. Venomous snakes (*see p.97*), and spiders and scorpions (*see p.82*), are also a risk in many areas.

There's plenty of crime, some of it violent, in most parts of east and central Africa, and political or terrorist violence in some border and other areas, so get reliable advice before visiting places off usual tourist routes. Traffic accidents – including ones involving buses and taxis – are very common and the cause of many injuries. Kenya's railways have quite frequent accidents, and there are occasional cyclones in some areas.

Sex safety The sub-Saharan HIV/AIDS epidemic (*see p.146*) has hit east and central Africa almost (but not quite) as hard as southern Africa. In three of the countries – Kenya, Malawi and Mozambique – between 13 and 15 per cent of adults (that's about one person in seven) have the HIV virus, and in Zambia the figure is over 20 per cent. But, as in other parts of the world, the infection rate tends to be higher in major urban areas – well over 20 per cent, for example, in Nairobi and Kenya's second city, Mombasa. And in many places half or more of all sex workers are HIV-positive. Uganda is regarded as the 'success story' of Africa's battle against HIV, but even there 5 per cent of adults are infected, although the trend is downwards.

Throughout the region, more women than men have HIV, and heterosexual contact is the main route of infection, followed by transmission from mother to child. Hepatitis B (*see p.148*) is also widespread, and is transferred both sexually and via contaminated blood. So it's vital to **always practise safer sex** (*see p.145*) and consider getting a hepatitis B vaccination (*see below*).

Vaccinations etc East and central Africa have many serious diseases that can be prevented if you're vaccinated. These are the vaccinations you should or must have – or at least consider – and precautions you should take:–

Cholera Vaccination isn't an international requirement any longer, and cholera in travellers is usually quite easily treated (*see p.44*), but some border posts may still demand a certificate of vaccination. The old vaccine isn't very effective, but newer ones are much more so; it's worth asking a travel clinic about these if you plan to travel extensively or an outbreak is in progress.

Hepatitis A All travellers to east and central Africa – indeed, any part of Africa – should have this vaccination (*see p.51*).

Hepatitis B Probably not necessary for short-term visitors, but if there's any chance of blood or sexual contact with local people, if you plan to take part in any hazardous activities that could cause injury, or if you're staying for an extended period (and so are more likely to need surgical or dental treatment, or even a blood transfusion), you should get vaccinated. (Blood supplies in this part of Africa can't be relied upon to be screened and safe; *see p.172*.)

Malaria There's a very high risk of catching malaria – mainly the sometimes dangerous falciparum type (*see p.107*) – all year round throughout almost all of east and central Africa, and certainly in all the countries covered here. The exceptions are highland areas of Kenya above about 2500m (8200ft) and parts of Tanzania above about 1800m (5900ft). There's little risk in Nairobi, but all other cities in these countries have malaria.

Chloroquine-resistant strains of malaria parasites exist in most areas, so the currently recommended antimalarial drugs (*see p.115*) are mefloquine ('Lariam'), doxycycline (eg, 'Nordox' or 'Vibramycin'), or atovoquine plus proguanil (combined in 'Malarone'). (If none of these is suitable, you may be prescribed chloroquine plus proguanil, but this combination doesn't give complete protection.) In any case, also be sure to take strict precautions to prevent mosquito bites, including covering up as much as possible of your body, applying mosquito-repellent containing DEET to all exposed parts, and sleeping under a mosquito net (preferably one treated with permethrin or a similar insecticide; *see p.75*).

Meningitis The region lies south of the sub-Saharan 'meningitis belt', but outbreaks of meningococcal meningitis (*see p.163*) are quite common – particularly during the dry season (generally December to June), but all year round in Kenya and Tanzania. In recent years, Malawi, Mozambique and Zambia have had the most cases. If you're travelling in the region during risk seasons – and particularly if an epidemic is in progress and/or you're visiting rural areas – you'd be well advised to get vaccinated. If you're unsure, discuss it with a specialist travel-clinic doctor.

Polio This still exists in east and central Africa, notably Zambia, but mainly otherwise to the north of these countries, in Ethiopia, Somalia and Sudan. However – and despite worldwide successes in eliminating the disease – it's advisable still to get a vaccination or booster before you travel (*see p.165*).

Rabies You could encounter rabid animals – especially dogs – anywhere in the region. As explained in the article on page 139, vaccination before you travel doesn't give complete protection, but it means that further jabs after a bite aren't so urgent. Given the poor medical facilities in most of this region (except perhaps Kenya's cities), it's probably worthwhile unless you're only going on a short holiday to modern tourist centres and avoid all contact with animals. Discuss it with a travel-clinic doctor.

Tuberculosis It's common throughout east and central Africa, so vaccination (or a booster) is generally recommended if you are likely to live in close proximity to local people during your stay. (American medical authorities prefer a system of testing for the disease before and after travel, followed by treatment if necessary; *see p.160*.)

Typhoid As this is common in the region, it's a jab worth getting – although it doesn't give full protection, so you still need to take care with food and drink (*see above*). One plus point is that the newer vaccines have fewer side-effects than the old typhoid ('TAB') vaccine (*see p.46*).

Yellow fever This dangerous disease is a real risk in most parts of east and central Africa. Even if there hasn't been a recent outbreak where you've been, you may need a vaccination certificate to get into all other countries in the region except Zambia, or into other parts of Africa and tropical America. (Children under 12 months old are generally excepted.) The vaccination is safe, effective and long-lasting (*see p. 123*), so everyone other than young children should have it before going anywhere in east and central Africa. A few people mustn't have the jab for medical reasons; in that case, take a doctor's letter to say so.

Others There are occasional outbreaks of plague in all these countries, but vaccination isn't usually warranted (*see p. 130*). Otherwise, you should make sure that all your childhood vaccinations are up to date, but especially tetanus and diphtheria (usually given as a combined jab; *see p. 166*). Flu epidemics can occur at any time of year, so older travellers and anyone else whose doctor advises a regular flu jab should be vaccinated against both this and pneumococcal disease.

Other medical risks Many tropical and other diseases (including common everyday ones like measles that exist everywhere) crop up in east and central Africa. Apart from those mentioned above, other risks include...

→ *Myiasis* (maggot infestation of the skin; *see p. 79*) caused by tumbu flies, mostly in rural areas, and *jiggers* (chigoes; *see p. 80*).

→ *Dengue fever* (*see p. 125*) in epidemics throughout the region, especially in urban areas; and *Rift Valley fever* (*see p. 128*) in many areas.

→ *Leishmaniasis* (*see p. 118*), especially in dry areas.

→ *Lymphatic filariasis* and other filarial diseases (*see pp. 131–132*).

→ The east African type of *sleeping sickness* (trypanosomiasis; *see p. 119*) in all countries, including in game parks and lodges. It's serious, so take precautions against tsetse-fly bites.

→ All forms of *typhus* plus *Crimean–Congo haemorrhagic fever* (*see pp. 137–139*).

→ *Lassa fever* and – much more rarely – *Ebola and Marburg viruses*, in isolated rural areas (*see p. 168*).

KENYA

Nairobi has best medical services in east Africa, but facilities are limited in rural areas.

Emergencies
Police **T** 999
Ambulance **T** 999; +254 (2) 336886; +254 (2) 501280; +254 (11) 312405
Air ambulance AAR **T** +254 (2) 717373; +254 (2) 717375.
Amref **T** +254 (2) 315454; +254 (2) 315455
Flying doctor **T** +254 (2) 501300

Health ministry/dept
Afya House, Cathedral Rd, Nairobi
T +254 (2) 717077

British consulates
British High Commission, Upper Hill Rd, Nairobi
T +254 (2) 271 4699
W *www.britain.or.ke*
Mombasa **T** +254 (11) 312312

Other consulates
Australian **T** +254 (2) 444 5034

Canadian **T** +254 (2) 214804

South African **T** +254 (2) 215616

US **T** +254 (2) 537800; +254 (2) 537809 (emergencies)
W *http://usembassy.state.gov/nairobi* (includes list of hospitals and doctors)

Hospitals/clinics
Kenyatta National Hospital, Nairobi
T +254 (2) 276300

Aga Khan Hospital, 3rd Parklands Ave, Nairobi
T +254 (2) 742531; +254 (2) 740000

PCEA Hospital, Kikuyu
T +254 (15) 432412

Mombasa Hospital
T +254 (11) 312191; +254 (11) 312099

Aga Khan Hospital, Mombasa
T +254 (11) 312953

MALAWI

Even in urban areas, medical facilities are only basic; elsewhere they're very limited or non-existent. Some medicines in short supply or unobtainable. Evacuation to South Africa or Nairobi is advisable for serious problems.

Emergencies T 199

Health ministry/dept
PO Box 30377, Capital City, Lilongwe 3
T +265 783044

British consulate
British High Commission, PO Box 30042, Lilongwe 3
T +265 772400; +265 772683

Other consulates
Canadian (Blantyre) **T** +265 645441; +265 645269; +265 644822

South African **T** +265 73722; +265 773597

US **T** +265 773166; +265 773343

Hospitals/clinics
Lilongwe Central Hospital
T +265 721555

Adventist Hospital, Presidential Way, Lilongwe
T +265 731049

Queen Elizabeth Central Hospital, Blantyre
T +265 630333

Adventist Hospital, Kabula Hill Rd, Blantyre
T +265 620488; +265 633095

MOZAMBIQUE

Medical facilities very limited and basic; many medicines unavailable. Immediate cash payment usually required. Evacuation to South Africa is advisable for many conditions.

Emergencies
Police **T** 119
Ambulance **T** 117 (*unreliable*)

Health ministry/dept
Av Eduardo Mondlane 1008, Maputo
T +258 (1) 427131

British consulates
British High Commission, Av Vladimir I. Lenine 310, Maputo
T +258 (1) 320111
Beira **T** +258 (3) 311763

Other consulates
Australian **T** +258 (1) 422780

Canadian **T** +258 (1) 492623

South African **T** +258 (1) 491614; +258 (1) 490059; +258 (1) 490547

US **T** +258 (1) 492797; +258 (1) 490723 (emergencies)

Hospitals/clinics
Sommershield Clinic, Maputo
T +258 (1) 493924

Otherwise, contact your embassy or consulate for information and advice

TANZANIA

Limited medical facilities, even in Dar es Salaam; Zanzibar clinics can treat only minor problems. Many medicines often unobtainable. Evacuation to South Africa or Nairobi is advisable for serious problems.

Emergencies T 999; 112
Flying doctor **T** +255 (51) 667063; +255 (51) 166610; +255 (51) 115823; or refer to Nairobi, Kenya (*see above*)

Health ministry/dept
PO Box 9083, Dar es Salaam
T +255 (22) 512 0261

TANZANIA (*continued*)

British consulate
British High Commission, Umoja House, Garden Ave, Dar es Salaam
T + 255 (22) 211 0101; +255 744 242242 (emergencies)
W *www.britishhighcommission.go.tz*

Other consulates
Canadian T +255 (22) 211 2831; +255 (22) 211 2863

South African T +255 (22) 260 1800

US T +252 (22) 266 6010
W *http://usembassy.state.gov/posts/tz1*

Hospitals/clinics
Muhimbili Medical Centre, Upanga, Dar Es Salaam
T +255 (22) 215 1351; +255 (22) 215 1367

Aga Khan Hospital, Ocean Rd, Sea View, Dar Es Salam
T +255 (22) 211 5151; +255 (22) 211 4090

Nordic Clinic, Valhalla House, Dar es Salaam
T +255 (22) 260 1650; +255 741 325569

Mnazi Mmoja Hospital, Zanzibar
T +255 (24) 543 1071

Kilimanjaro Christian Medical Centre, Moshi
T +255 (27) 54263; +225 (27) 52291; +255 (27) 52058

UGANDA

Medical facilities limited, even in Kampala, and very basic in rural areas. Many medicines in short supply or unobtainable. Evacuation to Nairobi often advisable.

Emergencies T 999 (Kampala; may vary elsewhere)

Health ministry/dept
Plot 6, Lourdel Rd, Wandegeya, Kampala
T +256 (41) 340884

British consulate
British High Commission, 10/12 Parliament Ave, Kampala
T +256 (78) 312000; +256 (75) 767777 (emergencies)
W *www.britain.or.ng*

Other consulates
Canadian T +256 (41) 258141

South African T +256 (41) 343543; +256 (41) 343560

US T +256 (41) 234142

Hospitals/clinics
Mulago Hospital, Kampala
T +256 (41) 541250

ZAMBIA

Reasonable care available in private clinics in urban areas, but public hospitals often understaffed and short of supplies. Very limited care in rural areas. Evacuation to South Africa or Nairobi advisable for serious problems.

Emergencies T 999

Health ministry/dept
Woodgate House, Cairo Rd, Lusaka
T +260 (1) 253040

British consulate
British High Commission, 5210 Independence Ave, Lusaka
T +260 (1) 251133

Other consulates
Canadian T +260 (1) 250833

South African T +260 (1) 260999

US T +260 (1) 250955; +260 (1) 252305 (emergencies)

Hospitals/clinics
Central Board of Health of Zambia, Ndeke House, Lusaka
T +260 (1) 253179

Churches Medical Association of Zambia, Ben Bella Rd, Lusaka
T +260 (1) 229702

University Teaching Hospital, Lusaka
T +260 (1) 253955

International Clinic, Nangwenya Rd, Lusaka
T +260 (1) 254819

General Hospital, Livingstone
T +260 (3) 320221

SOUTHERN AFRICA

Botswana, Lesotho, Namibia, South Africa, Swaziland, Zimbabwe

These six countries make up only a small corner of Africa, but they cover an area almost as big as the whole of western Europe, and range from the tropics to the warm temperate zone, from vast deserts (the Kalahari and Namib) to the landlocked Okavango swamp, from subtropical beaches to high plateaux and plains, and mountains up to almost 3500m (11 500ft) high.

Unless you keep to the tourist areas and cities of South Africa and to a lesser extent other big towns, you face many of the problems of other parts of Africa, including inadequate and overused medical facilities, the need to travel long distances for specialist care (South Africa's cities are major regional evacuation centres), and sometimes a scarcity of medications. Good medical insurance (including air ambulance and repatriation cover) is strongly advised even though free treatment is available in some places.

Everyday precautions So long as you take sensible precautions, food and water are generally safe in most parts of these countries except in rural areas. However, you can rely on safe tap water only in the capital in Lesotho and Namibia, and Zimbabwe's unstable situation may lead to water supply problems there. If in doubt, drink boiled, purified or reliable bottled water (widely available; *see p.32*) and use only ice made from similar water. Use pasteurised or sterilised milk and dairy products (or boil milk). In spite of such precautions, travellers' diarrhoea (*see p.34*) is quite common, and there have been oubreaks of cholera (*see p.44*) and typhoid (*see p.46*).

Respect the sun; remember that away from the coast much of the region is well over 1000m (3300ft) above sea level, and the summer sun can be extremely strong. So use a good sunscreen (*see p.56*) on exposed parts, wear a hat and expose yourself for only short periods at first.

There's bilharzia (schistosomiasis; *see p.102*) in fresh water in Botswana, Namibia, South Africa (particularly in the north and east), Swaziland (below about 1200m [4000ft]) and (to a lesser extent) Zimbabwe. So don't swim or paddle in lakes or rivers (well-chlorinated swimming pools are safe), and take care using a camp shower – eg, in game parks. There are venomous spiders, scorpions and snakes (*see pp.84 & 97*). Driving is dangerous in most of the region, and there are a lot of accidents, including collisions with wildlife. Violent crime is increasing in some cities in southern Africa.

Sex safety There has been a huge increase in HIV/AIDS in all of sub-Saharan Africa in recent years, but the situation in southern Africa is by far the worst – there were an estimated 636 000 AIDS deaths in 2001. Official UN estimates show that almost 40 per cent of adults in Botswana are HIV positive, and the figure is over 30 per cent for Lesotho, Swaziland and Zimbabwe, 22.5 per cent in Namibia and 20 per cent in South Africa. But these figures hide wide variations, with more than 50 per cent infected in many cities and 60 per cent among sex workers. HIV is mostly transferred by heterosexual contact here, and more women than men are infected in all these countries. Hepatitis B – spread by sexual contact and contaminated blood – is also widespread. More than anywhere else, take heed, and **practise safer sex** (*see p.145*).

Vaccinations etc Many serious diseases, preventable if you're vaccinated, are risks in southern Africa. These are the vaccinations you should (in some cases *must*) have – or at least consider – and precautions you should take:–

Cholera There have been large-scale outbreaks in southern Africa within the last decade. The old vaccine isn't very effective, and cholera is usually quite easily treated in travellers, so vaccination isn't normally recommended. But if you're travelling to a remote area where there's a current outbreak, or plan to spend time as an aid worker in a refugee camp, discuss with a specialist travel doctor getting one of the better new vaccines (*see p.44*).

Hepatitis A Vaccination is sensible for all travellers anywhere in Africa, especially if you're planning a long trip or visiting rural areas (*see p.51*).

Hepatitis B More debatable. Hep B is widespread in southern Africa, and in theory it's preventable by the same precautions that protect you from HIV (*see p.148*) – but you're also at risk if you have to have surgery or a blood transfusion. So vaccination isn't really necessary if you're visiting only South Africa (where blood supplies are generally good) and don't have unprotected sex, but it's very worthwhile otherwise, or if you're cautious.

Malaria Precautions – both preventive drugs and protection from mosquito bites (*see pp.75 & 107*) – are essential in most of the northern and north-eastern parts of southern Africa for at least part of the year. Malaria – mostly the potentially fatal *falciparum* type – is a risk as follows:–

→ **Botswana** Northern parts, including the Okavango; November to June.
→ **Lesotho** Malaria-free.
→ **Namibia** Northern parts; mostly November to June, but all year along the border with Angola.
→ **South Africa** Northern and north-eastern parts (including the Kruger National Park), and the coastal area of KwaZulu-Natal as far south as the Tugela River, about 85–100km (50–60 miles) north of Durban; all year, but risk greatest October to May.
→ **Swaziland** Throughout the lowland areas; all year, but risk greatest November to February.
→ **Zimbabwe** Everywhere below 1200m (4000ft), except in Harare and Bulawayo; all year along the Zambesi valley (including Victoria Falls), otherwise November to June.

Chloroquine-resistant malaria parasites are widespread, and the currently recommended pills for most of this region are melfoquine ('Lariam'), doxycycline (eg, 'Nordox' or 'Vibramycin'), or atovoquine plus proguanil (combined in 'Malarone'). (If none of these is suitable – and for some of the lower-risk areas of Botswana, Namibia and Zimbabwe – you may be prescribed chloroquine plus proguanil, but this combination doesn't always give complete protection.)

Meningitis You're well south of the African 'meningitis belt' here, but there have been odd outbreaks in Namibia and Zimbabwe. Discuss vaccination with a specialist travel-clinic doctor (see p.163).

Rabies You could encounter rabid animals in most parts of the region, but especially in eastern areas of South Africa. As explained in the article on page 139, vaccination doesn't give complete protection, but means that further jabs after a bite aren't so urgent. It's probably worthwhile if you're travelling extensively in the region. Discuss it with a specialist doctor.

Typhoid If you're planning on travelling in rural areas, this is a sensible precaution, but you still need to be careful about what you eat and drink as it doesn't give you complete protection (see p.46). But if you stick to big-city hotels and smart restaurants you're probably safe.

Yellow fever Nowhere in southern Africa has yellow fever, but you must have had a vaccination – and hold an official certificate to say so (see p.123) – to enter any of the six countries except Botswana, if you're travelling from somewhere where the disease exists (which basically means most of west, east and central Africa except Mozambique and Malawi, and the Americas from Panama to southern Brazil). Otherwise, you're liable to be delayed and vaccinated compulsorily. It's a safe, long-lasting vaccination worth having if you travel anywhere in sub-Saharan Africa. If you're one of the small group who shouldn't have the jab, make sure you've got an official letter to say so.

Others There are occasional outbreaks of plague, but vaccination is not usually warranted (see p.130). Polio (see p.165) has been all but eliminated from southern Africa, so vaccination isn't strictly needed, but it's always a good idea to keep your immunity up to date. The same applies to all the standard childhood vaccinations, but especially tetanus – which is usually combined with diphtheria (see p.166) and which all travellers should have. The same applies to tuberculosis vaccination (see p.160), although American doctors don't generally encourage this. Older travellers and anyone else whose doctor advises a regular flu jab should have both this and pneumococcal vaccinations before travelling to southern Africa.

Other medical risks Apart from those referred to above and the common diseases that can occur anywhere, risks in southern Africa include...

→ **Dengue fever** (see p.125) in occasional epidemics, especially in South Africa, Swaziland and Zimbabwe.
→ **Sleeping sickness** (African trypanosomiasis; see p.119) in Botswana and Namibia; avoid tsetse fly bites, common in game parks.
→ **Other insect- and tick-borne diseases** such as Rift Valley fever (see p.128), Crimean-Congo haemorrhagic fever (see p.139) and tick typhus (see p.137) – but these are rare in travellers to the region.

BOTSWANA

Medical facilities and care OK in towns, but basic in rural areas. Government hospitals supply free drugs, and other care at nominal cost, but medical insurance highly recommended. Transfer to South Africa best for specialist treatment.

Emergencies
Police T 999
Ambulance T 997; 911
Air ambulance MRI Botswana
T +267 301601 (emergency)

Health ministry/dept
Private Bag 0038, Gaborone
T +267 352000

British consulate
British High Commission, Private Bag 0023, Gaborone
T +267 395 2841

Other consulates
Canadian T +267 304411

South African T +267 390 4800

US T +267 353982; +267 357111 (emergencies)
W *http://usembassy.state.gov/posts/bc1* (includes list of medical facilities)

Hospitals/clinics
Princess Marina Hospital, Gaborone
T +267 353221

Gaborone Private Hospital, Mica Way
T +267 301999

Nyangabgwe Hospital, Doc Morgan Ave, Francistown
T +267 211000

Maun Hospital
T +267 686 0444

LESOTHO

Government and mission hospitals have basic facilities (not free to visitors). Serious and even many routine cases are best evacuated to South Africa; Bloemfontein is only 145km (90 miles) from Maseru.

Emergencies
Police T 123; +266 317263 (Maseru); +266 540209 (Mapoteng)
Ambulance T 121 (Maseru, Leribe and Butha-Buthe only); +266 312501
Flying doctor T +266 322329

Health ministry/dept
PO Box 514, Maseru 100
T +266 314404

British consulate
British High Commission, Linare Rd, Maseru 100
T +266 2231 3961
W *www.bhc.org.ls*

Other consulates
Canadian T +266 314187; +266 316435

South African T +266 2231 5758

US T +266 312666

Hospitals/clinics
Queen Elizabeth II Hospital, Maseru 100
T +266 314404

Maseru Private Hospital, Thetsane Industrial Area
T +266 313260

NAMIBIA

In major towns, facilities are second in the region only to those in South Africa. Care is expensive, so full medical insurance needed.

Emergencies
Police T 10111
Ambulance T 12111
Air ambulance See under South Africa

Health ministry/dept
Private Bag 13198, Windhoek
T +264 (61) 203 2801

British consulate
British High Commission, 116 Robert Mugabe Ave, Windhoek
T +264 (61) 274800

Other consulates
Canadian T +264 (61) 227417

South African T ++264 (61) 205 7111

US T +264 (61) 221061
W *www.usembassy.namib.com*

Hospitals/clinics
Windhoek Central Hospital, Harvey St
T +264 (61) 232270

Roman Catholic Hospital, 92 Stubel St,
Windhoek
T +264 (61) 237237

Rhino Park Day Hospital, Hosea Kutako
Drive, Windhoek
T +264 (61) 225434

Bismarck Medical Centre, 17 Kaiser
Wilhelm St, Swakopmund
T +264 (64) 402575

SOUTH AFRICA

Except in remote areas (from which
air evacuation is normal), standards
are equal to those in most developed
countries. Treatment free for
pregnant women and children under
six, but otherwise expensive, so full
medical insurance essential.

Emergencies
Police T 10111
Ambulance T 10117
Air ambulance MedicAir Specialty
Assistance T +27 (11) 452 4611;
0800 111261. South African Red Cross
T +27 (21) 418 6640 – *also flying doctor*

Health ministry/dept
Private Bag X9070, Cape Town 8000
T +27 (21) 465 7407

British consulates
Liberty Life Place Block B, 256 Glyn St,
Hatfield, Pretoria 0083
T +27 (12) 483 1400
W *www.britain.org.za*
Cape Town T +27 (21) 405 2400
Durban T +27 (31) 305 2920;
+27 (31) 2929
East London T +27 (43) 726 4430
Port Elizabeth T +27 (41) 363 8841

Other main consulates
Australian T +27 (12) 342 3781
W *www.australia.co.za*

Canadian T +27 (12) 422 3000
W *www.dfait-maeci.gc.ca/southafrica*

New Zealand T +27 (12) 342 8656

US T +27 (11) 644 8000 (Johannesburg)
W *http://usembassy.state.gov/pretoria*

Hospitals/clinics
Many; refer to local telephone directories

SWAZILAND

Low-cost care in government
hospitals, but facilities limited
outside Mbabane. Most visitors use
private facilities; full insurance
highly recommended. Specialised
emergency and many routine cases
may be transferred to South Africa.

Emergencies T 999

Health ministry/dept
PO Box 5, Mbabane
T +268 404 4016

British consulate
British High Commission, 2nd floor,
Lilunga House, Gilfillan St, Mbabane
T +268 404 2581

Other consulates
South African T +268 404 4651

US T +268 404 6441
W *http://usembassy.state.gov/mbabane*

Hospitals/clinics
Mbabane Government Hospital
T +268 404 2111

Piggs Peak Government Hospital
T +268 437 1111

Good Shepherd Hospital, Siteki
T +268 34133

ZIMBABWE

Good medical facilities in Harare
and Bulawayo; limited elsewhere.
Many medications unavailable.
Medical insurance essential for
adequate service. Political
instability may cause problems.

Emergencies T 999

Air ambulance Medical Air Ambulance
Service T +263 (4) 791074;
+263 (4) 790530; +263 (4) 790391

ZIMBABWE (*continued*)

Health ministry/dept
Kaguvi Building, Fourth St, Causeway, Harare
T +263 (4) 702368

British consulate
British High Commission, Corner House, Samora Machel Ave & Leopold Takawira St, Harare
T +263 (4) 772990; +263 (4) 774700
W www.britainzw.org

Other consulates
Australian **T** +263 (4) 253661
W www.zimbabwe.embassy.gov.au

Canadian **T** +263 (4) 252181

South African **T** +263 (4) 753147

US **T** +263 (4) 250593; +263 (4) 250595 (emergencies)
W http://usembassy.state.gov/zimbabwe (includes list of medical facilities)

Hospitals/clinics
Harare Hospital, Southerton
T +263 (4) 621111

Parirenyatwa Hospital, Causeway, Harare
T +263 (4) 794411

United Bulawayo Hospital
T +263 (9) 77388

WESTERN INDIAN OCEAN

Madagascar, Mauritius, Réunion, Seychelles

These islands range from idyllic holiday destinations to the poor developing nation of Madagascar. Medical facilities are pretty good in Mauritius, Réunion (with almost free care for many visitors; *see below*) and the Seychelles. But they are very basic (with widespread shortages) in Madagascar. You may need to be evacuated from any of the islands for serious conditions, and from Madagascar for almost anything except the most basic care. (Apart from South Africa and Kenya, Mauritius, Réunion and the Seychelles are themselves alternative evacuation destinations for moderately serious problems.) Even if you're just visiting Réunion and qualify for free treatment, it's advisable to get travel medical insurance that includes evacuation cover.

Everyday precautions There's a similar divide in respect of food and drink safety and many other aspects of health. You should **take care of what and where you eat and drink** in all the islands, except perhaps in the Seychelles and in major Mauritian hotels and resorts; but in Madagascar especially travellers' diarrhoea (*see p.34*) and related conditions are very common. It has also had recent outbreaks of cholera (*see p.44*). Hepatitis A (*see p.51*) is widespread in the islands. Only in the Seychelles, and in Port Louis (the capital) and the major tourist resorts of Mauritius, is tap water regarded as safe to drink. Elsewhere (and anywhere if you have doubts, including rural parts of Mauritius), you should boil or otherwise treat water (*see p.32*) for drinking, making ice or cleaning your teeth. Or use reliable bottled water, which is available in most places other than rural Madagascar. Use only pasteurised or sterilised milk and dairy products (or boil milk).

All these islands except the southern tip of Madagascar lie in the tropics, and the sun is very strong. (Antananarivo, Madagascar's capital, has a temperate climate due to its 1250m [4100ft] altitude, but for that very reason the sun is even stronger.) So treat it with respect: Use a high-factor sunscreen (*see p.56*), wear a hat and sunbathe for only short periods at first. The islands all have seasons of high humidity, when you need to beware of heat exhaustion (*see p.58*) – particularly on first arrival. Most are small, and onshore breezes usually temper the heat, but Madagascar – almost 1600km (1000 miles) long – is big enough to have both deserts and humid rainforests. All except the Seychelles may be hit by cyclones between about December and March.

Bilharzia (schistosomiasis; *see p.102*) is widespread in fresh water in Madagascar, so don't swim or paddle in any fresh water other than a well-chlorinated swimming pool there. It also has venomous snakes and spiders.

Sex safety Full official UN records aren't available, but it's clear that the sub-Saharan HIV/AIDS epidemic hasn't (yet) reached these islands, in all of which well under 1 per cent of the adult population is HIV-positive. (The highest measured rate is in Madagascar, with 0.3 per cent of adults infected.) However, infection rates are increasing, and hepatitis B (*see p.148*) is widespread; so it's still important to **practise safer sex** (*see p.145*) and consider getting a hepatitis B vaccination (see below). People wanting permanent residence or a working visa in Mauritius need an HIV test.

Vaccinations etc Again, Madagascar has the largest number of serious but vaccine-preventable diseases, but don't neglect vaccinations elsewhere; the ones you should have (or consider), and precautions to take, are:–

→ *Cholera* (*see p.44*) – especially for Madagascar and possibly Réunion.
→ *Hepatitis A* (*see p.51*) everywhere, except perhaps for short holidays at resorts in Mauritius or the Seychelles.
→ *Hepatitis B* (*see p.148*) everywhere if you may have sexual or blood contact with locals, take part in hazardous activities or stay long-term.
→ *Malaria* (*see p.107*) in Madagascar (mainly *falciparum* type) and northern rural parts of Mauritius (*vivax* type). Prophylaxis: mefloquine ('Lariam'), doxycycline or atovaquone plus proguanil ('Malarone') in Madagascar; none (but avoid mosquito bites) or chloroquine in Mauritius.
→ *Meningitis* (*see p.163*) – probably not necessary, even in Madagascar, but check with a travel clinic before you go, in case of local outbreaks.
→ *Polio* (*see p.165*) – only a few recent cases in Madagascar, but it's worth getting a vaccination or booster until it's fully eliminated worldwide.
→ *Rabies* (*see p.139*) – a risk only in Madagascar; pre-travel vaccination is probably worthwhile if you're staying long or travelling around the island, but you'll still need further vaccination if bitten by a rabid animal (eg, dog).
→ *Tuberculosis* (*see p.160*) – for those staying long-term (especially in Madagascar) in close contact with local people.
→ *Yellow fever* (*see p.123*) – not present in any of the islands, but an official certificate of vaccination is needed by all of them for anyone (usually except young children) travelling from or through a yellow fever area – including most of tropical Africa.

→ **Others** Make sure routine vaccinations are up to date, particularly tetanus and diphtheria (*see p. 166*) – usually combined – and, for older and some other travellers, flu and pneumococcal disease.

Other medical risks Apart from the diseases mentioned above (and common universal ones such as measles), other risks include dengue fever (*see p. 125*) in occasional epidemics; plague (*see p. 130*) in isolated areas of Madagascar; lymphatic filariasis (*see p. 131*); and sometimes Crimean–Congo haemorrhagic fever (*see p. 139*).

MADAGASCAR

Some well qualified doctors, but poor medical infrastructure. Medicines often unavailable, especially outside Antananarivo. Evacuation advisable for anything except simple problems.

Emergencies (may be unreliable)
Police T 17
Ambulance T 18

Health ministry/dept
Rue Jean Ralaemongo, Ambohidahy, 101 Antananarivo
T +261 (20) 223697

British consulates
British Embassy, Lot II I 164 Ter, Alarobia, Amboniloa, 101 Antananarivo
T +261 (20) 224 9378
Toamasina T +261 (20) 533 2548; +261 (20) 533 2569

Other consulates
Canadian T +261 (20) 224 2559

US T +261 (20) 222 1257

Hospitals/clinics
Hôpital Général de Befeletanana, Mahamasina, 101 Antananarivo
T +261 (20) 222384

Centre Hospitalier de Soavinandriana, Rue moss Soavinandriana, 101 Antananaviro
T +261 (20) 2241821

Espace Medical, Lot IV 0110 GA, Ambodivoma, Antananaviro
T +261 (20) 65825

MAURITIUS

Good medical care available, free in public hospitals and clinics.

Emergencies T 999
Medical assistance SAMU T 114

Health ministry/dept
Sir S. Ramgoolam St, Port Louis
T +230 201 1910

British consulates
British High Commission, Les Cascades Bldg, Edith Cavell St, Port Louis
T +230 202 9400
Rodrigues T +230 831 1766

Other consulates
Australian T +230 208 1700
W www.ahcmauritius.org

Canadian T +230 212 5500

New Zealand T +230 286 4920; +230 286 5579; +230 286 9414

South African T +230 212 6925

US T +230 202 4400
W www.usembassymauritius.mu

Hospitals/clinics
Sir S. Ramgoolam National Hospital, Pamplemousses
T +230 264 1661

Dr A.G. Jeetoo Hospital, Volcy Pougnet St, Port Louis
T +230 212 3201

Princess Margaret Orthopaedic Hospital, Candos, Quatre-Bornes
T +230 425 3031

REUNION

Overseas department of France; excellent medical care (for EEA citizens on same basis as in France itself; *see p.260*). Consular help usually from Mauritius.

Emergencies
Police **T** 17
Ambulance **T** 15
Air ambulance SAMU **T** +262 201515

Health ministry/dept
(Préfecture) Place du Barachois, 97400 Saint-Denis
T +262 407777

Hospitals/clinics
Centre Hospitalier Felix Guyon, Route de Bellepierre, 97405 Saint-Denis
T +262 905050

Centre Hospitalier Sud Réunion, RN2 Terre Sainte, 97410 Saint-Perre
T +262 359000

SEYCHELLES

Medical care good, but may be limited on outer islands.

Emergencies T 999

Health ministry/dept
Victoria Hospital, Mahé (*see below*)

British consulate
British High Commission, Oliaji Trade Centre (3rd Floor), Francis Rachel St, Victoria, Mahé
T +248 283666
W *www.bhcvictoria.sc*

Other consulates
US **T** +248 225256

Hospitals/clinics
Victoria Hospital, Mont Fleuri Rd, Victoria, Mahé
T +248 388000

TEMPERATE LATIN AMERICA

Argentina, Chile

From the tropical swamps of the Gran Chaco and (on the other side of the Andes) Chile's Atacama Desert – one of the driest places on Earth – these two long, narrow countries stretch to the stormy, cold tundra of Patagonia and Cape Horn. They're a bit more off the beaten track for many travellers than some of the countries farther north, but they also share fewer of the medical problems of their tropical neighbours. However, you still need full travel medical insurance (including evacuation and repatriation cover).

Everyday precautions Travellers' diarrhoea isn't such a problem as in the tropics, but it's still the most common illness to hit travellers. Tap water probably isn't safe to drink anywhere in Argentina, and only in the major cities and good tourist hotels in Chile. Elsewhere, boil or otherwise purify water for drinking, cleaning your teeth or making ice (*see p.32*), or use safe bottled water – which is generally available except in some isolated places.

The sun is very strong in the hotter northern areas and particularly at high altitude in the Andes. Treat it with great respect, use a high-factor sunscreen (*see p.56*), wear a hat and expose yourself for only short periods at first. On the other hand, cold exposure (*see p.61*) is more likely to be a problem in Patagonia, especially in winter, and in the mountains. Altitude sickness (*see* p.66) is always a risk if you go over about 2600m (8500ft) in the Andes, so be sure to acclimatise as you climb and go lower if you start to feel ill. Santiago is notorious for air pollution in winter (May to October) and dust in summer.

Sex safety About 0.7 per cent of the adult population is HIV-positive in Argentina (with the great majority in the Buenos Aires area) and about 0.3 per cent in Chile. Many people get HIV by gay or straight sex, but in both countries an increasing number become infected by injecting drugs with shared needles. Although the rates are lower than in many parts of Latin America, you should **always practise safer sex** (see p.145).

Vaccinations etc No vaccinations are required to enter Argentina or Chile, but there are rare outbreaks of yellow fever in north-eastern Argentina, near the borders with Paraguay, Brazil and Uruguay, and it makes sense to get vaccinated before going to that area (see p.123). There's a low risk of vivax-type malaria in the Gran Chaco region, near Argentina's boder with Bolivia and Paraguay (see p.107); the recommended preventive drug is chloroquine.

Rabies isn't a major problem, but there are rabid dogs in cities and suburbs in Argentina, so you might want to discuss vaccination with a travel clinic doctor. Hepatitis A vaccination is worthwhile for all travellers to South America (see p.51). The same applies to typhoid vaccination (see p.46) if you plan to travel outside major urban areas. Consider hepatitis B vaccination (see p.148), and also meningitis (see p.163) if there is one of the occasional epidemics of this disease occurring when you visit Chile.

Otherwise, it's as important here as anywhere to make sure your routine vaccinations are up to date – particularly tetanus and diphtheria (see p.166) and others generally given in childhood. The risk of tuberculosis in Argentina and Chile is generally low.

Other medical risks There aren't so many of these as in the tropics. Apart from common everyday diseases and those mentioned above, they include...

→ *Dengue fever* (see p.125), especially in urban areas of northern Agentina.
→ *Anthrax* (see p.167) if you have close contact with stock animals.
→ *Chagas disease* (see p.121) in northern rural areas (but rare).
→ *Leishmaniasis* (see p.118), especially in Argentina.
→ Various *worm infestations* (see p.49) in rural parts of Chile.

ARGENTINA

Medical facilities good in Buenos Aires but variable elsewhere; immediate cash payment often required.

Emergencies
Police **T** 101
Ambulance **T** 107

Health ministry/dept
Avenida 9 de Julio 1925 (Piso 4),
Buenos Aires
T +54 (11) 381 8911; +54 (11) 381 4435

British consulate
Dr Luis Agote 2412/52, Buenos Aires
T +54 (11) 4808 2200; +54 (11) 5331 7129 (emergencies)
W *www.britain.org.ar*

Other main consulates
Australian **T** +54 (11) 4779 3500
W *www.argentina.embassy.gov.au*

Canadian **T** +54 (11) 4808 1000
W *www.dfait-maeci.gc.ca/argentina*

New Zealand **T** +54 (11) 4328 0747

South African **T** +54 (11) 4317 2900

US **T** +54 (11) 5777 4533;
+54 (11) 4514 1830 (emergencies)

Hospitals/clinics
Hospital Municipal Juan Fernandez,
Av Cervino 3356, Palermo, Buenos Aires
T +54 (11) 801 5555

British Hospital, Perdriel 74,
Buenos Aires
T +54 (11) 4304 7758

CHILE

Good medical care available in major cities but variable elsewhere, especially in remote areas. Cash payment often required, except in some emergency departments.

Emergencies
Police **T** 133
Ambulance **T** 131

Health ministry/dept
Mac Iver 541, Santiago
T +56 (2) 630 0673

British consulates
British Embassy, Av El Bosque Norte 0125, Las Condes, Santiago
T +56 (2) 370 4100
W www.britemb.cl
Punta Arenas **T** +56 (61) 211535
Valparaiso **T** +56 (32) 213063

Other main consulates
Australian **T** +56 (2) 550 3500
W *www.chile.embassy.gov.au*

Canadian **T** +56 (2) 362 9660
W *www.dfait-maeci.gc.ca/chile*

New Zealand **T** +56 (2) 290 9802

South African **T** +56 (2) 290 9802

US **T** +56 (2) 335 6550; +56 (2) 330 3321 (emergencies)

Hospitals/clinics
Clinica Las Condes, Lo Fontecilla 441,
Las Condes, Santiago
T +56 (2) 210 4000

Fundacion Hospital San José Puerto Varas, Otto Bader 810, San José
T +56 (65) 232336

Hospital San Martin de Quillota, La Concepcion 1050, Quillota
T +56 (33) 310 023140

TROPICAL LATIN AMERICA

Belize , Bolivia, Brazil, Costa Rica, Ecuador and Galápagos Islands, Guyana, Mexico, Panama, Peru, Venezuela

You'll probably think first of the Andes, the lush Amazon jungle, the beaches of Cancún, Rio and other resorts, carnival, and the ruins of civilisations that flourished long before Europeans arrived. The tropics of Central and South America (plus the subtropical parts of Mexico) lure both tourists and adventure/eco-travellers – whether they want to take the 'Inca Trail' to Machu Picchu or check out the unique wildlife of the Costa Rican cloud forest.

There are luxury resorts and modern cities, but many local people in this huge region live in great poverty, and standards of medical care vary enormously. Among the countries listed on the following pages, first-class hospitals and other medical facilities exist only in Brazil (in cities), Costa Rica (in San José), Mexico (in major cities, especially the capital), Panama (in Panama City), Peru (in Lima and Cuzco) and Venezuela (in Caracas). Elsewhere – including in most provinical towns and all rural areas in these countries – facilities are adequate at best and very limited when it comes to more complicated needs. Evacuation by air to a major city, or to the USA or back home – which is very expensive – will probably be needed if you fall seriously ill, so I'd strongly advise you to get full medical insurance (including repatriation). None of the countries listed offers free medical care to visitors except for emergency care in Costa Rica, Panama and Venezuela

Everyday precautions It's no coincidence that one of diarrhoea's many nicknames is 'Montezuma's revenge'. The no. 1 complaint throughout the region is travellers' diarrhoea (see p.34), and hepatitis A is also common, so **take particular care with what and where you eat and drink** (see p.28). You can't rely on anywhere having safe tap water – even in tourist hotels and resorts – except perhaps in San José (Costa Rica) and in Panama City. Elsewhere, you need to boil water or purify it in other ways (see p.32), or use safe bottled water for drinking and cleaning teeth. (Bottled water is pretty widely available, except reportedly in parts of Bolivia.) Only use ice made from similar water, and consume only pasteurised or sterilised milk and dairy products (or boil milk).

Given the tropical/subtropical location, it's also no surprise that the heat and the strength of the sun are likely to trouble you if you come a from cooler climate. Be sure to allow your body to acclimatise to the heat and humidity when you first arrive (drinking lots of fluids; see p.58), and always treat the sun with great respect (see p.54). Use a high-factor sunscreen, wear a hat and expose yourself to the sun for only short periods at first; this is even more true in the high mountains – where the burning and skin-damaging ultra-violet light is very intense – than in beach resorts.

Cold and altitude are serious threats in the high Andes of Ecuador and particularly Peru and Bolivia. (Both Cuzco and La Paz are over 3000m [10 000ft] high.) If you visit these cities – or particularly if you trek the 'Inca Trail', which rises to 4200m (13 800ft), or visit Lake Titicaca at 3810m (12 500ft) – be very cautious of altitude sickness (see p.66); it can kill if you don't recognise or simply ignore the symptoms. (Coca-leaf tea-bags are widely sold as a 'herbal' antidote to altitude sickness in both Bolivia and Peru, but I can't vouch for their effectiveness; acetazolamide ['Diamox'] is a more conventional protective medication.) If you do get into trouble, air evacuation may be a problem at high altitude, so avoid an emergency by going lower if you start to feel unwell. Beware of hypothermia (see p.61).

There are a great variety of venomous and non-venomous snakes (see p.97), plus spiders and scorpions (see p.82), in the region, but they're much more of a hazard to local people than to visitors. In Mexico, the Durango scorpion stings thousands of people every year, and causes many deaths.

Sex safety HIV/AIDS is a significant problem in tropical Latin America, but overall it's not such a big problem as in the neighbouring Caribbean. Only in parts of Central America (including Belize) and in Guyana is the adult HIV-infection rate 2 per cent or more. Brazil has by far the largest number of HIV-positive people – more than 600 000, according to official UN estimates, representing 0.7 per cent of the country's adult population.

In most countries except Costa Rica, Mexico and Venezuela, straight sex is the main method of infection or is on a par with gay and bisexual contact; however, surveys in several of these countries have shown high infection rates in gay and bisexual men in major cities and that many gay men do also have sex with women. Shared use of dirty needles for injecting drugs is a significant problem only in Brazil and northern Mexico. The infection rate among sex workers ranges from as high as 44 per cent in Georgetown, Guyana, to very low figures in Bolivia, where registered sex workers must have regular check-ups. But **always take precautions** (*see p. 145*).

Vaccinations etc There are a lot of serious infectious diseases in Central and tropical South America that can be prevented (or made much less serious) by vaccination or other measures. These are the precautions you should (or in some cases *must*) take, or at least discuss with a travel doctor:–

Cholera Big cholera epidemics hit much of the region from time to time; the risk is lowest in Bolivia and Guyana. The normal 'El Tor' type (*see p.44*) is not usually very serious in travellers if treated properly. But if you're planning to travel far from good medical facilities during an epidemic, I'd recommend you discuss with a doctor getting one of the newer vaccines as protection. (The old vaccine isn't very effective, and isn't recommended.)

Hepatitis A Vaccination is sensible for all travellers to tropical Latin America, especially if you're backpacking outside the major cities (*see p.51*).

Hepatitis B Taking safer-sex precautions should protect you from sexual transmission of this virus, but if you're involved in a serious accident you may not be able to rely on safe, screened blood supplies for transfusion (*see p.172*). If you plan to take part in any risky physical activities, if you're working as a medical volunteer and are therefore likely to have blood contact with local people, if you're planning a long stay, or if you simply feel cautious, then hepatitis B vaccination is worth having (*see p.148*).

Malaria Precautions – both protection from mosquito bites and preventive drugs (*see pp.75 & 107*) – are essential all year round in at least part of all the countries covered here, except at high altitude (generally above about 2500m [8000ft]) and most big cities. Malaria (mainly *vivax* rather than the often more dangerous *falciparum* type, unless stated) is a risk as follows:–

→ ***Belize*** All regions, but risk is highest in the west and south.
→ ***Bolivia*** Mainly east of the Andes; *falciparum* type in the north-east.
→ ***Brazil*** Low risk of both *falciparum* and *vivax* types in most forested areas below 900m (3000ft) throughout the Amazon region except Belém City.

→ *Costa Rica* Low to moderate risk in rural areas below 500m (1650ft) near both the Pacific and Caribbean coasts; San José is malaria-free.

→ *Ecuador* Both *falciparum* and *vivax* types throughout the country below 1500m (5000ft), except in Guayaquil, Quito and the Galápagos Islands. The high-altitude tourist areas are malaria-free.

→ *Guyana* High risk of both *falciparum* and *vivax* types throughout the interior, and from time to time in the coastal belt.

→ *Mexico* Risk in some rural areas, mostly little visited by travellers. Highest risk in states of Chiapas, Quintana Roo and Tabasco in the south-east, and Sinaloa on the west coast. Moderate risk in Chihuahua, Durango and Sonora in the north, Nayarit on the west coast, and Oaxaca in the south. Low risk in Campeche in the south-east, and Guerrero, Michoacán and Jalisco in the south-west. Major cities and tourist resorts (including probably Cancún in Quintana Roo state) are malaria-free.

→ *Panama* Low risk only in provinces of Bocas del Toro in the north-west, and Darién and San Blas in the east (with some *falciparum* type in both). Panama City and the canal zone are malaria-free.

→ *Peru* High risk of both *falciparum* and *vivax* types in more than half of all administrative regions, except at high altitude. Main *falciparum* risk is in the Amazon Basin regions east of the Andes.

→ *Venezuela* Risk in rural areas in the southern two-thirds of the country, and in eastern coastal states of Sucre and Delta Amacuro. There's the *falciparum* type in jungle areas along and south of the Orinoco river.

For Mexico and Central America west and north of the Panama Canal, travel clinics usually recommend chloroquine or sometimes proguanil ('Paludrine') for malaria prophylaxis (see p.115). For the rest of Panama and in the other countries covered here, the recommended pills are usually mefloquine ('Lariam'), doxycycline (eg, 'Nordox' or 'Vibramycin') or atovaquone plus proguanil (combined in 'Malarone'). However, for travel only in Bolivia, Ecuador other than Esmereldas province (in the far north), eastern Panama, Peru and/or Venezuela, your doctor may suggest chloroquine plus proguanil.

Rabies There's a risk of rabies – especially from dogs and bats – throughout the region. Consider the advice in the article on page 139 about getting vaccinated before departure if you're going to spend a long time in the region or if you'll be travelling far from modern medical facilities.

Typhoid This is a risk throughout the region, particularly if you're travelling outside the cities and main tourist areas. In that case, vaccination is probably worthwhile, but doesn't give full protection (see p.46).

Yellow fever The only country covered here where you definitely don't need a vaccinaton (with an international certificate to back it up; see p.123) is Mexico. In addition, Costa Rica and Venezuela don't require visitors to hold a certificate, but you may need one if you're travelling on to other countries (see below). Certificates are required for all travellers from all 'infected areas' (which you can generally take to include Panama and most of tropical South

America, plus tropical Africa) to Belize, Bolivia, Brazil (travellers more than 9 months old), Ecuador (if more than a year old), Guyana (including travellers from Costa Rica and Venezuela) and Peru (if more than 6 months old).

In terms of your own protection, you should currently have a yellow fever vaccination if you intend visiting much of the interior of Brazil, eastern parts of Panama, or jungle areas of Peru below about 2300m (7500ft). But, to simplify things, I'd recommend you get vaccinated – it's reckoned to be pretty safe – if you intend to travel anywhere between Belize and southern Brazil.

Others There's an occasional outbreak of plague in small areas of Bolivia, Brazil, Guyana, Ecuador and Peru, but it's not common enough to make vaccination worthwhile for most travellers (see p. 130). Tuberculosis is quite common in Ecuador, Peru, Bolivia and Guyana, and to a lesser extent in Brazil, so you'd be well advised to make sure your BCG vaccination (see p. 160) is up to date, particularly if you expect to spend a significant time living among local people. (US authorities take a different approach.)

Otherwise, make sure that your standard childhood vaccinations are within date and get boosters if necessary; this particularly applies to tetanus (see p. 166), which all travellers should have (combined with diphtheria). (Polio has been eliminated in the Americas, so a booster is probably no longer needed.) Older travellers and anyone else who normally has a regular flu jab should have both this and pneumococcal vaccinations before visiting the region.

Other medical risks Many other diseases are common in the region. Apart from everyday universal diseases and those mentioned above, they include...

→ *Dengue fever* (see p. 125) throughout the region, with huge epidemics recently in some cities.
→ *Bilharzia* (schistosomiasis; see p. 102) in fresh water in Brazil and parts of Venezuela.
→ *Leishmaniasis* (see p. 118) throughout the region, but in Central America only in isolated areas.
→ *Chagas disease* (see p. 121) throughout the region, in rural areas.
→ *Lymphatic filiariasis* (see p. 131) and *river blindness* (onchocerciasis; see p. 132) in many areas.
→ *Brucellosis* (see p. 52) in most parts of the region.
→ *Respiratory diseases* in some areas because of air pollution (especially in São Paulo, Brazil) or high summer humidity.

BELIZE

Facilities limited, especially in rural areas; may need to evacuate to Mexico or USA for serious conditions. Cash payment often required, sometimes in advance.

Emergencies
Police T 911
Ambulance T 90

Health ministry/dept
East Block, Independence Hill, Belmopan
T +501 822325

BELIZE (continued)

British consulate
British High Commission, PO Box 91,
Belmopan
T +501 822 2146

Other consulates
Canadian T +501 231060

US T +501 227 7161
W www.usembassy.state.gov/belize

Hospitals/clinics
Karl Heusner Memorial Hopsital,
Princess Margaret Drive, Belize City
T +501 231548

BOLIVIA

Medical care adequate in large
cities, except for major emergencies.

Emergencies T 911
Police T 110
Ambulance T 118

Health ministry/dept
Plaza del Estudiante, La Paz
T +591 (2) 375471

British consulate
British Embassy, Av Arce 2732, La Paz
T +591 (2) 243 3424
W www.britishembassy.gov.uk/bolivia

Other consulates
Australian T +591 (2) 244 0459

Canadian T +591 (2) 241 5012;
+591 (2) 241 4517

US T +591 (2) 243 3812; +591 (2) 243 2540
or +591 (2) 772 3812 (emergencies)
W http://bolivia.usembassy.gov

Hospitals/clinics
Clinica Americana, Av 14 de Septiembre,
Obrajes, La Paz
T +591 (2) 783371

Hospital General, Av Saavedra 2245,
La Paz
T +591 (2) 367711

BRAZIL

Excellent medical care available in
major cities (although costs may be

very high), but more limited in rural
areas and especially in remote
regions (eg, much of Amazon).

Emergencies T 0
Ambulance T 0; 193
Air ambulance Golden Cross has
branches in major cities

Health ministry/dept
Esplanada dos Ministerios, Bloco G, 50,
Andar (Brasilia) 70058-900
T +55 (61) 315 2425

British consulates
British Embassy, SES Quadra 801, Lote
8, Av das Nações, 70408-900 Brasilia
T +55 (61) 225 2710
W www.reinounido.org.br
Belém T +55 (91) 222 5074
Belo Horizonte T +55 (31) 261 2072
Curitiba T +55 (41) 322 1202
Fortaleza T +55 (85) 466 8582
Manaus T +55 (92) 613 1819
Porto Alegre T +55 (51) 341 0720
Recife T +55 (81) 465 0230
Rio de Janeiro T +55 (21) 2555 9600
Rio Grande T +55 (53) 233 7700
Salvador T +55 (71) 243 7399
Santos T +55 (13) 219 6622
São Paulo T +55 (11) 3094 2700

Other main consulates (in São Paulo
unless stated)
Australian T +55 (11) 3849 6281
W www.embaixada-australia.org.br

Canadian T +55 (11) 5509 4321
W www.dfait-maeci.gc.ca/brazil

New Zealand T +55 (11) 3148 0616

South African T +55 (11) 3285 0433
W www.africadosulemb.org.br

US (Brasilia) T +55 (61) 312 7000;
+55 (61) 312 7400 (emergencies)
W www.embaixada-americana.org.br

Hospitals/clinics
Hospital Miguel Couto, Rua Mário
Ribeiro 117, Gávea, Rio de Janeiro
T +55 (21) 2274 6050

Hospital Adventista Silvestre, Ladeira
dos Guararapes 263, Cosme Velho,
Rio de Janeiro
T +55 (21) 2556 0212

Hospital das Clinicas da Faculdade de Medicina da Universida de São Paulo, Av Dr Enias de Carvalho Aguiar 255, Cerqueira Cesar, São Paulo
T +55 (11) 3069 6000

Hospital Albert Einstein, Av Albert Einstein 627/701, Morumbi, São Paulo
T +55 (11) 3845 1233

COSTA RICA

Good medical facilities in major cities but limited in rural areas. Treatment free in public hospitals.

Emergencies T 911
Police T 104
Ambulance T +506 225 1436;
+506 228 2187
Red Cross T 128

Health ministry/dept
Apartado Postal 10123-1000, San José
T +506 233 0333

British consulate
British Embassy, Edificio Centro Colon 11th Floor, San José
T +506 258 2025
W www.embajadabritanica.com

Other consulates
Canadian T +506 296 4149

South African T +506 222 1470

US T +506 220 3939; +506 20 3127
W http://usembassy.or.cr
(includes list of medical facilities)

Hospitals/clinics
Hospital San Juan de Dios, Calle 14, Av Central, San José
T +506 222 0166; +506 257 6282

Hospital CIMA San José
T +506 208 1000

ECUADOR (inc GALAPAGOS IS)

Medical care OK to good in main towns, but limited in rural areas. Said to be shortage of ambulances.

Emergencies
Police T 101
Ambulance T 911; 131

Health ministry/dept
Bldg A, Juan Larrea 445, Quito
T + 593 (2) 252 1411

British consulates
British Embassy, Av Naciones Unidas & Republica de El Salvador, Quito
T +593 (2) 297 0800
W www.britembquito.org.ec
Galápagos Is T +593 (5) 526157
Guayaquil T +593 (4) 256 0400 ext 318

Other main consulates
Australian T +593 (4) 680823

Canadian T +593 (2) 223 2114

US T +593 (2) 256 2890; +593 (2) 256 1749
W www.usembassy.org.ec

Hospitals/clinics
Eugenio Espejo Hospital, Av Colombia, Quito
T +593 (2) 222 4738

Luis Vernaza General Hospital, Julian Coronel & Escobedo, Guayaquil
T +593 (4) 256 0300

GUYANA

Limited facilities; drug shortages. Serious conditions need evacuation.

Emergencies
Police T 911
Ambulance T 913

Health ministry/dept
Lot 1, Brickdam, Georgetown, Guyana
T +592 226 1560

British consulate
British High Commission, 44 Main St, Georgetown
T +592 226 5881

Other consulates
Canadian T +592 227 2081

US T +592 225 4900; +592 226 2614 pager 6516 (emergencies)

Hospitals/clinics
Davis Memorial Hospital, 121 Durban St, Lodge. Georgetown
T +592 227 2041

St Joseph's Mercy Hospital, 130-132 Parade St, Kingston
T +592 227 2072

MEXICO

Good medical care available, especially in Mexico City and (to varying extent) other cities; may be limited in rural areas

Emergencies T 08 (Mexico City only; varies elsewhere)
Tourist helpline T 01800 903 9200

Health ministry/dept
Lieja 7, Col Juarez, Mexico City 06600
T +52 (5) 553 7670

British consulates
Usumacinta 30, Col Cuauhtémoc, Mexico City 06500
T +52 (55) 5242 8523
W www.embajadabritanica.com.mx
Acapulco **T** +52 (744) 841735
Cancún **T** +52 (998) 810100
Cuidad Juarez **T** +52 (656) 175791; +52 (656) 175088
Guadalajara **T** +52 (33) 3343 2296
Monterrey **T** +52 (81) 8356 5359
Oaxaca **T** +52 (951) 71742
Tijuana **T** +52 (666) 865320; +52 (666) 817323
Veracruz **T** +52 (229) 311285

Other main consulates
Australian **T** +52 (55) 5531 5225
W www.mexico.embassy.gov.au

Canadian **T** +52 (55) 5724 7900
W www.canada.org.mx

New Zealand **T** +52 (55) 5283 9460

South African **T** +52 (55) 5282 9260

US **T** +52 (55) 5080 2000
W www.usembassy-mexico.gov

Hospitals/clinics
American British Cowdray Hospital, Calle Sur 136 No 116, Mexico City
T +52 (55) 5230 8000

Hospital Americano, Ave Viento 15, Cancún
T +52 (998) 844 6133

Hospital Civiles de Guadalajara
T +52 (33) 3614 5501; +52 (33) 3614 7531

Hospital San José Tec de Monterrey, Av Morones Prieto 3000, Monterrey
T +52 (81) 8333 3600

PANAMA

Excellent standards of care in Panama City, but limited elsewhere. Free emergency treatment.

Emergencies
Police **T** 104
Ambulance **T** +507 225 1436; +507 228 2187

Health ministry/dept
Apartado 2048, Panama 1
T +507 225 3540

British consulate
British Embassy, Swiss Tower, Calle 53, Zona 1, Panama City
T +507 269 0866

Other consulates
Canadian **T** +507 264 9731; +507 264 7115
W www.dfait-maeci.gc.ca/panama

South African **T** +507 263 6900

US **T** +507 207 7000
W http://usembassy.state.gov/panama

Hospitals/clinics
Hospital Nacional, Av Cuba, Calle 38 y 39, Panama City
T +507 207 8100

Centro Medico Paitilla, Av Balboa, Calle 53, Panama City
T +507 269 0655

PERU

Standards of medical care adequate to good in Lima and other cities, but may be limited elsewhere. Cash payment often required.

Emergencies
Police **T** 105
Ambulance **T** 011; 5114

Health ministry/dept
Av Salaverry Cuadra 8 sin Jesus Maria, Lima
T +51 (1) 432 6242

British consulates
British Embassy, Torre Parque Mar Piso 22, Av Jose Larco 1301, Miraflores, Lima
T +51 (1) 617 3050

W *www.britemb.org.pe*
Arequipa T +51 (54) 241340
Cuzco T +51 (84) 226671; +51 (84) 239974
Iquitos T +51 (94) 222732
Piura T +51 (74) 305990
Trujillo T +51 (44) 235548;
+51 (44) 245935

Other main consulates
Australian T +51 (1) 222 8281
W *www.australia.org.pe*

Canadian T +51 (1) 444 4015
W *www.dfait-maeci.gc.ca/peru*

New Zealand T +51 (1) 222 5022

US T +51 (1) 434-3000; +51 (1) 434 3032
(emergencies)
W *http://usembassy.state.gov/lima*

Hospitals/clinics
Clinica Internacional, Washington 1475,
Lima
T +51 (1) 428 8060

Clinica Anglo-American, 3rd Block of
Salazar, San Isidrio, Lima
T +51 (1) 221 3656

Hospital Essalud, Av Anselmo Alvarez,
Cuzco
T +51 (84) 234724

VENEZUELA

Good facilities in private hospitals in
Caracas. Free emergency treatment
for travellers in public hospitals –
but these are of lower standard, so
insurance advisable. Facilities may
be limited in rural areas.

Emergencies T 171

Health ministry/dept
Parque Central, Torre Oests Piso 39-41,
DF Caracas
T +58 (2) 574 1876

British consulates
British Embassy, Torre La Castellana
Piso 11, Av La Principal de la Castellana,
La Castellana, Caracas
T +58 (212) 263 8411
W *www.britain.org.ve*
Maracaibo T +58 (261) 791 5589
Margarita T +58 (295) 262 4665
Mérida T +58 (274) 266 2022
Puerto La Cruz T +58 (81) 811011
San Cristobal T +58 (276) 347 1644
Valencia T +58 (241) 823 8401

Other main consulates
Australian T +58 (212) 263 4033
W *www.venezuela.embassy.gov.au*

Canadian T +58 (212) 264 0833
W *www.dfait-maeci.gc.ca/caracas*

New Zealand T +58 (212) 277 7965

South African T +58 (212) 991 4622

US T +58 (212) 975 6411;
+58 (212) 975 9821 (emergencies)
W *http://embajadausa.org.ve*

Hospitals/clinics
Hospital de Clinicas Caracas, Av
Panteon & Calle Alameda, San
Bernardino, Caracas
T +58 (2) 574 7432; +58 (2) 574 1187

Hospital Clinico Maracaibo, Urb La
Trinidad, Calle 59, Maracaibo, Edo Zulia
T +58 (61) 420842

THE CARIBBEAN

Bahamas, Barbados, Bermuda, Cuba, Dominican Repubic, Haiti, Jamaica, Puerto Rico, Trinidad and other islands

OK, so Bermuda isn't actually in the Caribbean Sea – and nor, for that matter are the Bahamas – but these sunny islands are traditionally grouped together and certainly share a similar appeal of beaches, beautiful coastal and inland scenery, clear waters and a warm (if sometimes rainy and windy) climate. They may not be the first choice for a highbrow holiday, but they're among the world's top spots for beach- or yacht-bumming, and for sports and other fun in the water and on land.

But, beneath the veneer of usually first-class tourist facilities, many places have the economy, infrastructure and other facilities of a developing country. Top-rank hospitals and other medical facilities do exist on some islands. On others they may be rated as adequate, but in many places you might well need to be evacuated to another centre (for example, the best facilities in the eastern Caribbean are probably on the French island of Guadeloupe) – or even back home or to the USA – for anything more than very straightforward care. Some islands give free medical care to British and some other nationals (*see listings on following pages*), but bear in mind the possible need for evacuation or repatriation and – certainly if you plan to travel through a number of islands, where entitlements vary – get good medical insurance.

Everyday precautions Travellers' diarrhoea (including amoebic dysentery; *see pp.34–43*) is quite common in the Caribbean, and there's hepatitis A especially in rural parts of the bigger islands to the north. So take care with what and where you eat and drink (*see p.28*). There are cases of ciguatera poisoning (*see p.48*) from time to time; avoid eating reef fish if there's been a recent outbreak. Tap water varies in quality; reports suggest that it's generally unsafe in Anguilla, Antigua, the Bahamas, Cuba, Dominica, the Dominican Republic, Guadeloupe, Haiti and St Kitts, and in rural parts of Jamaica. Safe bottled water is widely available, however, and if in doubt you should use it (or boiled or otherwise purified water; *see p.32*) everywhere – for drinking, for cleaning your teeth and for making ice. Use only pasteurised or sterilised milk and dairy products (or boil milk).

It almost goes without saying that the sun is strong here – all the islands except Bermuda and the northern Bahamas are within the tropics, and the sun is a major attraction. So treat it with great respect; use a high-factor sunscreen (*see p.56*), wear a hat and sunbathe for only short periods at first. Take sensible precautions if you engage in water sports (*see p.171*). Hurricanes are a risk in summer and autumn, and venomous spiders, scorpions and snakes live on a few islands. Beware the intensely irritating sap of manchineel trees, which grow at the edge of many Caribbean beaches (they're often signalled by a red warning sign); their fruits are poisonous, too.

Sex safety The Caribbean is second only to sub-Saharan Africa for the impact of HIV/AIDS, according to the UN, and hepatitis B is also common. In all the larger island nations except Cuba more than 1 per cent of the adult population is HIV-positive; the highest rates are in Haiti (6.1 per cent), the Bahamas (3.5 per cent), and Jamaica and Trinidad (both about 2.5 per cent).

In most of the islands, although HIV-positive men outnumber women, the main way of catching the virus is believed to be heterosexual and/or bisexual contact. (Research suggests that, as in some other regions, many gay men in the Caribbean also have sex with women, although the exact figures aren't known.) As elsewhere, sex workers usually have a much higher rate of infection than the rest of the population; for example, in the mid-1990s, a quarter of all the sex workers tested in Jamaica's main tourist centre, Montego Bay, were HIV-positive. Always **practise safer sex** (see p.145).

Vaccinations etc The only Caribbean island that, until recently, had yellow fever is Trinidad, where it used to crop up in the forested south-east of the island. It has quite recently been eliminated there, so you no longer need a vaccination for your own protection. However, Trinidad and Tobago and all except a few of the other islands demand a certificate of yellow fever vaccination as a precaution for everyone over the age of 12 months if they're travelling from an infected area (which includes Panama and most of tropical South America; see p.123). Exceptions, where you need no vaccination, are Bermuda, the Cayman Islands, Cuba, the Dominican Republic, Martinique, Montserrat and the Virgin Islands (British and American).

Malaria (see p.107) exists in the Caribbean only in the lowland and rural areas (excluding resorts) of Hispaniola (Haiti and western Dominican Republic). Except in some Haitian forests, the risk is low. It's the often dangerous *falciparum* type, but there's no evidence (yet) of any resistance to chloroquine, so this is the recommended prophylactic (protective) pill (see p.115). But you should still take precautions to prevent mosquito bites in both countries.

Other recommended vaccinations (apart from standard ones such as tetanus, diphtheria and measles) include:–

→ *Hepatitis A* (see p.51) in many areas.
→ *Hepatitis B* (see p.148), particularly if you might have sexual or blood contact with local people or plan to spend a long time and may have to have medical treatment, especially in Haiti or the Dominican Republic.
→ *Typhoid* (see p.46), especially if you're visiting less-developed regions.

Rabies vaccination (see p.139) is worth considering if you expect to have much contact with wild or domestic animals; consult a travel doctor.

Other medical risks Various other diseases occur in the Caribbean. Apart from common ones (eg, measles) and those mentioned above, they include...

→ *Dengue fever* (see p.125), including (rarely) the dangerous haemorrhagic version, in many of the islands. (I caught it myself in Grenada or Bequia.)

→ **Bilharzia** (schistosomiasis; *see p.102*) in fresh water in parts of Antigua, the Dominican Republic, Guadeloupe, Martinique, Montserrat, Puerto Rico and St Lucia, and sporadically elsewhere.

→ **Tuberculosis** (*see p.160*) if you have much contact with local people in the poorer areas; in the UK many people are vaccinated as routine.

→ **Filariasis** (*see p.131*) and **leishmaniasis** (*see p.118*) in some islands, but the risk is low for most travellers.

ANTIGUA

Basic medical care available, but serious cases need evacuation.

Emergencies T 911; 999

Health ministry/dept
Cross St, St John's
T +1 (268) 462 1600

British consulate
British High Commission, Price Waterhouse Centre, 11 Old Parham Rd, St John's
T +1 (268) 462 0008; +1 (268) 462 0009

Other consulates
US (agent) **T** +1 (268) 463 6531

Hospitals/clinics
Holberton Hospital, Hospital Rd, St John's
T +1 (268) 462 0251

Adelin Medical Centre, Fort Rd, St John's
T +1 (268) 462 0866

BAHAMAS

Good medical care in Nassau and Freeport, but limited elsewhere; cash payment often required.

Emergencies
Police **T** 911; + 1 (242) 322 4444
Ambulance **T** 911; +1 (242) 322 2221
Assistance **T** +1 (242) 326 4357

Health ministry/dept
Royal Victoria Gardens, East Hill St, Nassau
T +1 (242) 322 7425

British consulate
British High Commission, Ansbacher House (3rd Floor), Nassau
T +1 (242) 325 7471

Other consulates
Canadian **T** +1 (242) 393 2123

US **T** +1 (242) 322 1181

Hospitals/clinics
Princess Margaret Hospital, Shirley St & Elizabeth Ave, Nassau
T +1 (242) 322 2861

BARBADOS

Good care, but ambulance response may be slow. Free treatment (but not medicines) in hospitals and clinics for UK citizens. Otherwise, cash payment often required.

Emergencies
Police **T** 112
Ambulance **T** 115
Barbados Red Cross **T** +1 (246) 417 2727

Health ministry/dept
Jemmotts Lane, St Michael, Bridgetown
T +1 (246) 426 5080

British consulate
British High Commission, Lower Collymore Rock, Bridgetown
T +1 (246) 430 7800
W *www.britishhc.org*

Other consulates
Australian **T** +1 (246) 435 2834

Canadian **T** +1 (246) 429 3550

US **T** +1 (246) 431 0225
W *http://usembassy.state.gov/posts/bb1/wwwhcons.html*

Hospitals/clinics
Queen Elizabeth Hospital, Martindales Rd, St Michael, Bridgetown
T +1 (246) 436 6450

BERMUDA

Good medical care, but expensive.

Emergencies T 911

Health ministry/dept
Old Hospital Bldg, 7 Point Finger Rd,
Paget DV 04
T +1 (441) 236 0224

British consulate
(Governor) Government House,
Hamilton
T +1 (441) 292 3600

Other consulates
Canadian **T** +1 (441) 294 3611

US **T** +1 (441) 295 1342

Hospitals/clinics
King Edward VII Memorial Hospital,
Hamilton HM DX
T +1 (441) 236 2345

CUBA

Medical facilities limited; many
medications not available, so take
things you may need with you.

Emergencies T 26811

Health ministry/dept
Calle 23 No 301, Vedado, Havana
T +53 (7) 322561

British consulate
Calle 34 No 702/4 (between 7ma Av &
17), Miramar, Havana
T + 53 (7) 204 1771

Other consulates
Canadian **T** +53 (7) 204 2516

US (US Interests section, Swiss
Embassy) **T** +53 (7) 333551

Hospitals/clinics
Hospital 'Comandante Manuel Fajardo',
Calle Zapata & D, Vedado, Havana
T +53 (7) 552452

International Clinic,13 & 145 Glad Vista,
Santiago de Cuba
T +53 (22) 42589

DOMINICAN REPUBLIC

Limited medical and emergency
care outside Santo Domingo.

Emergencies
Police **T** 911
Ambulance **T** 911 (Santo Domingo).
Movi-med **T** +1 (809) 532 0000 (Santo
Domingo); +1 (809) 200 0911 (elsewhere)

Health ministry/dept
Ave Tiradente esq Calle San Cristobel,
Ensanche La Fe, Santo Domingo
T +1 (809) 549 4780

British consulates
British Embassy, Ave 27 de Fabrero 233,
Santo Domingo
T +1 (809) 472 7671; +1 (809) 472 7373;
+1 (809) 399 7599 (emergencies)
Puerto Plata **T** +1 (809) 586 4244

Other consulates
Canadian **T** +1 (809) 685 1136

US **T** +1 (809) 731 4294; +1 (809) 221 2171
W *www.usemb.gov.do/index.htm*

Hospitals/clinics
Centro Medico UCE University Hospital,
Santo Domingo
T +1 (809) 688 9511 (emergencies)

GRENADA

Medical care in St George's OK; cash
payment often required.

Emergencies
Police **T** 911
Ambulance **T** 434 (St George's);
724 (St Andrew's); 774 (Carriacou)

Health ministry/dept
Ministerial Complex, St George's
T +1 (473) 440 2649

British consulate
British High Commission, Netherlands
Bldg, Grand Anse, St George's
T +1 (473) 440 3222; +1 (473) 440 3536

Other consulates
US **T** +1 (473) 444 1173
W *www.spiceisle.com/usemb_gd*

Hospitals/clinics
St George's General Hospital
T +1 (473) 440 2051

GUADELOUPE

Excellent medical facilities. French overseas department, with same rights to treatment for EEA citizens as in France itself (*see p.260*).

Emergencies
Police **T** 17; +509 811155
Ambulance **T** 15; +590 876543

Health ministry/dept
(Préfecture) Rue Lardenoy, Basse-Terre
T +590 993900

British consulate
23 Rue Sadi Carnot,
97110 Pointe-à-Pitre
T +590 825757

Hospitals/clinics
Centre Hospitalier Régionale
Universitaire, Pointe-à-Pitre/Abymes
T +590 891010

HAITI

Very limited medial care, especially outside Port-au-Prince. Cash payment often required.

Emergencies
Police **T** 114
Ambulance **T** 118

Health ministry/dept
Palais des Ministères, Port-au-Prince
T +509 236248

British consulate
Hotel Montana, Port-au-Prince
T +509 257 3969

Other consulates
Canadian **T** +509 298 3050

US **T** +509 223 7011; +509 222 0200
W *www.usembassy.state.gov/haiti*

Hospitals/clinics
Hôpital Français, Port-au-Prince
T +509 222 4242; +509 223 9988

JAMAICA

Health care OK, especially in Kingston and Montego Bay. Cash payment often required.

Emergencies
Police **T** 119
Ambulance **T** 110

Health ministry/dept
2-4 King St, Kingston
T +1 (876) 967 1101

British consulate
British High Commission, Trafalgar Rd,
Kingston
T +1 (876) 510 0700
Montego Bay **T** +1 (876) 954 6394

Other consulates
Canadian **T** +1 (876) 926 1500

US **T** +1 (876) 935 6018; +1 (876) 929 4850

Hospitals/clinics
University Hospital of the West Indies,
Mona (7), Kingston
T +1 (876) 927 1620

Cornwall Regional Hospital,
Montego Bay
T +1 (876) 952 5100

MARTINIQUE

Excellent medical facilities. French overseas department, with same rights to treatment for EEA citizens as in France itself (*see p.260*).

Emergencies
Police **T** 17
Ambulance **T** 15; +596 751575
SOS Médecin **T** +596 633333

Health ministry/dept
(Préfecture) 80 Rue Victor-Sévère,
Fort-de-France
T +590 393600

British consulate
Rue du Phare, Fort-de-France
T +596 618892

Other consulates
US **T** +596 719690

Hospitals/clinics
Hôpital Pierre Zobda-Quitmann/La
Meynard, Fort-de-France
T +596 552000

PUERTO RICO

US territory. Good medical care, but expensive.

Emergencies T 911

Health ministry/dept
PO Box 70184, San Juan
T +1 (787) 274 7621

British consulate
Royal Bank Center Suite 807, 225 Ponce de Leon Ave, Hato Rey, San Juan
T +1 (787) 7758 9828

Other consulates
Canadian **T** +1 (787) 759 6629

Hospitals/clinics
Ashford Presbyterian Community Hospital, 1451 Ashford Ave, San Juan
T +1 (787) 721 2160

ST LUCIA

Facilities OK but somewhat limited. Cash payment often required.

Emergencies T 999

Health ministry/dept
Chaussee Rd, Castries
T +1 (758) 452 2859

British consulate
British High Commission, Francis Compton Bldg, Waterfront, Castries
T +1 (758) 452 2484

Hospitals/clinics
Victoria Hospital, Hospital Rd, Castries
T +1 (758) 452 2421

ST VINCENT & THE GRENADINES

Facilities rather limited, especially outside Kingstown and on outer islands. Cash payment often required.

Emergencies T 999

Health ministry/dept
Kingstown
T +1 (784) 456 1111

British consulate
British High Commission, Granby St, Kingstown
T +1 (784) 457 1701

Hospitals/clinics
Kingstown General Hospital
T +1 (784) 456 1185

TRINIDAD AND TOBAGO

Standards of health care OK on Trinidad but more limited on Tobago. Private facilities may demand proof of ability to pay.

Emergencies
Police **T** 999
Ambulance **T** 990

Health ministry/dept
42 Independence Square, Port-of-Spain
T +1(868) 627 0010

British consulate
British High Commission,
19 St Clair Ave, St Clair, Port-of-Spain
T +1 (868) 622 2748
W *www.britain-in-trinidad.org*

Other consulates
Canadian **T** +1 (868) 622 6232

US **T** +1 (868) 622 6371

Hospitals/clinics
Port-of-Spain General Hospital,
169 Charlotte St, Port-of-Spain
T +1 (868) 623 2951

Adventist Hospital, Western Main Rd, Cocorite, Port-of-Spain
T +1 (868) 622 1191

Tobago Regional Hospital, Fort St, Scarborough, Tobago
T +1 (868) 639 2551

NORTH AMERICA

Canada, United States

A whole continent of sights and experiences stretches from north of the Arctic Circle almost to the tropics, and from the seashores of the Gulf of Mexico (and almost all around the whole continent) to the 6194m (20 320ft) peak of Mt McKinley (Denali) in Alaska. There are vast wildernesses, many of them highly accessible, and of course some of the greatest cities on Earth. Unless you have an accident in one of the wilder places, you're never far from first-class medical facilities. However, even public hospitals charge, and you need (very) full medical insurance and a major credit card. You'll usually have to pay for all care, including ambulances and emergency treatment as well as everyday visits to a doctor's surgery (or 'physician's office' in American terminology). Many hospitals and doctors demand proof of medical insurance and/or a credit-card guarantee before giving treatment.

Everyday precautions Food and water are almost everywhere among the safest in the world, but (as anywhere) you need to be cautious about drinking water from streams in the wilds. Particularly in the southern half of North America, you should respect the sun and use a good sunscreen (*see p.56*), especially in summer. You'd be well advised to avoid some urban areas, particularly at night, where there may be violent and other street crime.

You can, of course, encounter extreme weather in any of the high mountains and in the north, especially in winter. There's a risk of hurricanes in summer and autumn near the east and Gulf coasts, tornadoes in summer especially on the Great Plains, and the deserts of the south-west get dangerously hot if you don't carry adequate water in summer. There are venomous snakes (*see p.97*), and spiders and scorpions (*see p.82*), especially in the south and south-west. Beware poison ivy and similar irritating plants (*see p.92*) in woods almost everywhere – and get a local to help you to recognise them.

Sex safety The USA was one of the first countries where HIV/AIDS was recognised, but has also led the research into remedies. Overall, there are estimated to be 890 000 HIV-positive people (0.6 per cent of the adult population) in the USA and 55 000 (0.3 per cent) in Canada. But anti-HIV drugs are very expensive, so AIDS in North America has become increasingly a problem of poor economic groups.

Black (African-American) people account for more than half of all new US HIV infections, and in some cities up to 30 per cent of black gay men are HIV-positive. (The leading route of HIV infection is still male same-sex contact, but the use of shared needles by drug-users and straight sex are increasingly important.) Many more men have the virus than women (who are mostly infected by heterosexual contact). In theory, HIV-positive people can be refused entry into the USA, but in practice only to those wanting long-term or permanent residence are tested for HIV. **Practise safer sex** (*see p.145*).

Vaccinations etc Visitors to Canada or the USA don't have to have any vaccinations, but make sure your routine childhood jabs – especially tetanus (see p.166) – are up to date. If you plan to spend a long time in woods where Lyme disease is common – mainly in the eastern USA – check if the vaccine, which was withdrawn in 2002, has become available again (see p.136).

Other medical risks North America is one of the world's lowest-risk areas for infectious diseases, but various outbreaks do occur – usually in specific regions – from time to time. Apart from Lyme disease (see above), there has been a big increase (although quite small actual numbers) in encephalitis caused by the West Nile virus (see p.134). Rabies (see p.139) – although rare – is increasing; it's carried by foxes, raccoons, skunks and other wild animals.

CANADA

First-class but expensive health care. Provincial governments' health insurance covers only Canadians and long-term residents (qualification period varies).

Emergencies T 911 or 0, depending on province

Health ministry
Brooke Claxton Bldg, Tunney's Pasture, Ottawa, Ontario K1A 0K9
T +1 (416) 341 5518

British consulates
British High Commission, 80 Elgin St, Ottawa, Ontario K1P 5K7
T +1 (613) 237 1530
W www.britainincanada.org
Also in *Dartmouth* (Halifax; Nova Scotia); *Montreal*; *Quebec City*; *St Johns* (Newfoundland); *Toronto*; *Vancouver*; *Winnipeg*

Other main consulates
Australian **T** +1 (613) 236 0841
W www.ahc-ottawa.org

New Zealand **T** +1 (613) 238 5991
W www.nzhcottawa.org

South African **T** +1 (613) 744 0330
W www.docuweb.ca/SouthAfrica

US **T** +1 (613) 238 5335
W www.usembassycanada.gov

Hospitals/clinics
Many; refer to local telephone directories

UNITED STATES

First-class private and (to varying standards) public care, but all charge (often heavily) – including for medicines, etc; insurance essential.

Emergencies T 911

Health dept
200 Independence Ave SW, Washington, DC 20201
T +1 (202) 619 0257; +1 (877) 696 6775

British consulates
British Embassy, 3100 Massachusetts Ave NW, Washington, DC 20008
T +1 (202) 588 7800
W www.britainusa.com
Also in *Anchorage*; *Atlanta*; *Cambridge* (Boston); *Charlotte*; *Chicago*; *Dallas*; *Denver*; *Glendale* (Phoenix); *Houston*; *La Jolla* (San Diego); *Los Angeles*; *Miami*; *Nashville*; *New Orleans*; *New York*; *Orlando*; *Philadelphia*; *Pittsburgh*; *Portland* (Oregon); *Salt Lake City*; *San Francisco*; *Seattle*; *Shawnee Mission* (Kansas City)

Other main consulates
Australian **T** +1 (202) 797 3000
W www.austemb.org

Canadian **T** +1 (202) 682 1740
W http://canadianembassy.org

New Zealand **T** +1 (202) 328 4800
W www.nzemb.org

South African **T** +1 (202) 232 4400
W www.saembassy.org

Hospitals/clinics
Many; refer to local telephone directories

THE MIDDLE EAST

Bahrain, Israel, Jordan, Kuwait, Qatar, Saudi Arabia, United Arab Emirates

You don't need me to tell you that this is a troubled and unstable part of the world, yet it has enormous riches to tempt travellers – including remains of some of the most ancient civilisations on Earth, sites significant to a number of religions, and the more physical appeal of sun, sand and usually clear, warm waters. Some countries in the region are definitely off-limits except to more intrepid travellers, but those covered here are to a greater or lesser extent welcoming at the time of writing. (However, wars or terrorism can change the situation in many of the countries at short notice).

Medical facilities in parts of most of these countries are relatively advanced, and most prescription medicines are generally available. However, care may be much more basic outside major urban areas. No free care is available except for residents in some countries, and immediate payment is often required for all treatments and medicines. So you should have full travel medical insurance (including evacuation cover) plus, often, access to cash.

Everyday precautions Travellers' diarrhoea (*see p.34*) – including dysentery and giardiasis (*see p.43*) – typhoid (*see p.46*) and hepatitis A (*see p.51*) are all common throughout the Middle East. There have also been outbreaks of cholera (*see p.44*) in some places (although not recently in any of the countries covered here) and cases of brucellosis (*see p.52*). So **take great care with what and where you eat and drink** (*see p.28*)

Tap water is very variable in quality. It's probably safe in most parts of Israel (but inquire locally about the West Bank, Gaza Strip and other occupied territories), Kuwait and Qatar, and in parts of the UAE including Abu Dhabi. Elsewhere boil or otherwise treat all water (*see p.32*), or use reliable bottled water in sealed bottles – which is widely available – for drinking, making ice and cleaning your teeth. Use only pasteurised or sterilised milk and dairy products (or boil milk, or mix dried or tinned milk with safe bottled water).

The sun is very strong in the whole region, especially in summer, and you should always use a high-factor sunscreen (*see p.56*), wear a hat and sunbathe for only short periods at first. Humidity is usually low, so take care not to get dehydrated; drink plenty of (safe) fluids and don't over-exert yourself, especially when you first arrive. The dry, dusty conditions may cause respiratory or sinus problems.

Bilharzia (schistosomiasis; *see p.102*) is a risk in fresh water in some parts of Saudi Arabia. (Chlorinated swimming pools are safe.) Seas and beaches in a few areas may be polluted, so make local inquiries before swimming. There are venomous snakes (*see p.97*) and scorpions (*see p.84*) in some rural areas, and road accidents are a real risk in many countries. Visitors are killed or injured in terrorist incidents from time to time, but statistically this is rare.

Sex safety Official HIV/AIDS statistics for the Middle East are patchy, but in general the proportion of HIV-positive people seems to be well below 1 per cent of the adult population. One significant fact is that, among 436 people with AIDS recorded in Saudi Arabia up to the end of 2000, two-thirds were male expats (of various, unstated nationalities) – who were generally sent back to their home countries. Hepatitis B is also widespread in the region, so **always practise safer sex** (*see p. 145*) and consider getting a hepatitis B vaccination (*see below*). All the countries except Israel demand an HIV test for all or some long-term residents and people wanting to work.

Vaccinations etc The risk of vaccine-preventable infectious diseases is not so high as in some parts of the world, but you should (or in a few cases *must*) get (or consider) certain vaccinations or take other precautions as follows:–

→ *Hepatitis A* (*see p.51*) – worthwhile for all visitors to the region.
→ *Hepatitis B* (*see p. 148*) – advisable if you may have sexual or blood contact with local people, plan to take part in hazardous activities or are staying for a long period. (Safe blood supplies are not always available.)
→ *Malaria* (*see p.107*) – *falciparum* type is a risk (all year) only in southern and some western parts of Saudi Arabia (but not Mecca or Medina). Recommended prophylaxis: chloroquine plus proguanil. Slight risk also in parts of UAE bordering Oman; no prophylaxis, or same as Saudi Arabia.
→ *Meningitis* (*see p.163*) – low general risk, but pilgrims on hadj or umrah pilgrimages to Saudi Arabia must have a recent certificate of vaccination, currently against the A, C, W-135 and Y strains.
→ *Polio* (*see p.165*) – no recent cases in these countries, but vaccination (or booster) is recommended.
→ *Rabies* (*see p.139*) – a risk except in Bahrain, Kuwait, Qatar and UAE; discuss vaccination with a travel clinic doctor unless you're staying only for a short period in resort areas and avoid all contact with animals.
→ *Tuberculosis* (*see p.160*) – exists in some Middle Eastern countries; consider vaccination if you will have close, prolonged contact with locals.
→ *Typhoid* (*see p.46*) – widespread and common, so get a vaccination (but still take precautions, as it's not 100 per cent effective).
→ *Yellow fever* (*see p.123*) – not a direct risk in the region, but certificate of vaccination required for travellers from infected countries (including most of tropical Africa and the Americas) entering Jordan (except those under 12 months old) or Saudi Arabia.
→ *Others* Make sure routine childhood vaccinations – especially tetanus and diphtheria (usually combined; *see p.166*) – are up to date. If you normally have a flu jab, get this and pneumococcal vaccination.

Other medical risks in the region include dengue fever (*see p.125*) in sporadic epidemics; leishmaniasis (mainly the cutaneous [skin] type; *see p.118*); and filariasis (*see p.131*), typhus (*see p.137*), Crimean–Congo haemorrhagic fever (*see p.139*) and other insect- and tick-borne infections (so take precautions against being bitten).

BAHRAIN

Good modern hospitals and clinics. Immediate cash payment may be required. Most medicines available without prescription.

Emergencies T 999

Health ministry/dept
PO Box 12, Manama
T +973 289810

British consulate
British Embassy, 21 Government Ave, Manama
T +973 574100; +973 960 2074 (emergencies)
W *www.ukembassy.gov.bh*

Other consulates
US **T** +973 273300
W *www.usembassy.com.bh*

Hospitals/clinics
Salmaniya Medical Complex, Manama
T +973 289083; +973 289090

International Hospital of Bahrain, Budayya Hwy, Manama
T +973 598222; +973 591666; +973 590575

American Mission Hospital, Shaikh Isa Al Kabeer Ave, Manama
T +973 253447

ISRAEL

Good modern hospitals and care; standards may be lower in occupied West Bank and Gaza. Emergencies may affect availability of facilities.

Emergencies
Police **T** 100
Ambulance **T** 101

Health ministry/dept
Ben Tabai 2 St, Jerusalem 91010
T +972 (2) 670 5705

British consulates
Migdalor Building (6th Floor), 1 Ben Yehuda St, Tel Aviv 63801
T +972 (3) 510 0166; +972 (3) 510 0497; +972 (3) 725 1222 (emergencies)
W *www.britemb.org.il*
Eilat **T** +972 (7) 634 0810

Jerusalem/Gaza/West Bank
T +972 (2) 671 7724; +972 (2) 541 4156 (emergencies)
W *www.britishconsulate.org*

Other main consulates
Australian **T** +972 (3) 695 0451
W *www.australianembassy.org.il*

Canadian **T** +972 (3) 636 3300
W *www.dfait-maeci.gc.ca/telaviv*

New Zealand
T +972 (3) 695 1869

South African **T** +972 (3) 525 2566; +972 5059 8074 (emergencies – mobile)

US **T** +972 (3) 519 7575; +972 (3) 519 7457; +972 (3) 519 7551 (emergencies)
W *www.usembassy-israel.or.il*
Jerusalem/West Bank **T** +972 (2) 622 7200; +972 (2) 622 7250 (emergencies)
W *www.uscongen-jerusalem.org*

Hospitals/clinics
Assuta Hospital, 62 Jabotinsky St, Tel Aviv 62748
T +972 (3) 520 1515; +972 (3) 520 1507

Hadassah Medical Organisation (University Hospital), Kiryat Hadassah, Jerusalem 91120
T +972 (2) 677 7111

Herzilya Medical Centres, 7 Ramat-Yam Rd, Herzilya-on-Sea 46851
T +972 (9) 959 2555; +972 (9) 959 2520

Yoseftal Medical Centre, Eilat
T +972 (8) 635 8011

JORDAN

Good but somewhat basic modern facilities and care available in major centres, but not in all rural areas. Evacuation may be needed for serious problems. Immediate cash payment often required.

Emergencies
Police **T** 191
Ambulance **T** 193

Health ministry/dept
Jabal al-Hussein, Medan Jamal Abed Alsnaser, Amman
T +962 (6) 566 5131; +962 (6) 560 7531

British consulates
British Embassy, Abdoun, Amman
T +962 (6) 592 3100; +962 (6) 592 6581;
+962 (6) 552 9999 – 'British Embassy 5'
(emergencies)
W www.britain.org.jo
Aqaba **T** +962 (3) 201 2525;
+962 (3) 201 3111

Other consulates
Australian **T** +962 (6) 593 0246

Canadian **T** +962 (6) 566 6124

New Zealand **T** +962 (6) 463 6720

South African **T** +962 (6) 592 1194

US **T** +962 (6) 592 0101; +962 (6) 592 0120
(emergencies)
W www.usembassy-amman.org.jo

Hospitals/clinics
Jordan Hospital, Queen Nour St, Amman
T +962 (6) 562 0777

Government Hospital, Zerka
T +962 (3) 83323

Aqaba Modern Hospital
T +962 (3) 201 6677

KUWAIT

Standards of medical facilities and
care variable; some very good, but
others not up to standards in some
other parts of the region. Immediate
cash payment sometimes required.

Emergencies T 777

Health ministry/dept
PO Box 5, 13001 Safat
T +965 245 8850; +965 245 8854

British consulate
British Embassy, Arabian Gulf St, Safat
T +965 240 3334; +965 240 3335
(emergencies)
W www.britishembassy-kuwait.org

Other consulates
Canadian **T** +965 256 3025

South African **T** +965 561 7988

US **T** +965 539 5307; +965 538 2097
(emergencies)
W www.usembassy.gov.kw

Hospitals/clinics
Amiri Hospital, Safat
T +956 245 0005

International Clinic, Salmiya
T +956 574 5111

QATAR

Basic modern medical care
available, but evacuation may be
needed for serious problems. Cash
payment often required.

Emergencies T 999

Health ministry/dept
PO Box 42, Doha
T +974 325005; +974 441555

British consulate
British Embassy, PO Box 3, Doha
T + 974 442 1991

Other consulates
South African **T** +974 436 6480

US **T** +974 488 4101
W www.usembassy.org.qa

Hospitals/clinics
American Hospital, C-Ring Rd, Doha
T + 974 442 1999

Hamad General Hospital, Doha
T +974 439 2222

SAUDI ARABIA

Basic modern medical care
available, but evacuation may be
needed for serious problems. Cash
payment often required.

Emergencies
Police **T** 999
Ambulance **T** 997

Health ministry/dept
Airport Road, Riyadh 11176
T +966 (1) 401 2220; +966 (1) 401 2392

British consulates
British Embassy, PO Box 94351, Riyadh
T +966 (1) 488 0077
W www.ukm.org.sa
Jedda **T** +966 (2) 622 5550;
+966 (2) 622 5557; +966 (2) 622 5558

SAUDI ARABIA (continued)

Other main consulates
Australian T +966 (1) 488 7788

Canadian T +966 (1) 488 2288;
+966 (1) 0292

New Zealand T 966 (1) 488 7988

South African T +966 (1) 456 4982
W www.southafrica.com.sa

US T +966 (1) 488 3800
W http://usembassy.state.gov/riyadh

Hospitals/clinics
Riyadh Central Hospital, Riyadh 11196
T +966 (1) 435 5555

International Medicare Group, Jeddah
T +966 (2) 651 4778

King Fahd Hospital, Medinah
T +966 (4) 823 3500

Al-Haj Street Health Centre, Mecca
T +966 (2) 536 8616

UNITED ARAB EMIRATES

Basic modern medical care
available in main cities; possibly not
in outlying areas. Evacuation may be
necessary for serious problems.

Emergencies T 344663 (Abu Dhabi)
Police T 999
Ambulance T 999; 998

Health ministry/dept
PO Box 848, Hamdan St, Abu Dhabi
T +971 (2) 633 0000

British consulates
British Embassy, PO Box 248, Abu Dhabi
T +971 (2) 632 6600. Emergencies: +971
(50) 624 1847 (mobile); +971 (2) 922 8441
(pager)
W www.britain.uae.org
Dubai T +971 (4) 397 1070. Emergencies:
+971 (4) 397 6790; +971 (50) 624 3774
(mobile); +971 (4) 929 2041 (pager)

Other main consulates (Abu Dhabi)
Australian T +971 (2) 634 6100
W www.austembuae.com

Canadian T +971 (2) 445 6969
W www.canada.org.ae

South African T +971 (2) 633 7565

US T +971 (2) 443 6691; +971 (2) 443 4457
(emergencies)
W www.usembabu.gov.ae

Hospitals/clinics
Abu Dhabi Central Hospital
T +971 (2) 621 4666

Al Baraha Hospital, Dubai
T +971 (4) 271 0000

Al Ain Medical District
T +971 (3) 762 7333

Al Sharjah Medical District
T +971 (6) 554 1117

SOUTHERN ASIA

Bangladesh, India, Maldives, Nepal, Pakistan, Sri Lanka

The Indian subcontinent has almost everything – and that's not including the
sights and sounds. From the beaches of Goa, the Maldives and Sri Lanka to
the world's highest mountains, from remnants of the British Raj and other,
earlier empires to monuments of several religions, it's one of the truly great
travellers' destinations. But even its best friends will tell you that in many
areas it smells, its big cities are among the most polluted on Earth, and
diseases of every kind surround you. You'll be lucky if you get through a trip
without a bout of travellers' diarrhoea (not for nothing is it dubbed Dehli
belly, the Kathmandu quickstep or the tandoori trots), but if you take sensible
precautions you should avoid more serious troubles.

In many things, including medical care, southern Asia is that old cliché, 'a land of contrasts'. High-tech industry exists alongside extreme poverty, and while first-class medical facilities exist in some large cities, in other areas you may be hard put to find even basic care up to the standards you're used to. If you get seriously ill you may need to be moved to one of the major cities, or even evacuated to Singapore or to Bangkok, Thailand. And if you get into trouble trekking in the Himalayas you may need expensive helicopter rescue just to reach Kathmandu, before transfer to a bigger centre. So make sure your travel health insurance and credit card can stand it – and remember that you'll have to pay for all treatment, often in cash in advance.

Everyday precautions Travellers' diarrhoea (see p.34) is the no. 1 problem in southern Asia, and it comes in all varieties, including dysentery and giardiasis (see p.43). The greatest risk is just before the monsoon. There's also hepatitis A and E (see p.51), brucellosis (see p.52), typhoid (see p.46) and cholera (see p.44), too. In this last case, it's not just the old, relatively mild 'El Tor' cholera strain, for which there are vaccines, but also the new virulent 'Bengal' strain; this has cropped up in all these countries except (so far) the Maldives. Probably more than anywhere else, therefore, **take extreme care with what and where you eat and drink** (see p.28).

Some visitors swear by keeping to a vegetarian diet – but you should avoid any uncooked salad or other vegetables and any fruit that you don't (or can't) wash in clean water and then peel. Whether you go veggie or not, make sure everything you eat is freshly cooked and piping-hot; no buffets or reheated 'chef's specials'! Most milk is unpasteurised, so should be boiled; avoid dairy products made from unpasteurised milk, including yoghurt.

Water's just as much of a problem. No tap water (or ice made from it), anywhere in the region except perhaps in resorts in the Maldives, is safe to drink without first being boiled or otherwise properly treated – read carefully the information on pages 31–33. Even bottled water, as explained there, can't be relied upon to be pure and uninfected unless you're certain that it's a genuine, imported, internationally-known brand in original sealed bottles (which may be difficult to find in many places). Nor is water from streams or wells safe. So this is one part of the world where I'd advise you to consider taking a water purifying kit, chemicals and/or an electric water-boiler element. Avoid lassi, a drink made from yoghurt, water and ice.

Your other big potential adversaries are of course the heat (often combined with high humidity in coastal areas) and the sun – which can be extremely fierce even outside the tropics, especially if you're at high altitude. Always use a high-factor sunscreen (see p.56), wear a hat and expose your skin for only short periods at first. Beware of heat exhaustion (see p.58), especially in the pre-monsoon period (April to June in most areas) and especially when you first arrive: Drink lots of (safe) fluids, and don't over-exert yourself.

In the Himalayas – even in the Kathmandu valley – strong sun can be combined with freezing conditions, and hypothermia (see p.61) and even frostbite (*see p.65*) are real risks to trekkers. But the most important threat, which you should take very seriously if you go above 2600m (8500ft) – Kathmandu itself is half this altitude – is altitude sickness (*see p.66*). Don't go alone; join a group led by an experienced guide, make sure you take acclimatisation breaks, and go lower if you develop the symptoms.

The UN recently rated southern Asia as having the most sewage-polluted seas on the planet, so take care where you swim, especially near big cities and towns, few of which have sewage-treatment plants. You may be OK at popular beach resorts in Goa, the Maldives and Sri Lanka, but take care not to swallow sea water and make sure that any swimming pool you use is well chlorinated. There's bilharzia (schistosomiasis; *see p.102*) in fresh water in some parts of India, but it's not a big problem as it is in Africa.

There are venomous scorpions and snakes (*see pp.84 & 97*) throughout the region (although snakes are rare in the Maldives). Hookworms (*see p.91*) are a risk if you go barefoot in poor, dusty areas or beaches where dogs roam, and you can pick up jiggers (chigoes or sand-fleas; *see p.80*) in western India. But for many travellers the greatest danger – especially in India and Pakistan – is from road traffic; Dehli alone has over 2000 road deaths a year. There are occasional cyclones in some areas (notably the Bay of Bengal).

Sex safety HIV infection rates in most of the smaller countries in southern Asia are low – 0.1 per cent of the adult population or less. But the story's different in Nepal (where 0.5 per cent of adults are HIV-positive, according to official UN figures) and India (0.8 per cent). Even India's percentage isn't particularly high, but when you take into account its huge population, the actual number of people with the virus – almost 4 million – is second only to the number in South Africa. This is bound to have a major impact on the spread of HIV/AIDS in the Asia-Pacific region and beyond. A particularly high proportion of sex workers are HIV-positive.

Rates of hepatitis B infection (*see p.148*) are also high in all these countries, so **always practise safer sex** (*see p.145*). (Blood supplies aren't adequately screened in southern Asia, so consider getting a hepatitis B vaccination [*see below*] and be very cautious about any blood transfusion; *see p.172*).

Vaccinations etc A lot of serious diseases prevalent in southern Asia can be prevented by vaccination. These are the jabs you should (in a few cases *must*) have, or at least consider, and the precautions you should take:–

Cholera New, effective vaccines are available against 'Classic' and 'El Tor' cholera, but not yet against the virulent 'Bengal' strain (*see p.44*). If you're staying for an extended period, discuss vaccination with a travel clinic doctor, but you'll still need to take precautions against catching the disease.

Hepatitis A A worthwhile jab for all visitors to the region (*see p.51*).

Hepatitis B It's worth getting vaccinated if there's any chance of blood or sexual contact with local people, if you'll take part in any hazardous activities that could cause injury, or if you're staying a long time (so are more likely to need surgical or dental treatment, or a blood transfusion; *see p.148*).

Japanese encephalitis exists in rural parts of Bangladesh, India, southern Nepal and Sri Lanka, particularly in rainy seasons (*see p.128*). It's potentially very dangerous, so get a vaccination if you plan to travel in these areas, especially during the monsoon – mainly between June and January.

Malaria exists throughout southern Asia *except* the Maldives, parts of India and Pakistan above 2000m (6500ft), parts of Nepal above about 1300m (4250ft; eg, Kathmandu), and in and just south of Colombo in Sri Lanka. It's mainly the *vivax* type, but there's also some *falciparum* malaria (*see p.107*), with drug-resistance in some places. Take precautions (including malaria pills and mosquito nets; *see p.75*) if you're visiting or passing through any other areas of the subcontinent.

The UN/WHO and British authorities recommend taking chloroquine plus proguanil as malaria prophyaxis (*see p.115*), except in south-eastern Bangladesh. The recommended drugs there (and for *all* malarial parts of southern Asia according to US authorities) are mefloquine ('Lariam'), doxycycline (eg, 'Nordox' or 'Vibramycin'), or atovaquone plus proguanil (combined in 'Malarone').

Polio Southern Asia is one of the few remaining parts of the world where polio still exists (*see p.165*). The risk is low in Bangladesh, the Maldives, Nepal and Sri Lanka, but its worth getting vaccinated (or getting a booster if you were vaccinated in childhood) before going to any part of the region.

Rabies This potentially fatal disease (*see p.139*) exists in all of southern Asia, and India has by far the world's highest death rate from rabid animal bites. Vaccination doesn't give complete protection, but it makes follow-up jabs after a bite less urgent (although still essential). So if you're going only to major cities with good medical facilities, or going on a short holiday to a tourist resort and avoid all contact with animals, you probably don't need a vaccination. But for other travellers it's a worthwhile precaution.

Tuberculosis It exists throughout the Indian subcontinent and is particularly common in Bangladesh, so BCG vaccination is usually recommended if you plan to stay in close proximity to local people. (American medical authorities follow a different procedure; *see p.160*.)

Typhoid This is common, and is a serious disease (*see p.46*), so vaccination is worthwhile even though it doesn't give 100 per cent protection. You still need to take care with food and drink (*see above*).

Yellow fever There's no direct risk of this in southern Asia, but all these countries are wary of importing the disease. They demand a certificate of vaccination for anyone (sometimes including children under 6 or 12 months old) coming from areas that are (or, in some cases, could be) infected – in general, anywhere in tropical sub-Saharan Africa and the tropical Americas from Panama to Brazil and Bolivia. It's a safe, long-lasting vaccination, and worth getting if you'll pass through any of the risk areas during your travels (*see p.123*). If you can't be vaccinated for medical reasons, get a doctor's letter to say so.

Others There are sporadic outbreaks of plague (*see p.130*), but vaccination is hardly ever necessary. Flu epidemics occur throughout the region, generally in winter and spring in the north, but at any time in the tropical areas. So older travellers and anyone else who's normally advised to have a flu jab should get one – and perhaps also one against pneumococcal disease – before travelling in southern Asia. Otherwise, make sure that all your routine childhood vaccinations are up to date – especially tetanus and diphtheria, usually given together (*see p.166*).

Other medical risks Various other diseases crop up in southern Asia. Apart from common ones (eg, measles) and those mentioned above, they include...

→ *Dengue fever* (*see p.125*) in epidemics, especially in urban areas.
→ *Leishmaniasis* (*see p.118*) everywhere except the Maldives and Sri Lanka, including the visceral form in some places.
→ *Lymphatic filariasis* (*see p.131*) in Bangladesh, India and the south-west coast of Sri Lanka.
→ *Typhus* (*see p.137*), rarely *Crimean–Congo haemorrhagic fever* (*see p.139*), and other tick-borne infections – so take precautions against tick bites and remove any ticks that do attach themselves (*see p.86*).

BANGLADESH

Very limited medical facilities, with poor standards, even in tourist areas. Evacuation necessary for all serious conditions.

Emergencies
Police T +880 (2) 861 6551;
+880 (2) 866551
Ambulance T +880 (2) 956 7734;
+880 (2) 955 5555

Health ministry/dept
Bangladesh Secretariat Building no 2 (3rd floor), Dhaka 1000
T +880 (2) 861 3639

British consulate
British High Commission, United Nations Rd, Baridhara, Dhaka 1212
T +880 (2) 882 2705; +880 (0) 11 858102 (emergencies)
W www.ukinbangladesh.org

Other consulates
Australian T +880 (2) 881 3101
W www.aushighcomdhaka.org

Canadian T +880 (2) 988 7091
W www.chcdhaka.org

US T +880 (2) 882 4700; +880 (2) 882 3805 (emergencies)
W www.usembassy-dhaka.org

Hospitals/clinics
Bangladesh Medical College Hospital, Dhanmondi, Dhaka
T +880 (2) 811 5843; + 880 (2) 911 8202

Holy Family Red Crescent Hopsital, Eskaton Garden Rd, Dhaka
T +880 (2) 831 1721

Dhaka Medical College Hospital, Bakshibazar, Dhaka
T +880 (2) 500121; +880 (2) 505025

INDIA

Good to excellent medical care available in major cities, but very limited or unavailable in rural areas.

Emergencies (New Delhi numbers; may vary elsewhere)
Police T 100
Ambulance T 102
Air ambulance ARMS, Kolkata (Calcutta)
T +91 (33) 2229 2922; +91 (33) 2246 7247;
+91 983 100 5000

Health ministry/dept
Nirman Bhavan, New Delhi 110011
T +91 (11) 2301 8863

British consulates
British High Commission, Shantipath, Chanakyapuri, New Delhi 110021
T +91 (11) 2687 2161
W *www.ukinindia.com*
Chennai (Madras) T +91 (44) 719 2151;
+91 (44) 719 2158 (emergencies)
Kolkata (Calcutta) T +91 (33) 2288 5172;
+91 (33) 2288 6536 (emergencies)
Mumbai (Bombay) T +91 (22) 2283 0517;
+91 (22) 2283 2330; +91 (22) 2283 3602

Other main consulates
Australian T +91 (11) 2688 8223
W *www.ausgovindia.com*

Canadian T +91 (11) 2687 6500

New Zealand T +91 (11) 2688 3170

South African T +91 (11) 2614 9411
W *www.sahc-india.com*

US T +91 (11) 2419 8000
W *http://usembassy.state.gov/posts/in1*

Hospitals/clinics
East West Medical Center, 38 Golf Links, New Delhi 110003
T +91 (11) 2629 3701

Tamilnad Hospital, Cheran Nagar, Chennai (Madras)
T +91 (44) 237 2522 1235

Asilo Hospital, Rajwaddo Mapusa, Goa
T +91 (832) 262372

City Hospital, Ashirvad Building, Margao-601, Goa
T +91 (832) 721707

Jaipuria Hospital, Jawaharlal Nehru Marg, Malviya Nagar, Jaipur
T +91 (141) 551460; +91 (141) 552034

Calcutta Medical College & Hospital, 88 College St, Kolkata (Calcutta) 700012
T +91 (33) 2241 4901

Bombay Hospital, Marine Lines, Mumbai (Bombay) 400020
T +91 (22) 2206 7676

MALDIVES

Good facilities and care available at hospitals listed. Consular help from Sri Lanka, India or Singapore.

Emergencies
Police T 119
Ambulance T 102
Air ambulance Coast Guard
T +960 325981; +960 338898

Health ministry/dept
Ameenee Magu, Malé 20-04
T +960 325311; +960 325312

Hospitals/clinics
Indira Ghandi Memorial Hospital, Malé (public; cash payment required)
T +960 316647

Abdurahman Don Kaleyfan (ADK) Hospital, Sosun Magu, Malé
T +960 313553

NEPAL

Very limited medical facilities; evacuation usually required for serious conditions. Helicopter rescue from Himalayas expensive; may be affected by terrorist attacks.

Emergencies
Police T 100
Ambulance T +977 (1) 226 359;
+977 (1) 226 403
Air ambulance See under India
Himalayan Rescue Association
Dhobichaur, Lazimpat, Kathmandu
T +977 (1) 440292; +977 (1) 440293

Health ministry/dept
Ram Shah Path, Kathmandu
T +977 (1) 224465; +977 (1) 225543

NEPAL (*continued*)

British consulate
British Embassy, Lainchaur, Kathmandu
T +977 (1) 410583; +977 (1) 411281;
+977 (1) 414588
W *www.britain.gov.np*

Other consulates
Australian T +977 (1) 371678

Canadian T +997 (1) 415193;
+997 (1) 415389

New Zealand T +977 (1) 412436

US T +977 (1) 411179
W *www.south-asia.com/USA*

Hospitals/clinics
Bir Hospital, Tundikhel, Kathmandu
T +977 (1) 221119; +977 (1) 226963;
+977 (1) 223 807 (emergencies)

Patan Hospital, Patan, Kathmandu
T +977 (1) 521 333

PAKISTAN

Medical care OK in major cities, but limited in rural areas. Prior cash payment often required.

Emergencies
Police T 15
Ambulance T +92 (51) 115

Health ministry/dept
Block C, Pakistan Secretariat,
Islamabad
T +92 (51) 213933

British consulates
British High Commission, Diplomatic
Enclave, Ramna 5, Islamabad
T + 92 (51) 220 6071; +92 (51) 282 2131
W *www.britainonline.org.pk*
Karachi T +92 (21) 587 2431

Other consulates
Australian T +92 (51) 282 4345

Canadian T +92 (51) 227 9100

New Zealand T +92 (21) 561 0198;
+92 (21) 561 0960 (Karachi)

South African T +92 (51) 226 2354;
+92 (51) 225 0411

US T +92 (51) 2080 2700
W *http://usembassy.state.gov/pakistan*

Hospitals/clinics
Shifa International Hospital,
Sector H-8/4, Islamabad
T +92 (51) 446801

Aga Khan University Hospital,
Stadium Rd, Karachi
T +92 (21) 493 0051

Doctors' Hospital, Lahore
T +92 (42) 530 2701

SRI LANKA

Limited medical facilities outside Colombo. Evacuation may be necessary for serious conditions.

Emergencies T +94 (1) 691095;
+94 (1) 699935

Health ministry/dept
385 'Suwasiripaya', Rev Baddagama
Wimalawansa Himi Mawatha, Colombo
T +94 (1) 698475

British consulate
British High Commission, 190 Galle Rd,
Kollupitiya, Colombo 3
T +94 (1) 437336; +94 (1) 451924
W *www.britishhighcommission.gov.uk/
srilanka*

Other consulates
Australian T +94 (1) 698767
W *www.srilanka.embassy.gov.au*

Canadian T +94 (1) 695841

New Zealand T +94 (1) 556701;
+94 (1) 585995

US T +94 (1) 448007; +94 (1) 447601
(emergencies)
W *http://usembassy.state.gov/srilanka*
(includes list of medical facilities)

Hospitals/clinics
General Hospital, Regent St, Colombo 8
T +94 (1) 691111; +94 (1) 693184
(emergencies)

Asiri Hospital, 181 Kirula Rd, Colombo 5
T +94 (1) 500608

Kandy General Hospital
T +94 (8) 233337

Lakeside Adventist Hospital, 40
Sangaraja Mawatha, Kandy
T +94 (8) 223466

SOUTH-EAST ASIA

Brunei, Cambodia, Indonesia, Laos, Malaysia, Philippines, Singapore, Thailand, Vietnam

To me, Malaysia and Singapore are where the Orient – with all the mystery and exoticism that name implies – begins. In many ways, it's a cleaner, more hygienic world than the parts of Asia farther to the west, but this view isn't altogether justified. Certainly you don't run quite such a risk of travellers' diarrhoea as you do in the Indian subcontinent, but there are plenty of exotic diseases around, particularly outside the major cities. Sadly, there's also come an increased risk of violence in this essentially peace-loving region.

Standards of health care vary hugely across south-east Asia. There are first-class facilities in Singapore (recently rated by the WHO as sixth-best in the world, well ahead of the UK, USA and other English-speaking countries) and Thailand (particularly in Bangkok). But they're extremely limited in such countries as Cambodia, Laos and Vietnam – especially outside capital cities – and you'll need to be evacuated to Singapore or Thailand (or back home) for specialist care. None of the countries covered here offers free or subsidised medical care to travellers except Malaysia (where government hospitals make no or only a nominal charge), so make sure you have full travel health insurance (including evacuation cover). In many places you'll have to pay cash, but in the more advanced countries a robust credit card will do – Singapore particularly is expensive.

Everyday precautions Even though food-borne diseases aren't as common as in, say, India, you still run the risk of travellers' diarrhoea (*see p.34*), including dysentery and giardiasis (*see p.43*). Typhoid (*see p.46*), hepatitis A (*see p.51*) and worms (*see p.49*) are also widespread, and there have been outbreaks of cholera in some areas (including the virulent 'Bengal' strain; *see p.44*). So **be very careful with what and where you eat and drink** (*see p.28*), especially outside the more developed cities and tourist resorts.

Tap water is safe to drink only in Singapore and perhaps in the major cities and resorts of Malaysia and Thailand. Elsewhere (and preferably in Malaysia and Thailand too) all drinking water should be boiled or otherwise treated (*see p.32*), or use reliable bottled water – widely available except in some rural areas – for drinking, making ice and cleaning your teeth.

The whole of south-east Asia lies within the tropics, and the sun is always strong. Use a high-factor sunscreen (*see p.56*), wear a hat and expose your skin for only short periods at first. Sheer heat is also a problem, particularly when you first arrive and particularly during the rainy seasons, when humidity is high. (These seasons vary with your location north or south of the Equator.) Avoid heat exhaustion (*see p.58*) by drinking plenty of (safe) fluids and not over-exerting yourself until you acclimatise. There are occasional typhoons in some areas.

The seas are a bit less polluted than around the Indian subcontinent, but avoid swimming near cities, towns and villages, where untreated sewage may be discharged, unless you're sure it's safe. Bilharzia (schistosomiasis; *see p.102*) exists in fresh water in certain areas – notably the Mekong Delta and some other parts of Vietnam, in parts of Cambodia, Laos and Thailand, in Sulawesi in Indonesia (low risk), and in the southern Philippines. It's not such a big problem as in Africa, but it's best to avoid swimming or wading in rivers or lakes in those areas. There are venomous snakes (*see p.97*) and marine stingers (*see p.99*) in the region, and leeches (*see p.88*) in forests.

Sex safety The rate of HIV infection varies widely, from very low figures in Brunei and the Philippines to almost 2 per cent of the adult population in Thailand and 2.7 per cent – 1 in every 37 people – in Cambodia. All routes of infection seem to be involved – gay and straight sex, sharing needles to inject drugs, and blood transfusions – with a particularly big increase in recent years among drug users. In both Cambodia and Thailand, a high proportion of sex workers (both women and men) are HIV-positive. So take heed, and **always practise safer sex** (*see p.145*). Be cautious about tattooing. If you want to stay long-term in the Philippines or Singapore, you'll need an HIV test.

There's also a high rate of infection with hepatitis B (*see p.148*), so consider getting a vaccination (*see below*). (Blood supplies are poorly screened in parts of south-east Asia, so avoid transfusions of local blood if at all possible; *see p.172*. If you're rhesus-negative, note that this blood group is rare here.)

Vaccinations etc A number of serious diseases that can be prevented by vaccination exist in south-east Asia. These are the recommended (in some cases compusory) jabs and other precautions you should take, or consider:–

Cholera New, effective vaccines are available against old strains of cholera, but not yet against the virulent 'Bengal' strain (*see p.44*). If you're staying for an extended period, discuss vaccination with a travel clinic doctor, but you'll still need to take precautions against catching the disease.

Hepatitis A A worthwhile jab for all visitors to the region (*see p.51*).

Hepatitis B It's worth getting vaccinated if there's any chance of blood or sexual contact with local people, if you'll take part in any hazardous activities that could cause injury, or if you're staying a long time (so are more likely to need surgical or dental treatment, or a blood transfusion; *see p.148*).

Japanese encephalitis exists throughout south-east Asia; it's prevalent mainly during the rainy seasons in Cambodia, Laos, Thailand and Vietnam, but all year in Indonesia, Malaysia and the Philippines. You're also more at risk in rural areas than in cities. It's potentially dangerous, however, so I'd advise you to get vaccinated (*see p.128*) if you plan to travel much in risky areas, especially during the monsoon.

Malaria This is also a risk in many (but not all) parts of the region, and includes the potentially dangerous *falciparum* type (*see p.107*). The pattern of drug-resistance also varies. Firstly, there's no malaria in Singapore; in cities and tourist areas of Indonesia (eg, Jarkarta, Yogyakarta and resort areas of Bali); in urban and coastal areas of Malaysia except Sabah and remote parts of peninsular Malaysia and Sarawak; in parts of the Philippines above 600m (about 2000ft) and some other places including Manila; or in cities and major tourist areas of Thailand (eg, Bangkok, Chiang Mai, Koh Samui, Pattaya and Phuket). There's a nil or low risk in major cities in Cambodia, Laos and Vietnam, and low risk in Brunei, but it exists everywhere else (including the tourist area around Angkor Wat in Cambodia). Generally speaking, if you're travelling through rural areas and anywhere not specifically listed above you should take antimalarial pills and avoid mosquito bites (see p.75).

The recommended prophylaxis in risk areas of peninsular Malaysia and the Philippines is chloroquine plus proguanil. In most other areas, you should take mefloquine ('Lariam'), doxycycline (eg, 'Nordox' or 'Vibramycin'), or atovaquone plus proguanil (combined in 'Malarone'). However, in some places – including western Cambodia (near the Thai border) and risk areas of Thailand (especially near the Burmese and Cambodian borders) – there's mefloquine-resistant malaria, and the first choice is doxycycline (see p.115).

Rabies You could encounter rabid animals – especially dogs, which commonly run wild in some areas – in most of south-east Asia except Singapore. As explained in the article on page 139, prior vaccination won't give you complete protection, but it makes it less urgent to get further jabs if you are bitten. So if you expect to travel through villages a long way from expert medical care, it's worth getting vaccinated before you go.

Tuberculosis exists throughout south-east Asia and is particularly common in Cambodia, so BCG vaccination is usually recommended if you plan to stay in close proximity to local people. (American medical authorities follow a different procedure; see p.160.)

Typhoid This is especially common in rural areas, and is a serious disease (see p.46), so vaccination is worthwhile even though it doesn't give 100 per cent protection. You still need to take care with food and drink (see above).

Yellow fever There's no risk of catching this in south-east Asia, but all the countries are wary of importing it. They demand a certificate of vaccination for anyone (over the age of 12 months old in the case of Brunei, Malaysia and Singapore) coming from infected regions – in general, anywhere in tropical sub-Saharan Africa and the tropical Americas south of Costa Rica. It's a safe, long-lasting vaccination, so it's worth getting if you'll pass through any of the risk areas during your travels (see p.123). If you can't be vaccinated for medical reasons, get a doctor's letter to say so.

Others Flu epidemics occur throughout the year in south-east Asia, so older travellers and anyone else who's normally advised to have a flu jab should get one – and perhaps also one against pneumococcal disease – before travelling in the region. Otherwise, make sure that all your routine childhood vaccinations are up to date – especially polio (*see p.165*), and tetanus and diphtheria (usually combined; *see p.166*).

Other medical risks Various other diseases occur in south-east Asia. Apart from common ones (eg, measles) and those mentioned above, they include...

→ **Dengue fever** (*see p.125*) in epidemics throughout the region.
→ **Leishmaniasis** (*see p.118*), although the risk is quite low.
→ **Lymphatic filariasis** (*see p.131*) in all areas.
→ **Trachoma** (*see p.159*) – but it hardly ever affects travellers.
→ **Typhus** (*see p.137*), occasionally **Crimean–Congo haemorrhagic fever** (*see p.139*) and other mite- and tick-borne infections – so take precautions against bites and remove any ticks or mites that do bite (*see p.86*).

BRUNEI

Facilities good for routine problems, but evacuation to Singapore is advisable for serious conditions. Occasional supply shortages. Immediate cash payment often required for treatment.

Emergencies
Police T +673 (2) 222333
Ambulance T +673 (2) 222555

Health ministry/dept
T +673 (2) 381640

British consulate
British High Commission, 2.01 2nd floor, Block D, Komplex Bangunan Yayasan, Sultan Haji Hassanal Bolkiah, Jalan Pretty, Bandar Seri Begawan BS8711
T +673 (2) 226001
W www.britain-brunei.org

Other consulates
Australian T +673 (2) 229435

Canadian T +673 (2) 220043
W www.dfait-maeci.gc.ca/Brunei

New Zealand T +673 (2) 331010

US T +673 (2) 229670; +673 (8) 730691 (emergencies)

Hospitals/clinics
Raja Isteri Pengiran Anak Saleha (RIPAS) Hospital, Jalan Tutong, Bandar Seri Begawan
T +673 (2) 242424

CAMBODIA

Facilities limited and basic; very poor outside Phnom Penh (including in Siem Riap). Evacuation advisable for serious conditions. Take any prescription medicines you may need with you. Immediate cash payment required for treatment.

Emergencies
Police T 118; +855 (23) 366841 (Phnom Penh); 012 893297 (Siem Riap)
Ambulance T 119; +855 (23) 724891 (SAMU); or call Calmette Hospital (*see below*)

Health ministry/dept
151 Kampuchea Krom, Phnom Penh
T +855 (23) 881405

British consulates
British Embassy, 27–29 Sreet 75, Phnom Penh
T +855 (23) 427124; +855 (23) 428295

Other consulates
Australian T +855 (23) 213470

Canadian T +855 (23) 213470

US T +855 (23) 216436

Hospitals/clinics
Calmette Hospital, 3 Monivong, Phnom Penh
T +855 (23) 426948; +855 (23) 724891

International SOS Clinic, Phnom Penh
T +855 (23) 216911

Siem Riap Hospital
T +855 (63) 963111

INDONESIA

Widespread medical facilities in cities, but standards of care may be low; Jakarta has best facilities. Low costs, but immediate cash payment often required. Evacuation advisable for serious conditions.

Emergencies
Police T 110
Ambulance T 118
Health ministry/dept
Jalan HR Rasuna Said 4–9, Jakarta
T +62 (21) 671 4711

British consulates
Deutsche Bank Building (19th Floor),
Jalan Imam Bonjol 80, Jakarta 10310
T +62 (21) 390 7484; +62 (811) 802435
(emergencies)
W *www.britain-in-indonesia.or.id*
Bali T +62 (361) 270601
Medan T +62 (61) 821 0559
Surabaya T +62 (31) 788 1418;
+62 (31) 788 4348

Other main consulates
Australian T +62 (21) 2550 5555
W *www.austembjak.or.id*

Canadian T +62 (21) 2550 7800
W *www.dfait-maeci.gc.ca/jakarta*

New Zealand T +62 (21) 570 9460

South African T +62 (21) 574 0660
W *www.saembassy-jakarta.or.id*

US T +62 (21) 3435 9000
W *www.usembassyjakarta.org*

Hospitals/clinics
Dr Cipto Mangunkusumo (Central)
Hospital, Jalan Diponegoro 71,
Jakarta Pusat
T +62 (21) 330 808; +62 (21) 314 4756

Pondok Indah Hospital, Jalan Metro
Duta 1, Pondok Indah, Jakarta
T +62, (21) 765 7525

Bali International Medical Centre, Jalan
Bypass Ngurah Rai 100X, Kuta, Bali
T +62 (361) 761263

Sanglah Hospital (Denpasar General
Hospital), Jalan Selatani 1, Sanglah,
Denpasar, Bali
T + 62 (361) 227911

Budi Mulia Hospital,
Jalan Raya Gubeng 70, Surabaya
T +62 (31) 534 1821; +62 (31) 535 2888

Dr Sardjito Hospital, Jalan Kesehatan 1,
Sekip Bulaksumur, Yogyakarta
T + 62 (274) 587333

LAOS

Very limited facilities. Cash only (no ATM machines). Take prescription medicines with you. All but most basic care best obtained in Thailand. (Ambulances from listed Thai hospitals can cross into Laos.)

Emergencies T 3590
Police T 191; +856 (21) 212706
Ambulance T 195 (Vientiane); or contact hospitals (*see below*)

Health ministry/dept
Simuong Rd, Vientiane
T +856 (21) 4013

British consulate
(British Trade Office, Vientiane)
T +856 (21) 413606

Other consulates
Australian T +856 (21) 413600
W *www.laos.embassy.gov.au*

US T +856 (21) 212581; +856 (20) 502016
(emergencies)
W *http://usembassy.state.gov/laos*

Hospitals/clinics
Mahosot Hospital and International
Clinic, Setthathirath Rd, Vientiane
T +856 (21) 214018; +856 (21) 214022

Setthathirath Hospital, TS (Ring) Rd,
Vientiane
T +856 (21) 413720

Australian Embassy Clinic (*for
Commonwealth citizens & families only*),
Nehru Rd, Vientiane
T +856 (21) 413603; +856 (21) 413600
(emergencies)

In Thailand, near border
AEK Udorn Hospital, Udorn Thani
T +66 (42) 324555

Nong Kai Wattana Hospital, Nong Kai
T +66 (42) 465201

MALAYSIA

Good facilities and care, especially in larger centres. Free or low-cost care in government hospitals; otherwise immediate cash or credit-card payment often required.

Emergencies T 999

Health ministry/dept
Jalan Cenderasari, 50590 Kuala Lumpur
T +60 (3) 269 85077

British consulates
British High Commission, 185 Jalan Ampang, 50450 Ampang, Kuala Lumpur
T +60 (3) 2170 2200; +60 (3) 2170 2345;
+60 (12) 322 0011 (emergencies)
W *www.britain.org.my*
Johor Bahru **T** +60 (7) 599 1301
Kota Kinabalu (Sabah) **T** +60 (88) 253333
Kuching (Sarawak) **T** +60 (82) 250950
Miri (Sarawak) **T** +60 (85) 475865;
+60 (85) 452736
Penang **T** +60 (4) 262 5333

Other main consulates
Australian **T** +60 (3) 2146 5555
W *www.australia.org.my*

Canadian **T** +60 (3) 2718 3333
W *www.dfait-maeci.gc.ca/kualalumpur*

New Zealand **T** +60 (3) 2078 2533

South African **T** +60 (3) 4024 4456

US **T** +60 (3) 2168 5000; +60 (3) 2168 4997
W *http://usembassymalaysia.org.my*

Hospitals/clinics
Kuala Lumpur Hospital, Jalan Pahang
T +60 (3) 2165 5555

Hospital Sultanah Aminah,
Jalan Skudai, Johor Bahru
T + 60 (7) 223 1666

Queen Elizabeth Hospital,
886500 Kota Kinabalu, Sabah
T +60 (88) 218166

Sarawak General Hospital (Hospital Umum Sarawak), Jalan Tun Abang Haji Openg, 93586 Kuchling, Sarawak
T +60 (8) 257555

Penang General Hospital (Hospital Pulau Pinang), Jalan Residensi 10990
T +60 (4) 229 3333

PHILIPPINES

Medical facilities OK, especially in private hospitals in larger centres; more limited in rural areas. Immediate cash payment (part often in advance) usually required.

Emergencies T 166

Health ministry/dept
San Lazaro Compound, Sta Cruz, Manila
T +63 (2) 743 8301

British consulates
British Embassy, Floors 15-17,
LV Locsin Building, 6752 Ayala Ave (corner of Makati Ave), Makati, Manila
T +63 (2) 816 7271; +63 (2) 816 7348
W *www.britishembassy.gov.uk/philippines* (includes list of doctors)
Cebu **T** +63 (32) 346 0525

Other consulates
Australian **T** +63 (2) 750 2850
W *www.australia.com.ph*

Canadian **T** +63 (2) 867 0001
W *www.dfait-maeci.gc.ca/manila*

New Zealand **T** +63 (2) 891 5358

US **T** +63 (2) 523 1001; +63 (2) 522 3242
W *http://usembassy.state.gov/manila*

Hospitals/clinics
Philippine General Hospital, Taft Ave, Ermita, Manila
T +63 (2) 521 8450

Makati Medical Center, Amorsolo & Della Rosa Streets, Legaspi Village, Makati, Manila
T +63 (2) 815 9911

St Luke's Medical Center, Cathedral Heights, 279 E. Rodriguez Sr Blvd, Quezon City (Metro Manila)
T +63 (2) 723 0301; + 63 (2) 723 0199

University of Santo Tomás Hospital, España Street, Manila 1008
T +63 (2) 731 3001

SINGAPORE

Excellent (but expensive) medical facilities and care at all levels (including networks of cooperating hospitals and clinics). Immediate cash or credit-card payment required.

Emergencies T 999
Air ambulance International SOS
T +65 6338 7800

Health ministry/dept
College of Medicine, Building 16, College Rd, Singapore 169854
T +65 6325 9220

British consulate
British High Commission, Tanglin Rd, Singapore 247919
T +65 6424 1270; +65 6731 6833 (emergencies)
W *www.britain.org.sg*

Other consulates
Australian **T** +65 6836 4100
W *www.singapore.embassy.gov.au*

Canadian **T** +65 6325 3200
W *www.dfait-maeci.gc.ca/singapore*

New Zealand **T** +65 6235 9966

South African **T** +65 6339 3319

US **T** +65 6476 9100
W *http://singapore.usembassy.gov*

Hospitals/clinics
National University Hospital, 5 Lower Kent Ridge Rd, Singapore 119074
T +65 6779 5555

Singapore General Hospital, Outram Rd, Singapore 169608
T +65 6222 3322

Gleneagles Hospital, 6a Napier Rd, Singapore 258500
T +65 6473 7222

Hospital/polyclinic networks
National Healthcare Group
T +65 6355 2788
W *www.nhg.com.sg*

Singapore Health Services
T +65 6225 0488
W *www.singhealth.com.sg*

THAILAND

Excellent medical facilities and care, especially in Bangkok (with Singapore, best in region). Variable in outlying areas.

Emergencies
Police **T** 191
Tourist police **T** 195; 199
Ambulance **T** 191
Air ambulance
Asia Air Ambulance **T** +66 (2) 957 6314
Si-Chang Helicopters **T** +66 (2) 535 5320; +66 (1) 927 8970 or +66 (1) 927 8971 (emergencies)

Health ministry/dept
Thanon Tiwanond, Amphoe Muang Nonthaburi, Bangkok 11000
T +66 (2) 590 1000; +66 (2) 591 8300

British consulates
British Embassy, 1031 Wireless Rd, Lumpini Pathumwan, Bangkok 10330
T +66 (2) 305 8333; +66 (2) 305 8273; +66 (2) 1144 – 'Pager 947362' (emergencies)
W *www.britishemb.or.th*
Chiang Mai **T** +66 (53) 242105; +66 (53) 242103

Other main consulates
Australian **T** +66 (2) 287 2680
W *www.austembassy.or.th*

Canadian **T** +66 (2) 636 0540
W *www.dfait-maeci.gc.ca/bangkok*

New Zealand **T** +66 (2) 254 2530

South African **T** +66 (2) 253 8473; +66 (1) 611 3514 (emergencies)

US **T** +66 (2) 205 4000; +66 (2) 205 4049
W *http://usa.or.th*

Hospitals/clinics
Bangkok General Hospital, 2 Soi Soonvijai 7, New Petchburi Rd
T +66 (2) 310 3000; +66 (2) 310 3456 (emergencies)

Bumrungrad Hospital, 33 Sukhumvit Soi 3 (Soi Nana Nua), Wattana, Bangkok 10110
T +660 (2) 667 1000; +66 (2) 667 2999 (emergencies)

THAILAND (*continued*)

Bangkok Adventist Mission Hospital,
430 Phitsanulok Rd
T +66 (2) 281 1422

Chiang Mai Ram Hospital,
8 Boonruangrit Rd, Chiang Mai
T +66 (53) 224851

Phuket International Hospital,
44 Chalermprakiat Ror 9
T +66 (76) 249400

Samui International Hospital,
Northern Chaweng Beach Rd,
90/2 Moo 2, Bophut, Koh Samui,
Surat Thani
T +66 (77) 230781; +66 (77) 422272

For hospitals in north-east Thailand, see under Laos (above).

VIETNAM

Medical facilities and care limited, with frequent shortages of medicines and supplies; may be non-existent in rural areas. Care for any serious conditions best obtained in Thailand or Hong Kong. Some medications may be unobtainable, so take prescription medicines you may need with you. Immediate cash payment required. (*Note*: Saigon is officially called Ho Chi Minh City.)

Emergencies
Police **T** 13
Ambulance **T** 15
SOS Assistance **T** +84 (4) 934 0555 (Hanoi); +84 (8) 829 8520 (Saigon)

Health ministry/dept
138A Giang Vo St, Hanoi
T +84 (4) 264416

British consulates
British Embassy, Central Building,
31 Hai Ba Trung, Hanoi
T +84 (4) 936 0500
W *www.uk-vietnam.org*
Saigon **T** +84 (8) 829 8433

Other consulates
Australian **T** +84 (4) 831 7755
W *www.ausinvn.com*

Canadian **T** +84 (4) 823 5500

New Zealand **T** +84 (4) 824 1481

South African **T** +84 (4) 934 0888

US **T** +84 (4) 831 4590; +84 (4) 772 1500 (emergencies)
W *http://usembassy.state.gov/vietnam*

Hospitals/clinics
Vietnam International Hospital,
Phuong Mai, Dong Da, Hanoi
T +84 (4) 574 0740; +84 (4) 574 1111 (emergencies)

AEA International Clinic,
65 Nguyen Du, District 1, Saigon
T +84 (8) 829 8424

Cho Ray Hospital,
201B Nguyen Thi Thanh,
District 5, Saigon
T +84 (8) 855 4138

THE FAR EAST

China, Hong Kong & Macau, Japan, South Korea, Taiwan

Some of the most complex and 'exotic' – to us Westerners – cultures on Earth are combined here with amazing landscapes (natural and man-made) and teeming, often highly polluted cities. There are plenty of medical hazards in east Asia, too, but also – except in smaller cities and rural areas of China in particular – usually good (and sometimes world-class) medical facilities. Care is often expensive, however, especially in Japan, so make sure you have full travel health insurance. Doctors and hospitals in some areas may demand cash payment.

Communication may be a problem in some places, particularly outside major cities, and there are some unexpected traps for the unwary. Japan, for example, bans the import of some prescription and non-prescription drugs, even if prescribed by your doctor and accompanied by a copy prescription. So if you have to take any regular medication, check with your nearest Japanese embassy or consulate before you go whether you may run into problems. (On a related subject, contraceptive Pills have only in very recent years been licensed in Japan, and are reportedly still very expensive there.)

Everyday precautions Travellers' diarrhoea (*see p.34*) and dysentery, including giardiasis (*see p.43*), are more or less common throughout east Asia – perhaps most common in less developed parts of China and least in Japan and urban Hong Kong and South Korea. Typhoid (*see p.46*) and hepatitis A (*see p.51*) are widespread – again, except in Japan – and there have been outbreaks of cholera (including the new and virulent 'Bengal' strain; *see p.44*) in China. There's also a risk of brucellosis (*see p.52*) and of worms (including flatworms from eating raw fish in Japan; *see p.49*). So **always be careful with what and where you eat and drink** (*see p.28*), especially outside Japan, Hong Kong and the more advanced cities.

Tap water is said to be safe to drink in Beijing, Hong Kong and all of Japan. Elsewhere (and perhaps in Beijing) all drinking water should be boiled or otherwise treated (*see p.32*). Or use reliable bottled water – widely available except in some rural areas – for drinking, making ice and cleaning your teeth.

Most of the region apart from Hong Kong and southern China and Taiwan is outside the tropics, but the sun is strong in summer. Use a high-factor sunscreen (*see p.56*), wear a hat and expose your skin for only short periods at first. Humidity is also often high in summer, so drink plenty of (safe) fluids. However, winters are extremely cold in northern and inland areas, and you need to take precautions against exposure (*see p.61*). You run a serious risk of altitude sickness (*see p.66*) in the mountainous parts of western and north-western China, including Tibet, unless you acclimatise properly.

The sea is badly polluted in some areas, so take care where you swim.

There's bilharzia (schistosomiasis; *see p. 102*) in fresh water in parts of south-east and eastern China – especially along the Yangtze River (Chang Jiang) and its tributaries; don't swim there except in a chlorinated pool. Many cities in the Far East – especially Tokyo and the major cities of China – have heavy air pollution, causing respiratory problems. There are typhoons from time to time in some areas.

Sex safety The rate of HIV infection in the region is generally low, at around 0.1 per cent (1 in 1000) or less of the adult population, but the sheer size of the Chinese population in particular means that huge numbers of people are infected – at least a million people, it's estimated, in China. There are much higher rates of infection among sex workers, and one survey suggests that many blood-donors in China are HIV-positive. As a result, UN agencies predict an AIDS explosion, with up to 10 million Chinese HIV-positive by 2010.

The situation is less critical in other parts of the Far East, but you should everywhere **practise safer sex** (*see p. 145*). South Korea and Taiwan demand HIV tests for long-term visitors. Hepatitis B is also widespread, except in Japan, so consider getting a vaccination (*see below*). Be cautious about tattoos and acupuncture. Blood supplies are poorly screened – particularly in China – so you should avoid the risks of a blood transfusion (*see p. 172*) if at all possible. (Note that rhesus-negative blood is rare in the Far East.)

Vaccinations etc A number of serious diseases that can be prevented by vaccination exist in parts of east Asia. These are the recommended (in a few cases compulsory) jabs and other precautions you should take:–

Cholera is a significant risk only in China, although there have been some cases in Japan and South Korea. New, effective vaccines are available against old strains of cholera, but not yet against the virulent 'Bengal' strain (*see p. 44*). If you're staying for an extended period, discuss vaccination with a travel clinic doctor, but still take precautions against catching the disease.

Hepatitis A Worthwhile for all visitors to the region, except Japan (*see p. 51*).

Hepatitis B Except for Japan, it's worth getting vaccinated if there's any chance of blood or sexual contact with local people, or of hazardous activities that could cause injury, or if you're staying a long time (so are more likely to need surgical or dental treatment, or a blood transfusion; *see p. 148*).

Japanese encephalitis exists throughout the Far East, although the risk isn't high. It's prevalent mainly between April and October. You're more at risk in rural areas than in good hotels in cities. It's a potentially dangerous disease, however, so it's a good idea to get vaccinated (*see p. 128*) if you plan to travel in risky areas/seasons, especially for an extended period.

Malaria is a risk only in some rural parts of southern China below 1500m (4900ft) – all year in the extreme south (up to 25°N), from May to December from 25 to 33°N, and from July to November north of 33°N – and (all year) in the northern parts of South Korea. There's no risk in urban areas or in

China's densely populated lowlands, but *falciparum* malaria (*see p.107*) exists in Hainan, Yunnan and possibly Guangxi provinces.

In these three latter areas the recommended malaria pills (*see p.115*) are mefloquine ('Lariam'), doxycycline (eg, 'Nordox' or 'Vibramycin'), or atovaquone plus proguanil (combined in 'Malarone'). Elsewhere in China's malarial zone and in Korea, chloroquine alone gives adequate protection. Avoid mosquito bites (*see p.75*). There's also a very slight risk in some rural parts of Hong Kong, but you don't need to take any malaria pills.

Rabies You could encounter rabid animals – especially dogs – in mainland Hong Kong (but not Hong Kong island), South Korea and especially China (where large numbers of people are said to be bitten). As explained on page 139, vaccination doesn't give complete protection, but it makes it less urgent to get further jabs if you are bitten. So if you expect to travel through areas far from expert medical care, it's worth getting vaccinated before you go.

Tuberculosis exists throughout east Asia, but there are very few cases in Japan or South Korea. BCG vaccination is probably advisable if you plan to stay in close proximity to local people elsewhere. (American medical authorities follow a different procedure; *see p.160*.)

Typhoid is a risk in rural areas, except in Japan, and it's a serious disease (*see p.46*), so vaccination is worthwhile even though it doesn't give 100 per cent protection. You still need to take care with food and drink (*see above*).

Yellow fever There's no risk of catching this in the Far East, but China and Taiwan (but not Hong Kong) demand a certificate of vaccination for anyone travelling from infected regions – in general, anywhere in tropical sub-Saharan Africa and the tropical Americas south of Costa Rica (*see p.123*). If you can't be vaccinated for medical reasons, get a doctor's letter to say so.

Others Flu epidemics are liable to occur mainly in the winter months (but all year in Hong Kong), so older travellers and anyone else who's normally advised to have a flu jab should get one – and perhaps also one against pneumococcal disease – before travelling in the region then. Otherwise, make sure that all your routine childhood vaccinations are up to date – especially polio (*see p.165*) and tetanus and diphtheria (*see p.166*).

Other medical risks Various other diseases occur in eastern Asia. Apart from common ones (eg, measles) and those mentioned above, they include...

→ **Dengue fever** (*see p.125*) in epidemics in southern China, Hong Kong and Taiwan – especially in urban areas.
→ **Leishmaniasis** (*see p.118*), although the risk to travellers is quite low.
→ **Lymphatic filariasis** (*see p.131*), mainly in rural areas.
→ **Trachoma** (*see p.159*), especially in China, but it rarely affects travellers.
→ **Typhus** (*see p.137*), occasionally **Crimean–Congo haemorrhagic fever** (*see p.139*) and other mite- and tick-borne infections – so take precautions against bites and remove any ticks or mites that do bite (*see p.86*).

CHINA

Excellent Western-style facilities in major cities; many hospitals in other large cities have *gaogang binfang* (VIP wards) that treat foreigners. Rural clinics may be reluctant to treat foreign travellers.

Emergencies
Police **T** 110
Ambulance **T** 120
Air ambulance MEDEX
T +86 (10) 6595 8510 (Beijing)
SOS International **T** +86 (10) 6462 9100 (Beijing); +86 (21) 6295 0099 (Shanghai)

Health ministry/dept
1 Xizhimen Nanhu, Beijing 100044
T + 86 (10) 6879 2114

British consulates
21st Floor, North Tower, Kerry Centre, 1 Guang Hua Lu, Beijing 100020
T +86 (10) 8529 6600; +86 (10) 6532 1961 (emergencies)
W *www.britishembassy.org.cn*
Chongqing **T** +86 (23) 6381 0321
Guangzhou (Canton) **T** +86 (20) 8335 1354; +86 1360 277 6806 (emergencies)
Hong Kong; Macau See below
Shanghai **T** +86 (21) 6279 7650; +86 (21) 6279 8130; +86 1380 162 0683 (emergencies)

Other main consulates
Australian **T** +86 (10) 6532 2331
W *www.austemb.org.cn*

Canadian **T** +86 (10) 6532 3536
W *www.dfait-maeci.gc.ca/china*

New Zealand **T** +86 (10) 6532 2731
W *www.nzembassy.com/china*

South African **T** +86 (10) 6532 0171

US **T** +86 (10) 6532 3431; +86 (10) 6532 3831; +86 (10) 6532 1910 (emergencies)
W *www.usembassy-china.org.cn*
(lists of medical facilities available by email from *AmCitBeijing@state.gov*)

Hospitals/clinics
Beijing Hospital, 1 Dahua Lu, Dongcheng
T +86 (10) 6513 2266

Beijing United Family Hospital, 2 Jiangtai Lu, Chaoyang
T +86 (10) 6433 3960

Beijing Union Medical College Hospital, 1 Shuaifuyuan, Wangfujing
T +86 (10) 6529 6207

International Medical Centre, S106 Lufthansa Centre, 50 Liangmaqiao Lu, Chaoyang, Beijing
T +86 (10) 6465 1561

AEA International Clinic, Ta Yuan International Building 2-2-11, 14 Liang Ma He South Rd, Beijing
T +86 (10) 6462 9112

Hua Sha Hospital (Foreigners' Clinic, 15th floor), Zong He Lou, 12 Wulumuqi Zhong Lu, Shanghai
T +86 (21) 6248 3986

International Medical Centre, 585 Jui Long Lu, Shanghai
T +86 (21) 6324 3852

Guangdong Provincial Peoples' Hospital, 96 Dongchuan Rd, Guangzhou (Canton)
T +86 (20) 8382 7812; +86 (20) 8384 9627 (emergencies)

Red Cross Hospital, 396 Tong Fu Zhong Lu, Haizhu, Guangzhou (Canton)
T +86 (20) 8444 6411 (emergencies)

HONG KONG & MACAU

Special Administrative Regions of China. Excellent medical facilities, especially in Hong Kong. Immediate cash payment often required.

Emergencies T 999
SOS International **T** +852 2428 9900

Health ministry/dept
Floors 5–8 Murray Building, Garden Rd, Hong Kong
T +852 2842 8747

British consulates
1 Supreme Court Rd, Central, Hong Kong
T +852 2901 3281; +852 2901 3000 (emergencies)
W *www.britishconsulate.org.hk*
Macau **T** +853 882797

Other consulates (Hong Kong)
Australian T +852 2827 8881
W *www.australia.org.hk*

Canadian T +852 5810 4321
W *www.hongkong.gc.ca*

New Zealand T +852 2525 5044

South African T +852 2577 3279

US T +852 2523 9011
W *www.usconsulate.org.hk*

Hospitals/clinics
Queen Mary Hospital, 102 Pokfulam Rd,
Hong Kong
T +852 2855 3111; +852 2595 6111

Queen Elizabeth Hospital,
30 Gascoigne Rd, Kowloon
T +852 2958 8888

Prince of Wales Hospital,
30-32 Ngang Shing St, Shatin, NT
T +852 2 645 1222; +852 2632 2211

Hong Kong Baptist Hospital,
222 Waterloo Rd, Kowloon Tong
T +852 2339 8888; +852 2339 8941

Kiang Wu Hospital, Macau
T +853 371333; +853 378311

JAPAN

Excellent (but expensive) medical
care, but communication problems
common. National health insurance
only for long-term visitors. Import
controls on some prescription and
over-the-counter drugs – check
with Japanese embassy if you need
to take regular medication with you.

Emergencies
Police T 110
Ambulance T 119
SOS International T +81 (3) 5213 9011
Tokyo English Life Line (TELL)
T +81 (3) 5774 0992
Japan Helpline T 0120 461997 or 0570
000911 (both free); +81 (3) 5780 1111
*Tokyo Metropolitan Health & Medical
Information Centre* T +81 (3) 5285 8181
(English available); +81 (3) 5285 8185
(emergency interpretation service)

Health ministry/dept
1-2-2 Kasumigaseki, Chiyoda-Ku,
Tokyo 100-8916
T +81 (3) 5253 1111

British consulates
British Embassy, 1 Ichibancho,
Chiyoda-ku, Tokyo 102-8381
T +81 (3) 5211 1100
W *www.uknow.or.jp/index_e.htm*
Hiroshima T +81 (82) 247 5151
Nagoya T +81 (52) 223 5031
Osaka T +81 (6) 6120 5600
Sapporo T +81 (11) 613 2123

Other main consulates
Australian T +81 (3) 5232 4111
W *www.australia.or.jp*

Canadian T +81 (3) 5412 6200
W *www.dfait-maeci.gc.ca/ni-ka*

New Zealand T +81 (3) 3467 2271
W *www.nzembassy.com/japan*

South African T +81 (3) 3265 3366
W *www.rsatk.com*

US T +81 (3) 3224 5000
W *www.tokyoacs.com*
(includes listing of English-speaking
doctors and hospitals)

Hospitals/clinics
Tokyo British Clinic, Daikanyama y
Building 2 F, 2-13-7 Ebishu-Nishi,
Shibuya-Ku, Tokyo 150-0021
T +81 (3) 5458 6099

Tokyo Medical and Surgical Clinic, Mori
Building 32, 2F, 3-4-30 Shiba-Koen,
Minato-ku, Tokyo 105-011
T +81 (3) 3436 3028; +81 (3) 3436 5024
(emergencies)

Fukuoka Emergency Medical Centre,
1-6-9 Momochihama, Sawara-ku,
Fukuoka
T +81 (92) 847 1099

Motonago Hospital, 8-13 Saijookamachi,
Higashi, Hiroshima
T +81 (82) 423 2666

Kyoto Shijo Hospital (Emergency
Hospital), 272-6 Shijo Horikawa-cho,
Higashihorikawa St, Shimogyo-ku,
Kyoto
T +81 (75) 361 5471

JAPAN (*continued*)

International Clinic, Dainagoya Bldg 3F,
3-28-12 Meiki, Nakamura-ku, Nagoya
T +81 (52) 541 9130

Osaka University Hospital,
2-15 Yamadaoka Suita, Osaka 565 0871
T +81 (6) 6879 5111

Hokkaido University Hospital, Kita 14-jo,
Nishi 5-chome, Kita-ku, Sapporo
T +81 (11) 716 1161

SOUTH KOREA

Good medical facilities. Immediate
cash payment often required.

Emergencies
Police **T** 112
Ambulance **T** 119
SOS International **T** +82 (2) 790 7561

Health ministry/dept
1 Choongang-dong, Kwachon-shi,
Kyonggi-do 427-760
T +82 (2) 503 7512

British consulates
British Embassy, 40 Taepyung-ro, 4
Chung-Dong, Chung-Ku, Seoul 100-120
T +82 (2) 3210 5500; +82 (19) 332 7344
(emergencies)
W *www.britishembassy.or.kr*
Pusan **T** +82 (51) 463 0041;
+82 (51) 463 4630

Other consulates
Australian **T** +82 (2) 2003 0100
W *www.australia.or.kr*

Canadian **T** +82 (2) 3455 6000
W *www.dfait-maeci.gc.ca/korea*

New Zealand **T** +82 (2) 730 7794
W *www.nzembassy.com/korea*

South African **T** +82 (2) 792 4855
W *www.saembassy.dacom.net*

US **T** +82 (2) 397 4114
W *http://usembassy.state.gov/seoul*
(inc. list of English-speaking facilities)

Hospitals/clinics
Samsung Medical Center,
50 Irwon-Dong, Gangnam-gu, Seoul
T +82 (2) 3410 2114; +82 (2) 3410 0200
(International Clinic)

Severance Hospital International Clinic,
134 Shinchon-Dong, Seodaemoon-Gu,
Seoul 120-752
T +82 (2) 361 5114; +82 (2) 361 6450

TAIWAN

Excellent medical facilities, often
with English-speaking staff.

Emergencies
Police **T** 110
Ambulance **T** 119

Health ministry/dept
110 Aikuo E Rd, Taipei 100
T +886 (2) 2321 0151

Consular assistance
*Most countries have no diplomatic
relations with Taiwan. For full consular
services, contact Hong Kong consulate.
The following offer restricted services:–*

UK (British Trade and Cultural Office,
8–10th floors, Fu Key Building,
99 Jen Ai Rd, Section 2, Taipei 100)
T +886 (2) 2192 7000
W *www.btco.org.tw*
Kaohsiung **T** +886 (7) 238 1034

Australian (Commerce & Industry
Office) **T** +886 (2) 8725 4100
W *www.australia.org.tw/index_en.asp*

US (American Institute in Taiwan)
T +866 (2) 709 2000
W *www.ait.org.tw*
(includes list of doctors and hospitals)

Hospitals/clinics
Adventist Hospital, 424 Pateh Rd,
Section 2, Taipei 105
T +886 (2) 2771 8151

National Taiwan University Hospital,
7 Chung Shan S Rd, Taipei 10016
T +886 (2) 2312 3456

Veterans General Hospital,
201 Shih Pai Rd, Section 2, Taipei 11217
T +886 (2) 2671 2121

Changhua Christian Hospital,
135 Nau-Hsiao Street, Changhua 500
T +886 (4) 723 8595

Chang Gung Memorial Hospital,
123 Dabei Road, Kaohsiung
T +886 (7) 731 7123

AUSTRALASIA AND THE PACIFIC

Australia, Fiji, Hawaii, New Caledonia, New Zealand, Papua New Guinea, Samoa, Solomon Islands, Tahiti, Tonga and other islands

Azure seas, brilliant sandy beaches, palm trees, coral reefs and sunshine – these are no doubt what first spring to mind when you think of the 'South Seas'. Add Australia's vast Red Centre, New Zealand's mountains, fiords, clean rivers and air, and both countries' unique animal life (if you discount the sheep and cattle!), and it's no surprise that the whole region is a favourite destination for holidaymakers and backpackers alike.

With some specific exceptions, it's a reasonably healthy destination, too. Some of the Pacific island groups are still very much developing nations and have limited health-care facilities outside their capitals, but their isolation from the rest of the world means that in many cases they have so far been spared some modern disease epidemics. Not all, however; Papua New Guinea, for example, has a rapidly growing HIV/AIDS problem and (together with the neighbouring Solomon Islands and Vanuatu) a serious risk of malaria. And there are some more or less unique – though pretty rare – risks in Australia, quite apart from the infamous sharks and marine stingers.

If you travel from certain countries only to Australia and/or New Zealand, you can benefit from those countries' health insurance schemes, but elsewhere you should have full travel health insurance – including evacuation cover. You may need to be transferred to the main centre if you get ill on one of the outlying island of a group – or, for any serious condition, to a regional centre such as Australia, New Zealand, Hawaii (a US state) or Guam (US territory).

Everyday precautions Food and water are usually safe in Australia, New Zealand and Hawaii, but standards in other small island territories vary. I don't have full data, but tap water also probably drinkable in major towns and resorts of Fiji. It's reportedly safe in Papua New Guinea's capital (Port Moresby) and in major hotels there, and probably also on some of the other more developed Pacific island territories. It's not reckoned to be safe to drink in Samoa, the Solomon Islands, Tonga and the outlying parts of Papua New Guinea, however, and should be boiled or otherwise treated (*see p.32*). Or – and this applies anywhere if you're in any doubt – use reliable bottled water, which is generally available except on some outlying islands or towns.

More or less the same pattern applies to food safety, but always **take care with what and where you eat** (*see p.28*). Travellers' diarrhoea (*see p.34*) is quite common on some of the islands. Reef and other fish may (rarely) pose a risk of ciguatera or scombroid poisoning (*see p.48*) – make inquiries locally. Worms are fairly common in the Pacific islands.

The sun is always very strong, except in winter in the southern parts of Australia and New Zealand (where, however, you'll get extra exposure to ultra-violet if you're skiing high in the mountains). Treat it with respect: Always use a high-factor sunscreen (see p.56), wear a hat and expose your skin for only short periods at first (and never when the sun is at its strongest). There are occasional cyclones. You also run the risk of cold exposure (see p.61) in winter in the colder parts of Australia and New Zealand.

There are sharks in the sea, but they very rarely cause fatalities or even injuries (see p.95). You're more likely to be stung – fatally, if you're very unlucky – by a venomous fish, jellyfish or other marine stinger (see p.99). But by far the greatest risk is of injury or drowning by the sea itself; treat the ocean surf and currents with even greater respect than the sun. Australia also has some of the world's most venomous snakes (see p.97) and spiders (see p.82), and dangerous crocodiles (see p.95) in the north.

Most of the region has a low crime rate, but there's a risk of violent crime in a few places, notably parts of Papua New Guinea and the Solomon Islands.

Sex safety Much of Australasia and the Pacific region seems to have a relatively low rate of HIV/AIDS, with around 0.1 per cent (1 in 1000) of the adult population HIV-positive, although the figure is more than double this in Hawaii. (I say seems because official UN figures aren't available for many of the smaller island territories.) Papua New Guinea has by far the biggest problem; nearly 1 per cent of adults are infected, and the rate is increasing fast. And a lot of people there also have 'traditional' STDs (see p.149).

Heterosexual contact is the main route of infection in Papua New Guinea, but in Australia and New Zealand, as in many advanced countries, HIV is passed on mainly by male gay sex – although at a declining rate, thanks largely to safer sex practices (see p.145). There's also a high rate of hepatitis B infection (see p.148) in the islands (much lower in Australia and New Zealand), so do **practise safer sex** and consider getting a hepatitis B vaccination (see below).

Vaccinations etc Malaria – mainly the potentially dangerous falciparum type (see p.107) – exists all year in the Solomon Islands, Vanuatu and all parts of Papua New Guinea below 1800m (5900ft). The recommended prophylaxis (protective pills; see p.115) is mefloquine ('Lariam'), doxycycline (eg, 'Nordox' or 'Vibramycin') or atovaquone plus proguanil (combined in 'Malarone'). Infection rates are high, especially in the Solomon Islands, so also take good care to avoid being bitten by mosquitoes (see p.75).

Most countries and territories in the region demand a certificate of yellow fever vaccination for travellers over 12 months old who arrive from areas infected with the disease. (These may include most tropical parts of Africa and the Americas; see p.123.) There's no risk of the disease itself here, however. Otherwise, the only vaccinations to consider getting are...

→ **Hepatitis A** (see p.51) if you're travelling extensively through the islands.
→ **Hepatitis B** (see p.148) if you're travelling through the islands and you may have blood or sexual contact with local people, plan to take part in hazardous activities, or may stay a long time.

→ **Tuberculosis** (see p.160) if you plan to stay in close contact with local people in Papua New Guinea.

→ **Typhoid** (see p.46) if you'll be travelling through rural areas of the less developed islands – but still take care with food and drink.

→ Boosters as necessary for childhood vaccinations, particularly **tetanus** and **diphtheria**, usually given together (see p.166), and **polio** (see p.165).

→ **Flu** and possibly **pnuemococcal disease** for older travellers and others who usually have a flu jab, especially if travelling during the southern winter in Australia and New Zealand (but all year in the Pacific islands).

Other medical risks Apart from those mentioned above and common illnesses that occur everywhere, other diseases you may encounter in the region include dengue fever (see p.125), except in New Zealand and most of Australia (it occurs rarely in the far north-east); filariasis (see p.131) in most of the south Pacific, but only rarely; rare outbreaks of Japanese encephalitis (see p.128) on some of the islands; and various mosquito-, tick- and mite-borne illnesses in Australia (see pp. 128, 134 & 138).

AUSTRALIA

Top-class medical facilities and care, free or at low cost to British, Irish, New Zealand and a few other nationalities through Medicare. Otherwise immediate cash or credit-card payment often required.

Emergencies T 000; 112 from some mobile phones
Poisons & bites information T 131126

Health ministry/dept
PO Box 9848, Canberra, ACT 2601
T +61 (6) 289 1555
Medicare information T 132011
Each state also has its own health dept

British consulates
British High Commission,
Commonwealth Ave, Yarralumba,
ACT 2606
T +61 (2) 6270 6666; +61 (2) 9285 6171
(emergencies)
W www.uk.emb.gov.au
Also in **Adelaide**; **Brisbane**; **Melbourne**;
Perth; **Sydney**

Other main consulates
Canadian T +61 (6) 6270 4000
W www.dfait-maeci.gc.ca/australia

New Zealand T +61 (6) 6270 4211
W www.nzembassy.com/australia

South African T +61 (6) 6273 2424
W www.rsa.emb.gov.au

US T +61 (6) 6214 5600
W http://usembassy-australia.state.gov

Hospitals/clinics
Many; refer to local telephone directories

COOK ISLANDS

Reasonable facilities on Rarotonga, but basic on outer islands. Serious cases will need evacuation.

Emergencies
Police T 999
Ambulance T 998

Health ministry/dept
PO Box 109, Raratonga
T +682 22664

British consulate
Muri Beach, Raratonga
T +682 26662

Other consulates
New Zealand T +682 22201

Hospitals/clinics
Raratonga Hospital **T** +682 22664

Dr Wolfgang Losacker, Banana Court Shops, Avarua, Raratonga
T +682 23306

There are also clinics on other islands

FIJI

Good care available for routine cases, but evcauation advisable for serious conditions. Immediate cash payment usually required.

Emergencies T 000

Health ministry/dept
88 Amy St, Suva
T +679 330 6177

British consulate
British High Commission, Victoria House, 47 Gladstone Rd, Suva
T 679 331 1033
W www.ukinthepacific.bhc.org.fj
(includes other Pacific islands)

Other consulates
Australian **T** +679 338 2211
W www.austhighcomm.org.fj

Canadian (Nadi) **T** +679 722400;
+679 721936

New Zealand **T** +679 311 1422

US **T** +679 314 4466
W www.amembassy-fiji.gov

Hospitals/clinics
Colonial War Memorial Hospital, Waimanu Rd, Suva
T +679 331 3444

Lautoka Hospital, Hospital Road
T +679 666 0399

GUAM

US territory, with good medical care at high cost. Major evacuation destination for north-west Pacific.

Emergencies T 911

Health ministry/dept
PO Box 2816, Agana 96910
T +1 (671) 735 7102

No British consulate

Other consulates
New Zealand **T** +1 (671) 646 7662

Hospitals/clinics
Guam Memorial Hospital, 850 Gov Carlos G. Camacho Rd, Oka, Tamuning
T +1 (671) 647 2555

HAWAII

US state, with excellent medical facilities at high cost. Major centre for evacuation from other islands.

Emergencies T 911

Health ministry/dept
1250 Punchbowl St, Honolulu, HI 96813
T +1 (808) 586 4400

No British consulate

Other consulates
Australian **T** +1 (808) 524 5050
W www.austemb.org

New Zealand **T** +1 (808) 547 5117

Hospitals/clinics
Queens Medical Center,
1301 Punchbowl St, Honolulu, HI 96813
T +1 (808) 538 9011

St Francis Medical Center,
2230 Liliha St, Honolulu, HI 96817
T +1 (808) 263 5500

For hospitals outside Honolulu, refer to local telephone directories

NEW CALEDONIA

Good medical facilities on main island, but limited on outer islands. Immediate cash payment often required. French territory, but no low-cost care for EEA citizens.

Emergencies
Police **T** 17
Ambulance **T** 15

Health ministry/dept
BP 3278, 98846 Noumea
T +687 243700

British honorary consulate
BP 362, 98845 Noumea **T** +687 282153

Other consulates
Australian **T** +687 272414

New Zealand **T** +687 272543

Hospitals/clinics
Hôpital Gaston Bourret, Rue Paul Doumer, Chir Viscrale, Noumea
T +687 256666; +687 256692
(emergencies)

NEW ZEALAND

First-class medical care and facilities, free or at low cost for British and Australian visitors. Otherwise, immediate cash or credit-card payment often required.

Emergencies T 111

Health ministry/dept
133 Molesworth St, Wellington
T +64 (4) 496 2000

British consulates
British High Commission, 44 Hill St, Thorndon, Wellington
T +64 (4) 924 2888; +64 (29) 924 2888 (emergencies)
W www.britain.org.nz
Also in *Auckland*; *Christchurch*

Other main consulates
Australian **T** +64 (4) 473 6411
W www.australia.org.nz

Canadian **T** +64 (4) 473 9577
W www.dfait-maeci.gc.ca/newzealand

US **T** +64 (9) 303 2724 (Auckland);
+64 (4) 462 6000 (emergencies)
W www.usembassy.org.nz

Hospitals/clinics
Many; refer to local telephone directories

PAPUA NEW GUINEA

Adequate routine and some emergency care in main urban centres, but very limited in outlying areas. Evacuation advisable for all serious conditions. Immediate cash payment often required.

Emergencies T 000 (not accessible in some areas); direct numbers vary
Air ambulance Niugini Air Rescue
T +675 321 7033

Health ministry/dept
PO Box 807, Waigani, Port Moresby
T +675 301 3601

British consulates
PO Box 212, Waigani, Port Moresby
T +675 325 1643; +675 325 1645;
+675 325 1659

Other consulates
Australian **T** +675 325 9333

Canadian **T** +675 322 2600

New Zealand **T** +675 325 9444

US **T** +675 321 1455

Hospitals/clinics
Port Moresby General Hospital, Boroko
T +675 324 8200

Angau Memorial Hospital, Lae
T +675 472 1211

Nonga Base Hospital, Rabaul
T +675 982 7333

SAMOA

Formerly Western Samoa. Limited medical facilities, but OK for routine problems. Serious cases best evacuated to Hawaii/New Zealand. Immediate cash payment required.

Emergencies T 999

Health ministry/dept
Apia **T** +685 21212; +685 22216

British honorary consulate
2nd Floor, NPF Building, Beach Rd, Apia
T +685 21895

Other consulates
Australian **T** +685 23411; +685 23412;
+685 23413; +685 25232

New Zealand **T** +685 21711

US **T** +685 21631

Hospitals/clinics
National Hospital, Ifiifi St, Apia
T +685 21212

SOLOMON ISLANDS

Basic facilities and medical supplies only available; very limited outside Honiara. Evacuation to Australia or New Zealand advisable for all serious conditions.

Emergencies
Police T +677 23666; +677 22266
Ambulance **T** +677 25566

SOLOMON ISLANDS (continued)

Health ministry/dept
PO Box 349, Honiara **T** +677 23600

British consulate
British High Commission, Telekom House, Mendana Ave, Honiara
T +677 21705; +677 21706

Other consulates
Australian **T** +677 21561

New Zealand **T** +677 21502

US **T** +677 23426; +677 27429

Hospitals/clinics
Central Hospital, Kukum, Honiara
T +677 23600

TAHITI (FRENCH POLYNESIA)

Good facilities in Papeete and on other main islands, but limited elsewhere. French territory, but no low-cost care for EEA citizens.

Emergencies
Police **T** 17
Ambulance **T** 15

Health ministry/dept
Papeete **T** +689 410651

British honorary consulate
Proprieté Boubée, Route Tuterai Tane, Pirae
T +689 419841; +689 424355;
+689 777197 (mobile – emergencies)

Other consulates
Australian **T** +689 468888

New Zealand **T** +689 540740

Hospitals/clinics
Hôpital Mamao, Papeete
T +689 466262; +689 420101

Clinque Cardella, Rue Anne-Marie-Javouhey, Papeete
T +689 428010

Bora Bora Medical Centre
T +689 677077

Moorea General Hospital, Afareaitu
T +689 562424; +689 562323

Uturoa General Hospital, Raiatea
T +689 663503

TONGA

Limited (but low-cost) medical facilities. Evacuation advisable for more serious conditions. Many medicines scarce on outer islands.

Emergencies T 911
Police **T** +676 70234 (Vava'u)

Health ministry/dept *See below*

British consulate
British High Commission, PO Box 56, Nuku'alofa
T +676 24285; +676 24395

Other consulates
Australian **T** +676 23244

New Zealand **T** + 676 23122

Hospitals/clinics
Vaiola Hospital (& health ministry), Taufa'ahau Rd, Tofoa, Nuku'alofa
T +676 21200

German Clinic & Pharmacy, Vahiaholo & Uelingitoni Roads, Nuku'alofa
T +676 22736

VANUATU

Formerly New Hebrides. Limited medical facilities, especially outside Port Vila. Evacuation advisable for serious conditions.

Emergencies
Police **T** +678 22222
Ambulance **T** +678 22100

Health ministry/dept
Private Mail Bag 009, Porta Vila
T +678 22512

British consulate
British High Commission, KPMG House, Rue Pasteur, Port Vila
T +678 23100

Other consulates
Australian & Canadian **T** +678 22777
W *www.vanuatu.embassy.gov.au*

New Zealand **T** +678 22933

Hospitals/clinics
Central Hospital, Seaside, Port Vila
T +678 22100

NORTH-WESTERN EUROPE

Austria, Belgium, Denmark, Finland, France, Germany, Iceland, Ireland, Luxembourg, Netherlands, Norway, Sweden, Switzerland, UK

If you're reading this in Britain, these countries are more or less on your doorstep, and you probably think of them as pretty risk-free, healthwise. Certainly, they all rank among the healthiest countries in the world to visit, but there are a few local risks that you may not face at home. They're all also among the top 20 per cent of countries for quality of health care (with France at the very top of the whole list), according to a recent WHO/UN assessment.

All the countries have either national health services or health insurance schemes that offer free or reduced-cost medical care – sometimes with various restrictions (*see the following pages*) – to their own citizens and some others. At the core of this scheme are the 15 EU countries plus Iceland, Liechtenstein and Norway; these 'EEA' countries offer medical care to each other's people on a reciprocal basis. Since June 2002, Switzerland has also had such a reciprocal agreement with the EU, but not with Iceland, Lietchenstein or Norway. Britain has quite separate reciprocal agreements with Australia, New Zealand and some other countries. (For more details, see *www.doh.gov.uk/traveladvice/treatment.htm*.)

In some cases, you simply get free or low-cost treatment; in others you may need to pay and then claim a refund. The key to getting treatment under the EEA scheme is form E111 (from a Post Office in the UK). Otherwise (and if you want to bypass waiting times in some countries) you should have full travel health insurance that covers private treatment. Note that the reciprocal agreements don't generally cover evacuation back home if you're ill.

Everyday precautions Food and water are almost everywhere among the safest in the world, but (as anywhere) you need to be cautious about drinking water from streams in the wilds. Only in a few rural areas of France is the tap water sometimes unsafe, but bottled water is widely available everywhere. BSE ('mad cow disease') – at one time widespread in British herds and blamed for brain degeneration in some people who had eaten beef – is believed to have been virtually eliminated from British beef by stringent controls in abbatoirs. The situation in some other European countries is still evolving, so if you're very cautious you might want to avoid eating beef. (Foot and mouth disease, which may be spread on footwear, leading to restrictions on people visiting farming areas during an outbreak, doesn't infect people.)

In southern parts of the region particularly, you should respect the sun and use a good sunscreen (*see p.56*) in summer. Cold exposure (*see p.61*) can be a threat in northern regions or at high altitudes even in summer. The Alps are the only mountains high enough to make altitude sickness (*see p.66*) a risk. Every country has some inner-city zones where violent crime is more common than average, but the region is in general pretty safe.

Sex safety The country with the biggest HIV/AIDS problem in terms of percentages is Switzerland, with 0.5 per cent of the adult population – 19 000 people – infected, according to official UN estimates. But by far the largest number of HIV-positive people are in France, where 100 000 (0.3 per cent of the adult population) have the virus. The infection rate is in the 0.1–0.2 per cent range in all the other countries except Finland, where it's even lower. In most countries, most people with the virus caught it via male gay sex, but in Ireland and Switzerland shared use of needles for injecting drugs is the leading cause. However, in many countries, the majority of *new* infections are from heterosexual contact. As always, the message is to **practise safer sex** (*see p. 145*). Anyone staying longer than 6 months in Germany has to have an HIV test, and in theory visitors to Britain can be tested on entry.

Vaccinations etc Nobody travelling to any of these countries has to have any vaccinations, and there's no malaria to worry about. However, you'd be well advised to update (if necessary) your routine vaccinations – particularly against tetanus (*see p. 166*), which is usually combined with diphtheria. The only other vaccination worth getting – if you're planning to hike, ride (on bike or horseback), camp or do other outdoor activities in forested areas of mainland Europe in spring and summer – is that against tick-borne encephalitis (*see p. 133*). (Also take precautions against tick bites [*see p. 86*], and remove ticks from your skin.) Much of the region is notoriously cold and damp in winter, and respiratory infections are common, so older travellers and any others who normally have a flu jab would be well advise to get one – and possibly also one against pneumococcal infections – before travelling.

Other medical risks Apart from those mentioned above and common universal ailments, very few diseases are a specific risk in north-western Europe. Lyme disease (*see p. 135*) – another tick-borne infection – exists in wooded areas, but is rarely serious. Rabies-infected wild animals (mainly foxes and some bats) live in mainland Europe (and a few infected bats also in the British Isles), but they very rarely pose any risk to travellers; rabies in domestic animals is extremly rare. Leishmaniasis (*see p. 118*) and West Nile virus (*see p. 134*) occur (also rarely) along France's Mediterranean coast.

AUSTRIA

Under EEA reciprocal scheme, small fixed charges payable for medicines and hospital stays. Only part of private fees refunded.

Emergencies T 122
Police **T** 133
Ambulance **T** 144

Health ministry/dept
Abteilung 11/D2, Radetzkystrasse 2, 1031 Vienna
T +43 (1) 711 724103

British consulates
British Embassy, Jauresgasse 10, 1030 Vienna
T +43 (1) 716130; +43 (1) 716 135151; +43 (676) 569 4012;
W *www.britishembassy.at*
Bregenz **T** +43 (5574) 78586
Innsbruck **T** +43 (512) 588320
Graz **T** +43 (316) 821 61621
Salzburg **T** +43 (662) 848133

Other consulates
Australian **T** +43 (1) 512 8580
W *www.australian-embassy.at*

Canadian T +43 (1) 531 383000
W www.kanada.at

New Zealand T +43 (1) 318 8505

South African T +43 (1) 320 6493
W www.southafrican-embassy.at

US T +43 (1) 31339
W www.usembassy-vienna.at

Hospitals/clinics
Numerous, in all cities and major towns

BELGIUM

Treatment and medicines must be paid for; about 75 per cent refunded under EEA reciprocal scheme. Ambulance costs not refundable.

Emergencies
Police T 112; 101
Ambulance T 112; 100

Health ministry/dept
Zwarte Lievevrouwtraat 3c,
Internetcel B634bis, 1000 Brussels
T +32 (2) 509 8219

British consulates
British Embassy, Rue d'Arlon 85,
1040 Brussels
T +32 (2) 287 6211
W www.british-embassy.be
Antwerp T +32 (3) 213 2125
Ghent T +32 (9) 235 721; +32 (9) 225 5427
Liege T +32 (4) 223 5832

Other consulates
Australian T +32 (2) 286 0500
W www.austemb.be

Canadian T +32 (2) 741 0611
W www.dfait-maeci.gc.ca/canadaeuropa/
belgium

New Zealand T +32 (2) 512 1040

South African T +32 (2) 285 4400
W www.southafrica.be

US T +32 (2) 508 2111
W www.usembassy.be

Hospitals/clinics
Numerous, in all cities and major towns

DENMARK

Most treatments free under EEA reciprocal scheme, but part of dental and medicine costs payable.

Emergencies T 112

Health ministry/dept
Slotsholms Gade 10-12,
1216 Copenhagen K
T +45 3392 3360

British consulates
British Embassy, Kastelsvej 36/38/40,
2100 Copenhagen
T +45 3544 5200
W www.britishembassy.dk
Aabenraa T +45 7462 3500
Aalborg T +45 9811 3499
Aarhus T +45 8730 7777
Esbjerg T +45 7911 1900
Fredericia T +45 7592 2000
Herning T +45 9722 0288
Odense T +45 6614 4714
Torshavn T +45 298 350077

Other consulates
Australian T +45 7026 3676
W www.denmark.embassy.gov.au

Canadian T +45 3348 3200
W www.canada.dk

South African T +45 3118 0155
W www.southafrica.dk

US T +45 3555 3144; +45 3555 9270
(emergencies)
W www.usembassy.dk

Hospitals/clinics
Numerous, in all cities and major towns

FINLAND

Charges and refunds under EEA reciprocal scheme vary with municipality; generally 50 per cent of cost of medicines refunded.

Emergencies
Police T 10022
Ambulance T 112

Health ministry/dept
Meritullinkatu 8, 00023 Helsinki
T +358 (9) 16001

FINLAND (*continued*)

British consulates
British Embassy, Itainen Puistotie 17,
00140 Helsinki
T +358 (9) 2286 5100
W *www.ukembassy.fi*
Aaland Is T +358 (18) 13591
Jyväskylä T +358 (204) 82150
Kotka T +358 (5) 234 4281
Kuopio T +358 (17) 265 7777
Pori T +358 (204) 164002
Oulu T +358 (204) 63373
Tampere T +358 (3) 256 5701
Turku T +358 (2) 274 3410
Vaasa T +358 (6) 282 2000

Other consulates
Australian T +358 (9) 447503

Canadian T +358 (9) 228530
W *www.canada.fi*

New Zealand T +358 (9) 615615

South African T +358 (9) 686 03100
W *www.southafricanembassy.fi*

US T +358 (9) 171931; +358 (9) 605414
(emergencies)
W *www.usembassy.fi*

Hospitals/clinics
Numerous, in all cities and major towns

FRANCE

About 70–75 per cent of approved
doctors', dentists' and hospital fees,
and 35–65 per cent of the cost of
medicines, refundable under EEA
reciprocal scheme.

Emergencies
Police T 112; 17
Ambulance T 112; 15

Health ministry/dept
8 Avenue de Ségur, 75700 Paris
T +33 (1) 4056 6000

British consulates
18bis Rue d'Anjou, 75008 Paris
T +33 (1) 4451 3100
W *www.amb-grandebretagne.fr*
Amiens T +33 (3) 2272 0848
Biarritz T +33 (5) 5924 2140
Bordeaux T +33 (5) 5722 2110

Boulogne-sur-Mer T +33 (3) 2187 1680
Calais T +33 (3) 2196 3376
Cherbourg T +33 (2) 3388 6560
Clermont-Ferrand T +33 (4) 7334 2429
Dunkirk T +33 (03) 2866 1198
Le Havre T +33 (2) 3519 7888
Lille T +33 (3) 2012 8272
Lorient T +33 (2) 9787 3620
Lyon T +33 (4) 7277 8170
Marseille T +33 (4) 9115 7210
Montpellier T +33 (4) 6715 5207
Nantes T +33 (2) 5172 7260
Nice T +33 (4) 9362 1356
St Malo T +33 (2) 2318 3030
Toulouse T +33 (5) 6115 0202
Tours T +33 (2) 4743 5058

Other main consulates
Australian T +33 (1) 4059 3300
W *www.austgov.fr*

Canadian T +33 (1) 4443 2900
W *www.amb-canada.fr*

New Zealand T +33 (1) 4501 4343

South African T +33 (1) 5359 2323
W *www.afriquesud.net*

US T +33 (1) 4312 2222
W *www.amb-usa.fr*

Hospitals/clinics
*Numerous, in all cities and major towns,
including:–*

American Hospital of Paris,
63 Boulevard Victor Hugo,
92200 Neuilly-sur-Seine
T +33 (1) 4641 2525

GERMANY

EEA reciprocal scheme operates
through insurance companies; gives
free medical or dental treatment,
and hospital treatment subject to
fixed daily charge. Small charge also
payable for medicines.

Emergencies
Police T 112; 110
Ambulance T 112

Health ministry/dept
Mohrenstrasse 62, 10117 Berlin
T +49 1888 4410

British consulates
British Embassy, Wilhelmstrasse 70,
10117 Berlin
T +49 (30) 204570
W *www.britischegebotschaft.de*
Bremen **T** +49 (421) 59090
Dusseldorf **T** +49 (211) 94480
Frankfurt/Main **T** +49 (69) 170 0020
Hamburg **T** +49 (40) 448 0320
Hannover **T** +49 (511) 388 3808
Kiel **T** +49 (431) 331971
Munich **T** +49 (89) 211090
Nuremburg **T** +49 (911) 240 4303
Stuttgart **T** +49 (711) 162690

Other main consulates
Australian **T** +49 (30) 880 0880
W *www.australianembassy.de*

Canadian **T** +49 (30) 2031 2470
W *www.kanada-info.de*

New Zealand **T** +49 (30) 206210

South African **T** +49 (30) 220 7310
W *www.suedafrika.org*

US **T** +49 (30) 832 9233
W *www.usembassy.de*

Hospitals/clinics
Numerous, in all cities and major towns

ICELAND

Fixed (reduced) fee payable under
EEA reciprocal scheme for medical
treatment and medicines (but not
dentistry). Hospital in-patient
treatment free; fee payable for
ambulance (subject to limit).

Emergencies T 112
Non-emergency medical help T 1770

Health ministry/dept
Laugavegi 116-1S-150, Reykjavik
T +354 545 8700

British consulates
British Embassy, Laufasvegur 31,
101 Reykjavik
T +354 550 5100
Akureyi **T** +354 463 0102

Other consulates
Canadian **T** +354 575 6500
W *www.canadaeuropa.gc.ca/iceland*

South African **T** +354 562 3300

US **T** +354 562 9100
W *www.usa.is*

Hospitals/clinics
Landspitali v/Hringbraut, Baronstigur,
Reykjavik 101
T +354 543 1000

IRELAND

Free medical and hospital treatment
and medicines under EEA scheme,
but must contact local Health Board.

Emergencies T 112; 999

Health ministry/dept
Hawkins House, Hawkins St,
Dublin 2
T +353 (1) 635 4000

British consulate
British Embassy, 29 Merrion Rd,
Ballsbridge, Dublin 4
T +353 (1) 205 3700
W *www.britishembassy.ie*

Other consulates
Australian **T** +353 (1) 664 5300
W *www.australianembassy.ie*

Canadian **T** +353 (1) 417 4100;
+353 (1) 417 4124
W *www.canadaeuropa.gc.ca/ireland*

New Zealand **T** +353 (1) 660 4233

South African **T** +353 (1) 661 5553

US **T** +353 (1) 668 7122; +353 (1) 688 9612
(emergencies)
W *www.usembassy.ie*

Hospitals/clinics
In Dublin and all major towns

LUXEMBOURG

Costs of treatment and medicines
refunded (but not always in full)
under EEA scheme; hospital
treatment subject to daily charge.

Emergencies
Police **T** 113
Ambulance **T** 112

LUXEMBOURG (*continued*)

Health ministry/dept
48 Rue Charles Arent, 1134 Luxembourg
T +352 445464

British consulate
British Embassy, 14 Blvd Roosevelt,
2450 Luxembourg
T +352 229864

Other consulates
Canadian **T** +352 2627 0570

US **T** +352 460123
W *www.amembassy.lu*

Hospitals/clinics
*Numerous in relation to size, in
Luxembourg-Ville and other major towns*

NETHERLANDS

Treatment by approved doctor or
hospital usually free under EEA
scheme, but not dental care. Part
of cost of medicines may be
payable by patient.

Emergencies T 112

Health ministry/dept
Parnassusplein 5, 2511 VX The Hague
T +31 (70) 340 7911

British consulates
British Embassy, Lange Voorhout 10,
2514 ED The Hague
T +31 (70) 427 0427
W *www.britain.nl*

Amsterdam **T** +31 (20) 676 4343

Other consulates
Australian **T** +31 (70) 310 8200
W *www.australian-embassy.nl*

Canadian **T** +31 (70) 311 1600
W *www.canada.nl*

New Zealand **T** +31 (70) 346 9324

South African **T** +31 (70) 392 4501
W *www.zuidafrika.nl*

US **T** +31 (20) 664 5661; +31 (20) 310 9499
(emergencies)
W *www.usembassy.nl*

Hospitals/clinics
Numerous, in all cities and major towns

NORWAY

Some or all of doctors' and hospital
fees covered under EEA scheme, but
not dental and prescription costs.

Emergencies
Police **T** 112
Ambulance **T** 113

Health ministry/dept
Einar Gerhardsensplass 3,
0030 Oslo
T +47 2224 9090

British consulates
British Embassy, Thomas Heftyesgate 8,
0244 Oslo
T +47 2313 2700
W *www.britain.no*
Ålesund **T** +47 7012 4460
Bergen **T** +47 5594 4705
Harstad **T** +47 7706 4631
Kristiansund (N) **T** +47 7167 5333
Kristiansund (S) **T** +47 3801 5068
Stavanger **T** +47 5152 9713
Tromso **T** +47 7762 4500
Trondheim **T** +47 7360 0200

Other consulates
Australian **T** +47 2247 9170

Canadian **T** +47 2299 5300
W *www.canada.no*

New Zealand **T** +47 6677 5330

South African **T** +47 2327 3220

US **T** +47 2244 8550
W *www.usa.no*

Hospitals/clinics
Numerous, in all cities and major towns

SWEDEN

Proportion of costs (or proportion
above a certain level) by approved
practitioners covered by EEA
reciprocal scheme.

Emergencies T 112; 90000

Health ministry/dept
Fredsgatan 8, 10333 Stockholm
T +46 (8) 405 1000

British consulates
British Embassy, Skarpögatan 6-8,
11593 Stockholm
T +46 (8) 671 3000
W www.britishembassy.com
Gothenburg T +46 (31) 339 3300
Malmö T +46 (40) 611 5525
Sundsvall T +46 (60) 164000

Other main consulates
Australian T +46 (8) 613 2900
W www.austemb.se

Canadian T +46 (8) 453 3000
W www.dfait-maeci.gc.ca/canadaeuropa/
sweden

New Zealand T +46 (8) 661 2625

South African T +46 (8) 243950
W www.southafricanemb.se

US T +46 (8) 783 5300; +46 (8) 783 5310
(emergencies)
W www.usemb.se

Hospitals/clinics
Numerous, in all cities and major towns

SWITZERLAND

You'll need to pay for treatment first,
but up to 90 per cent of costs
refunded under EU reciprocal
agreement. See www.doh.gov.uk/
international/switzerland.

Emergencies
Police T 117
Ambulance T 144

Health ministry/dept
3003 Bern
T + 41 (31) 322 2111

British consulates
British Embassy, Thunstrasse 50,
3005 Bern
T +41 (31) 359 7741
W www.britain-in-switzerland.ch
Basel T +41 (61) 483 0977
Geneva T +41 (22) 918 2400
Lugano T +41 (91) 950 0606
Montreux/Vevey T +41 (21) 943 3263
Valais T +41 (27) 480 3210
Zurich T +41 (01) 383 6560

Other main consulates
Australian T +41 (22) 799 9100
W www.australia.ch

Canadian T +41 (31) 357 3200
W www.dfait-maeci.gc.ca/canadaeuropa/
switzerland

New Zealand T +41 (22) 929 0350

South African T +41 (31) 350 1313
W www.southafrica.ch

US T + 41 (31) 357 7011; +41 (31) 357
7218 (emergencies)
W www.us-embassy.ch

Hospitals/clinics
Numerous, in all cities and major towns

UNITED KINGDOM

Free treatment by NHS doctors and
hospitals under EEA reciprocal
agreement and agreements with
Australia, New Zealand and some
other countries. Other visitors
entitled to free treatment in hospital
emergency departments only.

Emergencies T 999; 112

Health ministry/dept
Richmond House, 79 Whitehall,
London SW1A 2NS
T +44 (20) 7210 4850
NHS Direct (helpline) **T** 0845 4647
W www.nhsdirect.nhs.uk

Main consulates
Australian T +44 (20) 7379 4334
W www.australia.org.uk

Canadian T +44 (20) 7258 6600
W www.dfait-maeci.gc.ca/canadaeuropa/
united_kingdom

New Zealand T +44 (20) 7930 8422

South African T +44 (20) 7925 8910
W www.southafricahouse.com

US T +44 (20) 7499 9000
W www.usembassy.org.uk

Hospitals/clinics
Refer to local telephone directories

CENTRAL AND EASTERN EUROPE

Czech Republic, Hungary, Poland, Russia, Slovakia

It's ironic that the collapse of communism in central and eastern Europe in the late 1980s and 90s made it much easier to travel there, but in some places – particularly the former Soviet Union itself – standards of health care crumbled as fast as the state bureaucracy. However, things have been improving again in recent years, particularly in most of the big cities that Western travellers are most likely to visit. But ex-pats will tell you that local medical services are still sometimes a bit hit-and-miss, and often slow.

The former Soviet republics and satellites states covered here have state health services that offer free treatment (excluding medicines and sometimes dental treatment) to their own people and to some or all visitors. (This certainly applies to Brits; if you're from another country check before you go.) However, you'd be well advised to get full travel medical insurance that covers private medical care in Western-standard medical centres (and preferably private ambulance services too), particularly in Russia. You should also be covered for evacuation to the West (from many places, Berlin is the closest city with world-class facilities) if you need specialist treatment. Make sure that the travel insurance company you use has good arrangements for guaranteeing payments at short notice – you may find it difficult to get first-class treatment unless you can pay up-front or guarantee payment.

Everyday precautions Central and eastern Europe rank as intermediate in risk level for travellers' diarrhoea and dysentery (*see p.34*), and hepatitis A (*see p.51*) is also quite common. However, standards have improved a lot, especially in the central European countries. Even in Russia itself, many Western foods are now available, and you'll usually be OK in international restaurant chains. Elsewhere in Russia standards are variable, and you need to take care with what you eat and drink. Tap water is generally safe to drink in the Czech Republic, Hungary, Poland and Slovakia, but often not in Russia – even in big cities and tourist hotels – and you should use bottled water for drinking and cleaning your teeth. Water-borne giardiasis (*see p.43*) is quite common in Russia, especially among visitors to St Petersburg.

The seasons are extreme in this region – again, especially in Russia – and you need to be on your guard against cold exposure (*see p.61*) and even frostbite (*see p.65*) outdoors in winter. There are many more road accidents in some of these countries than in most of the West; if you're on foot, you particularly need to beware vehicles that ignore traffic signs and signals. Some cities have bad air pollution, causing respiratory problems, and street crime – sometimes violent – is a problem particularly in Poland and Russia.

Sex safety HIV/AIDS came relatively late to eastern Europe, but the epidemic there (and in former Soviet central Asia) is now the fastest-growing in the world, with a quarter of a million new infections in 2002 alone. Figures are far from complete (thanks again to the poor health infrastructure), but surveys here and there have shown a huge increase in HIV infection particularly among young people who inject drugs. (For example, in one Russian city, Togliatti, more than half of all drug-users were found to be HIV-positive, but three-quarters of them didn't know it.) Many sex workers are also drug-users, and many of them don't regularly use condoms.

Overall, the UN estimates that almost 1 per cent of Russian adults are HIV-positive, and the numbers are similar in several other former Soviet republics. There are high rates of infection with the 'old' STDs (see p.149), too. The situation is much less critical in the Czech Republic, Hungary, Poland and Slovakia, where the HIV infection rate is 0.1 per cent or less. But wherever you go in central and eastern Europe, **practise safer sex** (see p.145). Several countries demand an HIV test for long-stay visitors.

Vaccinations etc No vaccinations are required in order to enter these countries, but a number of vaccine-preventable diseases are relatively common there, and you'd be well advised to have jabs (or boosters if old vaccinations are now out of date) against the following:–

→ *Diphtheria* and *tetanus* (see p.166) – usually given as a combined jab. (There was a big diphtheria outbreak in eastern Europe in the 1990s)
→ *Polio* (see p.165), even though international orgnanisations are waging a pretty successful campaign to eliminate it worldwide.
→ *Tuberculosis* (see p.160), particularly if you expect to have close contact with local people (although US authorities take a different approach and don't usually advocate vaccination).
→ *Hepatitis A* (see p.51) and, particularly if you plan an extended visit or may have sexual contact with local people, *hepatitis B* (see p.148).
→ *Typhoid* (see p.46), especially if you plan to visit rural areas.
→ *Tick-borne encephalitis* (see p.133), if you plan to visit forested rural areas in spring or summer.
→ *Flu* and *pneumococcal disease* for older travellers and those usually advised to have a flu jab, especially if travelling in autumn or winter.
→ Consider a *rabies* jab (see p.139) if you're planning to visit rural areas where you may have contact with foxes, which carry the disease.

There's no risk of malaria or yellow fever in any of these countries, although malaria exists in some of the southern former Soviet republics (where chloroquine is the recommended preventive drug). Occasional outbreaks of meningitis (see p.163) have occurred in the region, so it makes sense to check with a travel clinic before departure and get a vaccination if necessary.

Other medical risks Apart from the diseases mentioned above and common illnesses that exist everywhere, the other risks you may face include several tick-borne infections in the forests – especially Lyme disease (see p.135) and, more rarely, tick typhus (see p.137) and Crimean–Congo haemorrhagic fever (see p.139). Take precautions against tick bites (see p.86), and remove any ticks that do attach themselves to you.

CZECH REPUBLIC

Medical facilities limited outside major cities. State medical care free for British visitors.

Emergencies
Police T 158
Municipal police T 156
Ambulance T 155

Health ministry/dept
Palackeho namesti 4, 12801 Prague 2
T +420 (2) 2497 1111

British consulate
British Embassy, Thunovska 14,
11800 Prague 1
T +420 (2) 5740 2111
W *www.britain.cz*

Other consulates
Australian T +420 (2) 5101 8350

Canadian T +420 (2) 7210 1800
W *www.canada.cz*

New Zealand T +420 (2) 2251 4672

South African T +420 (2) 6731 1114

US T +420 (2) 5753 0663; +420 (2) 5753 2716 (emergencies)
W *www.usembassy.cz*

Hospitals/clinics
American Medical Center,
Janovskeho 48, Prague 7 – Holesovice
T +420 (2) 807756

Na Homolce Hospital, Roentgenova 2,
15030 Prague 5
T +420 (2) 5727 1111

HUNGARY

Adequate medical care (free to British visitors in hospitals, clinics and doctors' surgeries), but language barrier often a problem.

Emergencies
Police T 112; 107
Ambulance T 112; 104

Health ministry/dept
Arany János Utca 6-8, Budapest 1051
T +36 (1) 332 3100

British consulate
British Embassy, Harmincad Utca 6,
Budapest 1051
T +36 (1) 266 2888
W *www.britishembassy.hu*

Other consulates
Australian T +36 (1) 457 9777
W *www.ausembbp.hu*

Canadian T +36 (1) 392 3360
W *www.kanada.hu*

New Zealand T +36 (1) 428 2208

South African T +36 (1) 392 0999
W *www.sa-embassy.hu*

US T +36 (1) 475 4400; +36 (1) 475 4703 (emergencies)
W *www.usis.hu/consular.htm*

Hospitals/clinics
The American Clinic, I Hattywhaz, Hattyu Utca 14, Budapest
T +36 (1) 224 9090

Medicover Center R-Klinika, Felss Zoldamali Utca 13, Budapest
T +36 (1) 325 9909; +36 (1) 325 9999

POLAND

Medical care OK, but not usually up to Western standards. Most treatment free for British visitors.

Emergencies
Police T 997
Ambulance T 999

Health ministry/dept
Ulica Miodowa 15, 00952 Warsaw
T +48 (22) 634 9600

British consulates
Warsaw Corporate Centre (2nd Floor),
Emilii Plater 28, 00688 Warsaw
T 48 (22) 625 3030
W *www.britishembassy.pl*
Gdansk T +48 (58) 341 4365
Katowice T +48 (32) 206 9801
Kraków T +48 (12) 421 7030
Lublin T +48 (81) 742 0101
Poznan T +48 (61) 851 7290
Szczecin T +48 (91) 487 0302
Wroclaw T +48 (71) 344 8961

Other main consulates
Australian T +48 (22) 521 3444
W www.australia.pl

Canadian T +48 (22) 584 3100
W www.canada.pl

New Zealand T +48 (22) 672 8069

South African T +48 (22) 625 6228

US T +48 (22) 628 3041; +48 (22) 625 0055
(emergencies)
W www.usinfo.pl

Hospitals/clinics
American Medical Centre,
Ul Wilcza 23/29, Warsaw
T +48 (22) 545 6161

British Embassy Medical Centre,
Al Roz 1, Warsaw
T +48 (22) 628 1001

Szpital Uniwersytecki w Krakowie,
Ul Strzelecka 3/5, 31503 Kraków
T +48 (12) 421 3751

RUSSIA

Although treatment in state
hospitals free for British visitors,
private treatment recommended as
hospital standards are low and
medical supplies in short supply.

Emergencies
Police T 02
Ambulance T 03

Health ministry/dept
3 Rakhmanovsky Pereulok,
Moscow 101431
T +7 (95) 923 8406

British consulates
British Embassy, Smolenskaya
Naberezhnaya 10, Moscow 121099
T +7 (95) 956 7200
W www.britemb.msk.ru
Ekaterinburg T +7 (3432) 564931
W www.britain.sky.ru
St Petersburg T +7 (812) 320 3200
W www.britain.spb.ru

Other main consulates
Australian T +7 (95) 956 6070
W www.australianembassy.ru

Canadian T +7 (95) 105 6000

New Zealand T +7 (95) 956 3579

South African T +7 (95) 956 3579

US T +7 (95) 728 5000
W www.usembassy.ru

(Note: Australia, Canada and the USA all
also have consulates in Vladivostok.)

Hospitals/clinics
American Medical Clinic (AMC),
1 Grokholsky Pereulok,129090 Moscow
T +7 (95) 933 7700

Euromed Clinic, Suvorovsky
Prospect 60, St Petersburg
T +7 (812) 327 0301

SLOVAKIA

Medical facilities adequate, but
language barrier may be a problem.
Most treatment free to British
visitors.

Emergencies
Police T 158
Ambulance T 155

Health ministry/dept
Limbova 2, 83752 Bratislava 37
T +421 (2) 5937 3111

British consulate
British Embassy, Panska 16,
81101 Bratislava
T +421 (2) 5998 2000; +421 (905) 601741
(emergencies)
W www.britishembassy.sk

Other consulates
Canadian T +421 (2) 5244 2175

New Zealand T +421 (1) 580 2001

US T +421 (7) 5443 0861;
+421 (7) 5443 3338
W www.usis.sk

Hospitals/clinics
Nemocnica s Poliklinikou Ruzinov,
Ruzinovska 6, Bratislava
T +421 (2) 4333 9500; +421 (2) 4333 8257

Kramare Hospital, Limbova 5, Bratislava
T +421 (2) 5477 3768; +421 (2) 5477 4060

SOUTHERN EUROPE

Croatia, Cyprus, Greece, Italy, Malta, Portugal, Slovenia, Spain, Turkey, etc

Many of these countries are among favourite summer destinations for family holidaymakers as well as student travellers and backpackers. Visitors are attracted by the sun, beaches and warm Mediterranean waters, often close to world-class cultural centres and ancient historical sites. A number of ailments are more common there than in north-western Europe, but they're mostly pretty safe places to visit, healthwise. Turkey is perhaps the riskiest.

All of the countries except Croatia, Slovenia and Turkey (which come in the 'good' category) also rank very highly for quality of health care, according to a recent WHO survey. Italy, Malta, Spain, Portugal and Greece (in order) all came in the top 10 per cent of countries – outranking the UK, Canada, Australia, USA and New Zealand. The EU members – Greece, Italy, Portugal and Spain, plus Gibraltar (British colony) – give free or reduced-cost medical treatment to people from other EEA countries (*see p.257*) on the same basis as their own citizens, but generally only in public hospitals or by approved doctors. (You'll usually need to take a form E111 with you.) For more details see the pages that follow. Greece in particular has a very slow and bureaucratic system. In Croatia, Malta and Slovenia also, medical treatment (generally in government hospitals and clinics; excluding prescribed drugs) are also free for UK and some other nationals. Otherwise, and for private treatment and repatriation anywhere, you need full travel health insurance.

Everyday precautions The risk of travellers' diarrhoea (*see p.34*) and hepatitis A (*see p.51*) is higher in some of these countries than in north-western Europe, although usually much lower than in, say, the Middle East. There have been big improvements in recent years, but some parts of the Mediterranean are still heavily polluted with sewage, so seafood can be a risk if it's not cooked properly. Generally take care with what and where you eat in the less developed parts of the region. Tap water is generally reckoned to be safe to drink in Croatia, Cyprus, Malta, Portugal and Slovenia, and in the main cities and resorts of the other countries except Turkey. (Otherwise, only in some rural parts of Greece, Italy and Spain is it likely to be unsafe, but you should be cautious about drinking water from streams everywhere.) Safe bottled water is generally available (and widely used).

The summer sun is strong throughout southern Europe, and you should always use a high-factor sunscreen (*see p.56*), wear a hat and expose yourself for only short periods at first. But remember also that you can get harsh winter weather in many areas – especially in the mountains – and cold exposure (*see p.61*) is far from unknown. The Mediterranean has virtually no tides and no ocean swell, but violent storms can brew quickly and cause dangerous seas, so check weather forecasts before going far from shore. There are stinging fish and jellyfish (as well as pollution) off some beaches, and heavy air pollution in some cities (eg, Athens, Ankara and Milan). Greece and Turkey have probably the highest rates of road deaths (in terms of population or distance travelled) in the whole of Europe.

Sex safety Italy, Portugal and Spain have the highest rates of HIV infection in southern Europe, accounting for 0.4–0.5 per cent of the adult population. In all three countries, the shared use of needles for injecting drugs is the major infection route, but infection via straight sex is increasing and it's important to **always practise safer sex** (see p.145). People wanting to work or stay long-term in Cyprus, Greece or Spain may need an HIV test.

Vaccinations etc The only vaccination needed for entry into any of these countries is against yellow fever (see p.123) if you arrive in Greece, Malta, or the Portuguese Atlantic islands of the Azores or Madeira from an infected area (which includes much of tropical Africa and the Americas); children under 9 or 12 months old are generally excused vaccination. The only part of the region where there's malaria (vivax type; see p.107) is south-eastern Turkey, near the border with Iraq (where few travellers go); if you do visit, you should take chloroquine as protection and also prevent mosquito bites.

Otherwise, you should make sure that your routine vaccinations (especially tetanus; see p.166) are up to date, and possibly get hepatitis A (see p.51) and typhoid (see p.46) jabs – particularly if you plan to visit rural areas in some countries. If you're going for a long period to less developed areas, discuss the need for a hepatitis B vaccination (see p.148) with a travel doctor; the same applies to a rabies jab (see p.139) if you may have contact with wild animals, and a polio booster (see p.165). Flu epidemics tend to occur in winter, so older travellers and others who normally have a flu jab should get this (and possibly one against pneumoccocal disease) before travelling at that time of year.

Other medical risks Apart from those mentioned above and common universal ills, only a few diseases are a specific risk in southern Europe. There are some cases of leishmaniasis (see p.118) in most of these countries, and outbreaks of louse- and flea-borne typhus (see p.137) and West Nile virus (see p.134) from time to time. Brucellosis (see p.52) is an occasional risk.

CROATIA

Good facilities but some medicines scarce. Free treatment (except medicines) for UK and some other visitors in public hospitals; private doctors may expect cash payment.

Emergencies
Police **T** 92
Ambulance **T** 94

Health ministry/dept
Ksaver 200a, 10000 Zagreb
T +385 (1) 1460 7555

British consulates
British Embassy, Ivana Lucica 4, Zagreb
T +385 (1) 600 9121
Dubrovnik **T** +385 (20) 324597
Split **T** +385 (21) 341464

Other consulates
Australian **T** +385 (1) 489 1200
W www.auembassy.hr

Canadian **T** +385 (1) 488 1200

New Zealand **T** +385 (1) 652 0888

US **T** +385 (1) 661 2400;
+386 (91) 455 2247 (emergencies)
W www.usembassy.hr

CROATIA (*continued*)

Hospitals/clinics
KBC Zagreb, Salata 2, 10000 Zagreb
T +385 (1) 455 2333

Klinicki Bolnicki Centar Rijeka,
Kresimirova 42, 51000 Rijeka
T +385 (51) 658111

CYPRUS

Good medical facilities and care but insurance recommended. (*Note*: Northern [Turkish] Cyprus is recognised as a separate state only by Turkey, and there's no other full diplomatic representation there.)

Emergencies T 199
Police **T** 112; 119
Ambulance **T** 112; 119

Health ministry/dept
10 Marcos, Drakos St, Nicosia
T +357 (22) 309503

British consulate
British High Commission,
Alexander Pallis St, 1587 Nicosia
T +357 (22) 861100
W *www.britain.org.cy*

Other consulates
Australian **T** +357 (22) 753001

Canadian **T** +357 (22) 775508

New Zealand **T** +357 (22) 590555

South African **T** +357 (22) 374411

US **T** +357 (22) 776400;
+392 669965 (office in Northern Cyprus)
W *www.americanembassy.org.cy*

Hospitals/clinics
Nicosia General Hospital, Nechrou Ave
T +357 (22) 801400

Famagusta General Hospital
T +357 (23) 821211

Larnaca New Hospital
T +357 (24) 630300

Limassol General Hospital
T +357 (25) 305333

Pafos General Hospital
T +357 (26) 240111

GIBRALTAR

Free medical (but not dental) care under EEA scheme, but not if you cross from Spain for treatment.

Emergencies T 999
Police **T** 199; 112
Ambulance **T** 190; 112

Health ministry/dept
17 Johnstone's Passage
T +350 48181

British consulate
(Governor's office) The Convent, Main St
T +350 45440

Hospitals/clinics
St Bernard's Hospital, Hospital Hill
T +350 79700

GREECE

Good medical facilities, especially in Athens and Thessaloniki, but nursing care may be inadequate. Free primary and hospital care (and low-cost medicines) under EEA scheme, but treatment may be very slow and inadequate, so travel health insurance recommended.

Emergencies
Police **T** 112; 100
Ambulance **T** 112; 166

Health ministry/dept
Odos Aristotelous 17, Athens
T +30 (210) 363 0911

British consulates
British Embassy, 1 Ploutarchou St,
10675 Athens
T +30 (210) 727 2600
W *www.british-embassy.gr*
Corfu **T** +30 (2661) 30055
Heraklion **T** +30 (281) 224012
Kos **T** +30 (242) 21549
Patras **T** +30 (261) 277329
Rhodes **T** +30 (241) 27247;
+30 (241) 22005
Syros **T** +30 (281) 82232; +30 (281) 88922
Thessaloniki (Salonika)
T +30 (231) 278006; +30 (231) 269984
Zakynthos **T** +30 (2695) 22906;
+ 30 (2695) 48030

Other main consulates
Australian T +30 (210) 645 0404
W *www.ausemb.gr*

Canadian T +30 (210) 727 3400
W *www.canadaeuropa.gc.ca/greece*

New Zealand T +30 (210) 687 4700

South African T +30 (210) 610 6645
W *www.southafrica.gr*

US T +30 (210) 777 3053
W *www.usembassy.gr*

Hospitals/clinics
Metropolitan Hospital, 9 Eth Makariou &
El Venizelou 1, N Faliro, 18547 Athens
T +30 (210) 480 9000

Athens Euro-Clinic, 9 Athanasiadou St,
Ambelokipi, 11521 Athens
T +30 (210) 641 6764

St Luke's Hospital, Panorama,
55236 Thessaloniki
T +30 (231) 342102

ITALY

Good medical care in cities and
major towns, especially in private
facilities. Reduced-cost care under
EEA scheme only from approved
doctors and hospitals.

(*Note*: Zero is part of area code, except
for mobile phone numbers, even when
calling from outside Italy.)

Emergencies T 112; 113

Health ministry/dept
Viale della Civilta, 00144 Rome
T +36 (06) 5994

British consulates
British Embassy, Via XX Settembre 80a,
00187 Rome
T +39 (06) 4220 0001; +39 (06) 482 5441;
+39 (06) 482 5400 (emergencies)
W *www.britain.it*
Bari T +39 (080) 554 3668;
+39 (336) 824917
Cagliari T +39 (070) 828628
Catania T +39 (095) 715 1864
Florence T +39 (055) 284133
Genoa T +39 (010) 416828
Milan T +39 (02) 723001

Naples T +39 (081) 423 8911
Palermo T +39 (091) 582533;
+39 (091) 326412
Trieste T +39 (040) 347 8303
Turin T +39 (011) 650 9202
Venice T +39 (041) 522 7207

Other main consulates
Australian T +39 (06) 852721
W *www.australian-embassy.it*

Canadian T +39 (06) 445981
W *www.canada.it*

New Zealand T +39 (06) 441 7171

South African T +39 (06) 852541
W *www.sudafrica.it*

US T +39 (06) 46741
W *www.usembassy.it*

Hospitals/clinics
*Numerous, in all cities and major towns,
including:–*

Rome American Hospital,
Via Emilio Longoni 69, 00155 Rome
T +39 (06) 22551

Salvator Mundi International Hospital,
Viale Mura Gianicolensi 67, Rome
T +39 (06) 588961

US Naval Hospital, Via Eduardo
Scarfoglio, 80125 Agnano, Naples
T +39 (081) 724 3666

MALTA

Excellent medical care, especially in
private facilities. Free treatment (but
not medicines) for UK visitors in
public facilities for up to 30-day stay.

Emergencies
Police T 112; 191
Ambulance T 112; 196

Health ministry/dept
15 Merchants St, Valletta, CMR 02
T +356 2122 4071

British consulate
British High Commission, Ta'Xbiex,
MSD 11 T +356 2323 0000
W *www.britain.com.mt*

Other consulates
Australian T +356 2133 8201

MALTA (*continued*)

Canadian **T** +356 2123 3121

New Zealand **T** +356 2143 5025

South African **T** +356 2138 0832

US **T** +356 2123 5960

Hospitals/clinics
St Luke's Hospital, Guardamangia Hill,
Guardamangia, MSD 09
T +356 2124 1251; +356 2123 4101

St James Hospital, St James Square,
Zabbar ZBR 05
T +356 2169 2002; +356 2169 2055

PORTUGAL

Good medical care, at reduced cost
under EEA reciprocal scheme.

Emergencies T 112; 115

Health ministry/dept
Alameda D. Alfonso Henriques 45,
1056 Lisbon
T +351 (21) 847 5515

British consulates
Rua de São Bernardo 33, 1249 Lisbon
T +351 (21) 392 4159
W *www.uk-embassy.pt*
Azores **T** +351 (296) 498115
Madeira **T** +351 (291) 221221
Portimão **T** +351 (282) 417800
Porto (Oporto) **T** +351 (22) 618 4789

Other main consulates
Australian **T** +351 (21) 310 1500
W *www.portugal.embassy.gov.au*

Canadian **T** +351 (21) 316 4600

New Zealand **T** +351 (21) 350 9690

South African **T** +351 (21) 319 2200

US **T** +351 (21) 272 3300
W *www.american-embassy.pt*

Hospitals/clinics
British Hospital,
Rua Saraiva de Carvalho 49, Lisbon
T +351 (21) 395 5067

Centro de Saúde de Vila do Porto,
Avenida de Santa Maria, Vila do Porto,
Santa Maria island, Azores
T +351 (296) 820100

Hospital Distrital de Faro,
Rua Leão Penedo Faro, 8000 Faro
T +351 (89) 891100

Centro Hospitalar do Funchal, Avenida
Luís de Camões, 9000 Funchal, Madeira
T +351 (291) 742111

SLOVENIA

Good medical treatment available,
free to UK and some other travellers
(excludes medicines).

Emergencies
Police **T** 113
Ambulance **T** 112

Health ministry/dept
Stefanova 5, 1000 Ljubljana
T +386 (1) 478 6040

British consulate
British Embassy, Trg Republike 3
(4th floor), 1000 Ljubljana
T +386 (1) 200 3910
W *www.british-embassy.si*

Other consulates
Australian **T** +386 (1) 425 4252

Canadian **T** +386 (1) 430 3570

South African **T** +386 (1) 200 6300

US **T** +386 (1) 200 5500
W *www.usembassy.si*

Hospitals/clinics
Klinicni Center Ljubljana (University
Medical Centre), Zaloska Cesta 2,
1000 Ljubljana
T +386 (1) 552 5050; +386 (1)543 1408

Splosna Bolnisnica Maribor (Maribor
General Hospital), Ljubljana Ulica 5,
2000 Maribor
T +386 (2) 321 1000

SPAIN

Good medical care, but make clear if
free/reduced-cost treatment under
EEA scheme wanted. Private fees
(including by doctors during private
consulation hours) not refunded,
even for emergencies, so full travel
health insurance advisable.

Emergencies
Police T 112; 091
Ambulance T 112; 085

Health ministry/dept
Paseo del Prado 18–20, 28071 Madrid
T +34 (91) 596 1000; +34 (91) 596 1515

British consulates
Paseo de Recoletos 7/9, 28004 Madrid
T +4 (91) 524 9700
W *www.ukinspain.com*
Alicante T +34 (96) 521 6190;
+34 (96) 521 6022
Barcelona T +34 (93) 366 6200
Bilbao T +34 (94) 415 7600;
+34 (94) 415 7711
Granada T +34 (958) 274724;
+34 (958) 221460
Gran Canaria T +34 (928) 262508
Ibiza T +34 (971) 301818;
+34 (971) 301816
Majorca T +34 (971) 712445;
+34 (971) 712085
Malaga T +34 (95) 235 2300
Minorca T +34 (971) 363373
Santander T +34 (942) 220000
Tenerife T +34 (922) 286863;
+34 (922) 286653
Vigo T +34 (986) 4371 33

Other main consulates
Australian T +34 (91) 441 6025
W *www.spain.embassy.gov.au*

Canadian T +34 (91) 423 3252
W *www.canada-es.org*

New Zealand T +34 (91) 523 0226

South African T +34 (91) 436 3780
W *www.sudafrica.com*

US T +34 (91) 587 2200
W *www.embusa.es*

Hospitals/clinics
*Numerous public and private, in all cities
and major towns, including:–*

Hospital Ruber Internacional,
La Maso 38, 28034 Madrid
T +34 (91) 730 2200

TURKEY

Medical facilities vary widely. Even
the best modern private hospitals
may not be able to treat serious
conditions. Take supplies of regular
prescription medicines you need
(including contraceptives) with you.

Emergencies T 112

Health ministry/dept
T.C. Saglik Bakanligi, Mithatpasa Cad 3,
06410 Sihhiye/Ankara
T +90 (312) 435 6440

British consulates
British Embassy, Sehit Ersan
Caddesi 46/A, Cankaya (Ankara)
T +90 (312) 455 3344
W *www.britishembassy.org.tr*
Antalya T +90 (242) 244 5313
Bodrum T +90 (252) 319 0093
Bursa T +90 (224) 220 2534;
+90 (224) 221 2984
Istanbul T +90 (212) 334 6400;
+90 (212) 334 6407
Izmir T +90 (232) 4635151
Marmaris T +90 (252) 412 6486 X 36/39

Other consulates
Australian T +90 (312) 446 1180
W *www.embaustralia.org.tr*

Canadian T +90 (312) 459 9200
W *www.dfait-maeci.gc.ca/ankara*

New Zealand T +90 (312) 467 9054

South African T +90 (312) 446 4056
W *www.southafrica.org.tr*

US T +90 (312) 455 5555
W *www.usemb-ankara.org.tr*
(includes lists of doctors and hospitals)

Hospitals/clinics
Ankara University Faculty of Medicine,
Ibni Sina Hospital, Sihhiye, Ankara
T +90 (312) 310 3333

Bayindir Hospital, Sogutozu, Ankara
T +90 (312) 287 9000

International Hospital, Istanbul Cad 82,
Yesilkoy, Istanbul
T +90 (212) 663 3000

American Hospital, Guzelbahce Sok,
Nisantasi, Istanbul
T +90 (212) 311 2000; +90 (212) 231 4050

Ege University Hospital, Narlidere,
Izmir Bornova, Izmir
T +90 (232) 259 5959;
+90 (232) 421 8620

AFTER YOU GET BACK HOME

Some conditions may appear weeks or months later;
do you need a routine check-up?

You're back to friends, family and – depending how long and how far you've been away – possibly reverse culture shock, itchy feet and a feeling of emptiness in your life; even post-trip depression. But have you brought anything more tangible, healthwise, back with you?

Many long-term travellers wonder if they should have a routine medical after their return, especially from the tropics. Even medical opinion is somewhat divided, but there are certain situations when it's advisable. Two things need stressing, however:–

→ **Don't forget to keep taking your malaria pills,** in most cases for four weeks after you leave an area where malaria exists (*see p.107*).

→ The symptoms of some travel-related conditions can take weeks or even months to appear. So if you get ill or any symptoms do develop, **for at least a year after you return home, tell (or remind) your doctor exactly where you've been**. If you were treated abroad, give him/her as many details as possible (ideally a written report from the overseas doctor or hospital). If s/he seems puzzled or you're not confident of his/her diagnosis, don't be afraid to ask for a referral to a tropical disease specialist.

Warning signs and symptoms

If you have actual symptoms, you need to see a doctor for diagnosis and treatment, not just a check-up, but symptoms are often rather vague. For example, hepatitis (*see pp.51 & 148*) may cause no more than tiredness and loss of appetite at first, so don't ignore symptoms because they're ill-defined. Post-trip symptoms you should certainly see a doctor about include:–

→ *Cough or sore throat* – common on return from travels, and may or may not indicate something serious; needs to be investigated.

→ *Diarrhoea* – often caused by an infection; possibly giardiasis or amoebic dysentery (*see p.43*) if persistent. See doctor if it lasts more than 36 hours.

→ *Fever* – often due to an infection and always needs investigating. If it's combined with chills, perhaps rigors (shivering), a headache or sometimes other symptoms, may indicate malaria. (Malaria symptoms can appear up to a year – rarely, even longer – but usually no more than three months after your return; this is serious.)

→ *Jaundice* – may be caused by hepatitis or malaria; both serious.

→ **Rash** – varies widely in type and cause; may need specialist investigation.

→ **Swellings or lumps** – need to be investigated.

→ **Ulcer or skin wound** that won't heal.

→ **Weight loss** – again needs investigating, as it can have many causes.

Routine examination

If you're feeling well, there's probably no need for a routine post-trip medical examination unless you may have been exposed to certain conditions. The main such conditions and situations (where there may be no symptoms at first even if you are infected) are:–

→ If you've had unsafe sex (*see p. 145*) with a new partner and fear the risk of infection, or have had a blood transfusion or surgical or dental treatment anywhere outside the developed world (Australia, Canada, western Europe, New Zealand, the USA and probably South Africa). There's a risk that you might have contracted hepatitis B (*see p. 148*), HIV (*see p. 146*) or another sexually-transmitted infection (*see p. 149*), and should have blood or other tests – but generally not for at least three months after exposure.

→ If you've come into contact with fresh water in a lake, pond or river anywhere in sub-Saharan Africa, the tropical Americas or anywhere else where bilharzia (schistosomiasis; *see p. 102*) is prevalent. You should have a routine blood test for the disease at least six weeks (and preferably three months) after the last possible date of infection.

Some doctors feel that more extensive screening tests are sometimes justified, particularly if there's a suspicion or worry that something's wrong, but a lack of clear symptoms, or if you've been to an area where certain worms or other parasites are common.

Stool tests – which should preferably be performed on a series of samples taken on different days – may reveal intestinal parasites. Blood tests may show if you have a filarial infection (*see pp. 131–132*). In either case, the sooner you receive treatment to eliminate the parasites the better. A full blood count may also suggest other infections which will need further investigation. A simple 'dipstick' urine test will show the presence blood, protein or sugar – any of which will also need to be investigated further.

A final point

If you're a blood donor, you should inform your blood centre if you've been travelling outside the developed world, and tell them about any infections or treatments you've received.

MEDICAL RECORD

Use the form on these pages to record your medical and insurance contact details, any pre-existing conditions and medications. Also fill in the dates of vaccinations, and when further doses and boosters are due. It's worth leaving a copy safe at home as well as carrying the book with you as you travel.

Self	Companion
Name	**Name**
Home address	Home address
Nationality	Nationality
Passport no	Passport no
Next-of-kin – name	**Next-of-kin – name**
Relationship	Relationship
Address	Address
T	T
E	E
Primary doctor/GP – name	**Primary doctor/GP – name**
Address	Address
T	T
E	E
Specialist doctor (if any) **– name**	**Specialist doctor** (if any) **– name**
Speciality	Speciality
Address	Address
T	E

Self	Companion
Travel insurance company	*Travel insurance company*
Address	Address
T	**T**
E	**E**
Policy no	Policy no
Emergency assistance company	*Emergency assistance company*
T (hotline)	**T** (hotline)
Medical problems/conditions	*Medical problems/conditions*
Allergies, drug reactions, etc	*Allergies, drug reactions, etc*
Regular medications (including dose & frequency)	*Regular medications* (including dose & frequency)
Blood group (ABO/Rh)	*Blood group* (ABO/Rh)

Vaccinations etc: Self	Companion
Malaria prophylaxis	**Malaria prophylaxis**
Generic name(s)	Generic name(s)
Proprietary name(s)	Proprietary name(s)
Dosage & frequency	Dosage & frequency
(1)	(1)
(2)	(2)
Start date	Start date
Finish date	Finish date
Cholera (vaccine name/type)	**Cholera** (vaccine name/type)
Dose 1/2/3	Dose 1/2/3
Booster due	Booster due
Diphtheria (with tetanus?)	**Diphtheria** (with tetanus?)
Dose 1/booster	Dose 1/booster
Booster due	Booster due
Flu	**Flu**
Dose 1/booster	Dose 1/booster
Booster due	Booster due
Hepatitis A (see also below)	**Hepatitis A** (see also below)
Dose 1	Dose 1
Dose 2	Dose 2
Booster due	Booster due
Hepatitis B (or A & B)	**Hepatitis B** (or A & B)
Dose 1	Dose 1
Dose 2	Dose 2
Dose 3	Dose 3
Booster due	Booster due
Japanese encephalitis	**Japanese encephalitis**
Dose 1	Dose 1
Dose 2	Dose 2
Dose 3	Dose 3
Booster due	Booster due

Self	Companion
Meningitis	**Meningitis**
Vaccine type/strains	Vaccine type/strains
Dose 1/booster	Dose 1/booster
Booster due	Booster due
Polio	**Polio**
Vaccine type	Vaccine type
Dose 1/booster	Dose 1/booster
Booster due	Booster due
Rabies (pre-exposure)	**Rabies** (pre-exposure)
Dose 1	Dose 1
Dose 2	Dose 2
Dose 3	Dose 3
Booster due	Booster due
Tetanus (with diphtheria?)	**Tetanus** (with diphtheria?)
Dose 1/booster	Dose 1/booster
Booster due	Booster due
Tick-borne encephalitis	**Tick-borne encephalitis**
Dose 1	Dose 1
Dose 2	Dose 2
Dose 3	Dose 3
Booster due	Booster due
Tuberculosis (BCG)	**Tuberculosis** (BCG)
Test/booster	Test/booster
Typhoid (with hepatitis A?)	**Typhoid** (with hepatitis A?)
Dose 1/2/3	Dose 1/2/3
Booster due	Booster due
Yellow fever	**Yellow fever**
Dose 1/booster	Dose 1/booster
Booster due	Booster due

Note: *This is not an official yellow fever certificate – obtainable only from clinic.*

Others	**Others**

WORD AND PHRASE FINDER

ENGLISH	FRENCH	GERMAN
1 Help!	1 Au secours!	1 Hilfe!
2 Emergency	2 Urgence	2 Notfall
3 I am/feel ill	3 Je suis malade	3 Ich bin krank
4 Ambulance	4 Ambulance	4 Krankenwagen
5 Doctor	5 Médecin; docteur	5 Arzt
6 Hospital	6 Hôpital	6 Krankenhaus
7 Accident	7 Accident	7 Unfall
8 Fracture	8 Fracture	8 Bruch
9 Blood	9 Sang	9 Blut
10 Unconscious	10 Évanoui	10 Bewusstlos
11 Ache/pain	11 Douleur	11 Schmerz
12 – bad/severe	12 – mal; grave	12 – schwer
13 – sharp/dull	13 – piquant/sourd	13 – stechende/dumpfe
14 Fever/feverish	14 Fièvre	14 Fieber
15 Nausea	15 Nausée	15 Übelkeit
16 Vomit/vomiting	16 Vomissements	16 Sich übergeben
17 Diarrhoea	17 Diarrhée	17 Durchfall
18 Cough	18 Toux	18 Husten
19 Rash	19 Éruption	19 Ausschlag
20 Bite	20 Piqûre; morsure	20 Biss; Stich
21 Here	21 Ici	21 Hier
22 Head	22 Tête	22 Kopf
23 Eye	23 Oeil (pl yeux)	23 Auge
24 Neck	24 Cou	24 Hals
25 Back	25 Dos	25 Rücken
26 Chest	26 Poitrine	26 Brust
27 Heart	27 Coeur	27 Herz
28 Arm	28 Bras	28 Arm
29 Hand	29 Main	29 Hand
30 Abdomen/stomach	30 Ventre; estomac	30 Unterleib/Magen
31 Leg	31 Jambe	31 Bein
32 Knee	32 Genou	32 Knie
33 Foot	33 Pied	33 Fuss
34 Pharmacy	34 Pharmacie	34 Apotheke
35 Painkiller	35 Calmant	35 Schmerzmittel
36 Antiseptic	36 Antiseptique	36 Antiseptikum
37 Antibiotic	37 Antibiotique	37 Antibiotikum
38 Condom/contraceptive	38 Préservatif	38 Kondom
39 Injection	39 Injection	39 Spritze; Injektion
40 X-ray	40 Radiographie	40 Röntgenaufnahme
41 Allergy/allergic	41 Allergie	41 Allergie
42 Diabetes/diabetic	42 Diabète	42 Zuckerkrankheit;
43 Flu	43 Grippe	43 Grippe [Diabetis
44 Heart attack	44 Crise cardiaque	44 Herzanfall
45 Heat/sun stroke	45 Coup de chaleur	45 Hitzschlag
46 Hepatitis/jaundice	46 Hépatite; jaunisse	46 Gelbsucht
47 Malaria	47 Malaria	47 Malaria
48 Pregnant/pregnancy	48 Enceinte	48 Schwanger
49 Sunburn	49 Coup de soleil	49 Sonnenbrand
50 STD/VD	50 Maladie vénérienne	50 Gesshlechtskrankheit

I can't pretend that this is an adequate substitute for a good command of the language of the country you're travelling in, or an English-speaking doctor. But I've chosen these words and phrases to help you to call for assistance if you need it and convey the urgency of your situation and basic symptoms.

	ITALIAN	PORTUGUESE	SPANISH
1	Aiuto!	Socorro!	¡Socorro!
2	Emergenza	Emergência	Emergencia
3	Mi sento male	Sinto-me doente	Me encuentro mal
4	Ambulanza	Ambulância	Ambulancia
5	Medico	Médico	Médico
6	Ospedale	Hospital	Hospital
7	Incidente	Acidente	Accidente
8	Frattura	Fractura	Fractura
9	Sangue	Sangue	Sangre
10	Privo di sensi; svenuto	Inconsciente	Inconsciente
11	Dolore	Dor	Dolor
12	– forte	– forte	– fuerte; intenso
13	– acuto/debole	– agudo/moinho	– agudo/apagado
14	Febbricitante	Febril	Con fiebre
15	Nausea	Náuseas	Nausea
16	Vomitare	Vômitos	Vómito
17	Diarrea	Diarreia	Diarrea
18	Tosse	Tosse	Tos
19	Eruzione cutanea	Erupção	Erupción cutánea
20	Puntura; morso	Picada; mordedura	Picadura; mordedura
21	Qui	Aqui	Aquí
22	Testa	Cabeça	Cabeza
23	Occhio	Ôlho	Ojo
24	Collo	Pescoço	Cuello
25	Schiena	Costas	Espalda
26	Petto	Peito	Pecho
27	Cuore	Coração	Corazón
28	Braccio	Braço	Brazo
29	Mano	Mão	Mano
30	Addome; stomaco	Estômago	Vientre; estómago
31	Gamba	Perna	Pierna
32	Ginocchio	Joelho	Rodilla
33	Piede	Pé	Pie
34	Farmacia	Farmácia	Farmacia
35	Analgesico	Analgésico	Analgésico
36	Antisettico	Antiséptico; antissético	Antiséptico
37	Antibiotico	Antibiótico	Antibiótico
38	Preservativo	Preservativo	Condón
39	Iniezione	Injecção	Inyección
40	Radiografia	Radiografia	Radiografía
41	Allergia	Alérgico	Alérgico
42	Diabete	Diabetes	Diabético
43	Influenza	Gripe	Influenza
44	Infarto	Enfarte	Infarto
45	Colpo di sole	Insolação	Insolación
46	Epatite; itterizia	Hepatite	Hepatitis
47	Malaria	Malária; paludismo	Paludismo
48	Incinta	Grávida	Embarazada
49	Scottatura solare	Queimadura de sol	Quemadura (de sol)
50	Malattia venerea	Doença venérea	Enfermedad venérea

English, French and Swahili will together make you understood in much of Africa; Spanish and Portuguese between them throughout South America; and German in eastern Europe. Indonesian and Malay are very similar, and I've also included the 'Romanji' transliteration of Japanese words.

	SWAHILI	INDONESIAN	JAPANESE
1	Msaada!	Tolong!	Tasukete!
2	Dharura	Darurat	Hijo
3	Naumwa	Saya sakit	Guai ga warui no desu
4	Ambulensi	Ambulans	Kyukyu-sha
5	Daktari	Dokter	Isha
6	Hospitali	Rumah sakit	Byoin
7	Ajali	Kecelakaan	Jiko
8	Mvunjiko	Retak	Zasho; kossetso
9	Damu	Darah	Chi; ketsueki
10	Hana fahamu	Tidak sadar	Ishiki fumei
11	Maumivu	Sakit	Itami
12	– mbaya	– berat	– hidoi
13	– makali/madogo	– keras/agak	– hageshi/nibui
14	Homa	Pening	Netsu
15	Kichefuchefu	Mual	Hakike
16	Tapika	Muntah	Hedo; modosu
17	Kuharisha	Diare; murus	Geri
18	Kikohozi	Batuk	Seki
19	Upele	Ruam	Hasshin
20	Uma	Gigitan	Kamare-kiz; sasare
21	Hapa	Di sini	Koko
22	Kichwa	Kepala	Atama
23	Jicho (pl macho)	Mata	Me
24	Shingo	Leher	Kubi
25	Mgongo	Punggung	Senaka
26	Kifua	Dada	Mune
27	Moyo	Jantung	Shinzo
28	Mkono	Lengan	Ude
29	Mkono	Tangan	Te
30	Tumbo	Perut	I; o-naka
31	Mguu	Kaki	Ashi
32	Goti	Dengkul	Hiza
33	Mguu	Kaki	Ashi
34	Duka la dawa	Apotik	Yakkyoku
35	Dawa za maumivu	Penawar sakit	Itamidome; chintsu-zai
36	Antiseptik	Obat antiseptik	Bofu-zai
37	Antibayotik	Obat antibiotik	Kosei-busshitsu
38	Kondomu	Kondom; kontraseptif	Sakku; kondomu
39	Kupiga sindano	Suntikan	Chusha
40	Eksirei	Sinar X	Rentogen
41	Inanidhuru	Alergi	Arerugii
42	Mgonjwa wa kisukari	Diabetik	Tonyo-byo
43	Homa ya mafua; flu	Influensa	Infuruenza
44	Maumvimu ya moyo	Serangan jantung	Shinzo hossa
45	Kuathiriwa na jua	Kelengar matahari	Nissha-byo
46	Homa ya manjano	Hepatitis	Kan'en; odan
47	[Homa ya] malaria	Malaria	Marariya
48	Mwenye mimba	Hamil	Ninshin
49	Kubabuka kaw jua	Terbakar matahari	Hiyake
50	Magonjwa ya zinaa	Penyakit kelamin	Sei-byo

USEFUL INFORMATION/CONTACTS

International

World Health Organisation
W *www.who.int/ith* (publication, *International Travel and Health*); *www.who.int/csr/don/en* (latest disease outbreak information)

International Society of Travel Medicine
W *www.istm.org* (includes directory of travel clinics in many countries)

UK

Foreign and Commonwealth Office
T +44 (20) 7008 1500 (general and emergencies); +44 (20) 7238 4503 (travel advice)
W *www.fco.gov.uk/travel* (travel advice); *www.fco.gov.uk/embassies* (contact details for consulates etc)

Department of Health
W *www.doh.gov.uk/traveladvice* (publication, *Health Advice for Travellers*); *www.doh.gov.uk/traveladvice/emerg.htm* (latest disease outbreak information)

Scottish NHS
W *www.fitfortravel.scot.nhs.uk* (travel health advice)

Blood Care Foundation
T +44 (1403) 262652
W *www.bloodcare.org.uk*

Travel Clinic, Hospital for Tropical Diseases, London
T +44 (20) 7388 8989
W *www.uclh.org/services/htd/travelclinic.shtml* (travel health advice and information on services)

Australia

Department of Foreign Affairs and Trade
T +61 (2) 6261 1111; +61 (2) 6261 3305 (emergencies); 1 300 555135 (emergencies; free within Australia)
W *www.dfat.gov.au* (general); *www.dfat.gov.au/consular/advice* (travel advice); *www.dfat.gov.au/missions* (contact details for consulates etc)

Canada

Department of Foreign Affairs and International Trade
T +1 (613) 944 6788 (general information and emergencies); +1 (613) 996 8885 (emergencies only; call collect); 1 800 267 6788 (toll-free within Canada)
W *www.dfait-maeci.gc.ca/travel/menu-en.asp* (travel advice); *www.dfait-maeci.gc.ca/world/embassies/cra-en.asp* (contact details for consulates etc)

New Zealand

Ministry of Foreign Affairs and Trade
T +64 (4) 439 8000 (general information and emergencies)
W *www.mfat.govt.nz* (general); *www.mfat.govt.nz/travel* (travel advice); *www.mfat.govt.nz/about/oseas* (contact details for consulates etc)

South Africa

Department of Foreign Affairs
T +27 (12) 351 1000 (general information and emergencies)
W *www.dfa.gov.za/travelling* (travel information); *www.dfa.gov.za/sa-abroad/salist.htm* (contact details for consulates etc)

USA

State Department
T +1 (202) 647 5225 (travel information and emergencies); +1 (202) 647 4000 (emergencies out of hours)
W *http://www.state.gov/travel* (travel information); *http://travel.state.gov/travel_warnings.html* (consular information sheets)

Centers for Disease Control
T +1 (877) 394 8747 (travel health hotline)
W *http://www.cdc.gov/travel* (comprehensive travel health advice)

INDEX

Acknowledgements

I'd like to express my thanks to everyone who helped to collect and check the information for this book, including of course to the Travel Clinic of London's Hospital for Tropical Diseases; to the researchers who compiled the data for Part three – Emily Fox, Anna Katz and Kate Weinberg; to Ben Murphy for compiling the index; to Emma Wright for proof-checking the words and putting me right in many other areas; and to Judith Robertson for designing the book on an impossible schedule.